MISSOURI
and the
Secession Crisis

MISSOURI
and the
Secession Crisis

A Documentary History

EDITED BY
DWIGHT T. PITCAITHLEY

The University of Tennessee Press / Knoxville

Copyright © 2025 by The University of Tennessee Press / Knoxville.
All Rights Reserved.
First Edition.

Library of Congress Cataloging-in-Publication Data

Names: Pitcaithley, Dwight T. editor
Title: Missouri and the secession crisis : a documentary history / edited by Dwight T. Pitcaithley.
Description: First edition. | Knoxville : The University of Tennessee Press, 2025. | Includes bibliographical references and index. | Summary: "This is the fourth volume of Dwight Pitcaithley's ongoing series of edited primary documents related to secession debates on the eve of the Civil War. Like Kentucky, Missouri ultimately voted to remain in the Union after contentious debates. While voters overwhelmingly embraced the Union, Missouri governor Claiborne Jackson did not—he established a government in exile and left the state government in control of the lieutenant governor. This fracturing reflected the intensely divided leadership of the state" —Provided by publisher.
Identifiers: LCCN 2025025181 (print) | LCCN 2025025182 (ebook) | ISBN 9798895270264 hardcover | ISBN 9798895270288 adobe pdf | ISBN 9798895270271 epub
Subjects: LCSH: Jackson, Claiborne Fox, 1806–1862 | Secession—Missouri—History—19th century—Sources | Missouri—Politics and government—1861–1865—Sources | Missouri—History—Civil War, 1861–1865—Sources
Classification: LCC E517 .M57 2025 (print) | LCC E517 (ebook) | DDC 977.8/03—dc23/eng/20250904
LC record available at https://lccn.loc.gov/2025025181
LC ebook record available at https://lccn.loc.gov/2025025182

For James Oliver Horton

CONTENTS

Timeline	ix
Acknowledgments	xiii
Editor's Note	xv
Introduction	xvii

Documents

1. Missouri General Assembly, January 1861	1
Robert Marcellus Stewart, January 3	1
Claiborne Fox Jackson, January 3	11
Commissioner Daniel Renouard Russell, January 18	20
2. United States Senate, January–February 1861	27
Trusten Polk, January 14	27
James Stephen Green, February 12	38
3. United States House of Representatives, December 1860– February 1861	49
John William Noell, December 12	49
Thomas Lilbourne Anderson, January 15	51
John Bullock Clark, January 26	60
John Richard Barret, February 21	68
4. Missouri State Convention, March 1861	93
Sample Orr, March 4	94
Commissioner Luther Judson Glenn, March 4	96
Alexander William Doniphan, March 5	101
John D. Coalter, March 5	106
Majority Report of the Committee on Federal Relations, March 9	110
Minority Report of the Committee on Federal Relations, March 11	117
Hamilton Rowan Gamble, March 11	122
James Hugh Moss, March 11	129
John Brooks Henderson, March 12	143
John Thomas Redd Jr., March 14	152
Thomas Tasker Gantt, March 14	158

    Abram Comingo, March 15 — 170
    Dr. Moses Lewis Linton, March 16 — 173
    Emilius Kitchell Sayre, March 16 — 177
    Uriel Sebree Wright, March 18 — 184
    George Youse Bast Sr., March 19 — 202
    Committee Response to Commissioner Glenn, March 21 — 205

5. Afterward, May–October 1861 — 221
    Claiborne Fox Jackson's Address to the General Assembly, May 3 — 221
    Claiborne Fox Jackson's "To the People of Missouri," June 12 — 226
    Missouri State Convention's Committee of Eight Report, July 29 — 229
    Missouri State Convention's "To the People of the State of Missouri," July 31 — 232
    Hamilton Rowan Gamble's Inaugural Address, July 31 — 240
    Claiborne Fox Jackson Convening the Rebel General Assembly, September 26 — 243
    Claiborne Fox Jackson's Address to the Rebel General Assembly, October 22 — 245
    Ordinance of Secession, October 28 — 247

Appendix 1. State Convention Delegates — 249
Appendix 2. Questions for Discussion — 253
Notes — 257
Bibliography — 287
Index — 291

TIMELINE

1860

November 6	Abraham Lincoln elected President of the United States
December 3	Second session of the Thirty-Sixth Congress convenes
December 20	South Carolina secedes
December 30	General Assembly convenes in Jefferson City

1861

January 3	Robert M. Stewart's last address to the General Assembly
January 3	Claiborne F. Jackson's Inaugural Address
January 9	The *Star of the West* repulsed off Morris Island, South Carolina
January 9	Mississippi secedes
January 10	Florida secedes
January 11	Alabama secedes
January 19	Georgia secedes
January 21	General Assembly passes bill authorizing election for state convention
January 26	Louisiana secedes
February 4	Washington Peace Convention convenes
February 4	Secessionist convention convenes in Montgomery, Alabama
February 6	Nathaniel Lyon arrives in St. Louis to reinforce the US Arsenal
February 9	Jefferson Davis elected Provisional President of the CSA
February 18	Election for Convention delegates
February 18	Jefferson Davis inaugurated as President of the CSA
February 23	Texas secedes
February 27	Washington Peace Convention concludes
February 28	State Convention convenes
March 4	Abraham Lincoln inaugurated as President of the USA
March 6	Confederate Congress authorizes raising 100,000 troops

Timeline for Secession Winter

March 19	State Convention adopts resolution denying cause for secession
March 22	State Convention adjourns
April 12–13	Confederate guns bombard Fort Sumter
April 15	Lincoln calls for 75,000 state militia
April 17	Jackson refuses to supply troops requested by Lincoln
April 17	Jackson begins planning to capture St. Louis Arsenal
April 17	Jackson requests artillery from Jefferson Davis
April 19	Jackson's letter to David Walker states he is in favor of secession
April 21	William S. Harney relieved of duty
April 22	Jackson calls for state militia to gather on May 3
April 23	Jefferson Davis sends requested artillery
April 25	St. Louis Arsenal arms shipped to Alton, Illinois
April 30	Lyon authorized to enlist 10,000 to protect Missouri
May 2	General Assembly reconvenes
May 3	Jackson requests reorganization of state militia
May 6	Camp Jackson established
May 6	Arkansas secedes
May 9	Confederate artillery arrive from Baton Rouge
May 10	Surrender of Camp Jackson
May 10	General Assembly passes militia bill
May 12	Sterling Price appointed commander of Jefferson City State Guard
May 20	North Carolina secedes
May 21	Harney/Price agreement
May 23	Virginia secedes
May 30	Harney replaced by Lyon
June 8	Tennessee secedes
June 11	Jackson/Price Lyon/Blair meeting
June 12	Jackson's "To the People of the State of Missouri" Proclamation
June 13	Jackson and others abandon Jefferson City
June 15	Lyon arrives in Jefferson City
June 16	Lyon leaves Jefferson City for Boonville
July 6	State Convention called back into session
July 20	Confederate government reconvenes in Richmond
July 22	State Convention reconvenes
July 31	Hamilton R. Gamble elected Governor

July 31	State Convention address to the people of Missouri
July 31	Gamble's Inaugural Address
July 31	State Convention adjourns until the third Monday in December
September 26	Claiborne Jackson issues call to reconvene the Missouri General Assembly
October 21	Missouri Rebel General Assembly convenes
October 28	Missouri Rebel General Assembly approves ordinance of secession
November 28	Confederate Congress admits Missouri into the Confederacy

1865

January 11	General Assembly abolishes slavery

ACKNOWLEDGMENTS

I am deeply indebted to a number of friends and colleagues who provided much welcomed assistance. John Andrews shared his immense knowledge of William Shakespeare in the explication of references to the Bard's writings. Jane Scott once again furnished clarification of antiquated nineteenth-century legal terms. William Eamon patiently explained the many references to classical literature. I am grateful for the friendship of Charles and Karen Dew and their sharing the newspaper transcript of Daniel R. Russell's speech found in chapter 1, and for clarifying a critical part of the original news script. Likewise, I need to thank my colleague Nick Sacco who not only willingly shared his research on John R. Barret, but also his deep understanding of Missouri's history; and provided valuable comments on the introduction. Historians William Piston and Jeremy Neely reviewed the entire manuscript and offered timely and useful critiques. I deeply appreciate the continuing support of Thomas Wells, Scot Danforth, and Jonathan Boggs at the University of Tennessee Press. Working with them has been a distinct pleasure. My wife, Sabette, has endured my many solitary hours working on this manuscript with good humor and equanimity. I thank her, yet again, for her patience, her keen editorial eye, and her love over five decades of marriage.

EDITOR'S NOTE

Justifications for the South's secession in 1860–1861 have long been debated in academic circles and vigorously argued in public forums. The puzzle of disunion is best addressed, however, by examining the speeches and documents produced by the nation's elected officials over Secession Winter. Those official addresses and papers were duly recorded by the various gatherings mentioned in the timeline above. All were published either immediately or soon after delivery. In total, the official documentation of secession amounts to over 12,000 pages. (See bibliography for the primary accounts referenced in this volume.) For various reasons, I limited my research on Missouri's conflicted reaction to secession to the speeches and proposals of elected officials, and purposely did not include newspaper articles or editorials. They have been used effectively in other accounts of secession. Focusing on the words of the senators and representatives and delegates to the numerous official gatherings following Lincoln's election allows an unfiltered examination of the presumptions and reasoning of those ultimately responsible for determining the fate of the nation. The speeches and pronouncements of Missouri's elected officials included in this collection were selected because they represent the remarkable diversity of opinions held by Missourians following Lincoln's election.

Understanding the motivations of those who advocated for and against secession is a challenging undertaking. Generally speaking, the official gatherings of elected officials in Missouri and elsewhere struggled with two questions: to what extent was the election of Abraham Lincoln a threat to the institution of slavery; and to what extent was the institution of slavery protected in the United States Constitution. Within that framework, one finds numerous thematic threads that illuminate the motivations for disunion. A visceral fear of abolition, the imagined loss of slavery, and the concomitant loss of white supremacy dominated southern anxiety following the Republican victory in 1860. Concerns over that party's pledge to prevent emigration with slaves into the western territories—a pledge never acted upon—formed a standard grievance against the North. Similarly, complaints that northern states were interfering with the return of runaway slaves, required by the Fugitive Slave Act of 1850, became commonplace. In order to justify leaving the Union, secessionists had to embrace an argument based on the compact theory of government. In response, Unionists countered that the Founding Fathers established a government designed to be perpetual, and a constitution that did not allow states to separate at will. To that end, amending the Constitution became yet another motif in the debates that dominated political discourse over Secession Winter.

Because of the extensive nature of Missouri's secession documents, I have included only the most germane of them. The speeches have been edited to emphasize the salient points of the debate and to omit redundant or incidental material. Instead of simple ellipses, however, I have provided the reader a sense of the omitted material by including explanatory comments within braces, i.e., {}. Many of the documents include brackets in the original to identify individuals or legislative procedures. For clarity, the editor's emendations are therefore included within braces. Some quotes could not be identified.

INTRODUCTION

Missouri's path through the tumultuous winter of 1860–1861 was unlike any other slave state's experience. It was the only state with strong political and commercial relationships north, south, and west. It was the only state to convene a convention that failed to vote for secession. It was the only state that would be governed by that same convention after its governor and a small portion of the General Assembly fled Jefferson City (and then the state) to align itself with the Confederate States of America. When Claiborne Fox Jackson took the oath of office on January 3, 1861, only South Carolina had seceded. The incoming governor, however, firmly believed Missouri should stand by her sister slave states. Holding strong secessionist sentiments, Jackson soon found himself in a distinct minority as the convention, which he had endorsed, consisted overwhelmingly of Unionists. When the convention voted on March 19 favoring a resolution declaring there was "no adequate cause to impel Missouri to dissolve her connection with the Federal Union," only George Bast, a farmer from Montgomery County, dissented. Following the Confederate bombardment of Fort Sumter in Charleston Harbor, and President Lincoln's call for a 75,000-man militia to quell the insurrection, Governor Jackson's Confederate sympathies became more evident. On the same day, April 17, that he refused to furnish the requested troops, he requested artillery from Confederate president Jefferson Davis.

Because St. Louis was home to a United States federal arsenal, the river town became the scene of confrontations (physical and political) that would determine the fate of the state for the rest of the war.[1] In 1861, St. Louis was predominately in favor of Union because of its large German population and its lucrative trade with non-slave states like Illinois just across the Mississippi River. The pro-southern element, however, was assisted by General William S. Harney, commander of the US Army's Department of the West, headquartered in St. Louis, who was known to sympathize with southern interests. As his department included supervision of the St. Louis Arsenal, he complicated his subordinates' plans to mobilize Unionist forces. In the face of Jackson's secessionist leanings and Harney's impediments, commander of the arsenal Nathaniel Lyon and US Representative Francis Preston Blair Jr. joined forces to keep Missouri in the Union. Lyon's move against Camp Jackson, that resulted in the surrender of the openly secessionist state militia, was a first act in the critical disruption of state control. After several failed attempts of conciliation between the governor and the Unionist Lyon, Jackson and other disunionists fled Jefferson City which was quickly occupied by United States forces. On July 22, the state convention reconvened and elected a temporary governor, Hamilton R. Gamble, who guided Missouri through the war years until his death on January 31, 1864. Missouri's journey through Secession Winter involved issues of state sovereignty, debates over the constitutionality of secession, proposals for compromise, concern over the Lincoln administration's presumed position on slavery, fear that its notion of white supremacy was threatened, and . . . a great deal of hyperbole.

Missouri had been at the forefront of constitutional issues involving the western territories and slavery ever since the 1820 compromise that created the state. The controversy cast a long shadow that influenced public conversations about the status of slavery in the country for the next several decades. The congressionally designated geographical line separating slave from non-slave populations served the country well until it didn't. By 1850, southern representatives in Congress decided that allowing territorial settlers to decide the issue of slavery for themselves was preferable to a congressional dictate. When the new approach worked well in Utah and New Mexico, but resulted in an antislavery referendum in Kansas, proslavery officials returned to the idea of reinstating the 36°30' Missouri Compromise line following the election of Lincoln. Guaranteeing slavery south of the parallel seemed a better approach than leaving the issue to the whims of settlers. The Missouri legacy included at least two additional elements. Missouri's initial 1820 constitution contained a provision that excluded free Blacks from entering the state. Northerners opposed to statehood argued that the clause violated Article IV, Section 2 of the Constitution which held that "The Citizens of each State shall be entitled to all Privileges and Immunities of Citizens in the several States." While northern resistance was eventually overcome by an obscurely written explanation by Henry Clay, the issue of Black citizenship simmered until Chief Justice Roger B. Taney's 1857 decision in the *Dred Scott* case; a case, it should be noted, that began a decade earlier in St. Louis's Old Courthouse.[2] Likewise, the debate over Missouri statehood resulted in a widely held perception that slavery could not be discussed without, in the words of historian Robert Forbes, "exposing unbreachable fissures in the Union." Thus, the less said about slavery the better.[3]

But the "slavery question" was one that could not be fully answered and remained a divisive issue in popular and political discourse until coming to a head with the election of Abraham Lincoln. The four decades following the Missouri controversy were plagued by national debates about the nature of the Constitution, federal versus state authority over slavery, Black citizenship, emancipation, colonization, the degree to which slaves as property were protected in the United States Constitution, and most specifically, the limits over Congress's authority to govern the territories. In time, the slavery issue evolved into a fundamental question: Is slavery a local institution protected by state legislation, or a national one protected by the United States Constitution?

***

The election of 1860 was presaged by the most politically turbulent decade in the history of the country. The problem that would simply not go away was that of the status of slavery in the western territories, an issue that presumably had been settled by Congress in 1850 when it admitted California as a non-slave state and divided the remainder of the Mexican Cession into the territories of New Mexico and Utah. Congress then had stipulated that the two territorial legislatures could decide to prohibit or permit the institution of slavery. (By the end of the decade both territories had passed legislation protecting and regulating the ownership of slaves.) In 1854, Congress upended the thirty-four-year prohibition of slavery north of the 36°30' parallel by allowing the territories of Kansas and Nebraska to permit slavery if they so chose. The resulting influx of pro- and antislavery settlers led to much violence and competing constitutions. (Statehood for Kansas was fought over in the territory, and in the halls of Congress, for the next seven years until it was finally admitted in January 1861.) In 1857, only days after the inauguration of President James Buchanan, the Supreme Court decided that Congress could not prohibit slavery in the territories (as it had done in 1820 with the Missouri Compromise and more recently in the Oregon Territory [1848] and a year later in the Minnesota Territory).[4] Presumably, however, territorial legislatures could prohibit slavery when preparing a constitution in anticipation of statehood as the issue of human bondage had been traditionally accepted as a prerogative of the states. Surprisingly, in spite of the Supreme Court's *Dred Scott* decision that Congress could not prohibit slavery in a territory, and in spite of the fact that slavery had already been authorized throughout the New Mexico Territory (that then stretched from Texas to California), the primary issue in the presidential election of 1860 revolved around the status of slavery in the western territories.

The Republican Party, in only its second appearance on the national political stage, nominated Abraham Lincoln in Chicago as its presidential candidate on a platform that proclaimed "the normal condition of all the territory of the

United States is that of freedom," that neither Congress nor territorial legislatures possessed the authority to "give legal existence to slavery in any territory of the United States." While reiterating the principles of the Declaration of Independence that "all men are created equal," the party also endorsed the time-honored custom that slavery was a local institution controlled by states and not the federal government. "That the maintenance inviolate of the rights of states," the fourth plank declared, "and especially the right of each state to order and control its own domestic institutions, according to its own judgment exclusively, is essential to that balance of power on which the perfection and endurance of our political fabric depend."

Unable to agree on the proper policy for slavery in the territories, Democrats split into northern and southern factions. Northern Democrats nominated Illinois Senator Stephen A. Douglas on a platform that supported the Supreme Court's 1857 decision in the *Dred Scott* case. Unofficially, however, Douglas personally persisted in the belief that territorial legislatures could bar slavery simply by not enacting protective legislation. Southern Democrats nominated James Buchanan's vice president, John C. Breckinridge, and announced that "all citizens of the United States have an equal right to settle with their property in a territory." Significantly, the platform stated that not only could any citizen emigrate to a territory, but that the federal government, if necessary, had the obligation to protect the rights of persons and property in the territories. Both factions advocated the acquisition of Cuba "on such terms as shall be honorable to ourselves and just to Spain," with the Breckinridge platform adding, "at the earliest practicable moment." The critical distinction between the federal government "not prohibiting" slavery, and actively "protecting" the institution in the territories, created an insurmountable rift between southern and northern Democrats.

The Constitutional Union Party, recently founded in 1859, entered the race with the simple declaration that it was the patriotic duty of all citizens to "*recognize* no political principles other than the Constitution of the country, the Union of the States, and the enforcement of the laws." Meeting in Baltimore, the party nominated Tennessean John Bell.

On November 6, 1860, the country's White male electorate demonstrated its moderate position on the issue of the day by electing Abraham Lincoln over Stephen Douglas by a 10 percent margin. John Breckinridge came in third edging out John Bell by 5 percentage points. In the Electoral College, however, Lincoln amassed a dominant 180 votes, Breckinridge followed with 72 while Bell bettered Douglas with 39. Tellingly, most voters favored a candidate other than Lincoln. Like Buchanan before him, Lincoln would enter the White House a minority president carrying only 39.8 percent of the popular vote.[5] A largely forgotten, but important result of the 1860 election was that Democrats retained control of the US Senate and regained the House of Representatives. For the first two years of the Lincoln administration, the legislative branch of government would be controlled by the opposition party.

The election results in Missouri were different, but still reflected a conservative bent. The state was the only one to vote for Stephen Douglas who narrowly beat John Bell by little more than 400 votes. Breckinridge followed with 19 percent; Abraham Lincoln garnered barely 10 percent. Significantly, 70 percent of the voters favored the moderate popular sovereignty policy of Douglas and the middle of the road, noncommittal platform of Bell.[6]

More directly relevant to the citizens of Missouri was the election of a new governor three months before the national contest. On August 6, Missourians elected Claiborne F. Jackson governor and Thomas C. Reynolds lieutenant governor. Having campaigned on a moderate platform that had endorsed Stephen A. Douglas for president, Jackson and Reynolds narrowly defeated the Constitutional Union Party candidate, Sample Orr, 47 percent to 42 percent. Reflecting the conservative faction of the electorate, supporters of John C. Breckinridge for president nominated former governor Hancock L. Jackson and James Gardenhire for governor and lieutenant governor. They carried just 11 percent of the vote.

Jackson played a cagey game. A decade earlier he, with the assistance of Missouri Supreme Court Justice William B. Napton, had developed and introduced into the Missouri legislature the Jackson-Napton Resolutions that unequivocally declared that Congress had no right to legislate against slavery in the territories and upheld the popular sovereignty policy for the territories endorsed by then Senator Stephen Douglas. The resolutions had been introduced when the United States Congress was debating how to organize the large expanse of land ceded by Mexico in 1848. While personally a supporter of John C. Breckinridge's platform of national protection for slavery in the territories, Governor Jackson believed he needed to adopt the more moderate position in order to win the governorship. Jackson's biographer, Christopher Phillips, noted that this duplicity was typical of Jackson and confirmed his "role as political chameleon."[7]

When Missouri's twenty-first general assembly convened on January 3, 1861, tradition held that the outgoing governor present a farewell speech as prelude for the incoming governor's inaugural address. Robert M. Stewart, who had succeeded Trusten Polk as governor in 1857, was a political moderate. While conflating abolitionists with the Republican Party, Stewart painted a dark, yet cautionary portrait. Abolitionism had not only invaded northern religions, he charged, but poisoned an entire generation by incorporating its message into "class books; set to music, and sung; caricatured with chains and scourges, exhibited in the print shops; wrought into plays, and acted upon the stage." Northern fanatics had "no sympathies for anything, but African slaves," and "have substituted for morals and religion a vile system of negrophilism, which culminates in all the crimes and horrors of amalgamation. . . ." While hyperbolically describing the Republican Party's policy toward slavery, Stewart was quick to point out that the offenses of the northern fanatics did not warrant disunion. Indeed, he posited that secession was "political heresy." "The very idea of the right of voluntary secession is not only absurd in itself, but utterly destructive of every principle on which national faith is founded." Missouri should acknowledge the services provided by the federal government including the postal service, military support on "our western frontier," and the millions of dollars "distributed from the Federal exchequer every year to support officers and contractors within the State." The outgoing governor concluded by recommending against "unwise and hasty action."[8]

Only a few hours later, Governor Claiborne F. Jackson mounted the podium and while agreeing with his predecessor about the threat to slavery posed by the incoming Lincoln administration, he concluded with a different message. The Republican Party, he began, has only one principle and that is "hostility to slavery." It was not political victory that it sought, but the domination of a section. With the party's possession of the Executive Branch, it would be only a short time before the party would control "all the other departments of the government." (The fact that more citizens had voted against Lincoln than for him, and that Democrats held on to the Senate and regained the House of Representatives in the last election, did not appear to factor into Jackson's political calculations.) With such a dire future awaiting Missouri, the state should issue a "timely declaration of her determination to stand by her sister slave-holding States, in whose wrongs she participates, and with whose institutions and people she sympathizes." Like many elected officials throughout the South, Jackson raised the specter of federal coercion: "Standing armies of mercenary soldiers, subject to the will of the Executive, are not the remedies for violated constitutions or laws."[9] In a conciliatory passage, the governor called for a convention of the slaveholding states to agree upon, and propose, constitutional amendments to the northern states "for their consideration and action." That this approach to amend the Constitution was not sanctioned by that document's Fifth Amendment, did not seem to concern the governor.[10] Jackson's effort to arbitrate the differences between the sections, however, was overshadowed by his latent determination to maneuver the state toward disunion. In his analysis of the address's most pointed passage—wherein Missouri's "honor, her interests, and her sympathies . . . determine her *to stand by the South*"—historian Christopher Phillips observed that Jackson had told his audience that "Missouri *was* the South."[11]

Two weeks after his inauguration, Jackson called the General Assembly to welcome Daniel R. Russell, a secession commissioner from Mississippi, and "confer" with him "in regard to the important objects of his mission." Russell was one of fifty-two commissioners sent by South Carolina, Mississippi, Alabama, Georgia, and Louisiana to persuade other slave states to join the secessionist cause.¹² Using embellished rhetoric typical of his fellow messengers of disunion, Russell announced that Mississippi had seceded because there was "a working majority in the North which is pledged to extinguish slavery." Would Missouri surrender, he asked, to "hordes of marauding Abolitionists?" While some of the legislators present applauded his plea to join the Confederacy, a majority, according to the only extant account, received it with "detestation."¹³

While the General Assembly pondered the advice of the state's new governor and Mississippi's secession commissioner, Missouri's delegation to the United States Congress offered their opinions on the election of Lincoln and the resulting march toward secession by the Deep South states. Collectively those senators and representatives could generally be described as conditional secessionists. While they voiced grievances against the northern states and their war against slavery that, to their minds, had been going on for decades, they favored constitutional compromises that would allow Missouri to remain in the Union. Some defended a state's right to secede, others did not. All believed that some sort of constitutional compromise should be explored. Most favored compromise along the lines suggested by Senator John J. Crittenden on December 18, 1860. At age seventy-four, Kentucky's senior senator, attempting to play the mediator role of his mentor, Henry Clay, had offered a constitutional amendment consisting of six articles that would have protected slavery in the southern part of the western territory, in federal installations throughout the South, and in the District of Columbia. It also prohibited Congress from interfering with slavery in the states and with the interstate transportation of slaves, more clearly defined the fugitive slave clause, and made the amendment unamendable by future Congresses.¹⁴ Crittenden's resolution quickly became the standard by which all other compromise solutions were measured. Between early December 1860 and April 13, 1861, elected officials proposed sixty-nine constitutional amendments in an attempt to avoid secession and war.¹⁵

On January 14, 1861, after the secession of four southern states, Missouri Senator Trusten Polk rose to comment on a resolution proposed by Virginia Senator Robert M. T. Hunter that the president of the United States ought to be authorized to retrocede southern forts then occupied by Confederate forces. Polk, a Yale-educated St. Louis resident and former governor, offered an analysis of the troubled state of affairs shared by many (but not all) Missourians. The presidential contest had been decided, he began, "sectionalism and anti-slavery fanaticism have triumphed." The senator then listed the causes for southern unrest as being the personal liberty laws passed by northern legislatures to interfere with the return of fugitive slaves, the Republican Party's "hostility to slavery," and President Lincoln's "dangerous dogma that . . . the negro is the equal of the white man." Southern complaints, Polk clarified, were not against the federal government, but in response to legislative action of certain northern states. A conditional Unionist who later committed to the Confederacy, Polk then introduced his own constitutional amendment that would have moved protections for the institution of slavery from the state to the federal level. Concessions must be made, Polk insisted, and be "made full and certain, and that without delay."[16] Polk's assessment was that even though the federal government was not to blame for the sectional unrest involving slavery, the Constitution must be amended to provide slaveowners national protection for their peculiar institution. Such concessions were the price Republicans were to pay for slave states to remain in the Union. Polk's amendment would have nationalized slavery and provided compensation to slave owners for unrecovered runaway slaves.[17] While Senator Polk and Governor Jackson aligned themselves against committed Unionists throughout the state, they were, as the crisis developed, in the minority. But their grievances clearly reflected the politically divided nature of that most northern slave state.

Missouri's junior senator, James S. Green, agreed that Republicanism was based on hostility to slavery, an antipathy "inculcated at the North through the instrumentality of politicians, teachers of schools, [and] tract societies." The senator favored the Crittenden amendment, but had no faith that the North would agree to it. Green also mentioned a resolution proposed by New York representative George W. Palmer that prohibited Congress from interfering with slavery in the states.[18] While labeling it, "a very fine resolution," the senator did not vote for or against such a prohibition (in a different form offered by Ohio representative Thomas Corwin) when it passed the Senate by the narrowest of margins on March 4 only hours before Lincoln's inaugural ceremony.[19] Green concluded his address by succinctly stating his position: Every state had a right to secede; if that right was exercised wrongly, the state alone was responsible; and if a state were to secede, all federal property would revert to that state. His final point included a conviction that every effort should be made to save the Union, but that if "all efforts fail, let us part in peace. . . ."[20]

At the other end of the US Capitol, Missouri's representatives weighed in on the issues confronting the country. On January 12, 1860, as numerous solutions were being proposed, John William Noell, from Perryville, offered one of the more unconventional. Concerned that the southern states no longer held sufficient power to "secure their peace and the safety of their property against the aggressions of the Federal Government," Noell proposed a constitutional amendment that would have abolished the office of the president and replaced it with an executive council consisting of three members elected by districts of contiguous states (presumably north, south, and west). Each member would be armed with veto power! How this council would actually work in reality, Noell did not explain. He also suggested that the political equilibrium between free and slave states could be accomplished "by a voluntary division on the part of some of the slave States into two or more States."[21] Noell seemed to be aware that when the United States annexed Texas in 1845, Congress included a stipulation that the Lone Star State could divide itself into as many as five states if it wished.[22] No other state possessed such an option.

Representative Thomas L. Anderson from Marion County, speaking on January 15 after the secession of South Carolina, Mississippi, Florida, and Alabama, warned his colleagues that "passion, prejudice, and fanaticism" had finally obtained supremacy over justice and reason, and if left unchecked would doom the country unless "the northern mind should undergo a change." Unlike Senator Green, he did not support the Crittenden amendment because it prohibited slavery north of the 36°30' parallel in spite of the Supreme Court's ruling in the *Dred Scott* case that had determined that slave owners had the constitutional right to take their slaves into any and all of the western territories. He urged northern representatives to propose amendments that would guarantee to the southern states "peace, safety, and security to them, and their property." The Union could be preserved, Anderson stipulated, if the North simply enforced the Fugitive Slave Law of 1850 and repealed its personal liberty laws, recognized slaves as property under the Constitution, allowed slave owners to travel anywhere in the country with their slaves (including the western territories), and "cease to abuse and denounce us." The time had arrived, he contended, when the "slavery question *must* be settled or this Union *must* be dissolved."[23]

The idea of nationalizing slavery, overtly recognizing slaves as property and moving protections thereof from the state level to the federal, was a concept that had grown throughout the decade. By mid-April, eleven similar constitutional amendments had been suggested by, among others, President James Buchanan, Missouri's Trusten Polk, Georgia's Robert Toombs, Virginia's former governor Henry A. Wise, and most famously by Mississippi's Jefferson Davis. On December 22, 1860, Senator Davis introduced an amendment that declared "property in slaves, recognized as such by the local law of any of the States of the Union, shall stand on the same footing in all constitutional and federal relations as any other species of property so recognized."[24] By identifying slaves as property, chattel slavery would be protected by the due process clause of the Fifth Amendment which held that no person shall "be deprived of life, liberty, or property, without due process of law." If nationalized, slavery would be legal throughout the United States. It was just this approach that the makers of the Confederate Constitution employed during the early months of 1861. By using phrases such as "property in negro slaves," "slaves and other property," and "property in said slaves," the new constitution of the Confederacy clearly assured the protection of slavery by the language of the Fifth Amendment which had been incorporated into the Montgomery charter as Article I, Section 9, Part 16.[25] None of the supporters of nationalizing slavery appeared to intuit that declaring slaves as property and only property would obviate the political advantage the South had in the US House of Representatives by virtue of Article 1, Section 2 of the Constitution (the three-fifths compromise), that gave slave states increased representation in Congress by counting a portion of their slave population.

Ten days after Anderson addressed the House of Representatives, John B. Clark from Howard County offered his thoughts on the state of the Union. While Clark would not opine on the constitutional right of secession, he forthrightly declared that the Republican Party and its platform of principles had encroached upon the constitutional rights of the southern states. Specifically, he complained that "Abolitionists and Free-Soilers" had, for thirty years, "assailed the institution of slavery in the southern States" and denied to the South "a common property in the Territories." The northern states, he claimed, had nullified the Fugitive Slave Act by obstructing the rendition of runaway slaves. Most egregious was the Chicago platform's declaration that "all men are free and equal," and that the doctrine of equality had been carried into effect in several northern states "where negroes are allowed to vote for President and members of Congress."[26] Clark supported the Crittenden Amendment, or something like it, which would give peace to the country and avoid the "pestilence, famine, fratricidal war, indeed, all the horrors of civil war." Unless southern rights were guaranteed by the Constitution, specifically "the right of protection of our peculiar property in slaves—without which we cannot live with you," Missouri would be forced to join the Confederacy.[27]

With only two weeks left in the legislative session, John R. Barret, representing St. Louis, offered the most intriguing speech offered by Missourians over Secession Winter. A native Kentuckian and graduate of St. Louis University, Barret had served four terms in the Missouri House of Representatives before being elected to Congress. As he rose to speak, six states had left the Union, and Texas would make that decision two days hence. The House of Representatives was more solidly Republican than at the beginning of the session, and the Senate had gained a Republican majority due to the departure of twelve southern senators. Barret's address moved quickly from pillorying abolitionists to attacking Republicans for believing that "all men are created equal," to pronouncing secession "unwise and selfish," to urging his Republican colleagues to offer compromise resolutions to restore peace to the country. In return for southern states' acceptance of Lincoln's victory, Republicans, to Barret's mind, would have to offer constitutional amendments protecting slavery.

Making no distinctions between Republicans and abolitionists, Barret assailed the party as being composed of "out-and-out, red-mouthed Abolitionists" (who believed it was the right of every slave to cut his master's throat), and "cunning and ambitious politicians who have embraced the "wicked, reckless, and lawless fanaticism of the Abolitionist." The party had succeeded in gaining possession of the general government (he erroneously raged), the result of which must be "the complete subjugation of the South, and the destruction of their institution of slavery." The leading idea of the party that was causing widespread fear throughout the South was the "Abolition doctrine" that all men are created equal! Barret devoted a significant portion of his address to the idea of Negro equality. "And now, the cardinal doctrine, the great leading central idea, the fundamental principle of Republicanism, has become the equality of the negro with the white man." Fear of losing the South's notion of white supremacy loomed large in the defense of the peculiar institution.[28]

Barret then shifted his focus and denounced the Deep South states for seceding. Disunion, he admonished, was a "remedy for no evil, real or imaginary." It could not be denied that the South had suffered "a long train of abuses by the anti-slavery party," but secession would not make the institution of slavery more secure, and would deny the slave states equal opportunity in the western territories. If the Republican Party should attempt to use federal power to attack slavery, then Missouri would have reason to object, but as it stood, the government in Washington was not the cause of southern grievance. In fact, he reminded his audience, the 1860 election had returned the House of Representatives to Democrats and maintained their hold on the Senate which "insured a constitutional check upon his administration." Nevertheless, Barret believed that the slavery issue should be settled sooner rather than later: "This is a proper occasion for the settlement of this pest question of slavery, *now and forever.*" He ended his address by urging Republicans to craft a constitutional compromise that would prevent war and secure the future of the South's peculiar institution.[29]

Barret, like others who represented the "Show Me" state, was mindful of the distinctive place Missouri occupied in the Union. As the most northwestern slave state, and one bordered by four non-slave states, he saw Missouri occupying the very "geographical center of this nation; she lies in the very highway of civilization, and in the march of empire." As the nation was quickly segregating itself into "southern" and "northern," Missouri (and the three other border states), saw itself because of its unique geographical position, as an arbiter, as mediator. As outgoing governor Robert M. Stewart observed during his farewell address to the General Assembly, "It would seem, indeed, that Missouri and her sister border States should be the first, instead of the last," to speak on the critical issues of the day.[30]

Back in Missouri, Unionism dominated the public spirit. On January 21, the General Assembly voted to call a convention to address the secession crisis and protect the "sovereignty of the State." A statewide election for delegates was scheduled for February 18 with those elected to gather at Jefferson City ten days later. While providing for an orderly election, the legislature also stipulated that if the planned convention proposed to change or dissolve the political relations with the federal government, it would not become valid "until a majority of the qualified voters of this State, voting upon the question, shall ratify the same."[31]

As the state prepared for the election, Governor Jackson prepared for secession. On January 18, he had warmly welcomed Mississippi's secession commissioner, Daniel R. Russell, presenting him to Jefferson City's influential citizens. The governor aggressively requisitioned arms from the Ordnance Bureau in Washington, and sent an emissary to the St. Louis Arsenal to ensure that any attempt by the governor to claim the arsenal's munitions upon the state's secession would not be resisted.[32]

Jackson's hopes for a prompt break with the Union, however, were frustrated by the will of Missouri's White male electorate. On election day, Unionist delegates received nearly 80 percent of the votes. While only four Republicans were elected, no avowed secessionist gained election to the convention. One month later, Missouri's representatives reaffirmed their attachment to the Union by voting 89 to 1 in favor of a resolution that read: "At present there is no adequate cause to impel Missouri to dissolve her connection with the General Government; but, on the contrary, she will labor for such an adjustment of existing troubles, as will secure peace as well as the rights and equality of all the States."[33]

Gathering on February 28, in the Cole County Courthouse, the delegates quickly elected former governor Sterling Price president, Robert Wilson vice president, and Samuel A. Lowe secretary. Before getting down to the business of protecting the state's sovereignty and institutions, the convention (having relocated to the St. Louis Mercantile Library over the weekend),[34] debated whether to allow a commissioner from Georgia to address the assembly. Former Constitutional Union Party candidate for governor, Sample Orr, spoke vigorously against allowing Luther Glenn to speak, reasoning that if he, Glenn, was presenting himself as an ambassador, he should have gone to Washington. Furthermore, Orr argued, the delegates had taken an oath to support the Constitution of the United States and of Missouri which forbade them from forming an alliance with any other state.[35] While Delegate Orr voted against allowing Commissioner Glenn to be heard, a majority of the members elected to listen to his presentation.

Like Mississippian Daniel R. Russell who had earlier addressed the General Assembly, Luther Glenn had been sent by Georgia as an apostle of disunion to persuade the convention delegates to secede from the United States and join the Confederacy. Glenn spoke passionately of the hostility of the northern people "towards the institutions and rights of the South," of the Republican Party's desire to prevent slave owners from settling in the western territories, and plotting for the eventual extinction of slavery. Believing there were antagonisms between the "civilizations" of North and South that could never be reconciled, Glenn hoped that Missouri would join Georgia in forming a "Southern Confederacy." Glenn's speech was met with mixed applause and hissing "which lasted for some time, and was subdued with some difficulty by the President."[36]

While commissioner Russell's speech on January 18 did not prompt a response from Missouri's secession-leaning General Assembly, the convention delegates could not pass up the opportunity to challenge Commissioner Glenn's foreboding predictions for the future of slavery. Delegate John B. Henderson representing Pike County proposed that a committee be formed to consider an appropriate rejoinder to Glenn. St. Louis attorney Thomas T. Gantt quickly agreed stating that while it was appropriate for the convention to listen "with fraternal kindness" to any citizen, Glenn's presentation required "an unequivocal declaration of dissent of the people of Missouri from the proposal which our sister State of Georgia offers through her messenger."[37]

When delivered on March 21, the committee's report was over twice as long as Glenn's address. It refuted not only the commissioner's claims, but also the compact theory of government on which the notion of secession was based. Referring to the "heresy of secession," the report denied that the Republican Party intended to interfere with slavery in the states citing the Chicago Platform and the recently passed Corwin amendment (introduced by Republicans), which prohibited Congress from interfering with or abolishing slavery in the states. Deflecting the charge that the Lincoln administration intended to prevent slaveholders from settling in the western territories, the report introduced the fact that the prior Congress, when totally controlled by Republicans, organized the territories of Dakota, Colorado, and Nevada without placing any restrictions on slavery.[38] Moreover, the Supreme Court's *Dred Scott* decision supporting the right to "carry slaves into all the public domain is to-day clear and undisputed." Missouri was not ready to "abandon the experiment of free government," the committee announced because of "imaginary ills" claimed by Georgia's secession commissioner. The report then presented a lengthy critique of the "false constructions of the Constitution," upon which South Carolina and other southern states had used the compact theory to justify disunion. The report concluded that Commissioner Glenn's argument in favor of secession, "whether viewed as a Constitutional right, a remedy for existing evils, or a preventive of anticipated wrongs, we find it in conflict with our allegiance to a good Government, and wholly inefficient to accomplish the ends designed."³⁹

The convention was clearly in no mood to entertain the possibility of secession. The Committee on Federal Relations, chaired by future governor Hamilton R. Gamble, had issued its report on March 9 which rejected disunion as a solution to the nation's problems. It found that the alienation between North and South was not based on any "actual injury" suffered, but in the "anticipation of future evils." The report stressed that southern grievances were aimed at the actions of northern states and pronouncements by the Republican Party, but not at any action of the federal government. There was no reason to believe, the report continued, that the Supreme Court would not continue to decide in favor of slave owners. Indeed, the rights of southern citizens were best adjudicated in the courts as they had been when addressing John Brown's 1859 failed raid on Harpers Ferry, Virginia.⁴⁰

The report concluded with five resolutions designed to articulate Missouri's position as a border state with strong allegiances north and south. The first stated unequivocally that "at present there is no adequate cause to impel Missouri to dissolve her connection with the Federal Union." A statement of support for the institution of slavery followed with an earnest desire that areas of disagreement "may be removed" and peace and harmony restored. A third resolution supported Senator Crittenden's constitutional amendment expanding protections for slavery, and a fourth called for a national convention (as authorized by Article V of the Fifth Amendment to the US Constitution) to propose constitutional solutions. In its final recommendation, the report stressed that "we therefore earnestly entreat as well the Federal Government as the seceding States to withhold and stay the arm of military power, and on no pretense whatever bring upon the nation the horrors of civil war.⁴¹ While the report met with the approval of a majority of the committee, John T. Redd, an attorney from Marion County, announced that he had a better plan of adjustment and would like to present a dissenting view when the convention next met.

As the delegates gathered after a Sunday break, John Redd presented his minority report (coauthored by Harrison Hough from Mississippi County) which argued that Gamble's assessment of the national crisis was too tepid. He wanted northern interference with the 1850 Fugitive Slave Act to be made much more explicit and John Brown's invasion of "the soil of Southern States," more forthrightly condemned. Redd and Hough agreed that Senator Crittenden's amendment would be satisfactory to Missouri, but that a convention of the eight remaining upper South and border states represented the best means for preserving the Union, reconciling conflicting interests, and "restoring peace and tranquility to the country."⁴²

Before the delegates began to debate the two reports, James Moss, an attorney from Clay County, introduced an amendment to the report's fifth amendment that read: "And further believing that the fate of Missouri depends upon the peaceable adjustment of our present difficulties, she will never countenance or aid a seceding State in making war on the General Government, nor will she furnish men and money for the purpose of aiding the General Government in any attempt to coerce a seceding State."[43] The possibility of adopting a position of neutrality during the coming conflict was considered by all four of the border states.

At the urging of his fellow delegates, Hamilton Gamble next took the podium to explain the rationale behind the development of the committee's report. He admitted to feeling "some embarrassment" in justifying the Unionist tone of the report because he had heard "no expression antagonistic to the Union" during the convention. Every action of the federal government had been to the benefit of Missouri and had demonstrated "every disposition to foster our interests as a State." He spent some time defending the recommendation for a national convention to "restore harmony between the conflicting portions of our Union," and rejecting the minority report's recommendation for a border state convention. One was "recognized by the Constitution," and the other was not. Gamble concluded by declaring that he had "discharged the duty of opening the debate, as chairman of the committee, and shall close, reserving to myself the privilege of again addressing the Convention, should it become necessary in the course of the discussion."[44] Gamble could not have known that before four months had expired, he would again be addressing the convention, but then as provisional governor.

The delegates considered the committee's reports (and Chairman Gamble's remarks) for the next week. They were aware that the Thirty-Sixth Congress had adjourned on March 4, not to reconvene until December, and had rejected Senator Crittenden's amendment in favor of Representative Thomas Corwin's that declared Congress had no authority to interfere with slavery in the states. The debate that ensued generally supported the Committee's assessment that the Deep South's concern for the future security of slavery was based on apprehensions of what the Lincoln administration might do, rather than on what the federal government had done. Many, while agreeing that some northern states had unconstitutionally prevented runaway slaves from being returned to their owners, argued that secession was "heresy," even "damnable heresy."[45]

One notable dissenting voice was that of John Redd. Three days after presenting his minority report to the Committee on Federal Relations, Redd, while not supporting secession for Missouri, argued that when "constitutional rights have been trampled under foot," states were justified in leaving the Union. To his mind, the actions of some northern states in obstructing the return of fugitive slaves were sufficient cause for secession. Redd invoked the oft used argument in defense of "southern rights" that the formation of the federal government was based on a theory of compact government. According to this view, states had retained full sovereignty when ratifying the United States Constitution. They had voluntarily agreed to join the union of states and could voluntarily leave. Under this concept, the federal government was the mere agent of the states that served to administer certain functions on their behalf. John C. Calhoun's 1832 belief in a state's ability to nullify a federal law sprang from this same doctrine.[46]

Redd qualified his remarks by insisting that while he believed states had the right to secede, he condemned the leaving of the seven Deep South states as "hasty and unwise." While he admitted the right of secession and believed that causes existed for its application, he opposed its "exercise, and I shall continue to oppose its exercise." He expressed concern that because of the Republican Party's war on slavery and its policy of nonextension of the institution into the territories, the fifteen slave states would soon ("in the next thirty years") be so outnumbered by non-slave states that they could ratify a constitutional amendment abolishing slavery throughout the United States.[47] The "handwriting is upon the wall," he announced, that a policy of exclusion from the territories would lead to the destruction of slavery as sure as the "sun will rise to-morrow."[48]

Delegate Thomas T. Gantt immediately took the floor to rebut Redd's constitutional assumptions. Gantt, a St. Louis attorney, argued that to assert that the nation was a confederation and not a union, was "political heresy." The Constitution replaced the Articles of Confederation to create a "more perfect union." Furthermore, Republicans were not abolitionists, he lectured, and should be judged solely on their platform from the past election. Its fourth plank clearly stated that they "would not interfere with slavery in the States in which it existed by virtue of the municipal law." The personal liberty laws of northern states, which were designed to protect Black citizens from being kidnapped, had been perverted to obstruct the return of runaway slaves; a clear violation of Article IV, Section 2 of the Constitution; but the most egregious of those were being repealed by the states themselves. Northern interference with the return of fugitives was, in his judgment, "aggressive in the first instance," but the retaliatory action of seven southern states, had "gone beyond the limits of a just defense." Regarding the territories, Gantt reminded his listeners that within the past month, the Republican-controlled Congress had organized three western territories without excluding slavery. For all the Republican rhetoric opposing the extension of slavery into the territories, such exclusion was not implemented. To Gantt's thinking, secession was clearly neither constitutional nor warranted.[49]

Uriel Wright, in one of the longest addresses of the convention, also attacked Delegate Redd's interpretation of the Constitution. If a state could dissolve its relationship with the federal government for any "clear and palpable" cause, who was to judge whether the implied violation of the Constitution was "palpable or not."[50] The presumption that a state retained authority sufficient to secede led Wright to discourse on the nature of sovereignty and the Constitution. In a civics lesson worthy of a university professor, Attorney Wright explained the divided sovereignty implicit in the nation's foundation document. The Founding Fathers distributed power between the several states and the federal government. States were sovereign in some respects, the federal government in others. Neither possessed complete sovereignty.[51] To believe in the notion of secession, to Wright's lights, was to believe in "national suicide."

Turning to the issue of slavery in the territories, Wright argued that the *Dred Scott* decision had settled the issue: "You have the right to carry slavery into all the Territories." Moreover, slavery had essentially been carried into all the land that natural law would allow. He commented on the absurdity of the South's obsession over Republican opposition to the extension of slavery into the territories by observing, "There is a party, in the North, who insist upon the Wilmot Proviso, where a Wilmot Proviso can never practically accomplish anything; and there are mad men in the South who insist upon the dogma of protection where there can never be a slave to be protected."[52] Furthermore, like Delegate Gantt, he reminded the convention that Republicans had only the month before organized three western territories without invoking the dreaded proviso. Wright, echoing several other delegates, then noted that if the deep South states had not "abandoned" Missouri, the Lincoln administration would have been powerless to pass legislation antagonistic to southern interests. In the event a "hurtful" law was passed, "the Supreme Court would denounce it." Had the South not succumbed to "this wild reign of *error*," the federal government would have remained, as it had for the past decade, in the hands of the proslavery Democratic Party.[53] Shortly after Wright concluded his lengthy address, the convention voted on the resolutions proposed by the Committee on Federal Relations (approving all by wide margins) and then adjourned to reconvene on December 16.

The will of Missouri's White male electorate, expressed through the convention delegates, had thus pronounced the state against both secession and the employment of military force by either the federal government or the Confederacy. But neutrality was not the favored path of Governor Claiborne Fox Jackson. An astute politician, Jackson realized that an overt push for secession was untimely given the convention's vote for neutrality. Instead, he planned to position himself as a staunch defender of state sovereignty while hoping that federal overreach would turn Missouri's citizens against the Union and into the arms of the Confederacy.[54] And he almost succeeded.

During the three weeks between the adjournment of the state convention (March 22) and the Confederate bombardment of Fort Sumter on April 12, Missouri fractured into pro-secession and pro-Union camps. Many of the state's citizens, alarmed that Kansas had been admitted to the Union on January 29 as a non-slave state and thus presumably offering sanctuary to runaway slaves, organized themselves into quasi-military companies called Minute Men. Alarmed by secessionist sentiment in the state and especially St. Louis, US Representative Francis Blair Jr., and Captain Nathaniel Lyon, an ardent antislavery Unionist assigned to the St. Louis Arsenal, recruited thousands of German citizens into Home Guard units.[55] A complicating factor in mobilizing support for Union, however, was the hostile relationship between Lyon and William S. Harney, the commander of the arsenal and Department of the West. A native Tennessean, Harney had married into the influential slave-owning Mullanphy family in 1833. Mary Mullanphy's father, John Mullanphy had been a successful businessman and an important philanthropist during the early development of St. Louis; and Mary's brother, Bryan, had been mayor between 1847 and 1848. Lyon suspected Harney of not being as solidly pro-Union as himself, as it was known that Harney held southern sympathies and many of his closest associates supported the Confederacy. Undoubtedly, Lyon also knew that Harney was related by marriage to Daniel M. Frost, the secessionist head of the Missouri State Militia.[56]

Growing tensions on both sides exploded on April 15 when President Lincoln, in response to the attack on Fort Sumter, issued a call for seventy-five thousand state militia troops to suppress the insurrection. When Governor Jackson received Secretary of War Simon Cameron's request for 3,123 men, his response was swift and emphatic: "Sir:—Your requisition is illegal, unconstitutional and revolutionary; in its object inhuman and diabolical. Not one man will Missouri furnish to carry on any such unholy crusade against her Southern sisters."[57] Jackson's defiance of a federal request sparked public displays of support for both secession and Unionism, and the state rapidly descended into political turmoil. Over the next two months Jackson's gambit failed to deliver Missouri to the Confederacy, and he and pro-secessionist members of his administration and the state legislature would abandon Jefferson City and head south toward Arkansas.

On the same day that Jackson refused to supply troops to the federal government, the governor began planning to capture the St. Louis Arsenal, and requested a shipment of artillery from Confederate President Jefferson Davis. Two days later he wrote to the president of the Arkansas state convention that Missouri would be ready to secede in "less than thirty days; *and will secede*, if Arkansas will only get out of the way and give her a free passage."[58] As the governor was stirring up the pro-Confederate elements in the state, Nathaniel

Lyon, then commander of the Department of the West and the St. Louis Arsenal (Harney having been relieved of duty on April 21), received authorization to muster into federal service the four regiments Jackson had failed to supply. By April 27, 2,500 volunteers had been sworn in, the majority of whom were of German extraction.[59] Believing that the arsenal's store of ordinance would be a tempting target for Confederate sympathizers and Jackson's state militia, Lyon also arranged for most the arms and munitions in the depot to be transported across the river to Alton, Illinois, and then by rail to Camp Butler near Springfield.[60]

As Missouri fractured, Jackson plotted to provoke Lyon and Blair into overplaying their hands with the intention of building resentment against the federal government and expanding secessionist sentiment. He reconvened the largely pro-secession leaning legislature, and on May 3, lectured the senators and representatives on the current state of affairs. "Fanaticism, sectionalism, and cupidity" in the northern states had resulted in the election of an administration that threatened to destroy the sovereignty of the states and was in the process of converting the federal government into an "overshadowing consolidated despotism." President Lincoln's call for troops in response to the bombardment of Fort Sumter "threatened a destructive war between the States." To protect the people of Missouri against the impending aggression, Jackson called for the reorganization of the state's militia and a "sufficient sum of money to place the State, at the earliest practicable moment, in a complete state of defence."[61]

Jackson commanded the overtly secessionist head of Missouri's militia, Daniel M. Frost, to provide for the state's defense. Frost, in turn, established Camp Jackson on the western edge of St. Louis (now part of St. Louis University) as a base for militia operations. At this point the trap was set. Although most of the arms in the St. Louis Arsenal had been moved to Illinois, Lyon, knowing that the Confederate artillery Jackson had requested had arrived on May 9, moved to prevent the presumed militia attack on the arsenal. During the afternoon of May 10, Lyon marched 6,500 men to Camp Jackson and forced the surrender of around 650 militia. While the surrender was peaceful (Commander Frost understanding that resistance would be futile), Lyon's next move enraged St. Louis' supporters of disunion. Dramatically wanting to demonstrate Union military superiority, the arsenal's commander began marching the state militia, now prisoners, six miles from Camp Jackson back to the arsenal.

While Lyon's intent was to illustrate the military might of the United States, his decision to parade his prisoners through St. Louis only provided fuel for the growing fire. Lyon's march from the arsenal to Camp Jackson had attracted throngs of curious onlookers, many of them anti-Unionist and anti-German supporters of the militia. Not long after the procession left the camp, the agitated bystanders began hurling rocks, bricks, and other found objects at Lyon's soldiers. Soon the hostilities escalated and several onlookers fired shots at the federal troops. The predominately German enlistees returned fire and chaos spread up and down the line. By the time Lyon was able to gain control over his men and halt the shooting, twenty-eight St. Louis citizens had been killed and seventy-five wounded. Two federal soldiers and three militia prisoners also were fatally shot.[62] The Camp Jackson affair ended quickly, but it reverberated throughout the city and state for weeks thereafter.[63]

That evening, Governor Jackson rushed to the General Assembly and reported on Lyon's actions of the afternoon. Fearing further federal advances against the state, the legislature quickly passed a military bill that gave the governor expanded authority over the state militia, and another that moved funds from Missouri's charitable institutions and schools to the militia. To lend prestige to the militia (now termed the Missouri State Guard), Jackson appointed the former president of the state convention, Sterling Price, commander with a rank of major general. Rumors that Frank Blair, now in charge of the First Missouri Regiment, was marching on Jefferson City, prompted Governor Jackson to send troops to destroy the railroad bridges over the Gasconade and Osage Rivers. The political divisions in state leadership became more obvious when Confederate flags were spotted flying over the governor's mansion and Missouri state militia headquarters in Jefferson City.[64]

The shifting political landscape grew even more complicated when General William S. Harney replaced Nathaniel Lyon as commander of the Department of the West. His anticipated arrival on May 11, may have been one of the motivating factors in Lyon acting precipitately in the Camp Jackson affair. Reaching St. Louis the day after Lyon's disastrous miscalculation, Harney desired to calm the roiling emotions in the city and promote equilibrium between the pro- and anti-Union factions. Averred neutrality was also favored by Governor Jackson who believed that some sort of détente would buy him time to consolidate the pro-secession sentiment throughout the state. At Harney's invitation, Jackson dispatched Sterling Price to St. Louis. The resulting Harney-Price agreement concluded on May 21, stipulated that as long as order was maintained, no federal military action would be taken. In spite of growing secessionist sensibilities throughout Missouri, and some overt harassment of Unionists around St. Louis, Harney had essentially granted the state a decree of neutrality.[65]

To exacerbate what was already high drama, Frank Blair, alarmed by Harney's seeming complicity in the face of rising hostility toward the federal presence in the state, arranged for the general's removal. In this show of military musical chairs, Nathaniel Lyon, once again, replaced Harney.[66] Significantly, Sterling Price, presuming that the reinstatement of Lyon meant that his agreement with Harney was no longer in effect, ordered his district commanders to accelerate militia enrollments in anticipation of a federal invasion from St. Louis.[67] Lyon, in turn, quickly enlisted additional troops and by June 1, had amassed over 10,000 volunteers and Home Guards. Concerned that the change in federal leadership would hasten hostilities, Governor Jackson, in an effort to preserve the peace and provide additional time for the organization of secessionist interests throughout the state, proposed a meeting with Lyon and Blair.[68]

In ordinary circumstances, such a meeting would have taken place in Jefferson City with the governor hosting. With Harney's removal, however, and Nathaniel Lyon and Frank Blair's influence now seemingly in the ascendancy, Governor Jackson agreed to meet in St. Louis after obtaining a guarantee of safe passage from Lyon. The gathering on June 11 at the Planter's House Hotel, included Jackson, Jackson's aide, Thomas L. Snead, Price, Blair, Lyon, and Lyon's aide, Major Horace Conant. Jackson and Price began the meeting by offering concessions that, they hoped, would lead to a state of neutrality throughout the state. Under their plan for appeasement the State Guard would be disbanded, no further arms would be requested from the Confederacy, and Confederate troops would be prevented from entering the state. In return, the recently mustered federal Home Guards would also be disarmed. The newly promoted Brigadier General Lyon listened impatiently unmoved from his commitment to Union, hatred for secessionists, and conviction of Jackson's duplicity.[69] The meeting ended without agreement and the long anticipated war had come to Missouri.

Not waiting for the promised escort by Lyon, Jackson and Price left the hotel and boarded a train for Jefferson City. On the way, Jackson formulated the final phase of his plan to paint the federal government as the aggressor leaving Missouri no alternative but to resist the "military despotism" of the Lincoln administration. With the assistance of his aide, Thomas L. Snead, the governor drafted a proclamation declaring the federal government the perpetrator of a "series of unprovoked unparalleled outrages" upon the "rights and liberties" of Missourians. Titled simply "To the People of Missouri," Jackson's declaration of June 12 listed the various ways the federal government had heaped "unbearable indignities" upon the citizens of the state. Chronicling the failure of the Price/Harney agreement and the rejection by Lyon of the terms offered in the recent meeting at the Planter's House Hotel, Jackson proclaimed that all "our efforts toward conciliation have failed." The "agents of the federal government in this State . . . are energetically hastening the execution of their bloody and revolutionary schemes for the inauguration of civil war in their midst, and for the military occupation of your State by the armed bands of lawless invaders, for the overthrow of your State Government, and for the subversion of those liberties which that Government has always sought to protect; and they intend to exert their whole power to subjugate you, if possible, to the military despotism which has usurped the powers of the Federal Government." The proclamation concluded by declaring that Missourians had no obligation to obey the "*Unconstitutional*" edicts of the Lincoln administration, and that they should rise, "and drive out ignominiously the invaders who have dared to desecrate the soil which your labors have made fruitful, and which is consecrated by your homes!"[70] Lyon's refusal to compromise was met with a forceful response by Governor Jackson.

During the next several weeks and months the Missouri drama only intensified. Reading Jackson's proclamation on the morning of June 13, Nathaniel Lyon characteristically decided to contain Missouri's secessionist leadership by marching to Jefferson City. Anticipating Lyon's attack, Jackson ordered his staff and a contingent of the state militia to evacuate the capital and move northwest to Boonville. Lyon's troops quickly followed and routed the State Guard causing Jackson and his small party to work their way slowly south to Carthage then on to Little Rock where he arrived on July 19. Sterling Price remained in Missouri sparring with Lyon's troops until August 10 when the impetuous Lyon attempted to attack Price's militia that had been reinforced by Confederate troops from Arkansas and Louisiana. Outnumbered two to one, Lyon led his troops to a resounding defeat at Wilson's Creek, and his own death.[71]

Jackson's departure from Jefferson City, left Missouri without an effective state government. On July 6, in order to fill the ministerial void, five members of the state convention that had adjourned on March 22, called the delegates back into session.[72] Reconvening on July 22, the assembly quickly established a Committee of Seven "for the purpose of reporting what action is necessary to be taken by this Convention in the present condition of public affairs in Missouri."[73] The committee's forthcoming preliminary report briefly traced the history of the state convention and then proclaimed that it had reconvened due to the "horrors of a civil war, inaugurated by the most gigantic and causeless rebellion of which modern history affords any example," brought on "by those who have been long plotting the overthrow of the Constitution and the disruption of the Union."[74] On July 29, the committee issued its final report that vacated the offices of governor, lieutenant governor, secretary of state, and members of the General Assembly, and announced that replacement officers be appointed by the convention to manage the affairs of the state until confirmed by a state-wide election in November. The convention would act as the state's legislative body until the same election on the first Monday in November when members of the General Assembly would be elected "by the qualified voters of this State."[75] The convention then duly elected Hamilton Gamble as president, Willard Preble Hall as lieutenant governor, and Mordecai Oliver as secretary of state. All three were elected by unanimous votes.[76]

Aware that the undertakings of the convention were rather unorthodox, the Committee of Seven (which was renamed the Committee of Eight when the delegates added Hamilton Gamble as chair) developed an address to the citizens of Missouri to explain its actions. Announced on July 31, the justification began by observing that the "most startling events have rushed upon us with such rapidity that the nation stands astonished at the condition of anarchy and strife to which in so brief a period it has been reduced." Finding no governing executive or body in Jefferson City to "maintain the internal peace of the State," or to exercise the ordinary functions of the "Executive department," it became the duty of the convention delegates to fill the void. The "evils that now afflict the State," the convention clearly laid at the feet of Governor Jackson and the pro-secession legislature whose acts clearly displayed a purpose "to engage in a conflict with the General Government, and to break the connection of Missouri with the United States." Remarking that the governor and other state officials had "fled from the seat of Government and from the State," the only logical remedy was to vacate the offices of the absent bureaucrats, appoint replacement administrators, and ask the voters to confirm that action early in November. In the judgment of the convention, its response to the secessionist acts of Governor Jackson were designed to vindicate the sovereignty of Missouri (a phrase repeated multiple times), and offered "the highest promise of peace and security to all her citizens."[77]

Having presented the convention's explanation of its efforts to maintain order and keep Missouri in the Union, Hamilton Gamble was sworn in as governor and delivered a short address. Admitting that he had made no "elaborate preparations" for an inaugural speech, Gamble offered his election as an "experiment that is about to be tried to endeavor to pacify this community and restore peace and harmony to the State." He and the convention had done their best to avoid civil war within the state and avoid secession. The state was, however, threatened with anarchy and "not merely a war between different divisions of the State, but a war between neighbors." Gamble urged the assembled delegates to join him in the work of attending to the "welfare of the State," and the "great work of pacification."[78] Due to the exigencies of war, the planned election to affirm the convention's appointment of Hamilton, Hall, and Oliver, and elect members of the General Assembly, did not occur until the fall of the following year. The November 1862 ballot returned Hamilton, Hall, and Oliver to office, and secured a majority of Unionists to Congress and to the General Assembly.[79]

Addressing the newly elected members of the legislature a month after the election in late December, Governor Gamble congratulated the assembled upon the fact that "at last a loyal General Assembly is convened." Gamble reflected on the "disloyal representatives" of the former General Assembly who conspired with Governor Jackson who employed "all the influence and power of his office to ruin a confiding people." Governor Gamble then praised the loyal citizens of the state who volunteered for service in the state militia (38,031) and United States Army (27,491). After covering several other subjects, the governor turned to the question of emancipation declaring that a "great rebellion against our Government exists, and its primary object is to inaugurate a Government in which slavery shall be fostered as the controlling interest." Because the war had reduced the number of slaves in Missouri and rendered "insecure" and diminished the value of those that remained, Gamble proposed a system of gradual, compensated emancipation. Such a process was sanctioned by the state's own constitution and, Gamble continued, was in line with the resolution of the slavery issue proposed earlier that month by President Lincoln.[80] While the Twenty-Second General Assembly deliberated over compensated emancipation, abolition in Missouri was not accomplished until early 1865, when a state constitutional convention passed an ordinance declaring the immediate and unconditional emancipation of all slaves in Missouri.[81]

Although having fled the state in June of 1861, Governor Jackson retained hopes of gaining additional support from Confederate President Jefferson Davis and the eventual union of Missouri with the Confederacy. After leaving the state, Jackson traveled through Little Rock and Memphis on his way to Richmond where he arrived on July 26. After two days of deliberations with Davis, Jackson received the promise of financial assistance once Missouri formally seceded. Satisfied, the governor in absentia returned to the boot heel of the state only to return to Memphis to plan a Confederate invasion of Missouri. By late September he was in Lexington where he issued a call for the General Assembly to reconvene on October 21, in Neosho, Newton County.[82]

By the fall of 1861, Jackson's absence from the state had allowed Missouri's Unionists to gain the upper hand. Major newspapers throughout the state rejected his former claims of desiring neutrality and blamed him directly for bringing the war to Missouri.[83] When the remnants of the General Assembly gathered in Neosho, the lack of a quorum did not prevent Governor Jackson from recommending that the assembled dissolve "all political connection between the State of Missouri and the United States of America." The federal government was determined to "trample upon our liberties, to violate our dearest constitutional rights, and in every manner known to tyrants, to insult, injure and afflict our people." Encouraged by the earlier support provided by Jefferson Davis, Jackson asked for an ordinance of secession, a provisional union with the Confederacy, and the passage of a law authorizing a special election to provide senators and representatives to the Confederate States of

America.[84] Six days later, the rump legislature passed the requested ordinance of secession declaring that the Lincoln administration had "utterly ignored the Constitution, subverted the government as constructed and intended by its makers, and established a despotic and arbitrary power instead." The federal government had invaded the state, made prisoners of the militia, forcibly occupied Jefferson City, and in league with "domestic traitors," was in the process of "seizing and destroying private property, and murdering with fiendish malignity peaceable citizens, man, women, and children."[85] Four months after abandoning Jefferson City, Jackson's government in exile finally achieved what he had hoped for in his inaugural address: a "declaration of her determination to stand by her sister slaveholding States, in whose wrongs she participates, and with whose institutions and people she sympathizes."[86]

Sources

The documentation of Missouri's handling of the secession crisis was dutifully recorded in the published proceedings of Congress and the state's General Assembly. The debates of the second session of the Thirty-Sixth Congress were captured in the *Congressional Globe* and are easily accessed at: https://www.loc.gov/collections/#anchor36. Published proceedings of Missouri's House and Senate can be found at: https://babel.hathitrust.org. The official records of the state convention are preserved in the Missouri State Archives, in Jefferson City: Office of the Secretary of State, Record Group 5.23. Printed versions of the convention's March and July 1861 sessions were published immediately by George Knapp, state printer. Lucius Chittenden, a delegate to the Washington Peace Conference from Vermont, recorded the deliberations of that gathering and published them in 1864 with the New York publisher, D. Appleton and Company. See bibliography for specific citations of relevant documents.

CHAPTER 1

MISSOURI GENERAL ASSEMBLY

January 1861

Robert Marcellus Stewart
January 3, 1861

A native of New York, Robert M. Stewart (1815-1871) studied for and was admitted to the New York bar in 1836. In 1839, he moved to Missouri and established his law practice in Bloomington and then St. Joseph. He was elected as a Democrat to the state senate in 1846 and served for ten years supporting public improvement projects. When the Missouri General Assembly selected Governor Trusten W. Polk to fill a vacant seat in the US Senate in 1857, Stewart defeated James S. Rollins in a special gubernatorial election. Although he defended slavery and attacked abolitionism, Stewart held moderate views on the issue of secession and has been described as an "Unconditional Union" man.[1]

Governor Stewart displayed his restrained views on the nation's crisis in his last address to Missouri's General Assembly by chastising the Republican Party for poisoning the northern mind against slavery and the South. Abolitionism had not only "invaded the pulpit, and polluted the pulpit," but it was "incorporated into class books, . . . caricatured with chains and scourges, . . . and wrought into plays, and acted upon the stage." At the same time, he lectured, many northerners were "friends of the Constitution and the Union" so Missouri should not act hastily as secession would be "suicidal." Voluntary secession, he opined, was "not only absurd in itself, but utterly destructive of every principle on which national faith is founded." Missouri should remain in the Union as long as "it can be made the protector of equal rights."

Message from the Governor by Mr. Tracy, his Private Secretary:
Gentlemen of the Senate and House of Representatives:

The closing day of another year—a year filled with interesting events, and foreshadowing others of still graver importance—called you together as the legal representatives of the people, to constitute the Twenty-First General Assembly of Missouri.

As the Chief Executive of the State, it is made my duty to communicate with you upon such subjects of present and pressing interest as should command themselves to your immediate attention and careful deliberation. First of all, I would unite with you in sentiments of profound gratitude to the Giver of all good, for His manifold blessings conferred upon us as a people, and in deprecating His wrath against our State and Nation.

Inasmuch as our Government is both general and local in its characteristics and jurisdiction, the Federal Constitution forming a *quasi* Constitution of each individual State, being openly and formally sworn to by all State officers, and the obligations to support it tacitly acknowledged by all the people, it is proper that our Federal relations, including our rights as a sovereign State and our obligations to the General Government, should be carefully considered and wisely acted upon. The very idea of an organized community implies that a portion of the individual rights must be surrendered for the common good. A man entirely isolated from his fellows might possess an indefeasible right to all his property; but the moment he becomes a subject of civil government, a portion of his acquired wealth must be used to support a system of domestic police, as well as other legitimate means of promoting the good order, happiness and prosperity of the community to which he belongs. On the same principle has been framed the league that binds together the States of the great American Republic, which, whatever may be its faults, is the noblest political fabric everreared by human hands. The first stones in this glorious temple were laid in wisdom, and cemented by the blood of the truest patriots the world has ever known.

Even at the first it was seen that a vast extent of territory, embracing within its bounds every variety of soil, climate, production, and resource, would require almost as great a variety in the local laws and institutions of the different districts. Hence the Federal Constitution was the child of compromise and concession. It gave to the General Government only such powers as should enable it to act for the general defense, and for the common good; whilst all such matters as related to local interests and institutions were left as the just prerogatives of the several States.

So long as these compromises were observed in good faith, and their conditions executed in a just and friendly spirit, their natural fruits appeared in the steady and rapid increase of population, wealth, and general prosperity, in every section of the Republic. The very diversity of interests seemed to produce a stronger political unity; the larger the bundle of sticks, the harder to break, so long as they remained bound together. Our country, in the vastness of its extent, and the variety of its interests, resources, and productions, seemed to possess the elements of a lasting union and independence. Each individual looked for a supply of the necessities, comforts, and luxuries of life to every section of the Republic. His manufactured goods must come from the East and North; his wheat and corn from the Middle and West; his rice from the Carolinas; his cotton from the South; his sugar from the Southwest; his furs and peltries from the Rocky Mountains; and, through the Golden Gate of California, the richer treasures of the new El Dorado. This condition of mutual dependence appeared to be the true element of a lasting fraternity of States. This idea was strengthened by the rapid increase of facilities for intercourse and communication, which, with bands of iron and currents of electric fire, have almost annihilated time and space, bringing the extremities of a vast continent into close neighborhood, the thirty millions of people within the limits of daily intercourse.

But without justice and good faith on the part of every member of this great Confederacy, these and a thousand other suspicious circumstances would be insufficient to perpetuate the existence of a political brotherhood. Unfortunately, justice and good faith have not been observed, and the seeds of discontent are rapidly producing the fruits of dissolution.

For many years there has been a party organization in one section of the Union opposed to the interests of another. The leaders and movers of this faction are infidels or fanatics in religion. Utopian in their social philosophy, and selfish and seditious in politics. Regarding themselves as wiser than the statesmen who formed our Government, and purer than the patriots and christians [sic] who established and defended it against the assaults of foreign foes, they have urged a relentless war of opinion against one half of the Confederacy, and strive to enforce their opinions by sending bands of robbers to steal our property, and murder our citizens.

In the first organization of this revolutionary faction they were so few in numbers, and so feeble in power, that the conservative portion of the nation, both North and South, manifested more contempt for their folly, than fear of their mischievous designs. But by the constant efforts of a corrupted press and a prostituted pulpit—the violent harangues and gross misrepresentations of crazed fanatics, male and female, black and white—the poison has been scattered throughout that whole section of the Confederacy, and a miserable faction has become a powerful party. Like every other kind of fanaticism, from witchcraft to Mormonism, it found no lack of teachers or disciples. Abolitionism not only invaded the sanctuary, and polluted the pulpit, but found its way into the nursery and school room, where it could poison a whole generation. It was incorporated into class books; set to music, and sung; caricatured with chains and scourges, exhibited in the print shops; wrought into plays, and acted upon the stage.[2]

While thousands of their own color and kind, under their own eyes, were reduced to an unnatural serfdom of poverty and toil, they had no sympathies for anything but the black slave, whose condition was far better than that of thousands in their own neighborhood. By the constant use of every engine of social influence, and the corruption of every fountain of social power, they gradually arose from the election of a constable to the election of a President. It is meet, too, that these Northern fanatics, who have no sympathies for anything, but African slaves, and who have substituted for morals and religion a vile system of negrophilism, which culminates in all the crimes and horrors of amalgamation, should remember "the pit from which they have been dug," and the sins that still cling to their skirts. The sale of their slaves originally furnished capital to start manufactories, and the labor of these slaves or their descendants still keeps their spindles turning.[3] Whilst they shed tears of hypocritical sorrow over the fancied sufferings of the slaves on the cotton and sugar plantations, they seize with a miser's greed upon the products of their labor, and "roll the sweet morsel under their tongues." They move heaven and earth to rescue a fugitive from the hands of his rightful owner, and fit out and man three-fourths of all the slave ships that prowl about the African coast.[4]

A strong and safe check to the domination of this ruthless and sectional power existed in the National Democratic party so long as it preserved its integrity. But, with the disruption and demoralization of this conservative power, the great bulwark of safety has been swept away, and the foul waters of fanaticism seem ready to deluge the land. For the first time in the history of the Republic, it is fairly divided into opposing sections by geographical lines, and a President has been elected by one section without a single vote from the other.[5] Nor is this the worst feature in the case; for the principles of the successful party are directly at war with our dearest interests—at war with what we consider to be a vital principle of our Federal Constitution—the right to occupy, with our property, and be protected in its possession, any of the common territory of the United States.

But these remarks are not applicable to all. Many of the Northern people are our friends, and friends of the Constitution and the Union, and disposed to do full justice to the claims of the South. In past years, the conservative masses of the North have stood by us, and fought with an unflinching and undaunted courage, even as a forlorn hope, against the avowed enemies of our institutions. Recent events indicate a healthy reaction, and I have reason to believe that a majority of our Northern neighbors will unite in giving proper guaranties to the South. The successful party has gained its present victory, not because a majority were abolitionists, but because they have been ruled and swayed by ambitious demagogues whose sole aim was the acquisition of political power, whether it resulted in the benefit or injury of the country. These selfish demagogues first courted the fanatics where they held the balance of power in local elections, and, thus proceeding step by step, have finally produced the present disastrous state of things. And here it is pertinent to propound a question to those who have been the movers and leaders in the Northern crusade against Southern rights and institutions; not to the infidels and socialists, the breakers of faith and blasphemers of God; but to those who have used abolitionism as a stepping stone to political power.

What do they expect to realize as the fruit of their victory? They have sowed the wind, and are now reaping the whirlwind. In one short month they have brought to the verge of destruction a glorious Union that required a century to build up, and, if demolished now, ten centuries could not reconstruct. The real authors of such a calamity will deserve and receive the execrations of the civilized world in all time to come. For years they have pursued, with a zeal worthy of a better cause, the traitorous work of undermining the foundations of the Republic. Novel writers, play actors, priests, peddlers, pedagogues, and political demagogues; the secular and religious press; the stump, the pulpit and the stage, have been brought into requisition for the accomplishment of their wicked designs; and now, when a whole continent is about to be involved in the horrors of a social and internecine war, we ask them to pause before the final blow is given. We ask them to inquire into the inevitable consequences of their doctrines and deeds before it is quite too late. And let us hope, too, that He who rules the hearts of men, and controls the destinies of the world, may send them wiser counsels and better thoughts, and that a returning sense of justice may lead to acts "meet for repentance," restoring the rights and conditions of good neighborship, and the peace of a distracted country.

It is no matter of marvel that such a state of things should cause not only dissatisfaction and disquietude, but the strongest feelings of opposition in the South. Hence we hear, not only the voice of alarm and solemn protestation against the evils that are likely to come with the rule of a purely sectional party, but stern resolutions of secession. Truly we have fallen upon evil times. A great crisis is not merely to be feared as approaching—it is already upon us. We see it in every man's face, we hear it in every man's voice. There is universal disquietude—a feverish unrest in the public mind—confidence between man and man is lost; a financial revolution precedes a political storm, and, with abundant crops and overflowing wealth, the whole country is on the verge of bankruptcy. The political sky is full of gloomy portents of coming evil; the old foundations seem sliding from beneath, and leaving us to drift out upon an ocean of untried experiment. If the fear of approaching dissolution brings such wide spread evils, what unspeakable calamities shall come with the reality itself!

Missouri occupies a position in regard to these troubles that should make her voice potent in the councils of the nation. With scarcely a disunionist, *per se*, to be found in her borders, she is still determined to demand and maintain her rights at every hazard. She loves the Union whilst it is the protector of equal rights, but will despise it as the instrument of wrong. She came into the Union upon a compromise, and is willing to abide by a fair compromise still; not such ephemeral contracts as are enacted by Congress to-day and repealed tomorrow; but a compromise assuring all the just rights of the States, and agreed to in solemn convention of all the parties interested.

Missouri has a right to speak on this subject, because she has suffered. Bounded on three sides by free territory, her border counties have been the frequent scenes of kidnapping and violence; and this State has probably lost as much in the last few years, in the abduction of slaves, as all the rest of the Southern States.[6] At this moment, several of the western counties are desolated, and almost depopulated, from fear of a bandit horde who have been committing depredations—arson, theft, and foul murder—upon the adjacent border.

Missouri has a right to be heard from her present position and power, as well as from the great calamities that a hasty dissolution of the Union would bring upon her. She has now a larger voting population than any other slave State, with prospective wealth and power far beyond any of her sister States.[7] With nearly seventy thousand square miles of territory, already inhabited by a million and a quarter of people, she has more arable land, of the first quality, than any other State in the Union; her territory is washed and intersected by rivers, whose fountains and tributary streams water half a continent, and whose mingled flood forms "an inland sea," extending more than a thousand miles to the ocean; her mineral wealth is far above the reach of computation; her commercial metropolis has already become the half-way house between the Atlantic and Pacific, and the great mart of trade for half a score of States and Territories; whilst our system of internal improvements is stimulating industry and effort, and rapidly filling up the vacant lands with intelligent, enterprising settlers. It would seem, indeed, that Missouri and her sister border States should be the first, instead of the last, to speak on a subject of this kind. They have suffered the evil and wrong, and should be the first to demand redress.[8] Is it quite proper that those who have suffered no pecuniary loss should initiate a proceeding of this kind, and say to us, by their premature action, that we do not know when to redress our wrongs, or defend our honor? Our people would feel more sympathy with the movement if it had originated amongst those who, like ourselves, had suffered severe loss and constant annoyance from the interference and depredations of outsiders.

As matters are at present Missouri will stand by her lot, and hold to the Union so long as it is worth an effort to preserve it. So long as there is hope of success she will seek for justice within the Union. She cannot be frightened from her propriety by the past unfriendly legislation of the North, nor dragooned into secession by the restrictive legislation of the extreme South. If those who should be our natural friends and allies undertake to render our property worthless by a system of prohibitory laws, or by re-opening the slave trade, in opposition to the moral sense of the civilized world, and at the same time reduce us to the humble position of a sentinel, to watch over and protect their interests, receiving all the blows and and [sic] none of the benefits, Missouri will hesitate long before sanctioning such an arrangement. She will rather take the high position of armed neutrality. She is, at present, able to take care of herself, and will be neither forced nor flattered, driven or coaxed, into a course of action that must end in her own destruction. If South Carolina and other Cotton States persist in secession, she will desire to see them go in peace, with the hope that a short experience of separate government, and an honorable re-adjustment of the Federal compact, will induce them to return to their former position. In the meantime, Missouri will hold herself in readiness, at any moment, to defend her soil from pollution, and her property from plunder by fanatics and marauders, let them come from what quarter they may. The people of Missouri will choose this deliberate, conservative course, both on account of the blessings they have derived from the Union, and the untold and unimagined evils that will come with its dissolution. Is it nothing to us that the postal system of the United States carries intelligence to every family in the State, and receives back, in postage, only a small portion of the expenditure? Is it a trifle to us that millions are distributed from the Federal exchequer every year to support officers and contractors within the State? Is it a matter of no consequence to our farmers that other millions are paid every year for stock and produce to support the army on our western frontier?

But far above this pecuniary view of the subject—quite beyond the reckoning of dollars and cents—is it nothing to be an American citizen?—a freeholder in the greatest and most powerful country on the globe?—part owner of a flag that has been baptized in the fire and blood of a thousand battles—a flag that now floats proudly on every sea, and in every port?—a countryman and kinsman of heroes and patriots, who fought and fell in the great struggle for liberty and right? Is there nothing in the memories of the past, the prosperity of the present, or the hopes of the future that should make us cling with a dying grasp to this last hope of the world—this proud temple of American liberty? But if the blessings we have derived from our government excite no desire for their preservation, then let the evils, crimes and horrors which must follow its dissolution, withhold us from hasty and inconsiderate action. First, though least in the category of evils that must come with secession, are those of a pecuniary nature.

The disruption of our present relations, the organization of an independent government, even without the natural consequences of civil war, will bring great and almost insupportable burdens upon the people. In addition to the loss of all the pecuniary benefits now derived from the General Government, the people must be unavoidably taxed for the means to inaugurate a new system. Depreciation of property; depression of trade, ruin of individuals and corporations; the withdrawal of gold and silver from circulation, the substitution of irredeemable paper for bankable funds; the loss of State credit, and the crippling or destruction of every public enterprise—these are amongst the positive evils of revolution, yet enough of themselves to destroy the hopes and crush out the energies of a great people. To these must be added the inevitable evils of taxation to support a respectable military force, a more thorough system of domestic police, an arrangement for the transportation and distribution of the mails, to provide for additional officers of government, and many other expenses. Those who are skeptical on this point, should reckon the expense of the three weeks' campaign just terminated, and then estimate the cost of a cordon of armed sentinels sufficient to protect a border of nearly one thousand miles. In this, as in most cases of fraternal strife, a conquest is the worst of all defeats. A single years' experiment of separate government, under these circumstances, would so impoverish the State and oppress the people, that the natural consequence might be looked for in a reign of anarchy or despotism. Our natural enemies, the Abolitionists, would attack us on three sides, and prey upon us whenever and wherever they could find the opportunity. Bickering, broil, battle, feud, and foray would prevail in all parts of the State; thousands of our best citizens would seek peace and quiet elsewhere, and Missouri would become like the lightening-scorched track of the Roman armies, where they "made a solitude, and called it peace!"

All our social, industrial, commercial, and educational interests would languish and die. The wheels of commerce would rust upon the rails, the hammer upon the anvil, the plow in the furrow. Farms would be untended; merchants idle; mechanics unemployed; our cities desolated as by a plague, and the country by a revolution. A few years of transition would put back Missouri a century in all the elements of moral and material progress, and finally leave her, as a wrecked Commonwealth, to drift out upon an unknown sea, on the ebbing tide of a popular revolution.

These things will be inevitable if we are forced into secession and revolution. You might as well attempt to turn back the shadow on the dial of time as to prevent the legitimate consequences of such a suicidal course. And will the planters, the slaveholders, merchants, miners and mechanics of Missouri surrender the fairest heritage on which the sun ever shown, in exchange for the mad chimera of secession, to be followed by revolution, battle and blood? Never!

Nor will Missouri be alone in the loss of property and the sufferings of her citizens, consequent upon the dismemberment of the American Union. In every section of the Republic, the same evils will prevail, in a modified or aggravated form. Public credit will become a myth, and the payment of public debts a miracle; the industrial pursuits that now bring contentment and prosperity to millions of hearth-stones, will be either destroyed or turned over to foreigners; our merchant ships will rot at their wharves, whilst the carrying trade of the world is transferred to other nations; the capitalists and operatives of Europe will furnish our manufactures, whilst the wheels of American factories and machine shops stand still, and the children of American artisans learn to utter the hopeless cry for bread!

It is not unlikely that those who have waged this political contest with the hope that it should end in bringing financial ruin and the horrors of a servile war to the South, may be the first to find their storehouses empty, and their firesides desolate. We commend to the lips of our enemies the poisoned chalice they had prepared for us, and when they have tasted its bitterness, may they then turn from their course, and learn to extend justice to those who have done them no wrong.

The very idea of the right of voluntary secession is not only absurd in itself, but utterly destructive of every principle on which national faith is founded. With such a doctrine in vogue, the idea of national credit is preposterous. When Texas came into the Union her large debt was paid by the National Government. Has she the right to retire from the compact the moment that the burden is removed from her shoulders? A large portion of our Territory has been purchased at the cost of hundreds of millions, and this money has been paid by all the States of the Confederacy. Has any State, composed of this purchased territory, a right to retire with a share of the property for which she has paid next to nothing? If this doctrine of secession holds good, our Government is without the first element of stability and is destitute of every feature of respectability. No foreign power will condescend to make treaties with us; no foreign nor even domestic capitalist will be simple enough to loan money to a dissolving partnership.

If the old Confederacy, which has enjoyed the confidence of the world for nearly a century, must lose her credit by giving countenance to this political heresy, what chance has a new Confederacy founded upon the practice of this very doctrine? In the absence of national credit, which must follow as the legitimate consequence of this doctrine of the right to secede at pleasure, how is it possible to prosecute war, build up national defenses, or foster works of domestic enterprise? It would be folly to declare war, for any number of States might withdraw from the compact, and avoid the expense of carrying it on. They might withdraw in anticipation of, or in time of war, and join the enemy with impunity.

It is idle to think of general secession without violence and blood. We might as well talk about amputating a limb without severing nerves or veins, or dying without pain. The different members of the Confederacy are bound together by a common origin, common language, and a common fortune in the past; united by the ties of commerce, social brotherhood, consanguinity, and mutual dependence upon each other for the comforts of life. We have grown to the strength and power of a vast empire, and our vital energies are now in full vigor. If dissolution should come, the death struggle will be as terrible as the dying energies are great.

Would the North-West consent to have the Mississippi blockaded either by foreign foes or domestic feud? Mr. Jefferson purchased this whole region of country from France in order to make this river a great highway for the nation. It belongs to the whole Republic, and the States of the great Western Valley will not consent to have their commerce cut off from the sea by one or two States lying near its mouth. This is one of a hundred examples that could be given to show that peaceable dissolution is a moral impossibility.

A strong reason for delay, reflection, and consultation is, that the great conservative masses of the people are not yet waked up to a knowledge of the mighty danger that threatens us. A majority of the State Legislatures and of Congress were elected in the midst of a popular furor, and their action will not be a fair exponent of the sober second thought of the people. The politicians now in power are not the men to settle this question. Let us turn from the selfish and helpless politicians, who are struck dumb at the magnitude of the calamity which their own folly has precipitated, and make one last appeal to the great conservative heart of the people. Give them a little time to rectify the errors into which they have been lured by the acts of ambitious and designing men, and all may yet be well.

Let us hope, then, that Missouri will "possess her soul in patience," occupying the high vantage ground which God and nature have bestowed; insisting upon all her rights, yet demanding nothing wrong; meting out condign punishment to the invaders of her soil, yet refusing to precipitate the destruction of our peace and prosperity by hastily cutting herself adrift from the sheet-anchor of our liberties. Whilst I would recommend the adoption of all proper measures and influences to secure the just acknowledgment and protection of our rights, and, in the final failure of this, a resort to the last painful remedy of separation; yet, regarding as I do the American Confederacy as the source of a thousand blessings, pecuniary, social and moral, and its destruction as fraught with incalculable loss, suffering and crime, I would here, in my last public official act as Governor of Missouri, record my solemn protest against unwise and hasty action, and my unalterable devotion to the Union, so long as it can be made the protector of equal rights.

{Governor Stewart concluded his address by commenting on domestic issues of railroads, banks, and education, among others.}

Source: *Journal of the House of Representatives of the State of Missouri, at the First Session of the Twenty-First General Assembly* (Jefferson City: W. G. Cheeney, Public Printer, 1861), 18–26.

Claiborne Fox Jackson
January 3, 1861

Born in Fleming County, Kentucky, Claiborne F. Jackson (1806–1862) moved to Missouri as a young adult, and engaged in the mercantile business in Saline County until 1836. Elected to the Missouri General Assembly in 1836, he served one term, before returning to the House in 1842 when he was chosen Speaker. He subsequently served in the Missouri Senate from 1848 until 1852. In 1856, he successfully managed the gubernatorial campaign of Robert M. Stewart. Four years later, Jackson won a narrow victory as a moderate over Constitutional Union candidate Sample Orr. With Abraham Lincoln's election, however, he abruptly altered his views, condemned the northern states as aggressors, and favored secession if the northern states proved unwilling to provide constitutional guaranties for the protection of slavery.[9]

Like Stewart, Governor Jackson believed the Republican Party posed a threat to the institution of slavery, and assumed that control of the executive department would soon be followed "by control of all the other departments of the government." In that event, Jackson believed that Missouri's "honor, her interests, and her sympathies point alike in one direction, and determine her *to stand by the South.*" For the time being, Jackson was content to recommend the calling of a convention of the slaveholding states so that amendments to the US Constitution could be agreed upon that would ensure the future protection of slavery.

Gentlemen of the Senate, and of the House of Representatives:
Assuming in your presence the office of Chief Executive Magistrate of the State, at a period when our whole country is in a condition of gloomy apprehension, I enter upon the discharge of the trust with which the people of Missouri have honored me, with deep convictions of its responsibility. Invoking the aid of that Almighty Being who has hitherto conducted us through perils of no ordinary kind, I can only promise to bring to the post assigned to me an honest devotion to my State, the Constitution of the United States, and to that Union which the Constitution was designed to perpetuate. My chief dependence, in hoping to accomplish anything promotive of the prosperity and security of the State, and contributory to an honorable, peaceful and satisfactory adjustment of our Federal relations, is upon the Representatives of the people, whom I meet here to-day. You, gentlemen, are here to pronounce the will of the people of Missouri; and it will be my pleasure, as it is my duty, to cooperate with you in the preparation and execution of such measures as will, in your judgment, advance the interest and sustain the honor of our State.

No man, who has observed the progress of events for many years past, could fail to perceive the approach of the crisis which is now upon us. Events have been tending in this direction, steadily but perceptibly; and if the present alarming disorganization of the government and dangerous division of the people are unexpected, it must be because the observer has labored under a lamentable misunderstanding of the nature of our government, and a fatal misconception of the character of the people. Upon questions of policy or expediency, no nation has exhibited a readier disposition to acquiesce in the expressed will of popular majorities than have the American people, in every stage of their progress; but they are jealous of their constitutional rights, and prompt to insist on their maintenance and preservation. They know full well that "the price of liberty is eternal vigilance;" and that to wait, with quiet submission, the insidious approaches of sectional despotism, when concealed under the forms of constitutional majorities, is to deprive themselves of all power of effectual resistance. They have not forgotten the lessons taught by their revolutionary ancestors, and are perfectly aware that the most odious and fatal absolutism is that which assumes the form of legitimate authority.

It is now forty years since the *Missouri question*, which startled the apprehension of one of our wisest statesmen, sounding in his ears as a "fire bell in the night," was finally disposed of.[10] Fifteen years after the adjustment of this controversy, under the instigation of emissaries from the headquarters of fanaticism in London, the slavery question was revived. The faction under whose auspicies [sic] it started was contemptible in numbers and power and isolated in position, seeking shelter for the propagation of its dogmas under the constitutional *"right of petition,"* and agitating Congress and the country under this perverted pretext. Acquiring strength from the countenance it received from a few prominent politicians, who were willing to sacrifice the permanent interests of their country for their own temporary aggrandizement, alliances were gradually formed with some one or two other of the political parties which divided the country, until a foothold was gained in the Federal Legislature. There we find it, first, resisting supplies to maintain the patriotic soldiers who, at the call of their country, were sustaining our flag on the plains of Mexico; then, controlling the disposition of our entire acquisitions on the Pacific, the fruits of that war, and appropriating that strip of country, south as well as north of the Missouri Compromise Line, to increase the strength of the predominating section; then, encouraging the colonization of Kansas, by State governmental intervention and Emigrant Aid Societies, against the spirit of the compromise upon which the Territorial bill was based; and finally, attaining its culmination in elevating to the head of the Federal Government the nominee and representative of the party.

I will not speak of the incidental outrages which have been perpetrated in the name of this party, by those whose powers of invention and vigor of execution have been drawn from a study of the precepts which their leaders have propagated and defended. The dissemination of incendiary pamphlets—the rescue of fugitive slaves—and the unparalleled atrocity of the Virginia invasion, are disclaimed as legitimate results of their leading political dogmas, and may only be attributed to them upon the principle that "he who sows the wind must reap the whirlwind."

But the prominent characteristic of this party, which pronounces its condemnation in the estimation of those who love their country, is, that it is purely sectional in its locality and its principles. The only principle inscribed upon its banner is hostility to slavery. Whatever adjuncts may have been drawn to it, from political or religious associations, the soul of the organization is now, where it was at the beginning, *hostility to slavery*. Its object has been openly avowed or disavowed as time, place and circumstances rendered expedient— not merely to confine slavery within its present limits—not merely to exclude it from the Territories, and prevent the formation and admission of any new slaveholding States—not merely to abolish it in the District of Columbia, and interdict its passage from one State to another; but to strike down its existence everywhere—to sap its foundation in public sentiment—to annoy and harrass, [sic] and gradually destroy its vitality, by every means, direct or indirect, physical and moral, which human ingenuity could devise. The triumph of such an organization is not the victory of a political party, but the domination of a section. It proclaims in significant tones the destruction of that equality among the States which is the vital cement of our Federal Union. It places fifteen of the thirty-three States in the position of humble recipients of the bounty, or sullen submissionists to the power of a government which they had no voice in creating, and in whose councils they do not participate.

It cannot, then, be a matter of surprise to any—victors or vanquished—that these fifteen States, with a pecuniary interest at stake reaching the enormous sum of at least three thousand five hundred millions of dollars, should be aroused and excited at the advent of such a party to power.[11] Their possession of the Federal Executive Department, destined soon to be followed, in the event of a silent acquiescence of the majority, by similar accessions, to the control of all the other departments of the government, is an event not likely to be overlooked by men who understand their rights, and have not yet been deprived of the power of maintaining them. Would it not rather be an instance of blindness and fatuity unprecedented, if the people and governments of the fifteen slaveholding States, under such circumstances, manifested a quiet indifference, and made no effort to avoid the destruction which threatened them? Is there nothing alarming in the fact that the whole power of the Federal Executive is pledged in advance for the subversion of the constitutional rights of nearly one-half of the Republic? History furnishes no example, nor can present observation point to the instance of any government on the face of the earth, whether created by the voice of the people or by the accident of hereditary succession, maintaining itself for any length of time with an administrative system hostile to the rights, the interests, the feelings and domestic quiet of nearly one-half of the nation, and that part distinguished by peculiarities of social organization and separated from the other by a geographical line. Are we to expect official appointees of the Federal Government to be opposed to the policy of the power which appoints them, and by which they are nurtured and sustained? Can the minority States, then, who have not contributed a single electoral vote to the elevation of the party to power who must soon control that government, look with unconcern upon the transplantation into their midst of thousands of Federal office-holders, exerting their influence, and the influence of their position, to break down the established social system of the States? Are these apprehensions diminished in the border States of the South and the South-West, where a nucleus for the accessions to abolitionism already exists, when the allurements of official station are to be the premium for treachery to their social and domestic policy? Such a condition of things is incompatible with the stability of any government, unless invested with the power and the will to sustain itself by the sword. It requires no extraordinary sensibility to injustice—no peculiar foresight to approaching danger—to be aroused at the approach of perils so apparent that the instinct of self-preservation, alone, is sufficient to warn against permitting their further advance.

Accordingly, we find the result of the recent Presidential election has already produced its natural effects. Throughout the entire slaveholding States of the Union, from Florida to Missouri, a feeling of discontent and alarm has manifested itself, more or less violent from the imminence of the danger, and the extent of the interest at stake. The cotton-growing States of the South, having a larger and more vital interest in jeopardy than the border States, are the first to awaken to a sense of insecurity. The sagacious Southern statesman is fully aware that his section, although necessarily the last victim, will be the greatest sufferer; that when the outposts yield, the citadel will not long afford safety. With them, the alternative is the maintenance of that institution which the Crown of Great Britain forced upon their ancesters [sic], or the conversion of their homes into desert wastes. With them, it is not a mere question of property, but what to them is dearer than property or life—their duty and honor are involved.

It has been said to be quite easy to bear the calamities of our neighbors with philosophical equanimity. Let us not illustrate this maxim by criticizing the precipitancy of the South. They are not the aggressors. They only ask to be let alone. If some have regarded their action as hasty, has not the occasion been extraordinary? I do not stand here to justify or condemn the action of South Carolina, who has already withdrawn her allegiance to the Federal Government. She is a gallant State, and will not forfeit that renown which a long list of distinguished dead has conferred on her history. When she unrolls that list—when she points to her Marions and Sumpters [sic] and Jaspers and Moultries and Laurenses and M'Donalds—her Pinckneys and Rutledges and Middletons—her Lowndes and Chevises and McDuffies and Hamiltons—her Haynes and Legares and Prestons and Butlers[12]—and to that preeminent statesmen who divided the public esteem with Webster and Clay[13]—her sister States, blessed with larger and more fertile territory, may well covet the glory of having given birth to such citizens, and may, at least, safely leave the honor of the State in the hands of their descendants. If South Carolina has acted in advance, let not her error lead to the more fatal one of an attempt at coercion.

The destiny of the slaveholding States of the Union is one and the same. So long as a State continues to maintain slavery within her limits, it is impossible to separate her fate from that of her sister States who have the same social organization. This decree of nature and necessity impresses itself upon the understanding without the aids of argument or illustration, and will not lose its force by any mutations to which our Federal Government may be subjected. In the event of a failure to reconcile the conflicting interests which now threaten the disruption of the existing Union, interest and sympathy alike combine to unite the fortunes of all the slaveholding States. The identity, rather than the similarity, of their domestic institutions—their political principles and party usages—their common origin, pursuits, tastes, manners and customs—their territorial contiguity and inter-commercial relations—all contribute to bind together in one brotherhood the States of the South and South-West. Missouri will not be found to shrink from the duty which her position upon the border imposes; her honor, her interests, and her sympathies point alike in one direction, and determine her *to stand by the South*. The products of our agriculture and manufactures find their principal market there;—our hemp, wheat, corn and flower, our horses, hogs and mules, and the manufactures already springing into existence and destined to augment the wealth and give stability to the prosperity of our commercial metropolis, must all go South for a market. Our only outlet to the ocean, through the natural channels of our great rivers, is through the South.

The estimated value of slave property now within the limits of our State falls but little, if any, short of one hundred millions of dollars.[14] Notwithstanding the active operations and assiduous exertions of a few anti-slavery propagandists, during the past ten years, and the number of slaves which high prices for cotton have drawn to the South, the increase in that portion of our population, as shown by the recent census, has been forty thousand. Are we prepared to annihilate a hundred millions of capital? or can we maintain a solitary, isolated position, as a slaveholding State, shut out from all access to the ocean, and flanked on either side by States who, in such a contingency, would look upon us with either hostility or distrust?

Propositions, looking to a number of new mixed Confederacies, are merely a reproof upon the dissolution of the present. If we can safely go into a new Union of a mixed character, why not remain in the present?

In considering the course proper to be pursued by this State, upon a contingency which events may yet render unnecessary, it is by no means unimportant to observe that any disposition evinced by Missouri, or any other large border slave State, to throw her weight into a non-slaveholding Republic, would close up all prospect of a reconciliation of present differences. The equilibrium of power between the slaveholding and non-slaveholding States is already gone. The weight of Kentucky or Missouri, thrown into the scale with the non-slaveholding States, increases the preponderance of the North, and drives the South to an adherence to a separate Southern Confederacy. The cotton growing States would then understand that the States on their border are prepared to submit to every aggression tending to affect slavery, and that in time they would only increase the number of States hostile to that institution. Missouri, then, in my opinion, will best consult her own interest, and the interest of the whole country, by a timely declaration of her determination to stand by her sister slaveholding States, in whose wrongs she participates, and with whose institutions and people she sympathizes.

These views are advanced, gentlemen, not upon a belief that all hope for the preservation of the present Union is lost, but upon a conviction, I believe, felt by all observers of passing events, that the time has arrived when a further postponement of their consideration would be unsafe and unwise. The issue of present embarrassments depends entirely upon the sentiments and action of the North. I trust there is patriotism left in our country sufficient to harmonize the conflicting views now in agitation, and place the existing Union on a basis consistent with the honor and safety of its constituent members. So far as Missouri is concerned, I do not fear to misrepresent the sentiments of her citizens by saying that they have ever been devoted to the Union, and will remain in it, as long as there is any hope of its maintaining the spirit and guaranties of the Constitution. But if the Northern States have determined on putting the slaveholding States on a footing of *inequality*, by interdicting them from all share in the Territories acquired by the common blood and treasure of all—if they have resolved to admit no more slaveholding States into the Union, contrary to the plain letter of the Constitution—if they mean to persist in nullifying that provision of the Constitution which secures to the slaveholder his property, when found within the limits of the States which do not recognize it, or have abolished it—they have themselves practically abandoned the Union, and will not expect our submission to a government on terms of inequality and subordination.

We hear it suggested, in some quarters, that the Union is to be maintained by the sword. Such suggestions, it is hoped, have sprung from momentary impulse, and not from cool reflection. The project of maintaining the Federal Government by force may lead to consolidation or despotism, but not to Union. Desperate politicians may hope to mend their fortunes by a civil war, and some men of honest intentions may fancy that the examples which history furnishes of successful usurpations of power, effected by the sword, may be safely imitated here. But our government stands upon the basis of *justice and equality*, and its existence cannot be prolonged by coercion. Standing armies of mercenary soldiers, subject to the will of the Executive, are not the remedies for violated constitutions or laws. Our British ancestors, in the worst times of their worst monarchs, would not submit to standing armies in time of peace; nor have their descendants so degenerated as to entrust to any Executive a mercenary army to be employed in enforcing obedience to an administration which has declared its hostility to an institution involving the rights and "domestic tranquility" of fifteen sovereign States of the Union. The first drop of blood shed in a war of aggression upon a sovereign State will arouse a spirit which must result in the overthrow of our entire Federal system, and which this generation will never see quelled.

As the ultimate fate of all the slaveholding States is, in my judgment, necessarily the same, their determination and action, in the present crisis, should be the result of a general consultation. To produce united action, there must be united counsel; and as the wrong is common to all, the redress for the wrong should be submitted to the consideration and judgment of all. It may not become me, therefore, to suggest what ought to be the *ultimatum* to be insisted upon by the slaveholding States. Candor compels me to say, however, that a mere Congressional Compromise is not to be thought of, and will only postpone and aggravate the evil, and will utterly fail to reach the disease. Experience shows too well that these compromises only lay the foundation for additional agitation. They are but laws, and, like all other laws, liable to be repealed; and their duration depends altogether upon the fluctuations of public opinion, operating through the representation of that opinion at Washington. The object of constitutional guaranties is to protect the rights of minorities; and it is to such guaranties, and not to legislative compromises, that the South must look for protection and security.

These questions must now be settled, and the powers and duties of the Federal Government, in connection with the existence of slavery in the States and Territories, put forever at rest. It is the interest of the whole country that these causes of dissension and irritation should be removed. Neither section has any right to expect a restoration of that harmonious cooperation in the advancement of the general welfare, which characterized the early stages of our national existence, by postponing or evading a full, frank and explicit understanding upon this subject. Its agitation hitherto has only served to inflame the public mind, to arouse all the angry passions, and keep the nation in a perpetual ferment; and if the gloomy and threatening aspect of affairs which this agitation has at length produced, shall happily terminate in a permanent, honorable and satisfactory adjustment, by means of constitutional amendments, the immense pecuniary losses already sustained will be more than compensated by a return of the country to her former career of prosperity, security and peace. If the Northern States are willing to remain with the South under a general government, where domestic slavery is to be regarded as entitled to its protection, instead of being the object of its hostility, they can have no reasonable objection so to declare in terms, and in a form which will leave no ground for cavil or misunderstanding. If they are not content with such an association, it is due to their own character, as well as to the rights of their associate States, that their determination should be made known.

For the purpose of ascertaining the final and deliberate judgment of each division of the country, and to carry that determination into effect, either by the addition of such stipulations to the Constitution as may be agreed on, or by a peaceable separation, if such should be the result, a Convention of the slaveholding States should be called. In such a Convention, the Southern States could agree upon such amendments to the Constitution as would secure to them their just rights, and in terms so explicit, that no difficulty could arise in the future as to the rights of either section. These amendments could be respectfully submitted to the Northern States for their consideration and action, and, in this manner, the whole question might be settled. As the ground of dispute is a single one, and a sectional one, the Convention to consider and adjust it must necessarily be sectional.

If it shall be proposed to establish a geographical line, there should, in my judgment, be at least a reciprocity of rights on either side of the line. If the Northern States shall insist upon excluding slavery from all Territory north of the compromise line, the South, upon every principle of justice, equality and right, should demand that slavery shall never be abolished south of the line, without the consent of the slaveholding States. By prudent and well directed efforts, I am not without hope that an adjustment alike honorable to both sections may be effected.

That such may be the issue—that our country may again advance in her career of unprecedented prosperity—that our Federal Government may again become, what its framers designed, "the sheet-anchor of our peace at home and safety abroad," and the State government continue to be "the most competent administrators of our domestic affairs, and the surest bulwarks against anti-republican tendencies," is, I am confident, the sentiment which animates you and all patriotic citizens. But, in the present unfavorable aspect of public affairs, it is our duty to prepare for the worst. We cannot avoid danger by closing our eyes to it. The magnitude of the interest now in jeopardy, both in reference to ourselves and our posterity, demands a prompt but deliberate consideration; and, in order that the will of the people may be ascertained and effectuated, a State Convention should in my view, be called immediately. Missouri is entitled to a voice in the settlement of the questions now pending in the country, and her position on these questions should be known. It may soon become necessary to send delegates to a Convention of the Southern States, or of all the States; and these delegates can only be instructed as to the determination of the State by an expression from the people through a State Convention. In this way the whole subject will be brought directly before the people at large, who will determine for themselves what is to be the ultimate action of the State.

In view of the marauding forays which continue to threaten our borders, as well as the general unsettled condition of our political relations, a due regard to our honor and safety requires a thorough organization of our militia. An active military force, well armed and held in readiness along our whole border, would afford that protection to persons and property which the citizens of our border counties have a right to demand, and which duty to them and to ourselves requires us to furnish. Allow me, in this connection, to allude to the promptness and efficiency with which the citizen soldiers of our commercial metropolis, under the lead of their gallant commander, responded to the call of my predecessor, to defend an exposed frontier from the ravages of a band of merciless outlaws. The expedition afforded no occasion by which military laurels could be gained; but the patriotism, ardor and endurance evinced by officers and men, furnish assurances of usefulness, whenever their country may call for their services.

{Governor Jackson concluded his address with observations on railroads, banking, agricultural resources, and the state's system of education.}

Source: *Journal of the House of Representatives of the State of Missouri, at the First Session of the Twenty-First General Assembly* (Jefferson City: W. G. Cheeney, Public Printer, 1861), 45–51.

Commissioner Daniel Renouard Russell
January 18, 1861

Daniel R. Russell (1821–1870) was appointed a secession commissioner by Mississippi Governor John J. Pettus.[15] During the war he served in the officer corps of the 20th Regiment, Mississippi Infantry. A glowing obituary described his speeches as "altogether unique, at one moment convincing the reason, at another stirring the emotions to a fever heat, and the next convulsing his audience with a never to be forgotten sense of the ludicrous in wit and satire of an order worthy of Hood or Hudibras."[16] His address was not captured in the House journal. This version was published in the St. Louis *Daily Missouri Democrat* a few days later.

Commissioner Russell argued, as conveyed by the reporter from the *Daily Missouri Democrat*, that Mississippi had seceded "because there was a working majority in the North which is pledged to extinguishing slavery." He envisioned a future with "hordes of marauding Abolitionists" invading Missouri. The Union was broken and if Missouri joined the southern Confederacy, she would become "the Empire State of the South." Russell's comments were apparently not met with much approval. The reporter, only cited as "K," sharply observed that if Mississippi "wishes to seduce other States into disunion, she must, in order to make any impression whatever, send abler men than Russell, who does not even possess ordinary ability as a speaker. He is a bad speaker in a bad cause."

Proceedings of the Joint Session on Friday Evening—Degrading Order of Lieut. Gov. Reynolds—Homage to a Secessionist—Manly Protest of Mr. Stevenson

DISCLOSING THEIR TREASON.

The proceedings of the joint session Friday evening, still further unfold the bold and treasonable designs of those unfortunately placed at the head of our State Government. Step by step they advance with their traitorous designs upon the Union and the safety and prosperity of the State.

This man Russell, the Commissioner from the independent repudiating State of Mississippi, has been here for some two weeks in close conference with the preeminent member of the dominant party—his hotel expenses doubtless paid out of the State treasury. Yet he has not been allowed to speak until now. He has even expressed himself annoyed that his name has been mentioned in certain papers, as the Commissioner, and as likely to make an address.

Treason against a good government never comes out boldly at first, lest it be crushed as the serpent under the heel of an indignant people. It must have time to work out its plans in deadly secret, and secure efficient co-operators ere it dares divulge itself boldly. It must be out of danger, also, in these modern times.

The time set for him to speak by his coadjutors was when, under false pretences, the calling of a State Convention had been secured; but he must not before, as it might alarm the people and frustrate that suicidal scheme. The Convention bill had passed—the time had come to develop its objects, and no better development could be made than the speech of a traitor to the Union, upon the very heels of its passage.

EXTRAORDINARY HONORS.

Not content, however, with introducing him as a mere Commissioner, he must be heralded and received with the most extraordinary honors, such as have never been accorded to any dignitary heretofore recognized by the Missouri Legislature. The Governor, by a special message, announced his presence at the Capital, though everybody knew he had been there for several days.

Joint resolutions were concurred in by both Houses, inviting him to a seat on the floor, and ponderous committees, vested with due dignity, were appointed to wait on him and escort him. The Governor, heads of departments, supreme judges, &c. were duly invited in the resolutions to attend.

Early in the evening the Hall of Representatives began to fill rapidly with members, citizens and ladies. The gallant Speaker, in his efforts to accommodate the expected Senators and the unprecedented rush and crush of *crinoline*, outdid himself in energy and displays of generalship in economising room. The reporters' tables were made to take a *side issue*, and little boys were duly warned that the chairs were reserved for those of a larger growth.

The grand opening scene commenced, the Speaker brought down his mallet and called the House to order.[17] Members who had not provided themselves with seats, were allowed the privilege of standing by the ladies. Shortly the shrill voice of the venerable doorkeeper announced the entrance of the Senate, headed by the Lieut. Governor, in all his dignity.[18] The Senators having taken their seats, the Lieut. Governor took the chair, and having announced that the object of the joint session was to receive a Commissioner from *our sister State* of Mississippi and to hear him, by invitation of the General Assembly, the committee were directed to wait upon that dignitary, and escort him, with all the honors, into the presence of the assembled dignity of the State of Missouri.

BOW TO GESLER'S HAT

But now transpired the most humiliating scene that has yet occurred in this secession movement. The Lieut. Governor, who never loses an occasion of displaying his newly fledged and accidental dignity, who "clothed in a little brief authority, plays such fantastic tricks before high heaven as makes the angels weep," *ordered* the members of the General Assembly to rise to their feet when the presence of the Commissioner from Mississippi was announced. This act of homage was never before required in the General Assembly of the State of Missouri, or ever performed. The Lieut. Governor did not even accord it to the present Governor, to whom he owes his present position, on the occasion of his inauguration. The hot indignant blood leaped to the cheek of every friend of the Union at this base homage to the secession power, and to a man of no power, intellect, ability or prestige.

Mr. Stevenson, of St. Louis,[19] demanded of the Lieutenant Governor if the General Assembly were required to do homage to a potentate.

Mr. Reynolds replied, "The member is out of order, and must take his seat."

The member demurred.

Mr. Reynolds reiterated his order to take his seat.

Mr. Stevenson offered to read the rules of the House, in which no such act of homage is required.

Mr. Reynolds changed his *order* to a *request*.

Mr. Stevenson having gained his point, sat down.

THE GRAND ENTREE OF THE FIERCE FIRE-EATER.

The commissioner made his appearance, escorted by the joint committee, and was warmly welcomed by the Lieutenant Governor. Not more than half the members did him the homage to rise—*not one of the St. Louis delegation of the House.*

HOW HE LOOKS.

The appearance of Mr. Russell is not such as to command respect even in a bad cause. Of medium stature; dark hair and complexion; low, narrow, retreating forehead; small sunken black eyes, with more of cunning than intellect manifested in them. He is certainly no type of the bold, chivalrous Southerner, but judging from his address, rather a type of the "whang-doodle" oratorical style. His address, taken from the inevitable text—"For he played upon a harp of a thousand strings," presented no new features, not even an argument, nor yet an original thought. The only striking feature was his style, it was very vehement.

CONDENSATION OF HIS SPEECH.

He presented himself before the General Assembly of the State of Missouri, to address it by the request of both Houses. He had been charged by the State of Mississippi to inform this State of its action in seceding from the Union, and to ask co-operation in the decided action of the seceding States. In encouragement of his position here to-night he would point to the inaugural of your Governor, to the elaborate debates in both Houses on the convention bill and its passage. He came here to plead the wrongs of the South, whose territory formed a vast empire.

It was his business to show that the action of Mississippi and other seceding States is justifiable. He was not a citizen of the United States, [hisses] but of the free and independent State of Mississippi. He did not glory in this. He had carried the flag of the Union, marched to its music on the battlefields of the Union, but recent occurrences had changed his thoughts and opinions on this subject. Many expressed their love to the Union in the recitals of "Hail Columbia," "Star Spangled Banner," and *even* "*Yankee Doodle*," but this was a poor way. Some ten years ago, when the dissolution of the Union was talked of in his State, he had acted as a Union man and had resisted it. The State of Mississippi would never have seceded from the Union *because of the non execution of the fugitive slave law, or the passage of personal liberty bills, or even on account of the election of Lincoln, or any other Northern measure against slavery.* It was because she had suffered long years of aggressions; because of the Kansas troubles, when we heard of your citizens being murdered and your property destroyed by raids of abolitionists from the North. He enlarged on Kansas greatly for the purpose of showing his sympathies for Missouri, and succeeded in showing himself a demagogue in every sense of the word.

Mississippi had seceded because there were a million and a half voters in the North, who would not be satisfied with anything less than the total extinction of slavery. Don't say that it is because of the speeches of that lying [sic] Jesuit of America, W. H. Seward,[20] or the foul slanders of the New York *Tribune*, that we take the step. It is because there is a working majority in the

North which is pledged to extinguish slavery. It is lamentably true that the Southern mind does not understand this question as it ought to do. He read from Mr. Lincoln's speech at the Cooper Institute, detached extracts to endeavor to prove his position.

He had seen many here who did not concur with him in secession views, who, however, acknowledged that the only question now was whether Missouri should give up slavery or not. He appealed only to pro-slavery men. He wanted no Black-Republicans, nor would he seek their acquaintance. [He might have added that Republicans did not seek the acquaintance of secessionists.] He had heard, since his arrival, that many members thought the action of seceding States too hasty. Why, Governor Letcher, of Virginia, in his message had made a lengthy complaint that South Carolina had not asked Virginia to co-operate with her.[21] The seceding States had been long asking the co-operation of the border States, but they had always been politely and kindly told to mind their own business. South Carolina, Florida, Alabama, Mississippi, and he hoped ere this time, Georgia had seceded. He had hoped that the sun which inaugurated Lincoln would shine upon all the slave States as free and independent of Black Republican rule. The South were determined to resist the rule of a numerical majority. There was no possibility of a reconciliation or compromise. The ultimatum the South demanded could not be granted by the North. We demand fraternal feeling, safety for our families and our property. We want no burning of our houses and cotton gins; no more Brown or Montgomery raids, etc.[22] Kentucky, Tennessee and Virginia must join the seceding States. Might he not express the hope that Missouri would stand by the South? Would Missouri surrender herself to hordes of marauding Abolitionists? She dare not do it. Missouri had been admitted by the compromise of the South, and that compromise had been the entering wedge to all the aggressions of the North. The South had carelessly admitted by that compromise that slavery was wrong; that was her great error.

He quoted from Washington, Jackson, Webster and Fillmore, detached sentences to prove the tendency of sectional parties to break up the Union. When fraternal feeling ceases, is not the Union virtually destroyed?

No Whig, no Democrat, no Union man—none but fanatical Abolitionists will say the course of Mississippi is not justifiable under the circumstances.

What evidence is there that there is a chance of reconciliation? In the Senate of the United States, the Crittenden resolutions had just been voted down, though loaded with concessions from the South. Every Northern Governor recently inaugurated had signified that no concessions should be made by the Republican party. Every Legislature of the North had talked of coercion. The South ought to arm herself for the conflict which he believed inevitable. Civil war was already inaugurated, and in less than ninety days the whole country would be involved in it. The guns from Fort Moultrie boomed forth this fact.[23]

The attempts to save the Union are useless; it is broken forever. The question now is, shall Missouri unite with a Southern Confederacy? Missouri would become the Empire State of the South. She is larger than any of the Southern States, her productions are more varied, her mineral resources greater. We will buy all of your products and you will be in the bosom of friends.

He paid a flattering, seductive compliment to St. Louis, was willing, glad to take her to his bosom, even with her 17,000 Republicans. He called her a jewel, the gem of the South, the Queen City, and defined her trade boundaries as extending to the Hudson Bay Company on the northwest and to Santa Fe on the Southwest.

EFFECT OF THE SPEECH

His remarks, delivered in vehement hate, without any argument or connection, though applauded by the faithful, were received with detestation by the great mass present. Upon leaving the hall many denunciations of his sentiments could be heard falling from the lips of Union loving men who are not yet prepared to give up the Union. The State of Mississippi if she wishes to seduce other States into disunion, must, in order to make any impression whatever, send abler men than Mr. Russell, who does not even possess ordinary ability as a speaker. He is a bad speaker in a bad cause.

K.

Source: St. Louis *Daily Missouri Democrat*, January 21, 1861.

CHAPTER 2

UNITED STATES SENATE

January–February 1861

Trusten Polk
January 14, 1861

Trusten Polk (1811–1876) was born in Delaware, graduated from Yale College in 1831, and commenced his law practice in St. Louis in 1835. Polk served briefly as governor in January 1857, but resigned having been elected to the US Senate where he represented the state from 1857 until January 10, 1862, when he was expelled as a "traitor to the United States" for his support of the Confederacy. During the war, he served in the Confederate Army as a judge in the military courts.

Polk began his address by observing that the complaints of the South were not against the federal government, but "against the action of certain States, and of the people of those States." Nevertheless, the people of the northern states had waged war against slavery for decades. In addition to the passage of personal liberty bills which "deprive their southern brethren of their undoubted rights under the Constitution," they had established underground railroads and "secret agencies" that work to "steal away slaves." Moreover, Polk charged, "Mr. Lincoln has announced the dangerous dogma that, in point of political rights, the negro is the equal of the white man." Soon the South could expect the entire power of the federal government to be brought to bear upon it for slavery's destruction. Polk did not recommend immediate secession, but a compromise that would involve "irrepealable amendments of the Constitution." His answer to the secession problem was a constitutional amendment of six parts that would have protected slavery in multiple ways, and obligated the federal government (not state governments) with enforcing those protections.

Mr. President, the circumstances which surround us are enough to force us to pause and to ponder. And if we do so, we shall perceive the cold shadow of events still more startling coming upon us in the future. Even now a vision of civil war begins to rise up before us; but we are not yet able to discern the form thereof.

Sir, I feel, for one, that we are in the midst of a crisis unprecedented in our history. It may be the very crisis of our country's fate.

Some affect to ignore it all; as, for instance, the Senator from Ohio, [Mr. WADE,][1] who first addressed the Senate.

Some, again, try to argue against it. That is the wisdom of the ostrich, which thinks to escape his pursuers by hiding his head in the sand.

Others still strive to allay apprehension. "Be still," they say; "there is no sufficient cause for danger." Grant it; and the danger is not thereby removed. What concerns us, and what we ought to be concerned about, is the magnitude of the evil. It matters not how trifling and insignificant the cause. A very small leak will sink a line-of-battle ship; and when the noble craft has gone down forever, it will not relieve the disaster to point out the smallness of the cause. You may tell me never [sic] so eloquently how she was able to battle with the storm-king on his own element, and to vanquish him; but the fact still remains that the gnawings of an insect has sunk her into the abyss. The American Revolution, says, Mr. Webster, was fought on a preamble. Is it not wiser and better to admit the truth, and look the danger full in the face? Then we may hope to prevent, or at least to avoid it.

"The prudent man foreseeth the evil, and hideth himself; but the fool passeth on, and is punished."[2]

But there are causes, Mr. President, for the perilous condition of affairs which is upon us. I know Senators say, "state your grievances; draw up your bill of indictment;" implying that there are no grievances, and that no bill of indictment can be drawn up. They are in error. They say, "you complain of the Government; and yet the Government has been, for most of the time, in the hands of the Democratic party." Here they are in error again. The complaint is not against the Government. To assume that it is, is a great mistake. To be sure, the action of the Government affecting the institution of slavery has been prejudicial to the South, and violative of its constitutional rights.

That was the case when the admission of my own State was resisted, and the Missouri restriction was enacted into a law. The South has borne the weight of that unconstitutional restriction for more than a quarter of a century. But she did not complain, because it was the work in part of southern men.

That was the case again in the passage of the Oregon territorial bill.³ President Polk, a southern man, deprecated the blow aimed against the rights of citizens of the slaveholding States by that bill as unjust and unequal. Yet, yielding to what he deemed the spirit of the Missouri compromise, he signed it. He signed it, because Oregon was north of the compromise line of 36°30′.

That, still again, was the case in the admission of California. California did not lie north of 36°30′; and her constituents did not tolerate slavery; and yet she was admitted into the Union, in violation of the spirit of the Missouri compromise.⁴ Moreover, the admission of California destroyed the equilibrium in the Senate between the slaveholding and the non-slaveholding States forever, and put the South at the mercy of the North.

But the complaint, I repeat, is not against the Government. It is against the action of certain States, and of the people of those States—States which are the parties to the constitutional compact, on which rests the Union of which they and their southern sisters are alike members.

They reap special advantages from the Union, in the protection it gives their manufacturing industry; in the bounties it lavishes upon their fishing interests; in the discrimination it imposes in favor of their commerce; in the millions of expenditures it pours annually into their lap; and they cry very loudly for its preservation, while at the very same time, they are violating the Constitution which supports the Union. They violate the compact on their part, and insist that their southern confederates shall be required, nay, coerced by force and by war, to keep it on their part; as if, in the language of Mr. Webster, "a compact broken on one side was not broken on all sides." They pass their personal liberty bills—there are some exceptions; I single them out, and honor them—bills in the very teeth of the Constitution, in contempt of it, and intended to deprive their southern brethren of their undoubted rights under the Constitution.

These bills not only do wrong and injury to their southern brethren, but they intensify the wrong by adding insult to the injury. They are passed in States where it has been admitted on this floor a fugitive slave scarcely ever goes—not one in forty years, according to the Senator from Vermont, [Mr. COLLAMER.]⁵ A high-spirited people may bear wrong, but it is quite too much to expect that they will bear with patience insult added to the wrong; and this, too, from those standing in the relation of friends and brethren. "It was not an enemy that reproached me," says the word of inspiration; "then I could have borne it; but it was thou, a man equal, my guide and mine acquaintance."

The fugitive escapes. Is he delivered up in obedience to the command of the Constitution? No, sir; he is harbored and secreted and hastened on his way. If the master is passing through the State, is he bid "God-speed" in the spirit of friendship and fraternity? On the contrary, his slave is enticed away by false promises, or is ravished from him by force. Underground railroads are established, stretching from the remotest slaveholding States clear up to Canada. Secret agencies are put to work in the very midst of our slaveholding communities, to steal away the slaves.

The constitutional obligation for the rendition of the fugitive from service is violated. The laws of Congress enacted to carry this provision of the Constitution into effect are not executed. Their execution is prevented. Prevented, first, by hostile and unconstitutional State legislation. Secondly, by a vitiated public sentiment. Thirdly, by the concealing of the slave, so that the United States law cannot be made to reach him. And when the runaway is arrested under the fugitive slave law—which, however, is seldom the case—he is very often rescued. It is said, that, in such case, when suits are brought against the rescuers, courts and juries will enforce the laws against them. But all this is accompanied by delay and vexation, and the most serious expenses—far exceeding the value of the slave. And even when judgment is obtained, it is, in many cases, valueless, for nothing can be made on the execution. The rescuers are either worthless negroes or equally insolvent white men. But worse than all, these rescues are always accompanied by violence, and consequently by the most imminent peril to the master. They are effected by mobs of excited and fanatical white men and reckless black men, themselves runaway slaves.[6]

Sir, I know gentlemen of my own State who have slaves in a northern city, worth thousands of dollars, who prefer to bear the loss of them rather than jeopardize their lives in attempting to recover them. The very case to which the Senator from Wisconsin [Mr. DOOLITTLE][7] alluded is a strong illustration. The slave was rescued by a mob, and the life of his master—whom I know well—was put in imminent peril. He has never recovered his slave; he has never recovered a dollar of his value, although he has spent more than his value in the endeavor. He has recovered judgment, and incurred costs, and that is all. And in this very case the supreme court of Wisconsin committed the judicial outrage of deciding the fugitive slave law unconstitutional.[8] And even yet the fruitless litigation is not ended. This lawlessness is felt with special seriousness in the border slave States. The underground railroads start mostly from these States. Hundreds of thousands of dollars are lost annually. And no State loses more heavily than my own. Kentucky, it is estimated, loses annually as much as $200,000. The other border States, no doubt, lose in the same ratio. Missouri much more.[9]

But all these losses and outrages, all this disregard of constitutional obligation and social duty, are as nothing in their bearing upon the Union, in comparison with the *animus*, the intent and purpose, of which they are at once the fruit and the evidence. They demonstrate that the authority of the Constitution has ceased to be respected at the North. That instead of fraternal feelings—instead of the good faith which ought to subsist between confederates—there are animosity and bad faith. And it is rendered worse still by the consideration that it was not so in the earlier and better days of the Republic. Then there were loyalty to the Constitution and kindness towards the South. These are now changed, it is to be feared, into disloyalty and hatred. If so, how remorseless is that hatred?

> "Earth hath no hate like love to malice turned,
> Nor hell a demon like a brother scorned.[10]

Is this a gloomy and portentous picture? I fear it is not equal to the sad reality. A worse picture is yet to be added.

These sentiments have become the animating spirit of a political party. They have found expression in its platform of principles; they have nominated candidates for the Presidency and Vice Presidency; and they have elected them by a strictly sectional vote.

The candidate just elected to the Presidency was the first man of his party to enunciate the dogma that there is an irrepressible conflict between the slaveholding and non-slaveholding States.[11] This house of the Constitution, made by our fathers, and which they supposed, by being divided into many apartments, was thereby rendered more commodious for a harmonious family of numerous and happy States; this Union, we have been told, is a house divided against itself. The Senator from Ohio, [Mr. PUGH,][12] not long since, showed, beyond cavil, that Mr. Lincoln in uttering that sentiment, had reference to slavery in the States; not merely in the Territories, but also and especially in the States.

Moreover, Mr. Lincoln has announced the dangerous dogma that, in point of political rights, the negro is the equal of the white man. In a speech made by him at Springfield, Illinois, on the 17th of July, 1858, he said: "I adhere to the Declaration of Independence. If Judge DOUGLAS and his friends are not willing to stand by it, let them come up and amend it. Let them make it read that all men are created equal, except negroes."

Again:

> My declarations upon this subject may be misrepresented, but cannot be misunderstood. I have said that I do not understand the Declaration to mean that all men were created equal in all respects. They are not equal in color; but I suppose that it does mean to declare that all men are equal in some respects; they are equal in their right to "life, liberty, and the pursuit of happiness." Certainly, the negro is not our equal in color—perhaps not in many other respects: still, in the right

to put in his mouth the bread his own hands have earned, he is the equal of every other man, white or black.

This needs no comment; its meaning is plain and unequivocal. I now beg call the attention of the Senate for a moment only to the platform upon which Mr. Lincoln secured his election. Considering the history and antecedents of this party, no man can doubt that the following portion of the second resolution was intended to be applied to negro slaves: "We solemnly reassert the self-evident truths that all are endowed by their Creator with certain inalienable rights, among which are those of life, liberty, and the pursuit of happiness; that governments are instituted among men to secure the enjoyment of these rights."

And that it denies that there can be any right of property in slaves, is clearly shown in the fifth resolution, in which it is declared that the present Democratic Administration has exceeded the worst apprehension of the convention, (the Chicago convention) among other things, "in construing the personal relation between master and servant to involve," as they say, "an unqualified property in persons." And again, the eighth resolution is as follows:

> That the normal condition of all the territory of the United States is that of freedom. That as our republican fathers, when they had abolished slavery in all our national territory, ordained that no person should be deprived of life, liberty, or property, without due process of law, it becomes our duty, by legislation, whenever such legislation is necessary, to maintain this provision of the Constitution against all attempts to violate it. And we deny the authority of Congress, of a Territorial Legislature, or any individuals, to give legal existence to slavery in any Territory of the United States.

Now, consider this in connection with the declaration made on the floor of the United States Senate in 1857, by the Senator from New York, [Mr. SEWARD,][13] who may be considered the leader of the party, that the Supreme Court of the United States must be reformed, which means that the national judiciary must be abolitionized; and is it not evident that the *writ of habeas corpus* might be brought into use to effect the liberation of the slaves in the slaveholding States? Is not such a purpose palpable, and such a result probable? What, then, could the slaveholding States expect, after the election of such a candidate upon such a platform, but that all the patronage and all the power of the Federal Government, in all its departments, would be brought to bear upon the institution of slavery in the South, in order to compass its destruction?

{Senator Polk here introduced a number of quotes from Republican newspapers and Republican Joshua R. Giddings emphasizing his point that the incoming party was hostile to the institution of slavery.}

Sir, at the formation of the Constitution, twelve of the thirteen States were slaveholding. And even Massachusetts herself had been a slaveholding colony; nor had she ever abolished slavery by any statute law. They all recognized the right of property in slaves.

The Constitution was adapted to the institution of slavery as it then existed, and was in accordance with the public sentiment of the whole country at the time. Accordingly, no man doubted that it recognized property in slaves, and was designed to protect it wherever the national flag was unfurled, on sea or on land. No question was made as to the right of the master to carry his slave with him into the common Territories of the Union. Even the men of Massachusetts would no doubt have conceded it. Its denial would have lessened the market, and consequently depreciated the price that the New England slave trader might get for the slaves he was importing from Africa by the ship-load. The flag of the Union protected this property on its passage from Africa to the slave States of the South. The treaties of the country with foreign nations specially stipulated for the indemnification of the loss of slaves. This was done in Jay's treaty.[14] It was done in the treaty of Ghent;[15] and the treaty for the acquisition of Louisiana recognizes and protects the right of property in slaves.[16]

But the times have changed. States have changed their institutions; and now eighteen of them are non-slaveholding—a majority in number, and the majority in population—and now the political power of the country is in their hands. But the Constitution is not changed. No amendment has been added to it on the subject of slavery. It remains exactly the same to-day that it was in 1789. Yet, Mr. President, what do we now behold? A political party has been organized upon the one central idea of hostility to slavery, and its ultimate and certain abolition in every section and State of our broad republic; and it has triumphed. It has wrought a revolution in the public sentiment of the country against slavery, and is about to inaugurate a revolution in the policy and administration of the Government for its extinction.

Mr. President, has the South no cause for alarm for the safety of her institutions, and the security of her rights? Is not her very existence at stake? How long could she retain the institution of slavery after the whole power of the Federal Government shall have been brought to bear upon her for its destruction? Think what could be effected by the Federal legislation. Abolition of slavery in the District of Columbia; abolition in the arsenals, dock-yards, and forts; outlawry of it on the high seas, and wherever the flag of the Union floats;

exclusion of it from the common Territories belonging equally to all the States; circumscribing it as with a wall of fire within the States.

Then let the long and strong arm of the Executive power of the Government be put forth for its extinction within the States. Sir, it will be mighty to the pulling down of the strongholds of southern institutions and rights. Against almost everything else but this, the South might protect herself. Cohorts of Federal office-holders, Abolitionists, may be sent into her midst to exert the patronage, influence, and power of their offices, and to plot and conspire against her property, her peace. Postmasters—more than thirteen thousand—with all their employees, controlling the mails and loading them down with incendiary documents. Add to these, land officers, surveyors of land, surveyors of ports, collectors of customs, assistant treasurers, judges and marshals, each of these, with all his employes, [sic] intent upon one aim. What institution could withstand such an invasion, such sapping and mining? Even the Senator from Ohio [Mr. WADE] is not surprised that the citizens of the slaveholding States should begin to arouse themselves from their supineness.

The slave property of the South, sir, is worth three and a half to four billion dollars. Is it to be expected that a brave and intelligent people would submit without resistance, without a murmur, to the destruction of such an amazing amount of property? Sir, no people, in any age of the world, in any country, or clime, under any form of government, has ever submitted to the destruction of a hundredth part of it without resistance and revolution.

But there is a more horrible result still to follow, especially in those States where the black slaves greatly outnumber the free whites. This I forbear to hold up to view. I draw a vail over it. Let not its horrors be even suggested to the imagination.

I am satisfied, Mr. President, that there exists, and is spreading among the masses of the citizens of the southern section of our Union, alarm in all the slaveholding States, real and profound alarm, for the safety both of their property and of the lives of their wives and children. The President {James Buchanan} has sketched this in the following sentences of his last annual message:

> The immediate peril arises not so much from these causes as from the fact that the incessant and violent agitation of the slavery question throughout the North, for the last quarter of a century, has at length produced its malign influence on the slaves, and inspired them with vague notions of freedom. Hence, a sense of security no longer exists around the family altar. This feeling of peace at home has given place to apprehensions of servile insurrection. Many a matron throughout the South retires at night in dread of what may befall herself and her children before the morning. Should this apprehension of domestic

danger, whether real or imaginary, extend and intensify itself until it shall pervade the masses of the southern people, then disunion will become inevitable. Self-preservation is the first law of nature, and has been implanted in the heart of man by his Creator for the wisest purpose; and no political union, however fraught with blessings and benefits in all other respects, can long continue, if the necessary consequence be to render the homes and the firesides of nearly half the parties to it habitually and hopelessly insecure. Sooner or later the bonds of such a union must be severed.[17]

This very alarm is one of the most intolerable of the grievances inflicted on the South by the ceaseless and systematic aggressions of Northern abolitionism and negroism. No people can consent to live in the midst of alarms by day, and terror by night. Last of all others will the American people of the slaveholding States of this Confederacy consent to it.

Sir, the "terror by night" is ranked by the sacred penman in the same category with "the arrow that flieth by day, and the pestilence that walketh in darkness, and the destruction that wasteth at noon-day."[18]

I am also satisfied, sir, that there is a settled purpose on the part of the people of the southern States to have the difficulties now brought upon them settled fully and forever, settled at once. Nothing short of this will meet the exigencies of the present crisis. And in order to such settlement, irrepealable amendments of the Constitution ought to be made, covering the following points:

1. Express and unequivocal recognition of the right of property in slaves.
2. A similar recognition of the right of the owner to take his slaves into the common territory of the United States, and to have his right of property in them protected by the Federal Government there, and wherever else its jurisdiction extends.
3. That Congress shall have no power to abolish slavery in places under its immediate jurisdiction situated within the limits of the States that permit the holding of slaves.
4. Nor within the District of Columbia, so long as slavery shall exist in either of the States of Virginia or Maryland, nor without the consent of the inhabitants, nor without just compensation first made to such owners as do not consent to such abolishment.
5. Nor shall Congress have power to prohibit or hinder the transportation of slaves from one State to another, nor to the District of Columbia, nor to a Territory of the United States.[19]
6. That, when the owner shall be prevented from retaking his fugitive slave, or when such fugitive shall be rescued from him by force, he shall receive compensation for the value of his slave.

All this the slaveholding States ought to have, and all this the non-slaveholding ought to be willing to concede. They ought to be willing to make these concessions, first, for the sufficient and commanding reason that they would relieve the common country.

Secondly. They are fully warranted by the Constitution as it now stands, and are in perfect concord with both its provisions and spirit. According to the opinion of the Supreme Court of the United States—the appropriate and the appointed tribunal for the arbitrament of such questions—the tribunal of last resort—they are guaranteed by the Constitution, as it was made by our fathers.

Thirdly. The Republican party has brought about the condition of things which has made such concessions necessary, and that same party ought to be ready to grant the concessions which are needed in order to remedy these evils. If they have done wrong, or inflicted injury, both justice and magnanimity require that they should make prompt and full reparation. In this, at least, you will receive the hearty and cordial cooperation of the Democracy of the North. The northern Democracy have always been willing to sustain the Constitution according to its true construction, and so as to secure to the citizens of the slaveholding States their just and equal rights.

Fourthly. You of the Republican party alone have the power to heal the dissensions which are dissolving the Union. The South cannot do it. The political power, adequate to the task, has passed out of their hands into yours. The northern Democracy are also unable to accomplish it. They can only aid you.

Fifthly. The northern States constitute the more populous and the more powerful section. Consequently you incur no danger by making the concessions.

Sixthly. You are the victorious and the dominant party, and you ought not to be willing to abuse your power to the oppression of the vanquished and weaker section. Nay, more; standing in a position where a want of generosity would be a reproach, you ought ever to be prompt to tender overtures.

And, lastly, the South asks no pecuniary advantage. She only demands safety. Can it be refused?

> {At this point in his address, Senator Polk observed that the Crittenden proposal regarding the territories was no solution because while slave owners were prohibited from settling north of the 36°30' line, nonslaveholders were not prohibited from settling south of it. Emigrant aid societies would invade New Mexico, as they had Kansas, and prevent slavery from being established there. The institution of slavery was important to Missouri and constituted wealth "of perhaps one hundred million dollars," and no state had suffered more from "Abolition incursions." He then

turned to the subject of coercion and argued, as had President Buchanan on December 3, 1860, that the federal government had no constitutional authority to use force to coerce a seceded state back into the Union. If coercion were attempted, Polk predicted, "you have inaugurated war—nothing less, nothing more.... But this would be the most wicked, horrible of all wars. It would be civil, internecine war; perhaps also servile war."}

In the dreary catalogue of wars that have cursed and depopulated and ravaged the earth, there is none which is a parallel to what such a war must be. The civil wars of the Roman Empire in ancient days, and those of the British in more modern, are no types of what this American civil war must be. It will be a war of sections—the North against the South, and the South against the North. It will be a war of families—son against father, brother against brother, and husband against his wife's brother. It will be bitter, bloody, remorseless, and exterminating. No man can tell when it will terminate, and no fancy depict its horrors, its universal devastation and ruin. The picture drawn by Mr. Burke of the havoc inflicted by Hyder Ali upon the Carnatic, will scarcely convey an adequate idea of it.[20]

Sir, is any Senator on this floor prepared to resort to coercion in order to achieve such results? Ought any Senator to be willing to deny to the South the constitutional concessions and guarantees necessary to maintain her rights and safety, at the risk of incurring these consequences?

Mr. President, for myself, I denounce the policy and the construction of the Constitution which must lead to such disasters. If we must separate, let us separate in peace. If Republicanism, having beaten down and subdued the gallant Democracy of the North, is determined, in spite of constitutional guarantees, in spite of social duties, in spite of justice and right, to exterminate the institution of slavery from every part of the soil of every State in the Union, or else to force the slaveholding States to go out of the Union, let our separation be without the shedding of blood.

> {Senator Polk ended his address by exhorting his colleagues to find a peaceful settlement of the crisis, to agree to "timely concessions," and prevent civil war. Believing that only northern states had the ability to forestall conflict, Polk concluded by appealing "from their Representatives to the sovereign people of the North; and may God grant to interpose for our country in this hour of her extremity and need."}

Source: *Congressional Globe*, 36th Cong., 2nd Sess., 355–60.

James Stephen Green
February 12, 1861

James S. Green (1817–1870), a native Virginian, moved to Missouri around 1838 and began his law practice in Monticello. He was elected as a Democrat to the Thirtieth and Thirty-First Congresses (1847–1851), served as chargé d'affaires to Columbia (1853–1854), and then in the US Senate from 1855 to 1861.

Senator Green's comments were in response to an amendment to a naval appropriation bill that would have directed $1,200,000 toward the construction of seven "steam screw sloops-of-war, of the second class." He cautioned against such an expenditure because of a depleted Treasury, but more importantly because he feared the naval ships would eventually be used to "coerce" seceded states. Green defended the right of secession and believed that all federal property within a seceded state reverted to the ownership of the state. A conditional secessionist, the senator believed that Missouri should only secede if the North continued its nonenforcement of the Fugitive Slave Law and refusal to acknowledge the constitutional right of property in slaves.

Mr. GREEN. Mr. President, it might be supposed that the line of my remarks is not appropriate to the present bill now pending before the Senate; but, under the circumstances growing out of the character of the speeches made on the pending amendment, I think them entirely appropriate. The exact subject-matter upon which the Senate must now act, and to which the attention of the Senate ought to be directed, is, the propriety of the appropriation of $1,200,000 to build seven new screw steamers of certain dimensions and draught. In itself, it would seem to be a matter of very small importance; but when the intent with which it is now urged is shadowed forth by its friends, it strikes the public mind with so much force that we cannot resist the occasion to meet them in the proper spirit. At a time when the Treasury is depleted; at a time when there is no actual necessity for an increase of our naval force; at a time when unfortunately, we have been driven into the market to borrow nearly seventy million dollars, in addition to a proposition to increase the duties upon all imported goods; and besides all this, when honest contracts are urged for payment, when the creditors of the Government are begging you to pay them, they are put off with the poor and miserable plea, that we have not money to pay; men who have credited this Government for eighty years, who have advanced money and have never received it back, are to be pushed aside on the poor plea that we are not able to pay them now, and when you undertake to pay them the plea is urged, also, that the Government is presumed always to be ready, and therefore you will not pay interest—in this contingency and under this state of things we are asked to appropriate $1,200,000 to build seven new steamers!

> {Senator Green continued here to argue against the necessity for building the ships at a time when the public coffers had been depleted by approving a "railroad to the Pacific" and funding the homestead bill. "Then you get up and say, give us $1,200,000 to build seven new steamers for war purposes, to coerce those States who deem themselves injured, and in the exercise of their sovereign rights, choose to say they may secede from the Union."}

Mr. President, it resolves itself into this question—not the protection of public property; not the enforcement of the laws; but, has any State a right to secede; and if she has the right under any circumstances and in any contingency, who is to be the judge of the circumstances that justify it? If the Federal Government is to be the judge, the right does not exist. That is a denial of the right. If the State is to be the judge, that is an admission of the right. Who then is to be the judge; and if a wrong decision is made, on whom does the responsibility fall, and what consequences are to follow? Talk to me about enforcing the law! Why, sir, there is no man in the United States but what says "enforce the law;" but enforce it where? Enforce it where you have jurisdiction; enforce it over your Union. That does not still meet the question; for if a State has the right to secede and does secede, she is no longer a part of the Union; and the enforcement of the law within the Union does not include the right to enforce it in a seceding State. Protect public property, you say? So say I. Whatever is public property, protect; protect it against John Brown and Montgomery and the Abolition hordes who rush into Missouri and Virginia. That is a different question. But what is public property? That property which is appropriated to public purposes *within the Union*; not property outside of the Union.

You have public property at Spezzia, on the Mediterranean; but I venture to say, that you will not send your Army and your Navy and your seven new steamers there, if the Government there says the circumstances of that country require you to desist. You have public property in the city of London, where your minister resides. You will not send your Army and your Navy there to protect it. You own it as a mere proprietor, and you are subjects to the local law, the law of Great Britain. You have public property in other parts of the world, but you cannot protect it with military power. You can negotiate and insist upon a protection of your rights; but that is all.

Have you public property in South Carolina? for I intend to reduce this question to its simple elements. I answer, you have not one single particle. The right to secede is a question that I postpone for after consideration. If, however, the right to secede is admitted, whatever forts, magazines, arsenals, or other public property had been purchased, made, constructed, or improved by the Federal Government, cease to be public property of the Union; they follow, necessarily, the action of the local sovereignty. Fort Sumter this day is wrongfully held by this Government; it is an act of war against the State of South Carolina. But you say, the Federal Government built it. I answer, yes; with the consent of the State. When? When that State was a part of the Federal Union. For whose benefit? To protect Washington city? No. To protect New York? No. To protect Boston? No. To protect Charleston? Yes. Now, a fort built for the purpose of protecting the city of Charleston, is, it seems, to have its ponderous guns turned and their frowning mouths directed against the very city for whose benefit it was erected.

Whose money paid for it? you may ask. I answer, the money of the Federal Treasury. You then will ask this additional question: if the Federal Treasury built the fort, and manned the fort, and armed the fort, although it was intended for the protection of South Carolina, can South Carolina, by an act of secession, reclaim that and take Federal property? I give you this answer: South Carolina contributed her due proportion for the building of all the forts; and she contributed as much to build Fort Columbus, and every northern fort, and every other southern fort as she did to build Fort Sumter; so that, in the adjustment of the accounts, there is no injustice done to any portion of the Union. She paid to build Fort McHenry, Fortress Monroe, Fort Columbus, and all the other forts stretching from her northern line around to the extreme West—even along the great lakes. She paid her full proportion; and if we paid our proportion for Fort Sumter. It is no injustice to divide.

For what object was it erected? It was erected to protect the city of Charleston and the State of South Carolina. But I will go a step further than that. I say there never was an instance in the history of the world, where a State seceded or revolutionized, when the act was complete, that any other State claimed the forts within her limits. I shall hereafter come to the point whether the act is yet complete or not; but I do say there never was an instance—you may search the records of the world—where a State revolutionizes or withdraws from an association of States, that any other Power claimed a fort situated in her limits.

Hence, when you talk about protecting the property of the United States, everybody will say that is right; but it leaves the question still unanswered, what is the property of the United States. When you talk about enforcing the laws within the jurisdiction of the United States, everybody responds, yes; but it leaves the question still unanswered, what are the limits of the United States. Hence, the whole of it, disguise it as you may, resolves itself into this one question: has the State the right to secede, and has the State, in fact, seceded? I challenge the world to meet that question, if you concede the right and the fact. There are two points in it: the *right*, and the *exercise* of the right. You may concede the right to all States; for if it exists with one, it exists with all. They are all on perfect terms with equality; every State in this Union acquired since the original thirteen formed the Confederation, is on exact terms of equality; and a Union not based upon terms of equality would not be worth preserving.

Individuals may rise in a community, violate the laws, and subject themselves to punishment; but that never meets the real question that we have to consider. Our Government is one of its own peculiar kind. This association of States is such a one as never existed before; and if broken up by the misconduct of its members, it will never have its counterpart. Individuals in a single Government can commit treason, can commit rebellion, can violate the laws. Individuals in an associated Government can do the same things. But in regard to a *State*—a member of the association—it brings up a different question for consideration. A county in a State is an integral part of the State; an individual of a State is an integral part of a State; but this Federal Government is, as expressed by Mr. Calhoun, a *multiple* of units.[21] Each State being an entirety, an entity, a thing of itself, having power to breathe and exist, it goes into this multiple by its own voluntary action.

> {Senator Green here continued to argue in favor of the right of secession. Only the "enlightened judgment of mankind" could judge the correctness of a state's decision to leave the Union. He commended South Carolina for its "honor and forbearance" in seceding. Green hoped the Mississippi River would not be "interfered" with if war were to come. "If we are compelled to divide," he lectured, "had we not better divide as honorable, thinking, and intelligent men, than as reckless brutes, governed alone by instinct?"}

It is said by many here that South Carolina has suffered no wrong; Maryland, Virginia, Kentucky, and Missouri, have suffered it. I know that Maryland, Virginia, Kentucky, and Missouri have suffered ten times as much as South Carolina ever did; I might say a hundred times as much; but the fact that she acts in advance, whether we consider it hasty or inconsiderate or not, proves that she is noble, patriotic, and true in her impulse. She is acting for our benefit. We may think a different policy would have been better, as I do think; but it shows her regard for a great question involving all of us together; and not only all of us, but the whole of the human race. It is not a question of slaves only. The very principle that will permit them to attack one species of property against the Constitution, and break it down, will justify them in taking another species of property and confiscating that also. The agrarianism of the North will spread from the success of their attempt to break down slavery in the South; and every property holder in New York and Boston is as much interested in repressing this attack upon private property as I am. Let the populace rise; let the mob gather; let the impulse be given to them, and they will say: "Why shall one man have $15,000,000, and we stand here starving and begging for bread?" This feeling will be engendered. Law-abiding, orderly, good people ought, therefore, to repress every thing that leads to it. We of the South ought to repress it; you of the North ought to repress it; and, if it be not repressed, the consequences will come home to you in a more fearful degree than they can possibly come to us.

While Missouri has suffered so much, she has been the last to act; yet that State will act. The action, however, of Kentucky, of Virginia, I am sorry to say it, and of Tennessee, has been of the most disastrous character. It has done no harm to Missouri; but it has stimulated northern men to make speeches, such as the KING of New York, very violent, domineering, demanding, threatening, after he hears the returns from Tennessee.[22] I am sorry that Virginia has lagged behind. If all these border States, as they are called, had come right up to the mark at once, we should have had a settlement, or a peaceful separation; and we shall never have it until that is done.

Some persons say these southern States were precipitate. Grant it; I will not stop to quarrel about that. What are we to do? Take things as we find them, and shape our action according to the necessities of the case. We do not make the rain; but if it rains we put up an umbrella over our heads. We do not make the sun shine, but yet we will raise a parasol to protect us from its rays. We did not make South Carolina go out of the Union. It may have been hasty, for aught I know. I will not say it was or not. What shall we do? Take that course which is best calculated to preserve our rights, either in the Union or in a new one. What course ought that to be? For every State to go out together—I mean all the slaveholding States. Do you say we desert our northern friends? No. Our warm sympathies, our high admiration for them will be as lasting as time; but we can best serve them by serving ourselves in this matter; because if the fifteen States were all to recede from the Union, associate together, and say to the North, "do this and we are with you again," the North would concede it to us; but if some are going off, and we are hesitating and higgling and doubting, it makes the North so confident in its power, that they say, let South Carolina, Georgia, Alabama, Mississippi, and Florida go. Very well. Just as sure as you let them go, others will follow; and what other States will follow? Every slaveholding State, except Delaware, Maryland, and Virginia. I am afraid of old Virginia. She is so hesitating, so timid, walking on egg-shells, and afraid she will mash them;[23] but, just as sure as you live, if no adjustment on honorable terms is made in a satisfactory manner, Missouri, Arkansas, and Kansas will go. [Laughter.] Yes, Kansas. Do not be surprised at the use of the term. Montgomery does not rule there now. He can make his raids upon Missouri, and be driven back; they can make attacks from Iowa and be driven back; but the material interests of Kansas will force her to link her fortunes with Missouri.

But for the hot-bed plants that have been planted in Kansas, through the instrumentality of the Emigrant Aid Society, Kansas would have been with Missouri this day; and when these hot-bed plants die out—as they are fast dying out, and sending petitions to the Senator from Massachusetts, begging for bread, that they are starving—as soon as they die out, the homogeneous character of the people will gradually bring them back into the arms of Missouri. They are begging for bread and begging for an independent State government; and then saying, "If you will not give us bread, give us land; we are starving." I might ask the question, can you eat land? But it shows it is all a trick, a fraud gotten up through this Emigrant Aid Society. It will die out. Every attempt at fraud will be exposed sooner or later; and this miserable attempt is now being exposed, and the people are beginning to comprehend it. Even the traveling agents, who have gone abroad begging for contributions to relieve poor, starving Kansas, have received more rifles, more lead and powder, than they have bread and meat. These are facts that I can prove in a court of justice. I know what I say; and no one who is acquainted with the subject will contradict me. Do you not see, therefore, it is all a preparation to attack Missouri? I was informed by the Governor of Kansas, two weeks before the thing took place, that he was in fearful apprehension that Montgomery would make an attack on Missouri, or the Cherokee nation, and so on down to Texas, for that was a part of their plan. It was to circumscribe slavery and break it down through the Cherokee nation, through the Choctaw nation, through the Creek nation, in the borders of Arkansas, and then into Texas; and that plan is not yet given up. It is smothered; it sleepeth for the time; but it will be revived again, unless we are prepared to meet it.

Now, Mr. President, what ought we to do? Live in what we call a fraternal relation, yet compelled to keep arms in our hands, or submit to depredations upon our property? At the beginning of this session, I suggested the propriety of having an armed police, controlled by the States, paid from the Federal Treasury, to prevent these invasions and enforce the fugitive slave law all along the line separating the slaveholding from the non-slaveholding States. It was met with derision. Very well. When we divide, as divide we must, we shall have the same thing to do; but we shall have it to do in a larger degree. We shall have to raise a very large army, and a strong military force, each watching the other; and the slightest interruption may lead to a collision which will involve the whole country in a bloody war. If my suggestion had been received, something might have been done; but my suggestion was only intended as a means to check action and give time for reflection; for if the sentiment expressed by the North in the election of Mr. Lincoln is the settled judgment of the North, and if the practice of the North in stealing our negroes is the settled practice of the North, I would not live with you one day; I would divide this hour, this minute. There are men, it is true, who say they would not steal a slave; but they would not prevent anybody else from stealing one. There are men who say they have no objection to the fugitive slave law; but will they aid to execute it? Not one. Is not there, then, that dangerous, miserable sentiment we cannot tolerate and live in unity with?

Perhaps it will be said the House of Representatives passed a very fine resolution yesterday.[24] We have a right to notice the official proceedings of the House. They passed a resolution that they would not interfere with slavery in the States, and also that they did not intend to do it, embracing two points: first, they would not do it, and second, they did not intend to do it. Now, I wish to call the attention of the Senate to a little circumstance that took place in this body not twelve months ago. I asked the question of several northern Senators: why do you wish to circumscribe slavery? Why does it affect you to prevent the expansion and spreading of it in the new Territories? The answer was, by hemming it in, the slaves will gradually become so numerous, that slavery will become so unprofitable or dangerous that the master, perforce, will emancipate—thus seeking to accomplish by indirect means the very thing they swear in the House they do not desire to do by direct means. That is the purpose of every member of this Senate on the Republican side. If it is not, I would like for some one to rise and answer me. They have avowed it. No one has denied it. I have charged it upon them. Some of them were honest enough to confess it. Others chose to sit mute under the charge, thereby giving it a confession. Therefore, to say, "We do not intend to make a direct attack upon your State, but we will bring to bear a train of circumstances that will break down slavery in your State," is just as base and as infamous as if you raised an army to attack us in the State. You are attacking the State of Missouri every day.

When you talk of enforcing the fugitive slave law, you know it is not done; and when you say you occasionally enforce it, you know also that nineteen out of twenty never come to the cognizance of the law.

Mr. SEWARD.[25] How would you enforce the law in respect to those that never come to the cognizance of the law.

Mr. GREEN. I will tell you. Your abolition societies pay fifty dollars a head for every one stolen and taken to the North. I would punish those societies; and if you were a Union-loving people, and observed your oath, you would do it. [Applause in the galleries.]

The PRESIDING OFFICER. The galleries will be cleared, if the disturbance is repeated.

Mr. GREEN. Why, sir, no rogue ever had a good opinion of the law, when he felt the halter draw. I believe that is in Hudibras, somewhere.

Mr. ANTHONY.[26] Something like it.

Mr. GREEN. Now, sir, it is not simply the courts, not simply the liberty bills, not simply the official acts, of which I complain. These are but the bloom, as the miners would say, that blossom out. It is the deep-seated mind, the sentiment that has been inculcated at the North through the instrumentality of politicians, teachers of schools, tract societies, and everything that you can conceive of, which underlies those popular political indications, stronger than all of it. There is not one that dares run counter to it; and when our noble friends over on this side have stood up so manfully, they have been cut down as with a sharp scythe, one by one, until every one must go; and why? Because there is a sentiment inculcated there which is in direct conflict with their opinions. You have got to go, [to Mr. BRIGHT;][27] you have already gone, [to Mr. FITCH;][28] and every one of you will go. Yes, sir, as the Senator from New York said, the "irrepressible conflict" will go on. What did he mean by that doctrine? I do not suppose he meant a bloody war, for he is not a man of war; he is a man of words. What kind of conflict, then, did he mean? Why, a continual agitation of the question, until they get us in such trepidation and fear that, out of regard for personal safety, we would sell our negroes, or emancipate them, or run them off, and gradually work it down, Missouri first, Maryland next, Virginia next, until you crowd them down to the last extremity. That is the "irrepressible conflict;" and yet his friends in the other House vote that they do not intend to interfere with slavery in the States.

> {Senator Green here announced that he favored John J. Crittenden's proposed amendment, but had no hope that it would honored in the North. "We cannot have peace," he proclaimed, until northern attitudes toward slavery were disclaimed. "I say we must have a retraction of northern sentiment, or a separation." A civil war was a frightful eventuality to contemplate, "but we are gradually drifting along up to the fearful catastrophe."}

Now, Mr. President, we have a fearful responsibility resting upon us. This Senate cannot amend the Constitution. This Senate can make no adjustment. This Senate had better let the subject sleep. All that is said is calculated to stimulate one side or the other. We had better make the ordinary appropriations, and let the people and the States, through proper conventions, undertake the work of adjustment. It is no use to say that no adjustment can be made; it is no use to say an adjustment can be made. It is a very doubtful question to solve. We, as a Senate and as a Congress, can do no good; yet the motive that prompts the resolutions of the Senator from Kentucky is good, and I commend it only for this reason: it may, perhaps, hold the country still long enough for that reflection which will bring the northern mind right. Without that change in the northern mind, I would not accept any constitution to be associated with any such people as they have proved themselves to be in the past.

If we can quiet the public mind; if we can throw out suggestions which will induce the North to pause and say, they will enforce the fugitive slave law, they will guaranty us the protection of our rights, they will secure to us all that the Constitution now promises; and if we see there is a disposition to do what they say—then, indeed, I would love this Union. We have grown with time; we have increased with age; we have prospered under every circumstance; we have over thirty million people; we have productions innumerable; we have commerce, manufacturers, civilization, Christianity, and advancement in all that makes a people good and great. War will reverse the action of all this, and throw us back; war will brutalize; war will barbarize; war will throw us back more than a century, in the short space of five years. It demoralizes the people; it eats up the substance of the people; it brutalizes the feelings; and it is the last resort, but sometimes a fearful necessity.

Now, Mr. President, the object of my few remarks is this: as this proposed amendment to the naval bill comes at such an inopportune time; comes when we have no money in the Treasury; and comes from those who are refusing to do justice to little claimants because they have no money; comes when we do not need it; and comes with an avowal that it is intended to coerce the weaker States—I think I am compelled to oppose it on the general principles which I have announced. I shall continue to do so; and, whether successful or not, time will prove whether it will accomplish the ends that the friends of the measure expect.

No threats, no petitions, no demands but justice. Let the whole of the southern States act together as a unit, and act speedily, and negotiate with the North as equals. Sir, I would not take a proposition that we had forced upon the North. The North ought not to take a proposition that they had forced upon the South. I want to negotiate as equals—the fifteen southern States the equals of the eighteen on the other side.

Several SENATORS. Nineteen.

Mr. GREEN. Nineteen now; but that other one is going to be on our side; and that is the reason I let Kansas pass so easily.[29] Mr. President, everybody desires an adjustment; everybody desires peace and harmony; everybody desires a continuance of the Union; but when we come to talk about what is the

Union, and what are our rights in it, we commence to differ. Let us go to work and settle the question, if we can. Do it, and every slaveholding State will join at once. Let them come together in concert, make their propositions as honorable States to the others. If, then, we cannot agree, our separation is permanent and peaceable.

This is my whole purpose; and I will state, in conclusion, my positions:

First. That any State has a right to secede.

Second. If that right is exercised wrongfully, the State alone is responsible.

Third. When any State does *in fact* secede, all the fixtures in her limits belong to the State.

Fourth. Every effort to save the Union and preserve the peace of the country, should be made before any other remedy is resorted to. And finally, when all efforts fail, let us part in peace, and let each section pursue the course and line of policy deemed best for the good of the people; and to the God of justice, not of war, I commit the fate of our beloved country.

The PRESIDING OFFICER. The question is: "Will the Senate concur in the amendment made as in Committee of the Whole?"

Mr. MASON[30] called for the yeas and nays; and they were ordered; and being taken, resulted—yeas 27, nays 17; as follows:

{Here senators were listed as voting yea or nay.}

So the amendment was agreed to.

Source: *Congressional Globe*, 36th Cong., 2nd Sess., 865–69.

CHAPTER 3

UNITED STATES HOUSE OF REPRESENTATIVES

December 1860–February 1861

John William Noell
December 12, 1860

John W. Noell (1816–1863) was born in Bedford County, Virginia; moved to Perryville, Missouri, in 1833; and was admitted to the bar a decade later. He served in the state senate from 1851 until 1855, before being elected as a Democrat to the Thirty-Sixth Congress. He successfully ran for reelection in 1862 as an Unconditional Unionist and served until his death on March 14, 1863.

Representative Noell was one of two Missourians to propose a solution to the sectional crisis in the form of a constitutional amendment, the other being Senator Trusten Polk. While the majority of the sixty-nine amendments suggested over Secession Winter were designed to directly protect the institution of slavery, Noell designed his amendment to achieve regional equity within the executive branch. Instead of one president, Noell envisioned three (presumably representing the North, South, and West) each "armed with a veto power." Other elected officials to suggest an executive office solution included Ohio Representative Clement Vallandigham who proposed that the United States be divided into four sections (North, South, West, and Pacific) and that a majority of electors in each section be required to elect a president. Virginia Representative Albert Gallatin Jenkins suggested whether a "dual executive" might better protect the interests of the South, while Pennsylvania Senator William Bigler proposed that the president should hold his office for a six-year term and not be eligible for reelection. In a related proposal, Hugh French Thomason, a delegate to Arkansas's state convention, proposed that the president and vice president would be chosen "alternately" from a slaveholding and nonslaveholding state, "but, in no case, shall both be chosen from slaveholding or non-slaveholding states."[1] Additionally, Noell suggested that the House Committee of Thirty-Three explore the possibility of creating "equilibrium between the free and slave States in the Senate," by the "voluntary division on the part of some of the slave States into two or more States." He was presumably remembering that when Texas had been admitted in 1845, it retained the option of dividing itself into as many as five states if it wished.[2]

Whereas there now exists, on the part of the people of the southern States of this Union, a well-founded appreciation that they no longer hold the power in the Federal Government necessary to secure their peace and the safety of their property against the aggressions of the Federal Government, should it become the will of the people of the northern States to assail them through the Federal Administration or by hostile legislation; and whereas security and peace, held by one section at the mere will of another, cannot be safely relied on; and whereas the great material interests of the country, in every section, are involved in the safety of the Union and the perpetuity of the Constitution on such terms as will give every section the means of protection against the aggressions of other sections: Therefore,

Be it resolved, That the select committee of thirty-three be instructed to take into consideration the propriety and necessity of abolishing, by amendments to the Constitution, the office of the President of the United States, and of establishing, in lieu thereof, an executive council, to consist of three members to be elected by districts composed of contiguous States as near as practicable; each member of said council to be armed with a veto power, such as is now vested in the President of the United States; and if such plan be deemed practicable by said committee, that they report to this House such details thereof as may be necessary to accommodate the same to the existing Constitution of the United States.

Be it further resolved, That said committee be also requested to take into consideration the means necessary (if any can be devised) to restore the equilibrium between the free and the slave States in the Senate of the United States; and particularly whether this end can be accomplished by a voluntary division on the part of some of the slave States into two or more States.

Source: *Congressional Globe*, 36th Cong., 2nd Sess., 78.

{Representative Noell was not a major participant in the political debates over Secession Winter. His other contribution to compromise was to present several memorials from his constituents urging a settlement of the sectional crisis. On February 2, 1861, he offered the following:}

Mr. NOELL. I desire to present three memorials from my constituents in reference to existing difficulties; one from citizens of Dent county, and another from citizens from Phelps county, Missouri, both signed by the farmers and workingmen of those counties, asking Congress to adopt the Crittenden propositions. The third memorial is from Lucy A. James and thirty-five other ladies of Phelps county. They come here not in the spirit of dictation, but as the descendants of those honored women who showed their devotion to the country in the days of the Revolution, asking this House to take such measures as may avert the calamities which now threaten the country, and in which those nearest and dearest to them will be involved.

The memorials were received, and laid on the table.

Source: *Congressional Globe*, 36th Cong., 2nd Sess., 710.

Thomas Lilbourne Anderson
January 15, 1861

Thomas L. Anderson (1808–1885) was born near Bowling Green, admitted to the bar in 1828, and practiced law in Franklin and Palmyra. He was elected as a member of the American Party to the Thirty-Fifth Congress and as an Independent Democrat to the Thirty-Sixth and served from 1857 to 1861. Returning to Missouri, he resumed his law practice in Marion County.

Representative Anderson began his address by observing that the South had "submitted for years to the assaults, injustice, inequality, oppression, and misrepresentations of our northern neighbors" and that "passion, prejudice, and fanaticism, have finally obtained the supremacy over justice and reason." The slavery issue must be settled, he insisted, "or this Union *must* be dissolved." Anderson ended by calling on the people of the North to propose amendments to the Constitution that among other things would recognize property in slaves, allow slaveowners to travel throughout the country (including the territories) with their slaves, and expedite the return of fugitive slaves.

Mr. ANDERSON, of Missouri. Mr. Chairman, I propose to submit to the consideration of this House some remarks upon the subject of our national difficulties. I shall aim to do so with that calmness, frankness, and deliberation which the importance of the occasion demands; avoiding the utterance of anything calculated or designed to irritate the feelings of any party in this House, or add to the terrible excitement that now prevails throughout the whole extent of this nation. It may be truly said, that we are in the midst of a great revolution that is hurrying us on with fearful rapidity to the disruption of all the ties that bind this Confederacy together. The fact cannot be disguised that we are now standing upon the crumbling brink of political ruin; that this once happy and glorious Union of States is now virtually severed; that the ensign of our country's greatness and glory has ceased to float from the flagstaff of four sovereign States. But the other day our Confederates—South Carolina, Florida, Mississippi, and Alabama—did, by solemn ordinances, announce to the world that they are absolved from all allegiance to the General Government. That other southern States will follow in rapid succession, unless some just and peaceful remedy is speedily devised, is undeniably true. How many stars are to be blotted out from the flag of our Union time will speedily disclose. The public mind at the South has been preparing for years for the existing state of things. With many of us it produces no surprise. Long have we witnessed the gradual development of the causes that would inevitably produce the results that are now upon us. Many of the statesmen and patriots of the land have, again and again, warned our countrymen of the "mining and sapping process" that was going on, which, if persevered in, must eventually destroy the noble edifice constructed by our fathers. But the voice of wisdom and patriotism has been unheeded; passion, prejudice, and fanaticism, have finally obtained the supremacy over justice and reason; and unless the "sober second thought" of the people of the northern States, or their Representatives here, shall induce them to discard their prejudices, and speedily award to the people of the southern States their just and constitutional rights, all is lost.

I can assure you, Mr. Chairman, that there is an irreversible determination on the part of the people of the slaveholding States to have this slavery agitation quieted, this slavery controversy definitively settled. We have submitted for years to the assaults, injustice, inequality, oppression, and misrepresentations of our northern neighbors. Unless these things cease, we are constrained, by our self-respect, our love of peace, and the security of our property, to absolve ourselves from all connection with them.

This Government was formed by our fathers, "to establish justice, insure domestic tranquility, provide for the common defense, promote the general welfare, and secure the blessings of liberty to ourselves and our posterity." In some of these great objects, so far as the slaveholding States are concerned, it has utterly failed. Our slave property is becoming less secure and less valuable every day. The guarantees of the Constitution afford us but little or no protection. In many of the slave States we are sustaining heavy losses every month, with no means of redress. Those losses, with the present feeling and sentiment abroad in the land, must still increase. Many of our slaves are now impressed with the idea that, after the inauguration of Mr. Lincoln, they are to be free. This impression makes them restless and discontented; renders our homes, our wives, and our children unsafe. Surely no rational man expects us to live with such a state of things in our midst. We cannot; we will not. Our devotion to the Union, our veneration for the achievements of our ancestors, our recollection of their heroic deeds, their perils and sufferings, cannot induce us to submit to the wrongs and injuries that are now being inflicted upon us in the name of the Constitution and the Union. We have borne them for years, still cherishing the patriotic hope, hitherto delusive, that a returning sense of justice would induce the North to recede from the "irrepressible conflict." We have again and again asked to be let alone in the enjoyment of our rights and our property; again and again warned our fellow-citizens of the disastrous consequences that must surely ensue, if they persisted in refusing to us that peace and security which the Government was pledged to afford us. These warnings on our part they have regarded as idle threats, and consequently our demands have not only been unheeded, but they have recklessly and imperiously pushed on in the accomplishment of their unjust and unconstitutional purposes, thereby furnishing us with conclusive evidence of their unfaltering determination to destroy the institution of slavery.

> {Representative Anderson here quoted a US senator who, according to Anderson, proclaimed after the election, that "thanks be to God, we stand with the slave power beneath our feet. . . . We are in power with the Army and Navy at our command, and they shall submit; we rule and they shall obey." To this comment, Anderson responded, "The freemen of the South who, under such circumstances, would not assert and maintain his just and constitutional rights, in the Union if he can, out of it if necessary, is a fitter representative of a Russian serf than an American citizen."}

These expressions of feelings and sentiment, exhibited by the dominant party in all the non-slaveholding States, satisfy us that we are a doomed people in the Union, unless the northern mind should undergo a change; of which, I apprehend, there is scarcely a glimmering hope.

The result of this constant and unceasing attack upon the institution of slavery has now culminated in the election of a man to the Chief Magistracy of the nation who has not only been ceaseless in his opposition to the institution, but who has deliberately declared that "this nation cannot exist half free and half slave;" that "it must be one or the other—all slave or all free"—elected as a sectional candidate, upon the main idea of his hostility to the institution of slavery, upon a platform declaring it to be a relic of barbarism,[3] with a distinct avowal that we shall be denied all participation in the Territories of the United States; that it must be placed "where the public mind can rest in the belief that it is in the course of ultimate extinction;" that it shall never expand; that it shall be confined to its present limits, thereby insuring its final destruction. The Constitution, according to his interpretation of it, is no interposition to the accomplishment of these ends. The guarantee of one of the plainest provisions of that instrument has not only been disregarded, but nine or ten States have enacted legislative acts designed and intended to prevent the execution of the "fugitive slave act" made for the preservation of our property, in conformity to an express provision of the Constitution. And one of these States but the other day—yes, Pennsylvania, the Keystone of the Federal arch—solemnly and deliberately, in view of the impending perils that now environ our Union, refused to repeal its unjust and unconstitutional legislation.[4] With all these evidences before us, and numberless others, of the ultimate annihilation of our property and the destruction of our rights, is there any class of men so blinded by passion, prejudice, or fanaticism, as to suppose for a moment that we will remain in the Union, and submit to these wrongs? If the people of the non-slaveholding States were occupying our position, educated in thought, feeling, and sentiment as we are, with $4,000,000,000 worth of property vested in slaves, could they—would they submit? Never; no, never! Why not, then, exemplify that golden rule, so necessary to the peace and happiness of the world: "Do unto others as you would they should do unto you" under like circumstances.

I am not here to-day to utter threats or menaces—that day has passed away—I am uttering that which you know, and I feel to be true. You know, as well as I do, that this slavery agitation is rapidly culminating in the overthrow of one of the noblest Republics that earth ever beheld; and nothing short of the most expansive and exalted patriotism, sustained by the most godlike forbearance on the part of the people of the slave States, has preserved it thus long.

Missouri, the State that I have the honor in part to represent, though assailed upon every side—suffering more injury from the enemies of slavery than any other State in the Union—was disposed to bear these wrongs, so long as there was a reasonable hope for their redress, and allow to the people of the free States time to reconsider their action, and finally determine whether their prejudices against our institution, for which they are not responsible, and which should not concern them, are stronger than their love for the Union. If they still value the Union, and are desirous of preserving it, all they have to do, is to give us that which our fathers left us—peace, security, equal rights, and equal privileges, under the Constitution of our common country. If you will repeal your "personal liberty bills;" recognize property in slaves; enforce the execution of the "fugitive slave act;" permit us, as did your fathers, to travel through the country with our property unmolested; let us go to the Territories of the United States—property for which we shed our blood and paid our money—with our slaves, and have them protected while the country remains in a territorial condition; cease to interfere with slavery where it now exists; cease to abuse and denounce us—then fraternal relations can be restored between us, *and upon no other terms*; then the Union can be preserved; the States that have seceded reunited; and we still march on to further attainments in greatness and renown. The enjoyment of these constitutional guarantees by us does not interfere with any of your rights, retard your prosperity, lessen the value of your property, or endanger your lives, and those of your wives and your children; while, on the other hand, they are necessary to secure to us these rights and blessings.

In the event of a denial of these constitutional rights to the people of my State, I see no other alternative but servile submission and degradation on the one hand, or secession on the other; which of the two she will choose, I think there can be no doubt. It is evident that she cannot be injured in any of her social, commercial, or material interests, by uniting with a southern confederation. Possessing her immense territory—unsurpassed in climate, the richness of her soil, the variety of her productions, the extent of her minerals, with a larger population than any of her southern sisters, save one, she certainly would, under the fostering care of that Government, become one of the greatest and wealthiest States in the new confederation.[5] She would furnish the South with horses, mules, cattle, hogs, hemp, lead, iron, copper, and a large amount of manufactured articles, protected as she would be, by a moderate tariff for revenue; she would, to a great extent, get rid of the competition she now has, in that market, from the non-slaveholding States. We certainly have nothing to lose, so far as our material interests are involved, by connecting our destiny with our southern friends. Then, and I fear not till then, will we have our rights protected, and escape from the continual strife, troubles, and annoyances to which we are constantly subjected by our northern neighbors. But, notwithstanding all these things, our loyalty and attachment to this Union is such, that we prefer to remain a part of this great Confederacy, if our rights can and will be protected, and we permitted to enjoy our property in peace and security. If this boon is to be denied us, Missouri will not long hesitate to go where her honor and her interest invite her to go.

I regret, however, that candor compels me to say, that I entertain serious apprehensions that the North will never again concede to us our just and full constitutional rights—never permit us to live upon terms of peace and equality; that her hostility to the institution of slavery is so violent and uncompromising, that she will never again cease to assail it as long as it exists in the Union. The North, however, should remember that the result of such a course is the inevitable dismemberment of the Union, and the eternal postponement of a reconstruction of the Government. Momentous events, now thronging rapidly upon us, must surely satisfy you of the unfaltering determination of the South, whether in or out of the Union, to defend and preserve her slave property, at every sacrifice of blood and treasure that may be demanded.

We are told that the difficulties between the North and the South should be compromised, in order that the Union may be preserved. Sir, I greatly desire that this Union shall be saved; there is no personal sacrifice that I would not make to perpetuate this Union for all time to come, with the provisions of the Constitution fully and fairly enforced. Without the guarantees of that instrument, I hesitate not to say that the Union is a curse, and the Government a despotism. What compromise do you suppose the South will ever make, yielding more than is surrendered by the amendments proposed by the eloquent and patriotic Senator from Kentucky?[6] That proposition is so liberal as to exclude us, with our property, from three fourths of the Territories of the United States, while you are allowed to occupy, equally with us, the remaining one fourth, south of 36°30′ and enjoy an equal right with us, in the formation of State constitutions south of that line. And although the Supreme Court of the United States—the ablest and most impartial tribunal known to the country—uninfluenced by party clamor and party feeling, have decided that we have the right, under the Constitution, to go to all the Territories of the United States with our slave property, and have it protected; still, patriotism, an ardent love for the Union formed by our fathers, constrain us to yield and accept the proposition—you have refused, and I doubt not, will continue to refuse, and thereby rend asunder all the ties that bind the Union together. Be it so; the responsibility, with all its fearful consequences, will rest upon you, not us.

> {Here Representative Anderson called for a convention of the border slave states that would recommend constitutional amendments that set "at rest the agitation of the slavery question forever." In the meantime, Missouri should arm its militia and make preparations for the defense of the state.}

Mr. Chairman, I propose now to say a few words to my friends in the slaveholding States that still remain in the Union. We are evidently in the midst of a great crisis, involving considerations of the deepest and most profound interest. Never was an occasion presented to intelligent men that demanded the exercise of more coolness, firmness, deliberation, wisdom, and prudence, than the present. What means this movement in which we are engaged? In the language of another, "it means that this confederation of States shall be broken up, and its fragments scattered; that the flag which has carried our name so proudly all over the globe—the signal of hope and protection to the oppressed everywhere—shall be struck, and known no more among the nations of the earth; it means the overthrow of our national greatness, the extraction of our national hope." Let civil war attend it, and "it means spreading all over our land social alienations; the sundering of families and friends; mistrust, jealousy, commercial derangement, loss, wrong, violence, injury, retaliation; all this it means and much more that can be imagined."

> {Anderson expressed his opinion that the secession of the "Gulf States was too hasty and precipitate." Their action, he argued, placed the border states "at the very threshold of danger."}

Our friends of the extreme South should have remembered that the slave States bordering on the free States have been the great sufferers in this conflict. We have lost a thousand times as many negroes as the cotton States, in consequence of the faithlessness of a portion of our northern neighbors. The very district that I represent—bordering on the State of Illinois, with her tens of thousands of true constitutional men—has lost more slaves through the instrumentality of the underground railroad than any one of the Gulf States; yea, more, I suspect, than the whole of them combined;[7] and yet my constituents are unwilling to break up the great Confederacy of States, to separate from our friends in Illinois and other States, who have been fighting our battles—who have endeared themselves to us by their noble efforts and self-sacrificing struggles in defense of our constitutional rights—until further efforts are made to obtain from the non-slaveholding States justice, security, and the full enforcement of the guarantees of the Constitution.[8]

> {Anderson here entered into a lengthy entreaty to his southern colleagues to exhaust all reasonable efforts to "obtain our rights in the Union." Blame for the unsettled state of the country he laid fully at the feet of the northern states for "assailing" the institution of slavery at every turn. He ended with a plea to amend the Constitution "so as to protect their [the seceded states] rights, and guarantee peace, safety, and security to them, and their property, and they will return to us again."}

I now appeal to the Representatives of the non-slaveholding States to propose amendments to the Constitution that will secure to the South her just and equal rights; that will stop forever all agitation upon the subject of slavery; give to the country quiet and repose. Surely the fearful and extraordinary circumstances that now surround us, big with the destiny of this great nation, should induce us to do it. Is there a Representative in this Hall so devoid of patriotism, so utterly insensible to the mighty interests involved in this conflict—social and fraternal, political, financial, and commercial—as to refuse a measure that will not only prevent anarchy and bloodshed, but will carry joy and gladness to every part of our distracted country? Refuse it; heed not the voice of wisdom and patriotism, and terrible will be the responsibility that will rest upon you. Could I this day appeal directly to the great masses of the northern people, the response would be heard: "let it be done!" Reason and common sense declare that the people of the free States should have nothing to do with the subject of slavery. It does not concern them; it is no business of theirs. It is property secured to us by the Constitution, which they do not choose to hold. It is ours; and we alone should possess the right of managing, governing, and controlling it, as to us may seem wisest and best. Sir, the time has arrived, in the judgment of the southern people, when the slavery question *must* be settled or this Union *must* be dissolved. The fiat has gone forth from the entire South; and you may rest assured that there is now no escape from it. The crisis is upon us. It must be met. Sir, if action is postponed until seven or eight States secede, and establish another Confederacy, the inevitable result will be that the remaining slave States will unite with them or form a central Republic, leaving New England, the source of all our woes, to take care of herself as best she may. The border States will be forced, by the love of self-preservation, thus to act. If not, we should be completely in the power and under the subjection of our avowed enemies; with them we could not—we would not—remain.

> {Representative Anderson encouraged his colleagues to adopt amendments to the Constitution and "pledge anew our devotion to the Union." He warned against any attempt to obstruct the navigation of the Mississippi River and devoted a long portion of his address warning the federal government against coercing the states, of resorting "to force to compel a sovereign State to remain in the Union and submit to Federal authority."}

Whether secession or revolution be the remedy by which an injured State is to redress her wrongs, I do not deem it important, at this time and under existing circumstances, further to inquire. Four sovereign States have not been deterred; nor will it change the purpose of any other States that may determine to disrupt the ties that bind them to this Union—call it secession or revolution, peaceable or bloody—it will not delay their action one moment. They conscientiously believe that they are now striking for the security of their homes and their altars, for the safety of their wives and their children; and be the consequences never [sic] so terrible, they have coolly and deliberately made up their minds to meet them with that determined will and unyielding purpose that should ever characterize men born, raised, and educated in the atmosphere of liberty and freedom—men who know how to appreciate their rights and how to defend them. The terrors of civil war, now threatened by their enemies, with all its hideous and dreadful results, will not affright them from the protection and preservation of their rights, and the repudiation of a Government that denies to them justice and equality under a common Constitution.

If, in the providence of God, it should come, the fearful responsibility of invoking bloodshed, anguish, grief, and eternal alienation, will rest upon the Republican party. The last hope of a reconstruction of this Government will forever disappear, the moment one drop of blood is spilt upon southern soil to force any State into submission. That moment every southern star will fall from the Federal constellation, and the scattered fragments of this Union will be covered with a blood-stained mantle, upon which will be written, in letters of inextinguishable fire, the words, "Eternal separation." Then the last shriek of the American eagle will be heard amid the clash of arms and the din of battle.

Sir, I fondly cherish the hope that peaceful counsels will yet prevail; that these dreadful consequences may be averted, and that the people of the non-slaveholding States—who alone can save this Union—will yield up their prejudices and fanaticism upon the altar of their country; and, without hesitation, tender to the southern States, in a spirit of noble magnanimity and exalted patriotism, what they believe most conscientiously to be their just and equal rights. Thus this mighty Government, made by our fathers, can be saved, and by no other means; thus the gloom and sadness of this hour can be dispelled; thus the sinking hopes of a great nation can be revived; thus the lovers of freedom can be made to rejoice throughout the civilized world; thus joy and gladness, peace and prosperity, may again be restored to the inhabitants of this great Republic, and the echo returned by the patriots of other lands.

Source: *Congressional Globe*, 36th Cong., 2nd Sess., 397–401.

US House of Representatives

John Bullock Clark
January 26, 1861

John B. Clark (1802–1885) was born in Madison County, Kentucky, admitted to the bar in 1824, and practiced law in Fayette. He served as a Democrat in the Missouri House of Representatives (1850–1851), and in the US Congress from 1857 until 1861 when he was expelled for "disloyalty to the Union." Clark represented Missouri in both the first and second Confederate congresses and later served as brigadier general of Missouri's Confederate state troops.

Representative Clark began by tracing the rise of the antislavery movement in the country claiming that for more than thirty years abolitionists and Free-Soilers "have assailed the institution of slavery in the southern States." Clark continued in this vein adding that since the formation of the Republican Party, the South has "had no peace." He voiced especial concern that the Chicago Platform had declared that all men were free and equal, and several northern states, acting on "this doctrine of negro equality" allowed free Blacks to vote for president and members of Congress. Focusing on the Republican Party's opposition to slavery in the western territories, Clark proposed that the Crittenden amendment or something like it was the only hope of restoring peace to the country. Without the right of protection to our peculiar property in slaves, he concluded, "we cannot live with you."

THE CRISIS

The SPEAKER. The hour has arrived for resuming the consideration of the special order, which is the report of the select committee of thirty-three on the disturbed condition of the country.[9] On that question the gentleman from Missouri [Mr. CLARK] is entitled to the floor.

{Representative Clark here introduced a long explanation of the "causes which have led to the present difficulty." He included the Compromise of 1820, the annexation of Texas, Wilmot Proviso, and the Compromise of 1850. The elected officials from that time, during those moments of difficulty "rose above the propositions of mere partisans to that of statesmen and patriots, to save a sinking and bleeding country." "Then," he observed, "the

Republican party was formed, which has so rapidly increased, that now they have elected their candidate for the Presidency."}

Now, Mr. Speaker, I ask this House, is it any wonder that the South is excited? We are equals in this Union; and we claim the same constitutional rights, and claim to be entitled to the same constitutional guarantees, that any other portion of the Confederacy possesses. From the time that the Republican party was formed, as I have told you, we have had no peace. The country has been excited continually from that time until now. These evils have increased until they have reached a culminating point, and it now depends upon the action of this party whether this Government is to continue and this Union be preserved, or whether it is to be destroyed. State after State has seceded and withdrawn;[10] their Representatives have vacated their seats in this Hall. Sir, those empty seats speak with an eloquence which should command the attention of patriots of all parties.

What has produced this state of things? Who have produced it? Have the South ever imposed upon the North? Have they ever initiated any proceedings to take from the North their political rights in the Territories, or their rights of person and property anywhere? I deny that anything can be produced to show that any portion of the southern States have made encroachments, in any respect, upon the northern section of the Union.

Against all these encroachments of the North upon the South, the South have complained. Sometimes they have threatened; but for the greater part they have held up the Constitution, and have shown the structure and framework of the Government, and under them have asked the North to give them the equality to which they are entitled under the Constitution. They have asked the North not to trespass upon the constitutional rights of their section. But, not withstanding, the North have persisted in their course of wrong and oppression.

Sir, it has been asked by some if the election of Mr. Lincoln was any cause for a dissolution of the Union? I say emphatically, that I do not consider that it is a sufficient cause of itself. The election of a President is in no case a sufficient cause. I believe in the power, the intelligence, and the integrity of the American people. I recognize the Constitution of my country as a bond of union; and when I take the oath to support that Constitution, I take an oath, in my judgment, to bow to the majority and will of the people constitutionally expressed. But while I make this admission, I want to tell my northern friends of the Republican party, that it is not the election of Mr. Lincoln alone which has created this alarm in the South. The facts which I have named; the history which I have given; the encroachments which I have alluded to, connected with the opinions which Mr. Lincoln is known to entertain; the platform of principles upon which he was elected; the construction which he gives to the Constitution and to the decision of the Supreme Court, looking to the use of the executive arm of this Government, and of the power of the party which has, in years gone by, trespassed, as we think, upon our constitutional rights;—these, all these, are what give us alarm, and admonish the South to look out in time to secure additional constitutional guarantees for their safety, peace, and happiness. When we had the executive and judicial arm, and the legislative power of the Government, although these encroachments were advancing upon us, we had the power; and that power we could exercise to secure our safety, having the fortress of the Constitution. The different departments of the Federal Government upon our side gave us safety and repose. When we lost the executive power of the Government, and it was transferred to the Republican party, the South began to look around for means to strengthen their fortress, or to change their position.

In this connection I wish to say, that whether a State has a constitutional right to secede, or whether the action of a State in seceding is revolutionary, I shall not consume the time of the House to discuss. I consider that no State, and no citizens of a State, will ever secede from the Federal Government until their grievances are too heavy to be borne; and when that is the case, all admit that they have the right of revolution, and can change their form of government whenever they please. Whether, then, it be secession or revolution, it is useless now to inquire or discuss. We have to deal with the facts before us; and, if we can, to arrest the progress of that revolution, save the country, and keep the stars and stripes of this blessed Union floating. Nothing now remains for the patriot but to address himself to the work of healing the breach between the two sections of this Confederacy. Five States have gone out of the Union; whether rightfully or wrongfully, they have denied the Federal authority, and have set up their own jurisdiction. We have to deal with this fact.

We were asked, the other day, by the gentleman from Ohio, [Mr. SHERMAN,][11] what the Republican party had done? Said he: "what have we done, except to elect our President?" We claim that they have done a great deal; and when I answer the gentleman's question, I want it distinctly understood that I do not impugn the motives of any one, nor do I design to make a personal application of my remarks to any particular member of the Republican party. The question asked was: what has been done giving the South cause of complaint? I answer that the Abolitionists and Free-Soilers of the free States have, for more than thirty years, assailed the institution of slavery in the southern States. They deny to us a common property in the Territories; those Territories acquired equally by our blood and treasure as by yours, making it a condition that we shall migrate to them only with such property as is recognized in the free States. A gentleman on the other side of the House said the other day that they imposed no restrictions upon the South; that when the citizens of the free States moved into the Territories they carried no slaves with them; and that they were willing to permit the slave States to carry there all they carried. The doctrine of the Constitution is, that each State has a right to regulate its domestic affairs in its own way, to establish its own institutions, and to recognize as property whatever its citizens see proper, in the formation of their fundamental law; the doctrine of the Constitution is, that the citizens of each State shall have the same rights and privileges as the citizens of the several States. The Territories were acquired, by the several States; and it is, therefore, a violation of good faith, and of our constitutional rights, to restrict our citizens from carrying into the common Territories whatever is regarded as property in the States whence they emigrate.

The North have enacted laws in many of their States nullifying the provision of the Constitution of the United States for the rendition of fugitive slaves, refusing the use of their jails for the custody of the prisoners, and making it a penal offense for any one to aid in the execution of the fugitive slave law. Justice requires that I should say here, that there seems to be a disposition in many of the free States to repeal those obnoxious laws. They have not yet, however, been repealed in more than one or two States. I hope they will all be repealed without delay.

> {At this point, Representatives from Pennsylvania took issue with Clark's comments. Jacob K. McKenty observed that a bill was currently before the legislation to "repeal the obnoxious sections of the act." David Kilgore, a representative from Indiana, inquired whether the Pennsylvania personal liberty laws were passed by Democratic Legislatures. While the makeup of the legislature that passed the law was not clarified, Thomas Florence, of Pennsylvania, offered that the governor who signed the bill "was also a Democratic Governor." Benjamin Franklin Junkin, also of Pennsylvania, added that there had been an 1847 law on Pennsylvania's books preventing jails from being used for those accused of assisting runaway slaves, but that that law had been repealed in 1852.}

Mr. CLARK, of Missouri. I never said that Pennsylvania had such a law, and I never thought so; for I am in the habit of reading the statutes of Pennsylvania and of most of the other States, and I never supposed that Pennsylvania had such a law.

The Republican party of the North have declared in their national convention, as a solution of the slavery question—and they have elected a President pledged to that doctrine—that all men are free and equal; and this doctrine of negro equality is carried into practical effect in the States of New York, Massachusetts, and Ohio, where negroes are allowed to vote for President and members of Congress. Associations have been organized in many of the free States, without rebuke from the Republican party in any organized form, to steal our slaves and to prevent their recapture. To show that such associations are countenanced in high places, I have only to instance the refusal of the Governor of Ohio, upon a late occasion, to give up persons charged with negro stealing, on the requisitions of the Governors of Kentucky and Tennessee, on the ground that negro stealing is not a crime in the State of Ohio. Citizens from your States have invaded southern soil for the purpose of liberating slaves, and have murdered unoffending citizens; and the people in many localities in your States have, in public meetings and otherwise, bestowed praise and eulogium upon the assassins; and the Executives of several States have refused to deliver up parties implicated in the treason. Many distinguished members of the Republican party have declared their intention to remodel the Supreme Court, and to put it on the side of freedom. They have declared that their party power shall be used for the expansion of freedom and the contraction of slavery; and that with Lincoln's election American slavery is at an end. They have, in many of the free States, arrayed the schools, churches, and presses with great unanimity against the South; and the idea is inculcated by them that it is the duty of the people to exterminate slavery at any sacrifice and at all hazards. They have flooded the South with seditious anti-slavery pamphlets and papers calculated to create servile insurrection, and to endanger the safety of our homes and families. By the fanaticism of the North, we have been forced to separate from you in some of our churches and other religious institutions.

These are things of which the South complains, whether truthfully or otherwise history will record. In addition to all this, Mr. Lincoln has been elected to the Presidency with his sentiment that he was opposed to the exclusion of the negro from the polls; with the sentiment that the Union, part slave and part free, was like a house divided against itself, which could not stand; with the sentiment proclaimed by him that those who deny freedom to others cannot long, in the providence of God, retain it themselves. All these things, taken in connection with the past history of the party, have alarmed the South. These are the things that have culminated in producing the disruption which now exists in the withdrawal of the southern States.

Mr. FARNSWORTH.[12] I desire to correct the gentleman from Missouri. I do not think he can find any passage in any speech of Mr. Lincoln where he ever declared himself in favor of negro suffrage.[13]

Mr. CLARK, of Missouri. Oh yes; I can find that he has said what amounts to the same thing.

Mr. FARNSWORTH. I think the gentleman is mistaken.

{Here Representative Clark introduced several quotes from Lincoln declaring that "all men are created equal," that he would vote in favor of prohibiting slavery in the territories in spite of the *Dred Scott* decision, and that "Those who deny freedom to others deserve it not for themselves, and under a just God cannot long retain it." Clark and Representative Benjamin Stanton from Ohio then engaged in a dialogue on interpreting the Constitution and "whether it is the constitutional right of each State to maintain its own construction, even by a dissolution of the Confederacy and civil war."}

Mr. CLARK, of Missouri. If Mr. Lincoln would say a word upon that point himself, he could quiet the apprehensions of the people on the subject in a moment; provided what he said was in favor of obeying the decision of the court. He could quiet the fears of the country, or prepare them for what inevitably would come.

Mr. STANTON.[14] Now, if the gentleman will allow me, I will take but a moment of his time.

Mr. CLARK, of Missouri. No, sir; I cannot yield further. Mr. Speaker, I was going on to remark that, notwithstanding all these complaints, which, in our judgment, we have abundant cause to make, the people of the State which I have the honor in part, to represent, still continue to maintain their loyalty to the Union of these States. The question to which I wish now to address myself is, what will relieve the apprehensions of the people of the South? What will restore peace to the country? What will give strength to the Union? What will calm these troubles? What will give peace and repose and confidence and safety, and again reunite our once prosperous country?

In this connection, Mr. Speaker, without adverting to any particular argument, permit me to say it here—to announce it from my place—that I believe the measures called the Crittenden proposition would give peace to the country. That proposition, sir, establishes nothing more than the Missouri Compromise, as originally understood. It does nothing more than to give protection to persons and property in the territory lying south of the line of 36°30'. If gentlemen are sincere in desiring the Union to be preserved; if they are sincere in saying they are willing the South should have equal constitutional rights in the Union; if they are sincere in saying they would do nothing in derogation of the rights of the South, here is an opportunity, by adopting that proposition, to carry into effect their promises, and to immediately produce a state of feeling that would culminate in the safety and reunion of the whole country, in my humble judgment. I ask gentlemen of the Republican party, why can you not consent to submit that proposition to the people? Are you afraid of the people?

I believe, that if this proposition were to be submitted to the sovereign people of this country, it would be carried by acclamation. But, if the people of the country are with the Republicans of this House, and opposed to that proposition, you then run no risk by submitting it.

Mr. HOARD.[15] Suppose it is submitted to the people, and they vote it down: would the gentleman then be satisfied?

Mr. KILGORE.[16] I understand the gentleman from Missouri to say that the Crittenden proposition is nothing more or less than the Missouri compromise. I wish to ask the gentleman whether that proposition does not constitutionalize slavery south of that line, and whether the Missouri compromise did?

> {Here ensued a conversation among Clark, Hoard, and Kilgore on the Crittenden amendment. Representative Clark responded to Hoard's question by stating that if the Crittenden resolutions were not approved in a popular vote, "I would then be content to remain in the Union." He continued by asserting that while he loved the Union and the "stars and stripes," the South must have its constitutional rights, "upon terms of equality in all the departments of the Government; for we will remain with no people, and in no Union, or in any Confederation, as inferiors."}

Mr. CLARK, of Missouri. I tell gentlemen upon the Republican side of the House that now is the time, if they desire to preserve the hopeless dissolution of this Confederacy. Missouri, Kentucky, Tennessee, Arkansas, Virginia, Maryland, Delaware—we are the border States; we claim to be the conservative portion of this Union; and we not only claim to be the conservative portion of this Union, but we are the sufferers as border States. We have borne our sufferings with patience, but the people of these States are now moving. My own State has provided for a convention to take into consideration what remedy they shall provide. I have confidence in the people of the State of Missouri. I have known them long. I have lived among them all my life, and I know them to be a brave and loyal people, understanding what are their rights, and possessing the nerve to maintain them. I have full confidence that the convention soon to assemble there will protect the honor, the safety, and the interests of my State. It does not become me to point out the course of policy they ought to pursue. But, sir, I tell the Republican party that, unless something be done soon to allay the existing excitement, and to restore harmony to the country—unless, sir, they evince some spirit of conciliation and compromise, and pass some measure of adjustment like the Crittenden proposition, the Union will be severed. Unless something is done, the border States, when they assemble by their commissioners in convention, will cooperate with their southern brethren, unless they can have secured to them the rights guaranteed by the

Constitution—the right of protection to our peculiar property in slaves—without which we cannot live with you.

The border States are not in favor of precipitate action. They have already shown that they are not. We have made no threats; but, sir, we are not the less determined to act at the proper time, as becomes a free and brave people. Missouri will not shrink from the responsibility imposed upon her. If our constitutional rights shall be resisted and denied to us, and the Union be dissolved, let gentlemen of the North be not mistaken or deceived: the border States will confederate with the States with which they are homogeneous in population and institutions. But we beg to be relieved from such a dire alternative. We implore the party in power to adjust the present difficulties by granting the South her constitutional rights. Now is the accepted time; now peace may be secured with honor; now the Union may be preserved; and it is with you, gentlemen of the Republican party, to do it. Delay, put it off longer, quibble over these technicalities, and it may be too late.

The SPEAKER. The gentleman's hour has expired.

Mr. GILMER[17] obtained the floor.

Mr. CLARK, of Missouri. I ask that my time be extended. I have not yet finished all I have to say.

The SPEAKER. Is there objection? There was no objection, and it was ordered accordingly.

Mr. CLARK, of Missouri. I thank the House for its kindness.

Mr. Speaker, I want to remark that it is, in my opinion, the duty of the border States—Virginia, Kentucky, Tennessee, Missouri, and Arkansas—to consult together. We have the same population and the same interests, and our destiny is inseparable. Missouri is pledged by resolutions, known as the Jackson resolutions—their author being our present Governor—passed in 1849, that she would be found cooperating with the slaveholding States if the constitutional rights of the South were denied by Congress.[18] I understand that our first duty, the first duty of the border States, is cooperation. Their ultimate destiny will be determined by the action of their respective conventions about to assemble. It is in the power of this Congress to save the Union.

While I love the Union; while I avow my devotion to it; while my constituents are devoted to it; while they all deprecate disunion, and would do everything not dishonorable to avoid pestilence, famine, fratricidal war, indeed, all the horrors of civil war; yet, sir, we are resolved to have our rights. We are resolved to have all the rights guaranteed to us by our forefathers. We are resolved not to be placed upon terms of inequality and inferiority. If we cannot secure our rights in the present confederation, we will be compelled to confederate where they can be secured.

Source: *Congressional Globe*, 36th Cong., 2nd Sess., 577–80.

John Richard Barret
February 21, 1861

Born in Green County, Kentucky, John R. Barret (1825–1903) moved to St. Louis around 1839 and graduated from St. Louis University in 1843. A lawyer by profession, he represented St. Louis County in the Missouri House of Representatives for four terms (1852–1858), and served in the US House of Representatives as a Democrat from 1859 until 1861. During the war, Barret sided with the Confederacy negotiating prisoner exchanges and acting as liaison between Sterling Price's Army of the Trans-Mississippi and the Confederate government in Richmond. After Appomattox he moved to New York City where he engaged in numerous occupations.[19]

Representative Barret's address, delivered only two weeks before the conclusion of the Thirty-Sixth Congress, presents a puzzling mixture of hyperbole and dispassionate logic. While protesting against the secessionist movement in the South arguing that secession is "a remedy for no evil, real or imaginary," and that there is "no complaint against the Government," Barret spent the majority of his time railing against the North, abolitionists, and specifically the Republican Party. In his castigation of Republicans, he colorfully described half as "out-and-out, red-mouthed Abolitionists, . . . who carry the Bible in their hands, religion on their tongues, and hell in their wicked hearts." The other half were "cunning and ambitious politicians, . . ." small demagogues and pitiful pettifoggers," who employed the "wicked, reckless, and lawless fanaticism of the Abolitionist." It was clear to this first-term congressman that those northern "fanatics" had taken control of the federal government and would soon subjugate the South and destroy its "institution of slavery."

Barret concluded by asking what "shall be done to restore peace, happiness, and prosperity?" The question of slavery must be settled, "now and forever." Republicans alone, he insisted, could solve the problem they had created. The country had turned to New York Senator William H. Seward, Barret opined, "believing that he who has raised could easily rule the storm," but "he (Seward) furnishes no remedy for relief."

In his rush to censure Republicans as abolitionists and William H. Seward as offering no solution to the South's complaints, Barret carefully omitted the fact that president-elect Lincoln had repeatedly announced that he had no interest in interfering with slavery in the states and "no lawful right to do so," a point Lincoln reaffirmed in his first inaugural address. Representative Barret also failed to note that the official position of the Republican Party was the continuance of slavery in the states. To that end, Senator Seward (Barret's "acknowledged leader" of the Republican Party) had introduced a constitutional amendment on Christmas Eve 1860 designed to prohibit Congress from interfering with slavery in the states. A few days later, Republican Charles Francis Adams had introduced a similar amendment that was formally adopted by the Committee of Thirty-Three. The Republican chair of the Committee, Thomas Corwin of Ohio, later replaced the Adams amendment with Seward's, and on February 28 the Seward-Adams-Corwin amendment passed the House and on March 4 received the approval of the US Senate. In his inaugural speech later that day, Abraham Lincoln referenced the passage of the amendment and observed that he had "no objection to its being made express, and irrevocable."

In addition to painting Republicans as abolitionists, Representative Barret spent a considerable portion of his speech explaining why the southern people had cause to fear the incoming administration. Like Senator Trusten Polk and Representative John Clark before him, Barret appealed to the white supremacist views held by the majority of White southerners (and not a few White northerners). Quoting from various Republicans and the Chicago Platform, he stressed that the "fundamental principle of Republicanism, has become the equality of the negro with the white man."

STATE OF THE UNION

—

SPEECH OF HON. J. R. BARRET, OF MISSOURI, IN THE HOUSE OF REPRESENTATIVES,

February 21, 1861.

The House having under consideration the report from the select committee of thirty-three—
Mr. BARRET said:
Mr. SPEAKER: In 1783, George Washington, in a letter to the Governors of the several States,[20] used the following language: "There are four things

which I humbly conceive are essential to the well-being, I may even venture to say to the existence, of the United States as an independent power: 1. An indissoluble Union under our Federal head. 2. A sacred regard for public justice. 3. The adoption of a proper peace regulation. 4. The prevalence of that pacific and friendly disposition among the people of the United States which will induce them to forget their local politics and prejudices."

In 1787, acting upon this advice from the Father of his Country, whom to love was the delight of the whole nation, the people of the United States, in order to form a more perfect Union, establish justice, insure domestic tranquility, provide for the common defense, promote the general welfare, and secure the blessings of liberty to themselves and their posterity, did ordain and establish our blessed Constitution. To say that those who formed that sacred instrument were good and great, is not enough. They seemed inspired from above—special messengers from the very throne of the Eternal; bearers of the high and holy mission of teaching to all the earth the true doctrines of self-government.

The Constitution, as a peace regulation, would, in all things, be complete; and the Union thus formed, under one Federal head, would be indissoluble, if there existed a sacred regard for public justice and such a friendly and pacific feeling among the people as to induce them to forget their local politics and prejudices.

George Washington seemed impressed with this idea when, in 1796, he, in the most affectionate, solemn, and earnest manner, warned his countrymen against every attempt to alienate one portion of the people from the rest, and enjoined upon all the constant love of liberty, and especially the preservation of the unity of the Government, as the palladium of our political safety and prosperity.[21]

In utter disregard of the warnings and injunctions, in direct conflict with the spirit of the Constitution and the principles of public justice, a party was formed in the North, founded entirely upon local politics and prejudices, and with the avowed object of making war upon southern institutions. And in 1820, upon the application of Missouri for admission as a State, an issue, based upon geographical discriminations, was directly made, which endangered, even at that early day, the very existence of the Union. It may be well to call attention to the views of Mr. Jefferson,[22] upon this proposition and the party making it, as he is one of the *fathers of the Republic*, to whom this anti-slavery party now delight to refer.

In a letter to Mr. Monroe,[23] of March 3, 1820, he says: "The Missouri question is the most portentous one which ever threatened our Union. In the gloomiest moment of the revolutionary war, I never had an apprehension equal to that I felt from this source."

In his writings, volume seven, he says: "The question is a mere party trick;

the leaders of Federalism, defeated in their schemes of obtaining power, by rallying partisans to the principle of monarchism—a principle of personal, not of local division—have changed their tact and thrown out another barrel to the whale. They are taking advantage of the virtuous feeling of the people to effect a division of parties by geographical lines; they expect this will insure them, on local principles, the majority they could never obtain on principles of Federalism."

In a letter to Mr. Adams,[24] January 22, 1821, he says:

What does the holy alliance, in and out of Congress, mean to do with us on the Missouri question? And this, by the way, is but the name of the case: it is only the John Doe and Richard Roe of the ejectment. The real question, as seen in the States afflicted with this unfortunate population, is, "are our slaves to be presented with freedom and a dagger?" For, if Congress has the power to regulate the conditions of the inhabitants of the States within the States, it will be but the exercise of that power to declare that all shall be free.

In a letter to La Fayette,[25] November 4, 1823, he says: "On the eclipse of Federalism with us, although not its extinction, its leaders got up the Missouri question under the false front of lessening the measure of slavery, but with the real view of producing a geographical division of parties which might insure them the next President."

To Mr. Holmes,[26] April 22, 1820:

I have been among the most sanguine in believing that our Union would be of long duration. I now doubt it much, and see the event at no great distance, and the direct consequence of this question. My only comfort and consolation is, that I shall not live to see it; and I envy not the present generation the glory of throwing away the fruits of their fathers' sacrifices of life and fortune, and of rendering desperate the experiment which was to decide, ultimately, whether man is capable of self-government. This treason against human hope will signalize their epoch in future history as the counterpart of the model of their predecessors.

This momentous question, like a fire-bell in the night, awakened me and filled me with horror. I considered it, at once, as the knell of the Union. It is hushed, indeed, for the moment; but this is a reprieve, only, not a final sentence. A geographical line, coinciding with a marked principle, moral and political, once conceived and held up to the angry passions of men, will never be obliterated; and every new irritation will mark it deeper and deeper.

For peace and for the Union, the South upon this question made a compromise of their rights which even the Constitution would not justify.

But this compromise did not secure peace. It was a "reprieve only," and not a "final sentence." It was but a temporary success of sectionalism, which encouraged more thorough organization. On the 30th January, 1832, the Anti-slavery Society of New England was formed. This was an association, not professedly political, having for its object the abolition of slavery by moral means. The delightful amusement of witch-burning had been played out, and so industrious and puritanical a people could not remain idle. In 1848, these humanitarians, assisted by politicians, succeeded in getting up another national agitation, which once more threatened the Union, until peace was restored by the compromise of 1850. Afterwards, a union of politicians, with the various anti-slavery societies, formed the Republican party, an organization wholly sectional in its character, determined upon effecting the ultimate extinction of slavery, regardless of plighted faith and national obligations.

This party is now under the management of two distinct classes. The first is composed of the out-and-out, red-mouthed Abolitionists, who believe that it is the right and duty of every slave to cut his master's throat. These are the bold and desperate men who attempt to carry out practically the great leading ideas and moving principles of the Republican party. They are men who would have rejoiced to see John Brown President, Hinton Rowan Helper Vice President, and Dred Scott Chief Justice of the Supreme Court of the United States.

Mr. KILGORE.[27] I desire to ask the gentleman a question.

Mr. BARRET. I am unwilling to be interrupted. After concluding my remarks, I will answer any questions the gentleman may desire to ask.

Mr. KILGORE. I wanted to ask if the gentleman includes all the members of the Republican party in that category?

Mr. BARRET. I decline yielding the floor. I say most prominent among this Abolition class, are preachers of the Gospel, men making pretense of much true piety and Christian charity.

> "When devils will their blackest sins put on,
> They do suggest at first with heavenly shows,
> "How smooth and even they do bear themselves!
> As if allegiance in their bosoms sat,
> Crowned with faith and constant loyalty.
> "They are meek, and humble mouth'd;
> They sign their place and calling, in full seeming,
> With meekness and humility.[28]

They carry the Bible in their hands, religion on their tongues, and hell in their wicked hearts. The second class is made up of cunning and ambitious politicians. Believing it necessary to their success, they have succeeded in forming sectional parties—parties distinctly northern and southern, slavery and anti-slavery; and to this end they have employed with marked effect, the wicked, reckless, and lawless fanaticism of the Abolitionist; and while they appropriate the *service* to their own purposes, they would have us believe that they condemn the *servants*. From this second class of managers proceed all the artful platforms, so cunningly devised as to reveal just enough to hold the Abolitionist, and to conceal just enough to catch the more moderate, and the good men who are sometimes found in the Republican party.

I shall say nothing of the small demagogues and pitiful pettifoggers who make themselves so prominent now in the hour of party success. They are but the light, surface material, drawn by the Republican current from every eddy. They are without size and substance, and float upon the tide; because its influx may raise, while its reflux can never lower them.

Under this management, the Republican party has combined States against States, and arrayed section against section, until, by the power of numbers, by a sectional plurality, led on by party drill, and by the stimulus of pay and rations, and under the inducement of coveted honors, fat salaries, and the sweets of patronage, place, and power, and at the same time penetrated and fired with the delicious idea that they were moving in the cause of human rights, and of the equality of man, have succeeded in getting possession of the General Government.

The South, the defeated section, believing that this geographical party, in its very nature, is inimical to them, and that their main object in taking possession of the Government is to use all its powers and patronage in carrying out their leading idea—which must result in the complete subjugation of the South, and the destruction of their institution of slavery—have become alarmed, and they ask for further guarantees of their safety. They ask only their rights under the Constitution, but they want such explanatory amendments as will prevent the perversion of that instrument into the means of their own destruction.

Now, what is that leading idea, and have the southern people any cause for fear? In 1859, Mr. SEWARD said of the Republican party, of which he is the acknowledged leader and originator: "The secret of its assured success lies in the fact that it is a party of one idea—the idea of equality; equality of all men, before human tribunals and human laws, as they are equal before divine tribunals and divine laws."

On previous occasions he had used similar language. At Buffalo, in 1856, he said: "If all men are created equal, no one can rightfully acquire or hold dominion over, or property in, another man, without his consent. If all men are created equal, one man cannot rightfully exact the service or the labor of another man, without his consent. The subjugation of one man to another by force, so as to compel involuntary labor or service, subverts that equality between the parties which the Creator established."

In the Senate, on the 11th of March, 1850, he said: "All this is just and sound; but assuming the same premises—to wit, that all men are equal by the law of nature and of nations—the right of property in slaves falls to the ground; for one who is equal to the other cannot be the owner of property of that other. But you answer that the Constitution recognizes property in slaves. It would be sufficient, then, to reply, that the constitutional obligation must be void, because it is repugnant to the law of nature and nations."

These sentiments had been proclaimed by the Anti-Slavery party in every convention, and they were not only not disclaimed by the party at Chicago, but emphatically reasserted in the following resolution: "That the maintenance of the principles promulgated in the Declaration of Independence, and embodied in the Federal Constitution, 'that all men are created equal; that they are endowed by their Creator with certain inalienable rights; that among them are life, liberty, and the pursuit of happiness; that to secure these rights, Governments are instituted among men, deriving their just powers from the consent of the governed,' is essential to the preservation of republican institutions."

To this bold enunciation of the real Abolition doctrine of the party some timid man made objection; but this objection was soon dispelled by that great leader of the party, Mr. Giddings, of Ohio.[29] He would not allow any dodging, and advocated the resolution with feeling. He said, and truthfully: "The Republican party was founded on this doctrine of negro equality; that it grew upon it, and existed upon it. When you leave this truth out, you leave out the party."

Mr. Curtis, of New York,[30] in advocating the resolution, declared: "That the words were truths by which the Republican party lives, and upon which alone the future of this country in the hands of the Republican party is passing."

In the nomination and election of Mr. Lincoln, the future of this country did pass into the hands of the Republican party upon the doctrine of negro equality. Judging from his speeches, we must regard Mr. Lincoln as the very embodiment of the sentiments of Mr. Giddings and Mr. Curtis, and of the Abolition party generally. Listen to his words at Chicago, in 1858: "My friends, I have detained you about as long as I desired to do, and I have only to say, let us discard all quibbling about this man or the other man, this race, that race, and the other race being inferior, and therefore must be placed in an inferior position, discarding our standard which we have left us; let us discard all these things, and unite as one people throughout the land, until we shall once more stand up declaring that all men are created equal."

He makes it still stronger in the same speech: "My friends, I could not, without launching off upon some new topic, which would detain you too long, continue to-night. I thank you for this most extensive audience you have furnished me to-night. I leave you, hoping that the lamp of liberty will burn in your bosoms until there shall be no longer a doubt that all men are created free and equal."

Afterwards, at Galesburg, Mr. Lincoln said: "I believe that the entire records of the world, from the date of the Declaration of Independence up to within three years ago, may be searched in vain for a single affirmation, from one single man, that the negro was not included in the Declaration of Independence."[31]

Mr. Lincoln will not be content with an admission of the abstract equality of men, but wishes to reduce it to practice. The Illinois Journal, of September 16, 1856, contains the following, which is prefaced: "We are indebted to Mr. Lincoln for a verbatim report of the speech:"

> That central idea, in our political opinion, at the beginning was, and until recently continued to be, the equality of men. And although it was always submitted patiently to whatever inequality there seemed to be as a matter of actual necessity, its constant working has been a steady progress towards the practical equality of all men.
>
> Let past differences as nothing be; and with steady eye on the real issue, let us reinaugurate the good old central ideas of the Republic. We can do it. The human heart is with us; God is with us. We shall again be able, not to declare that all the States, as States, are equal, nor yet that all citizens, as citizens, are equal; but renew the broader, better declaration, including both these and much more, that all men are created equal.—*Speech at banquet in Chicago.*

On the 10th of October, 1854, at Peoria, Illinois, he used the following language:

> What I do say is, that no man is good enough to govern another man without the other's consent. I say this is the leading principle, the sheet anchor, of American republicanism. Our Declaration of Independence says: "We hold these truths to be self-evident: that all men are created equal; that they are endowed by their Creator with certain inalienable rights; that among these are life, liberty, and the pursuit of happiness. That to secure these rights Governments are instituted among men, deriving their just powers from the consent of the governed." I have quoted so much at this time merely to show that, according to our ancient faith, the just powers of Governments are derived from the consent of the governed. Now, the relation of master and slave is *pro tanto*[32] a total violation of this principle. The master not only governs his slave without his consent, but he governs him by a set of rules

altogether different from those which he prescribes for himself. Allow all the governed an equal voice in the Government; and that, and that only, is self-government.—*Howell's Life of Lincoln*, p. 279.³³

The stump orators in slave and free States all advocated the claims of Mr. Lincoln upon this doctrine of negro equality; and prominent among these was a Dutch upstart,³⁴ who went from city to city, insulting the people of this country by explaining to them their Declaration of Independence. If that Declaration did not mean to place the negro upon an equality with the white man, this is his opinion of that sacred instrument. I quote his own words:

> There is your Declaration of Independence, a diplomatic dodge, adopted merely for the purpose of excusing the rebellious colonies in the eyes of civilized mankind. There is your Declaration of Independence, no longer the sacred code of the rights of man, but a hypocritical piece of special pleading, drawn up by a batch of pettifoggers, who, when speaking of the rights of men, meant but the privileges of a set of aristocratic slaveholders, but styled it 'the rights of man' in order to throw dust in the eyes of the world, and to inveigle noble-hearted fools into lending them aid and assistance. There are your boasted revolutionary sires, no longer heroes and sages, but accomplished humbuggers and hypocrites, who said one thing and meant another; who passed counterfeit sentiments as genuine, and obtained arms, and money, and assistance, and sympathy, on false pretenses! There is your great American Revolution, no longer the great champion of universal principles, but a mean Yankee trick—a wooden nutmeg—the most impudent imposition ever practiced upon the whole world.³⁵

Mr. Speaker, there are in the Declaration of Independence many self-evident truths. Why should the Chicago platform contain that one concerning equality? Was it the expression of a sentiment honestly entertained, or was it a mere pretense to draw the honest elector into the support of the party by false pretenses?

But they say these principles, promulgated in the Declaration, are embodied in the Constitution. The Declaration announces the fact that all men are created equal, and entitled to life, liberty, &c. The Constitution returns the fugitive slave to his master. Is this a case of principle, promulgated in the one and embodied in the other? Then, for which are the Republican party: for the promulgation or the embodiment?

Sir, I do not believe in that interpretation of our bill of rights. Our forefathers, in the promulgation of a great international principle of human freedom, never intended to establish a law paramount to the Constitution itself, declaring their own slaves entitled to their freedom, and themselves law-breakers in holding them in bondage. That there should be a prejudice against slavery in the minds of northern men, is but natural; and for it I make due allowance. But that prejudice has grown into a sickly sentimentality; into a wild, wicked, and dangerous fanaticism; into a social and political disease; a great national curse. And now, the cardinal doctrine, the great leading central idea, the fundamental principle of Republicanism, has become the equality of the negro with the white man. Hence the persistent denunciation of slavery in the States; hence the establishment and encouragement of underground railroads; hence the personal liberty bills; hence the bloody strife in Kansas; hence the devilish raids upon our border; hence the incitement to civil war, and the excitement of servile insurrection.

The Republicans believe that whether promulgated by the Declaration, or embodied in the Constitution, the negro is the equal of the white man, and entitled by the higher law to his freedom; that slavery is the sum of all villainies; that thieves are less amenable to the moral code than slaveholders; "that slavery is a sin against God and a crime against man, which no human enactment or usage can make right; and that Christianity and patriotism alike demand its abolition." They believe, with Mr. SUMNER,[36] that—"Slavery is a wrong so grievous and unquestionable, that it should not be allowed to continue; nay, that it should cease at once; nay, that a wrong so transcendent, so loathsome, so direful, must be encountered wherever it can be reached; and the battle must be continued without truce or compromise, until the field is entirely won."

That it is the object of the Republican party to abolish slavery in the States, I need only read from the organs and leaders of the party, and from Mr. Lincoln himself.

The Chicago Democrat, of the 11th of August, 1860, is suggestive:

> Blair is a Republican of the radical school. He is a Republican of the Seward, the Sumner, and the Lincoln school. He believes in making the States all free. He believes slavery to be an evil and a curse, and that the duty of the Federal Government is to prevent its extension.
>
> While the great doctrine of the duty of the Federal Government to make 'the States all free' thus receives indorsement in a slaveholding State, shall the Republicans of the free States lower their standard of principle?
>
> The day of compromising, half-way measures, has gone by. The people are determined to force the politicians up to the point of making the States all free. If the politicians are not prepared for this, they must get out of the road. Unless they do, they will be run over....
>
> The year of jubilee has come! Already is the child born who shall

live to see the last shackle fall from the limbs of the slave on this continent. Universal emancipation is near at hand.

The only class of people who are standing in the way of the accomplishment of this great work are the office-hunters—the fossils and the flunkeys of the North. They cannot, or will not, see that the path of duty is the path of safety; and they prefer party to principle. Such men would have the Republican party in the free States lower its standard, and pretend not to be devoted to the extinction of slavery everywhere, while our gallant Republicans in the slave States are winning victories upon this very principle, in the face of the slave power.

But the great heart of the Republican masses revolts against such hypocrisy and such truckling. They throw their banner to the breeze, inscribed with Lincoln's glorious words, "The States must be made all free;" and under it will march on to victory after victory, conquering and to conquer.

In October, 1855, Mr. SEWARD said: "Slavery is not and never can be perpetual. It will be overthrown either peacefully and lawfully under this Constitution, or it will work the subversion of the Constitution together with its own overthrow."

Helper,[37] in a work indorsed by sixty-eight members of this Congress, has fully exposed the intentions of his party. He says:

But we are wedded to one purpose, from which no power can divorce us. We are determined to *abolish slavery at all hazards*, in defiance of all opposition, of whatever nature, which it is possible for the slaveocrats to bring against us. Of this they may take due notice, and govern themselves, accordingly.—Page 149.

Abolition is but another name for patriotism, magnanimity, reason, prudence, wisdom, religion, progress, justice, and humanity.—Page 118.

The oligarchs say we cannot abolish slavery without infringing on the right of property. Again we tell them we do not *recognize property in man*. . . . Impelled by a sense of duty to others, we would be fully warranted in emancipating all the slaves *at once*, without any compensation whatever to those who claim to be their absolute owners.—Page 123.

Of you, the introducers, aiders, and abettors of slavery, we demand indemnification for the damage our lands have sustained on account thereof: the amount of damage is $7,544,118,825; and now, sirs, we are ready to receive the money, and if it is perfectly convenient to you, we would be glad to have you pay it in specie. It will not avail you, sirs, to parley or prevaricate. We must have a settlement. Our claim is just, and overdue.... It is for you to decide whether we are to have justice peaceably, or by violence; for, whatever consequences may follow, we are determined to have it, one way or the other. Do you aspire to become the victims of white non-slaveholding vengeance by day, and of barbarous massacres by the negroes at night?

Would you be instrumental in bringing upon yourselves, your wives, and your children, a fate too horrible to contemplate? Shall history cease to cite as an instance of unexampled cruelty the massacre of St. Bartholomew,[38] because the South shall have furnished a more direful scene of atrocity and carnage? Now, sirs, you must emancipate them, [slaves,] speedily emancipate them, or we will emancipate them for you.—Pages 126, 128.

The great revolutionary movement which was set on foot in Charlotte, Mecklenburg County, North Carolina, May 20, 1775, has not yet terminated, nor will it be, until every slave in the United States is freed from the tyranny of his master.—Page 95.

But we are wedded to one purpose, from which no earthly power can divorce us. We are determined to abolish slavery, at all hazards, in defiance of all opposition, of whatever nature which it is possible for the slaveocrats to bring against us. Of this they may take due notice, and govern themselves accordingly.—Page 149.

The pro-slavery slaveholders deserve to be at once reduced to a parallel with the basest criminals that lie fettered within the cells of our public prisons.—Page 158.

No opportunity for inflicting a mortal wound in the side of slavery shall be permitted to pass us unimproved. Thus, terror-engenderers of the South, have we fully and frankly defined our position. We have no modifications to propose; no compromises to offer; nothing to retract. Frown, fret, foam, prepare your weapons, threat, strike, shoot, stab, bring on civil war, dissolve the Union. Sirs, you can neither foil nor intimidate us; our purpose is as firmly fixed as the eternal pillars of heaven; we have determined to abolish slavery, and, so help us God, abolish it we will.—Page 187.[39]

As early as 1837, Mr. Lincoln seemed as sound on some of these propositions as Helper. He was then a member of the Illinois Legislature; and on the 12th of January Mr. Ralston introduced the following resolutions:

Resolved by the General Assembly of the State of Illinois, That we highly disapprove of the formation of abolition societies, and of the doctrines promulgated by them.

Resolved, That the right of property in slaves is sacred to the slaveholding States by the Federal Constitution, and that they cannot be deprived of that right without their consent.

Mr. Lincoln voted against them. (See House Journal, p. 243.) In 1839, still a member of the Legislature, he voted against the following resolution: "That the General Government cannot do indirectly, what it is clearly prohibited from doing directly; that it is the openly declared design of the Abolitionists of this nation to abolish slavery in the District of Columbia, with a view to its ultimate abolishment in the States;" . . . "and that, therefore, Congress ought not to abolish slavery in the District of Columbia."—*House Journal,* p. 126.

Such votes, such expressions, by the President elect and his party, leave us no longer in doubt as to their intentions; and what Mr. Clay[40] said of the anti-slavery party in 1838, is true of the Republican party in 1861. We have only to insert New Mexico, in place of Florida, to make the application complete:

> With the Abolitionists, the rights of property are nothing; the deficiency of the powers of the General Government are nothing; the acknowledged and incontestable powers of the States are nothing; civil war, a dissolution of the Union, and the overthrow of the Government in which are concentrated the fondest hopes of the civilized world, are nothing. A single idea has taken possession of their minds, and onward they pursue it, overlooking all barriers, reckless and regardless of consequences. With this class the immediate abolition of slavery in the District of Columbia, and in the Territory of Florida, the prohibition of the removal of slaves from State to State, and the refusal to admit any new States comprising within their limits the institution of domestic slavery, are but so many means conducing to the accomplishment of the ultimate but perilous end at which they avowedly and boldly aim, are but so many short stages in the long and bloody road to the distant goal at which they would finally arrive. Their purpose is abolition, universal abolition—peaceably, if they can; forcibly, if they must.—*Appendix Globe,* vol. 7, p. 355.[41]

I know that many of the Republican party shrewdly disavow any intention to interfere directly with slavery in the States. It would be too great a strain of the higher law, even, to justify so flagrant an outrage. But the same object can be accomplished indirectly. Admit no more slave States. Then, according to Mr. SUMNER, "slavery will die, like the poisoned rat, of rage, in his hole."

Create dissatisfaction among the slaves in the border States; induce them to seek refuge in the free States; prevent their recapture and return, by personal liberty bills; and slave property will be thus rendered so insecure, unprofitable, and even dangerous, in the border States, that they will rid themselves of it; and once free, it is expected that those States will cooperate in making an amendment to the Constitution, providing for the ultimate extinction of slavery throughout the land.

Abolition of slavery, directly or indirectly, is demanded by the people of the North.[42] Men high in authority, leaders of party, preachers, teachers, editors, judges, lawyers, law-makers, State and national, openly avow it; and no scheme has yet been suggested, however unconstitutional; no plan has yet been attempted, however wicked and infernal, which looked towards the freedom of a negro, which has not met with approval in the ranks of the Republican party. Many of that party believe that the design of John Brown was founded in the deepest wisdom and benevolence, and executed in unrivaled heroism, integrity, and self-forgetfulness; that his life was a complete success, his death an unparalleled and most honorable triumph; that the blood of John Brown appeals to God and humanity against slaveholders; that the heart of this nation, and of the civilized world, will respond to that appeal in one defiant shout: "resistance to slaveholders is obedience to God."

John Brown was a true, practical Republican. He considered the negro an equal of the white man. He believed slavery a sin against God, and a crime against man. He believed in the insurrectionary and bloody schemes promulgated by the distinguished Republican Hinton Rowan Helper, and cordially indorsed by sixty-eight Republican members of this Congress.[43] He believed with the Republicans of Natick, "that it was the right and the duty of slaves to resist their masters, and the right and duty of the people of the North to incite them to resistance, and to aid them in it." Theodore Parker[44] says: "John Brown sought by force what the Republican party works for with other weapons; the two agree in the end, and differ only in the means."

I know that there are many members of the Republican party who blame John Brown. Of such I may say:

> They know the right, and they approve it, too;
> Condemn the wrong, and yet the wrong pursue.[45]

The Republican party has one million eight hundred and fifty-eight thousand two hundred voters in the North, and only twenty-seven thousand and thirty-two voters in the South. It could hardly be more sectional. They have gained possession of the Government.[46] As to what will be their policy, we can judge only from the sentiments expressed by their leaders and their party organs.

On the 13th day of August last, Mr. SEWARD used the following language, which, from him, and under the circumstances, is full of meaning:

> What a commentary upon the wisdom of man is given in this single fact that, fifteen years only after the death of John Quincy Adams,[47] the people of the United States, who hurled him from power and from place, are calling to the head of the nation, to the very seat from which he was expelled, Abraham Lincoln, whose claim to that seat is that he confesses the obligation of that higher law which the sage of Quincy proclaimed, and that he avows himself, for weal or woe, for life or death, a soldier on the side of freedom in the irrepressible conflict between freedom and slavery.

He afterwards said: "I tell you, fellow-citizens, that with this victory comes the end of the slave power in the United States."

Helper, on page 183 of his book, reduces this sentiment of his distinguished leader into a more practical shape. He says: "Once for all, within a reasonably short period, let us make the slaveholders do something like justice to their negroes, by giving each and every one of them his freedom and sixty dollars in current money."

The wheels of Government are to be moved with a high hand. For years have we been warned of this intention. Mr. SEWARD said, in the Senate, March 3, 1858: "Let the Supreme Court recede. Whether it recede or not, we shall reorganize that court, and thus reform its political sentiments and practices, and bring them into harmony with the Constitution and the laws of nature."

Massachusetts, through one of her distinguished Senators, [Mr. WILSON,][48] sustained this doctrine: "We shall change the Supreme Court of the United States, and place men in that court who believe, with its immortal Chief Justice, John Jay, that our prayers will be impious to Heaven while we support and sustain human slavery."

Through one of her Representatives, [Mr. BURLINGAME,][49] she has gone even further: "When we shall have elected a President, as we will, who will not be the President of a party, but the tribune of the people, and after we have exterminated a few doughfaces from the North, then, if the slave Senate will not give way, we will grind it between the upper and nether millstones of our power."

From these and many like expressions of the leaders of the Republican party, the southern people have concluded that the administration of Mr. Lincoln will abolish slavery in the District of Columbia; that they will prevent inter-State slave trade, restrict slavery in all the Territories, reorganize the Supreme Court, and put the Government actually and perpetually on the side of freedom.[50]

I know that it is claimed that the only object of the Republican party is to prohibit slavery in the Territories. And, according to the gentleman from Ohio, [Mr. SHERMAN,] no sane man would for a moment suppose that slavery could ever go north of the 36°30', and hence the only practical issue was, as to the existence of slavery in New Mexico. This, then, is a statement of the case. Two different forms of labor exist in this country, bond and free. The Constitution does not prescribe, or proscribe, either, for the Territory of New Mexico. The people of the South claim the right to take their bondmen into New Mexico. The people of the North deny the existence of any such right. Upon a fair submission of this question to the voters of the whole country at the election in November last, there were, in the free States, 1,574,091, and in the slave States, 1,257,195—total, 2,831,286 voters, who were of opinion that a citizen of the United States had a right to take his bondman into New Mexico, or any other Territory of the United States; while there were in the free States 1,858,200, and in the slave, 27,032, voters—total, 1,885,232, who were of a different opinion.[51] This opinion of the South had already been sustained by a decision of that august tribunal, the Supreme Court of the United States, which, by the very Constitution, is a coordinate branch of this Government, and its decisions are final, and the supreme law of the land. There are not more than seven slaves now in New Mexico, and such are its climate and soil that it cannot possibly be a free State; and yet, the gentleman from Ohio considers the question of slavery in New Mexico the all-important one upon which, as he says, the Union is being disrupted, and State after State is going out.[52]

Was it the whole end aim of the Republican party to make this Territory free? Was it for this that nearly three million people placed themselves upon sectional ground, and arrayed North against South? Was it for this that they went through with a protracted, expensive, and laborious canvas? Was it for this that they brought about a sectional agitation, a hostile feeling, which threatens the very existence of the Union? Was it for this that they sought the possession of the General Government, and the reorganization of the Supreme Court? I deny that such a respectable number of Republicans even, however excited, however prejudiced, could be so greatly moved by so pitiful an object. If the position of the gentleman from Ohio be correct, the existence of the Republican party is dependent upon the *status* of New Mexico on the slavery question, and the determination of that would, as a matter of course, put an end to the politics of that party, and to the party itself.

The gentleman from Ohio is not the only distinguished Republican who believes that the sole object of his party is the prohibition of slavery in the Territories; nor do I stand alone in the opinion that, if that be true, the party must soon cease to exist. Mr. Bates, of Missouri,[53] a prominent candidate before the Chicago convention for President, thus spoke in the rotunda at St. Louis, August 10, 1856:

> The Republican party is not a mere array of men. It is a hasty agglomeration made up of the odds and ends of every other party that ever existed at the North. Mr. SEWARD, ever an eminent Whig and unquestionably a man of ability, is one of its leaders. He was that distinguished Whig, he is that distinguished Republican. At the North, whole slabs of the American party have united with the new organization, and it is now animated by an ardent enthusiasm which furnishes proof of its transitory nature. In proportion to its ardor will be the shortness of its life. Its only aim is the prohibition of slavery in the Territories; and even if it should succeed in accomplishing its object by a congressional enactment, its whole force and vitality would be exhausted in the effort, and it would decline.

Of this party, Mr. H. WINTER DAVIS,[54] the distinguished member from Maryland, and a candidate for the Vice Presidency in the Chicago convention, spoke as follows, in this House, January 6, 1857:

> The Republican party was a hasty levy *en masse* of the northern people to repel or revenge an intrusion by northern votes alone. With its occasion it must pass away. Within two years, Kansas must be a State of the Union. She must be admitted with or without slavery, as her people prefer. Beyond Kansas, there is no question that is practically open. I speak to practical men. Slavery does not exist in any other Territory; it is excluded by law from several, and not likely to exist anywhere; and the Republican party has nothing to do, and can do nothing. It has no future. Why cumbers it the ground?
>
> No, Mr. Speaker, a party organized under such circumstances, composed of such materials, announcing such sentiments, fighting such battles, must have an object far beyond the prevention of slavery in a Territory where it can never exist.
>
> Sir, the restriction of slavery in the Territories is but one of the means. The great end to be accomplished is, as Mr. Lincoln says, the ultimate extinction of slavery. At any rate, the South fears that this is the object, and that the whole power and patronage of the Government will be used in its accomplishment; and moved by this fear, and by actual wrongs, the cotton States, exercising the right claimed by Massachusetts in 1814, and afterwards upon the annexation of Texas, have thrown off their allegiance to this Government and declared their independence.

It is not to be denied that the seceding States, yea, the whole South, have been subjected to a long train of abuses by the anti-slavery party. An incessant war has been made upon them, because slaveholders; their constitutional rights have been denied them; their slaves constantly interfered with; and laws made for their protection have been purposely obstructed; and now, it would seem to be the purpose of this anti-slavery Republican party, not only to destroy the value of $4,000,000,000 worth of their property, but to convert it into the means of their own destruction. In vain they have warned the northern people against this unholy crusade; in vain have they remonstrated against the obstruction of the laws; in vain have they appealed to the generous sympathies of their brethren, asking only for the peaceful enjoyment of rights guaranteed by the Constitution. Their warnings, remonstrations, and appeals have been answered only with repeated injuries. Wrongs like these, if inflicted by the Government, would be just cause for revolution. Such grievances could only be redressed by a resort to arms. But this Government has done no wrong. There is no complaint against the Government. On the contrary, all unite in the opinion that it is the best form of government ever instituted among men. The southern confederacy have adopted it; and now, after our dismemberment, it is the only plan of government upon which there is the slightest hope for a reconstruction.

But besides, the Government has provided a mode of redressing the grievances which this sectional minority has imposed upon the South. The very election which raised a sectional President into power, manifested the existence of a national conservative element which insured a constitutional check upon his administration, and its certain termination at the end of four years. An opposition which, if united, could have defeated that election, could surely have protected themselves, under the Constitution and in the Union, against the aggressions of any sectional minority.

Under these circumstances, I now enter my solemn protest against the action of the seceding States. It was, in my opinion, unwise and selfish, an irreparable injury to themselves, an act of cruel injustice to the middle and border slave States, and to the General Government, and of gross ingratitude to a million and a half of gallant men of the North, who have made every sacrifice and dared every danger in support of the Constitution and in defense of southern rights. Has it ever recurred to our precipitate brethren of the South that those northern friends, like themselves, owe allegiance to their respective States, and that, by secession, they leave a noble army of northern conservatives, with all their valor and devotion, to be swept down by the assaults of resistless numbers, to rise no more forever? By this hasty act, they have forced upon the border States the fearful alternative of submission, on the one hand, to a power which could at any moment override all their rights; or rebellion, secession, and civil war, on the other, which, in their exposed position, would be their utter ruin. In my judgment, such a respectable number of States, so vast in extent, with a population so large, and an interest so great, were entitled to some consideration at the hands of those States for which, in all their struggles against northern aggression, they had been a cloud by day and a pillar of fire by night.

But this disunion, while it may bring upon the country the direst of all calamities, is a remedy for no evil, real or imaginary. It cannot render slave property more secure, or in any manner perpetuate it. It yields up forever the equal participation in the Territories by the slave States, while it furnishes no greater protection for slavery where it exists. In the Union, the South, with a minority North, were stronger than even a united South could possibly be out of the Union, with or without arms. The cotton States should, therefore, have remained in the Union. Then, if this northern party—formerly Abolition, now Republican—should attempt to reorganize the Supreme Court, and make of it a machine to sustain their bad morals and worse politics; if they should fasten upon the Government the doctrine of the higher law, and employ all its patronage and power in an organized and direct attack upon slavery, then would we make war, not against the Government, but against its enemies; then might we fight, under the Constitution, against those who would subvert it; fight for this beautiful capital, hallowed in its very name, location, and in all its associations; fight for the archives, the flag, the honor of this great nation.

But, whether secession, disunion, revolution—call it what you will—be right or wrong, is not now the question. It exists; it is all around and about us. It has shocked and unsettled every department of the Government, and paralyzed business in all its branches. Its baleful influence has spread sorrow and gloom, disaster, and destitution, over the whole land.

The question now is: what shall be done to restore peace, happiness, and prosperity? Who can, who will save the country from the threatened doom?

The gentleman from Ohio [Mr. SHERMAN] appealed to the border States to "arrest the tide, which, but for them, would in a few days place us in hostile array against each other." Believing that the border States, free and slave, understood practically this question of slavery, about which the pestiferous States of South Carolina and Massachusetts only theorize, I took upon myself the responsibility of calling those States together, that they might counsel with each other.

The committee appointed by those States agreed almost unanimously upon a plan of adjustment; but when that plan was in substance proposed in the House of Representatives, the gentleman and his party voted unanimously against its consideration. At that time the border slave States occupied a position for effective interference; but the rejection of a proposition so reasonable, so just, weakened their confidence in their northern brethren. And that confidence was not in the slightest restored by the gentleman from Ohio, when, in a speech "alternately gentle as the dews and as boisterous as the thunder," he accompanies his pleas for peace with a recommendation of war, and meets all propositions of conciliation with promised adherence to the Chicago platform.

It is difficult to tell what these border States will do. The elections lately held are no proper indices of their intentions. Having large interests involved, they take time for consideration. Although not consulted by the cotton States, they choose to consult one another. But let the North be assured of one thing: that those border States are unanimous in the opinion that this is a proper occasion for the settlement of this pest question of slavery, *now and forever*.

But, sir, while I can speak for no other, I can say but little even for my own State. Missouri occupies the geographical center of this nation; she lies in the very highway of civilization, and in the march of empire. She now contains a white population equal to that of Florida, South Carolina, Alabama, and Mississippi, combined; and for her future greatness she looks to the North, to the South, to the East, and to the West. Sir, Missouri was born of the Union; she was rocked in the cradle of the Union; she has grown up, lived, and prospered in the Union, and she loves the Union with unceasing devotion; but not a Union of the North with a fragment of the South, but the Union as our fathers made it—a Union of all the States in one grand and glorious Republic. Thus situated, thus interested, Missouri claims the right to criticise the conduct of her sister States, North and South. But, if the doctrine of coercion obtain, and the attempt be made to whip the cotton States into *self*-government, then Missouri will be found side by side with the other border slave States in armed resistance. And I now say to our northern friends, beware. And I say this not in a spirit of menace, but of solemn warning.

Long before the 6th of November, South Carolina declared that she would not submit to the election of a sectional President. This was treated as an idle threat; and the taunting reply was, that South Carolina could not be kicked out of the Union. When Congress assembled, and it became evident that she would secede, and would, most likely, be followed by all the other cotton States, the country was suddenly awakened to the real danger, and was at once convulsed with fear. In the Senate, and in this House, committees were constituted, of able men, and the many propositions looking to the safety of the country were laid before them, but nothing of a practical nature was accomplished. In the emergency, all eyes are turned to the distinguished Senator from New York, believing that he who had raised could easily rule the storm. After many long weeks of painful anxiety, that Senator comes forward and coolly tells us that all this is nothing more than might be expected; that in two or three years, when the lightening-flash and the thunder-clap have subsided into a perfect calm, he may recommend something in the shape of a small Franklin rod for the protection of the people.[55] Like a physician called to see a patient, writhing, almost, with the agonies of death, he furnishes no remedy for relief, but delivers a very learned lecture on the subject of pathology in the sick room. The danger increases; State after State goes out; "The Union must and shall be preserved," is the borrowed eloquence of every Republican orator. The Government is disrupted, and civil war threatens the destruction of thirty million people and to cover the whole land with desolation. Our rulers tell us that they wish to test the strength of the Government; that they wish to see whether we have any Government at all. Commerce is destroyed, manufactures ruined, and business of all kinds prostrated; until the people, the rightful sovereigns of the nation, the makers of Government, and its rulers, are reduced by desperation to the humble position of petitioners, and, by thousands and by tens of thousands, they earnestly ask their own *servants* for concession, for compromise, for peace; to all which, they receive the slighting reply that *it is very likely that Mr. Lincoln will adhere to the Chicago platform.*[56] And now, when the dreadful issue is forced upon us, and the question is: "Union or no Union; Constitution or no Constitution; Government or no Government; country or no country;" the President elect says that "there is nothing wrong;" that "nobody is hurt;" "keep cool;" "there's no crisis; and if there is, it is all artificial;" while his Premier amuses himself and entertains the Senate by spinning cunning rhetoric into pointless platitudes and useless generalities.

Republicans, I once more give you warning. You have complete control of this Congress, and in your hands rests the destiny of this nation. Your Chicago platform is not a panacea for all the ills which now afflict us. It was made in time of peace and prosperity, and not in time of revolution and adversity. It was intended only as a basis of party action, and admirably adapted to party ends. What if it should now be abandoned, utterly destroyed? Your Greeleys, your Sewards, your Giddingses, could easily make for you another, and far better suited to the times. And now let me remind you that the election of your candidate for President was not the adoption of your platform. The disruption of the Democratic party, the dissatisfaction with the present Administration, and that restless spirit which always desires change, contributed to your success in procuring a plurality of the votes for your candidate, while there was a majority of nearly a million against your platform.

But you say the flag has been dishonored, the Constitution violated, the Union endangered, the Government defied; and you cry for war, and invoke the potential arm of Federal power to avenge all wrongs and enforce obedience. You forget that this is not a Government of force. The Union, so necessary to the establishment of the Government, was founded in the affections, which are stronger to bind a people together than any written Constitution or confederated authority. While this Government thus formed is all-powerful for good, it is impotent for evil. It was made for common defense and general welfare; but the Constitution does not provide for making war upon the very power that gave the Government existence. What if the misguided people of Charleston, in a moment of precipitation and excitement, did open a fire upon *their portion* of a common flag?[57] What if they had blotted out the star which represents their own State—South Carolina? You now tolerate in your ranks hundreds of men who, but a few years ago, marched under a flag with only sixteen stars. Your Vice President elect has made speeches under such a flag. Your respect for the Constitution has greatly increased of late. It was a distinguished Republican who, but a short time ago, pronounced that Constitution the fountain of all our evils. And for years your party has taught obedience to a higher law, and not to the Constitution of the United States.

But, all at once, you have become great lovers of union. You abuse disunion in others, while you tolerate men in your ranks who were willing to let the Union slide; men who have declared that they considered the Union a lie, an imposture, a covenant with death and an agreement with hell. If you so love the Union, why will you not do something to save it. Since there is no longer a question in regard to slavery in the Territories, the Republican party would have to fall back upon its abolitionism but for this Union question. And now, while they regard disunion as the best move ever made towards abolition, they find it necessary, for political effect, to pretend much devotion to the Union. But the other day, one of the Republican leaders said, "we can win on Union, but we cannot win on compromise." Have we come to this? Our difficulties are not to be adjusted, the Union is not to be saved, because the party in power wishes to convert the very distresses of the country into political capital.

Sir, we have indeed fallen upon strange times. But yesterday we were told that Governments were instituted among men, deriving all their just powers from the consent of the governed. That, inasmuch as the negro had not given his assent to this Government, his enslavement is a sin against God, and a crime against man. Now, this is a Government of force, of supreme power, of which even the consent of the white man forms no constituent element. But a short time ago we were told by the Senator from New York that, between free and slave labor, there was an irrepressible conflict; now he says, "that the different forms of labor, if slavery was not perverted to purposes of political ambition, need not constitute any element of strife in the Confederacy." But a short time ago we were told that it was necessary to protect the Territories from slavery, and to drive back the slave power which was threatening the invasion even of the free States. Now, says the great leader of the Republican party, "there is no fear of slavery anywhere; and the protection of the Territories from slavery has ceased to be a practical question.{"}

Gentlemen of the Republican party, this is no time for trifling; no time for diplomacy; no time for promoting political dogmas, and advancing partisan interests; no time for trying to preserve doubtful political consistency. Questions of grave moment force themselves upon you. Shall a sacrifice be made of our house, race, lineage, and blood, for those of a strange clime? Shall every seven white men cut each other's throats for the sake of one negro? Will you disregard all ties of consanguinity, and use all your endeavors to ruin ten million of the noblest race on earth, under the pretext of benefiting about one third that number of the most degraded? Shall this free, glorious, happy America throw away all her grand achievements, and tear from her brow the wreath of science, commerce, politics, and war, and no longer stand forth the loveliest of all the nations? Shall this model Republic, having no model on earth, cease forever to be an example worthy of study and imitation? These are important questions, and you alone can decide them. As I have before said, you hold in your hands the destiny of this great nation.

The formation of the Union by the adoption of the Constitution was celebrated with deep, passionate enthusiasm throughout the original colonies. "'Tis done, we have become a nation," was the exultant boast of the whole people. And that was but the dawn of the day which promised glory and happiness to all our America. A few months ago that day was at noontide, and we in the full realization of all its blessed promises. If now, in our calamity, the same spirit of concession, compromise, and patriotism, which formed the Union, should secure its preservation and its establishment for all time as the palladium of our political safety and prosperity, and if that proud bird of liberty should once more take his flight, bearing the sacred motto of "*E Pluribus Unum*," in letters of ever-living light, the whole earth would be illuminated with joy and gladness. The loud shout of a freeman's exultation would break from the deep forests of Maine, and mingle with the harmonious strains of gratitude wafted over the golden plains of California. Thirteen infant colonies rejoiced over the birth of this nation; thirty-four grown up States, empires within themselves, with their thirty million people, will rise up in one grand, national jubilee over its preservation. But if, in spite of all appeals, and regardless of all obligations, partisan feeling and small politics shall overrule concession, compromise, patriotism, be assured that whole columns of curses, rising from the bosoms of an agonized and outraged people, will ascend to Heaven against those would not save, as against those who would destroy, a nation's happiness, a nation's prosperity.

Mr. Speaker, there are many propositions in the hands of the committee of thirty-three which would restore peace to this country, and I have done all in my humble power to secure their adoption. I have had the honor of being taunted by men from the North, and men from the South, as a Union-saver.

Would that it were in my power, by a word, by a vote, by any act, by any sacrifice, to save this beautiful and holy house of our fathers; and that I could thus win this proud title, which, though bestowed in derision, is a title worth dying for; worth having lived for.

Source: *Congressional Globe*, 36th Cong., 2nd Sess., Appendix, 246–50.

CHAPTER 4

MISSOURI STATE CONVENTION

March 1861

On January 21, 1861, Missouri's General Assembly determined that a state convention should be called "to adopt such measures for vindicating the sovereignty of the State and the protection of its institutions, as shall appear to them to be demanded." Section ten of the act provided that if the convention voted to change the political relations between the state and the United States, such resolution would only be valid when a majority of the "qualified voters of this State, voting upon the question, shall ratify the same."[1] On February 18, as the Confederate States of America inaugurated Jefferson Davis as its president, Missouri's White male voters elected 104 delegates to meet in Jefferson City ten days later. Deliberating from February 28 until March 22, the gathering, dominated by Unionists, never held a direct vote on secession. Near the end of the conference, the delegates agreed on a resolution that stated "at present there is no adequate cause to impel Missouri to dissolve her connection with the General Government." Only George Bast, from Rhineland in Montgomery County, dissented. On the third day of the convention, after having elected officers and establishing committees, the delegates considered the appropriateness of receiving Luther Glenn, a secession commissioner from Georgia. The short discussion took place at almost the same time that Abraham Lincoln was delivering his inauguration address in Washington.

Sample Orr
March 4, 1861

> Born in Tennessee, Sample Orr (1816–1896) represented Green County in the state convention. A local judge and farmer by profession, Orr was the nominee of the Constitutional Union Party in the 1860 Missouri gubernatorial election. During the war he served as a major in the Green County Regiment of the Missouri Home Guard.
>
> In this short speech, Delegate Orr objected to secession commissioner Luther J. Glenn being permitted to address the convention. Having taken an oath to support the Constitution of the United States and the state of Missouri, Orr believed that the "mission of this gentleman to be to ask us to violate the oaths we have voluntarily taken." Orr vowed to vote against hearing Commissioner Glenn and did, but was overruled by his colleagues who voted 62 to 35 in favor of hearing Glenn's address.

Mr. ORR. I am as able to withstand the arguments of a gentleman from Georgia, or an abolitionist from the North, as any gentleman here, but I am here representing in part a district composed of a people who are as liberal and as virtuous and as hospitable to strangers, as any other gentleman that is here today. I am also here to discharge the duties that I have voluntarily placed myself under in relation to the oath I took the other day. I have taken an oath that I will support the Constitution of the United States, and of the State of Missouri. I hold in my hand here a communication from Mr. Glenn, in which he says the people of Georgia, in Convention assembled, appointed commissioners to several States now in this Union, for the purpose of forming a Southern Confederacy. Now, from his communication I understand the mission of this gentleman to be to ask us to violate the oaths we have voluntarily taken—to ask us to co-operate with the Southern seceding States in doing—what? In perpetuating the blessings of this Government? No, sir; but to aid in tearing to pieces the best Government the sun has ever shown upon. He is here today, and called an ambassador by some. By others a commissioner. If he is an ambassador he has missed the right city. He should have gone to Washington. If he is here as a commissioner from a sister State, then the oath we have taken forbids that we should form an alliance with any other State in the Confederacy. Therefore, I shall oppose, for one, hearing this gentleman in Convention at all. I am willing to hear the gentleman, and treat him with all the respect that a citizen of a State that has long acted with us demands. Now, I am asked by some gentlemen, "Would you be so discourteous as to refuse to allow a citizen of another State to enter your house?" I say the citizen of a sister State, whether born in this or in a foreign land, who comes to my house in the image of his God, and I, not knowing anything of his intentions, the latch-string will always hang out for him, and he can come in; but if he comes to my house, and sends in a communication which shows to me that he intends to break up the peace of my family, he won't come in if I can help it. [Loud cheering outside the bar, and a few hisses.]

THE CHAIR. (Rapping loudly with his hammer.) I will have the lobby cleared if there is any more cheering.

Mr. ORR. I hope no demonstrations will be made on one side or the other. We stand here probably in the most eventful day that has ever been known in our history. Events will date from this day which will long be remembered. To-day the inaugural address of Abraham Lincoln will be delivered, and much of the weal or woe of this nation depends on that address to-day; and in all probability the action we may take during the next hour will not only seal the destinies of Missouri, but blight the prospects of civilization. We stand here on the banks of the greatest river in the world, and a river I never will consent to have cut in twain by this government. We stand here to-day, in the midst of a city that will one day be the great commercial and manufacturing city of civilization, and I am unwilling to do anything which will blast its progress in the future. Now in regard to this gentleman from Georgia, I am willing to do what is right. I intend to vote against hearing this gentleman make a speech in our body, because I believe I am right, and that in so doing I am not acting discourteously. I do not believe the district I represent on this floor would have ever sent their representatives here, if they had declared to the people when before them as candidates, that they were coming to receive a proposition from seceding States, in order to go out and form a Southern Confederacy. I do not believe, if they had told the people that they were coming here to haul down the stars and stripes and run up the Palmetto flag, that they intended to swap the American eagle for the pelican, that they had determined to barter off "Yankee Doodle" for the African song "Dixie"—I do not believe, if they had done this, that a solitary individual would have been elected. Then, Mr. President, I shall vote against receiving this commissioner from Georgia, or from any State whatever. We are here—for what purpose? Not for secession—not for the purpose of tearing up this Government, because the people that have elected us have given, I don't know what majority, but Mr. Vest[2] says in his speech a majority of 80,000, for the Union. I am not fearful this body is going to be influenced by the gentleman from Georgia, or any gentleman that may come from South Carolina, Florida, or any of the seceding States, or even from Great Britain, which, I believe, seceded seventy-five or eighty years ago. Then I am not afraid this body is going to vote a secession ordinance, for if they do, the people of Missouri will vote it down. Without occupying further time, but acting in view of the responsibility resting upon me, I shall vote against receiving this Commissioner. I am willing he shall come here, and I am perfectly willing to adjourn and hear him speak, but if we invite a gentleman from a seceded State to address us, who asks this Convention to assist in breaking up this Union and form a Southern Confederacy, I shall vote against it, whether any other gentlemen does so or not.

Source: *Proceedings of the Missouri State Convention Held at Jefferson City and St. Louis, March, 1861* (St. Louis: George Knapp & Co., Printers and Binders, 1861), 14–15.

Commissioner Luther Judson Glenn
March 4, 1861

Luther J. Glenn (1818–1886) graduated from the University of Georgia in 1841, represented Henry County in the state legislature, and served as mayor of Atlanta from 1858 to 1860. He married Mildred Lewis Cobb younger sister of Howell Cobb, secretary of the treasury in the James Buchanan administration. During the war he served in Cobb's Legion (organized by Thomas Reade Rootes Cobb, younger brother of Howell Cobb) before being appointed commander of the Post of Atlanta, which he surrendered to United States forces on May 3, 1865.

Luther Glenn was one of fifty-two secession commissioners appointed by Deep South states to spread the disunion message throughout the slaveholding South. Those "apostles" of secession addressed state legislatures and conventions, wrote letters to and met with governors, and spoke to the southern public in meeting halls and on the streets.[3] Glenn was typical of those men as he stressed the presumed goal of the Republican Party to abolish slavery. Repeatedly citing the Chicago Platform (but, like Representative Barret, never citing the fourth plank assuring states the right to regulate slavery according to their "own judgment"), he attempted to assure his audience that Republicans would exclude slave owners from moving into the western territories in spite of the 1857 decision of the US Supreme Court in *Dred Scott v. Sandford*. He hoped that Missouri would come to the same conclusion as Georgia had that Lincoln and the Republican Party were determined to put slavery "in a course of ultimate extinction."

Mr. GLENN, after having been introduced to the President and the Convention, spoke as follows:

COMMISSIONER GLENN'S SPEECH.

Mr. President and Gentlemen of the Missouri Convention: On the 19th day of January, a Convention of the people of the State of Georgia adopted an ordinance of secession, which I beg leave to read and present to this Convention. They also adopted a resolution appointing commissioners to the various States, which I will read. [Mr. Glenn here read the ordinance of secession passed by the State of Georgia, and the resolution referring to his appointment as Commissioner.] Under that resolution, gentlemen of the Convention, I had the honor to be appointed a Commissioner from the State of Georgia to the State of Missouri, and having read and presented to you the ordinance of secession and the resolution, my duty might be considered as having been performed. It is, perhaps, however, due alike to the State which I represent and the State of Missouri, that, with your permission, I shall accompany the execution of my duty with a few brief remarks. I propose to trespass upon your patience but a short time.

Georgia has not assumed this position because of any dissatisfaction with the Constitution, because of any dissatisfaction with the General Government when administered in accordance with the spirit of that Constitution. If her Northern confederates had been true to that instrument, if they had carried out the Federal Constitution according to its spirit and letter, Georgia, having been among the first to adopt the Federal Constitution, would have been among the last to have abandoned the General Government. The causes which have operated to induce and impel the State of Georgia, one of the old thirteen States, one of those which passed through the fire and blood of the Revolution, to sever the ties that bound her to the Government of her fathers, have been enunciated, and read and understood of all men.

I do not, gentlemen, propose to enter into anything like a detailed history of the rise and progress, and present position of the anti-slavery feeling in the North. To do so would be a reflection upon your intelligence—an abuse of your indulgence, and an assumption on my part of an unnecessary task.

The first occasion upon which this feeling of hostility among the people of the Northern States assumed a position of hostility was, I believe, the application of your own people, then a Territory, for admission into the Federal Union. With the history and result of that struggle you are familiar. I need not recite it. Without assuming a political aspect of organization, the Abolitionists a few years after this event formed societies; they established newspapers at different points. In New York, Boston and other places, they began to teach the mind of the rising generation. They began to preach their doctrines from the pulpit, and but a few years elapsed before this anti-slavery feeling had so far overcome and taken possession of the religious mind of the North that (as you remember in 1844) they deposed from office one of their ablest men, to-wit: Bishop ANDREW, of Georgia, for no other reason than that he had intermarried with a lady in Georgia who was possessed of a few negroes in her own right. It was then, you recollect, that the Southern Methodists dissolved their connection with their fanatical brethren of the North.[4] The same feeling and spirit of opposition to the Southern interests and institutions—the same fanatical spirit if you please—entered into the Baptist church and soon after brought about an effective separation of that denomination. And, in truth, gentlemen of Missouri, so far has this feeling taken possession of the mind of the North, that at this time there are but few places and few churches to be found on the Northern soil, where the Southern church, however pure and upright and devoted to its cause, would be allowed to proclaim its holy mission. As might have been expected, this feeling entered into the political organization of the country. The Abolition party of the North, for many years, only held the balance of power between the political organizations of the country, but it soon took possession of one of them and you know, as every man knows who has read the history of the political parties of the country, that the untimely end of the old Whig organization was attributable alone to this cause. Even Mr. Clay,[5] with all his power, and with all his influence could not save the Whig organization from the withering effects and influence of this party. Gentlemen, some years thereafter another political organization, the American party, arose—as was said, on the ruins of both the old political organizations, discarding the evils of both, and combining the virtues of both. It lived for a while, so long as it was confined within the limits of State Governments, and you remember that no sooner than the delegates of this party from the North and South, in 1856, met in convention in the city of Philadelphia, than they disagreed and differed in reference to the slave question, and it was then that the delegates from the Northern States, or most of them withdrew and went into a convention with those of more congenial principles and tastes in the city of Pittsburgh, and there Mr. FREMONT[6] was nominated. You remember the platform upon which he was nominated, I will not take up your time by reading it. You will remember that the principle therein advocated was that it was the duty, the right and power of Congress to exclude the men of the South with their property from the common territory of the Union. You will further remember, gentlemen, what a contest there was in the election that followed. You vividly recollect that struggle, and that it was only after the most superhuman effort on the part of the Democratic party, the conservative portion of the people of the North, that Mr. BUCHANAN[7] was elected.

Well, gentlemen, four years passed away. Within that time does the anti-slavery feeling of the North subside? Is there any abatement of hostility of the Northern people towards the institutions and rights of the South? Why, within those four years what have the people of Georgia seen and witnessed? They have witnessed the formation of Emigrant Aid Societies for the purpose of sending men into the common Territories of the country for no other object than to exclude the men of Georgia and men of Missouri therefrom with their property. In that same time they have witnessed their own people shot down, and the soil of Kansas moistened with the blood of your own people, for no other crime than the assertion and vindication of their own constitutional rights. Within that time, gentlemen, we have seen the Governor of a non-slave-holding State refusing to deliver a fugitive from justice upon the demand of the Governor of the State of Kentucky, for the reason, as they hold, that it is no crime to entice your slaves to leave you. Within that time Georgia has witnessed more than sixty Representatives of this organization at the North, endorsing and recommending the infamous sentiments contained in the Helper Book, and but for the indomitable perseverance of one of the Missouri Representatives in urging his resolution to that effect, she would have witnessed one of the men who endorsed the book elevated to the Speakership. She has witnessed, moreover, within these four years almost every State North of Mason and Dixon's line pass under the influence and power of the Republican organization of the North. She has seen within that time the true men, the constitutional men of the North cut down one after another, and in every case and on every occasion where the opportunity has occurred, every true and constitutional man in the Senate of the United States, with but one exception within the last four years, has been swept away and his place filled and occupied by a Representative of the Republican party.

She has seen within that time, as I have already stated, the States of the North pass under the influence and into the hands of this organization. It has seen their Executive, their Judicial and their Legislative Departments—all their offices, from the highest to the lowest, from the constable up through every intermediate grade to the Executive—filled with the representatives of the Republican organization. Not only so, but within these four years, Georgia has seen an organized band descending upon the soil of Virginia, taking possession of the arsenal and property of the Government, and there pouring out the blood, shedding the innocent blood, of Virginia's citizens, for the avowed purpose of liberating the slaves of the South.

But, gentlemen, these four years have passed away, and the Republican organization—a sectional organization—existing alone in the Northern States; with the exception of a few thousand votes in the South; I say this organization, sectional, geographical—an organization against the formation of which, the Father of his Country warned the American people, met in Convention at the city of Chicago, and there proclaimed and published a platform of principles to the world. And, gentlemen, this same platform is to be found one in spirit and in object, to the one which was adopted in Pittsburgh in 1856; whereby it is asserted that Congress has the power and right, aye, and that it is its duty, to exclude the Southern man and his property from the Territories, belonging alike to the North and the South, to the East and the West. They nominated their candidates on this platform. They go before the people—the ides of November roll around—what is the result? Mr. Lincoln and Mr Hamlin are elected by an overwhelming majority of the popular vote in the North.

Now, gentlemen, we have not only to look to the platform of this party for the principles and objects which they avow, but we must also look (and so the State of Georgia has done) to the principles and objects avowed by the candidates who have been elected by the Republican organization. Mr. Lincoln, the President elect, subscribes to the platform adopted in Chicago. Not only so, but he avowed the principles contained in it long before he was nominated, and enunciated the doctrine that Congress had the power to exclude the Southern man from going into the Territories with his property. He said that if he were a member of Congress he would *vote* to effect this exclusion, regardless of the decisions of the Supreme tribunal of the country. Not only so, but he avowed the irrepressible conflict. Georgia saw all this and declared that the Northern mind would never become easy and quiet upon this question until it was satisfied that slavery was put in a course of ultimate extinction. Georgia has looked to his published declarations and opinions in order to ascertain the objects and views and opinions of the Republican organization. Not stopping there, she has looked to the declarations of the representative men of the Republican organization. She has looked to the views and opinions as expressed by Mr. Seward, Mr. Sumner, Mr. Wilson[8] and others, both in and out of Congress, for the purpose of arriving at and ascertaining what was the ultimate object of the Republican organization in reference to the institution of slavery. She has not confined herself to them, but in order to ascertain more clearly, if you please, the object, she has gone into the county meetings and State Conventions, which may probably be a more true reflex of the principles and objects of the party, than the declaration of its representative men, and considered their action and resolutions. Looking at all these things—looking at the national platform; at the county and State platforms; at the declarations published of Mr. LINCOLN himself; at the declaration and avowals of the representative men of his party, Georgia came to the conclusion that it was the avowed object of the Republican organization to put slavery and the government upon such a track as that slavery might ultimately be put in a course of ultimate extinction—that it was their object to surround the slaveholding States with a circle of free States, and thereby cause the institution (to use their own language) to sting itself to death. Seeing these things, believing, gentlemen of Missouri, that there was no hope in the future—looking to the end and seeing nothing but danger and destruction to her people and her best interests—aye, seeing that there was an antagonism, an irreconcilable antagonism, if you please, between the two sections of the country—believing, if you please, that there is a difference in principles, of civilization between the North and South, and feeling that this difference would never be reconciled, Georgia thought it best there should be a peaceable separation. Hence, gentlemen, she has adopted her ordinance of secession,[9] and she invites all slaveholding States to unite with her, and among them the State of Missouri—to unite with her in forming a Southern Confederacy—believing that, if they all will unite in forming a Southern Confederacy, we shall thereby have a government combining, as it were, every variety of soil and climate, embracing, as it will, a people homogeneous in views, in feelings, in sympathies and interests. With a government securing equal rights to all and every State and citizen, she thinks that a future will be presented full of power and greatness to the Union, of happiness and prosperity to the people.

Mr. President and Gentlemen of the Convention. In the name of my State and for myself individually, I beg you to accept my grateful acknowledgment, for the kind reception and respectful hearing you have given me, (mingled applause and hissing among the audience, which lasted for some time, and was subdued with some difficulty by the President.)

Source: *Proceedings of the Missouri State Convention Held at Jefferson City and St. Louis, March, 1861* (St. Louis: George Knapp & Co., Printers and Binders, 1861), 17–20.

Alexander William Doniphan
March 5, 1861

Alexander W. Doniphan (1808–1887) was born in Maysville, Kentucky, graduated from Augusta College in 1824, and established a law practice first in Lexington, Missouri, and later Liberty. He served in the state legislature as a Whig in 1836, 1840, and 1854. During the war with Mexico, as colonel of the 1st Regiment of Missouri Mounted Volunteers, he assisted Stephen Watts Kearny in the capture of Santa Fe and, as directed by Kearny, drew up the papers creating a code of laws for New Mexico. Known as the Kearny Code, the document established a civil government in New Mexico in accordance with the United States Constitution. Doniphan then led his troops south through El Paso and captured the city of Chihuahua. (Doniphan Drive and Doniphan Park in El Paso are named for Doniphan as is Doniphan Road in Fort Bliss.) After attending the Washington Peace Conference and the Missouri state convention, he declined to take up arms for either side.[10]

Missouri's delegates to the Washington Peace Conference included, John D. Coalter, Waldo P. Johnson, Aylett H. Buckner, Harrison Hough, and Doniphan. Colonel Doniphan was not an active member of the Washington Peace Conference offering brief comments only twice; once on the topic of a national convention of all states, and again stating his opposition to the international slave trade.[11] When invited, along with John D. Coalter, to report on the Washington Peace Conference, Doniphan observed that the Crittenden amendment was the best solution to solving "the question of negro slavery," but was voted down. No other proposed amendment came close to giving "such guarantees to slaveholding States that are now in to remain, and induce the States that are now out eventually to come back."[12]

By Mr. GRAY.
Resolved, That Col. A. W. Doniphan be requested to address the Convention in reference to the action of the Peace Convention.
Adopted.
Mr. DONIPHAN. I hardly know what gentlemen desire I shall address them about. As for the action of the Convention, its conclusions and the amendments proposed to the Constitution of the United States, all these have been published in all the journals, and, of course, have been subjected to the inspection of the gentlemen of this Convention. If it is desired to know the attitude Missouri assumed there, why, of course, if it be the pleasure of the convention, Judge Hough,[13] a member of this Convention, or Judge Coalter,[14] whom I see in the lobby, or myself, can give the Convention our opinion in relation to the matter now or any other time.
VOICE—Now!
Mr. DONIPHAN. Mr. President and Gentlemen of the Convention: I was appointed as one of the delegates from the State of Missouri to go to a Conference that has been called a Peace Congress—a Conference recommended by the State of Virginia, in which she had asked a conference with her sister States in relation to the difficulties and embarrassments that now surround this Government, and the Legislature of my State thought proper to designate me as one of the individuals to represent the interest and honor of our State in that Convention. I went there entertaining an opinion that I presume is in

accordance with the opinions of a large majority of the members of this Convention: namely, that the disintegration, or rather the revolution in progress in this Government now, was caused by one single element of strife—that we have no other cause for the difficulties that now agitate and disturb the country save the question of negro slavery—that our nation was never more prosperous in all the great elements that constitute a free and happy people than it is now; that our commerce was extending and as prosperous as it ever has been; that our sails whitened every sea, and our flag floated under every sky; that we were respected at home and abroad, and involved in no conflict with any foreign nation; that while we were standing in peaceful relations to all the rest of the world; while we were in the most prosperous condition that a nation could enjoy; while we were blessed with abundance at home; while the great Valley of the Mississippi in which we live, and whose centre we occupy, extends from the crest of the Alleghanies to the crest of the Rocky Mountains, and now feeds starving millions of the world from overflowing granaries, and clothes the naked with its cotton; that while, therefore, we were in the most prosperous condition, with our commerce, agricultures and manufactures continually increasing, there was nothing to interrupt this prosperity with the exception of this solitary question agitating us at home—the question of negro slavery. It naturally occurs to every reflecting mind that in order to restore harmony and union, that question must be removed from the arena of politics—that there can be no restoration of harmony, peace and quiet unless that question is removed. That question has interposed between the North and the South and created a division, and you may plaster it together as you please; you may try Spalding's glue[15] or anything else in the world but you cannot bring it together until this question is removed, and when this question is removed it will unite itself. The question has been raised, what is the best plan to remove this difficulty? It is well known that in all governments like this, originating in equality, having that as the very essence and foundation of our institutions—for this government, in its revolution, was unlike that of any other, for the reason that but one single sentiment pervaded the hearts of our fathers—one single, vital sentiment, and that was that all men are born free and equal, that are capable of self-government—that is what distinguished it from all other revolutions in the world, and on that principle the Government was framed, the principles of equality among States and individuals, and of equal protection to property; and when we have this removed, of course the very essence, foundations and pillars of this Government are destroyed and it can no longer exist. Now, if there is truth in all governments, it is that nationality and sectionalism cannot exist at the same time; they are entirely antagonistic and cannot flourish healthfully in the same body politic. Sectionalism itself destroys, withers and crushes out nationality. If there is sectionalism at the South in the shape of slavery propagandism, or at the North in the shape of abolitionism, nationality cannot exist, and the vital element of the whole Union is crushed out. This sectionalism does exist. For twenty years it has been growing upon us North and South. There have been fiery spirits in one portion of the North who have administered aliment to discontented spirits in another portion of the Union, and this has gone on until a gulf has been created between the North and South which has broadened and deepened until a revolution has now separated one portion from the other. The object, therefore, is to destroy sectionalism. It has now assumed a gigantic shape. It has now culminated in the election of two men to power, both of whom live in the North, and have been placed on a platform which is antagonistic to the South—entirely, in its whole aspect, antagonistic to one portion of the nation. And take out from the platform this antagonism to the South and the essence of that party is destroyed. I do not say that the whole blame devolves upon the North. I admit many imprudent men have done many imprudent things at the South, calculated to inflame the minds of men at the North. But we must take matters as they are—we must take this revolution as it is—and we find that this revolution has grown out of the triumph of sectionalism, and that triumph has weakened the cords that bind us together, and disintegration is the natural consequence.

We talk of the revolution inaugurated at the South, but no revolution has been inaugurated there. The revolution in this Government has been progressing for the last twenty years, and it has progressed until it culminated last fall in the triumph of this sectional party. That is the revolution that has destroyed our nationality and equality—a revolution that was successful on the 6th day of November last—a revolution that has caused the falling off of States in the South and the disintegration of this Government. The falling off of these states is not the cause but the consequence of the revolution that preceded it—it is nothing more. As well or as logical would it be to say that when the lightning cleaves its way through the forest and destroys the branches and rich foliage of some mighty oak that the falling away of its branches and the withering of its foliage is the cause of the destruction of that tree. It is not the withering of this foliage or the falling away of those branches that causes the destruction of that oak, but it is the bolt from heaven that shattered and destroyed its elements of vitality. It is this sectionalism that has stricken down the nationality of this Government; it is this sectionalism that has grown up like a upas[16] and poisoned everything around it, which has been the cause of the revolution that is now destroying the vitality of this Government. And in order to restore it back, and unite the parts that have been thrown off, you must remove this apple of discord upon which this sectional party have fed and fattened, during its entire progress. To do that, we felt that it was essential that amendments should be adopted to the Constitution that should settle this question now and forever. The Crittenden amendments were offered, and I deem these amendments as being the thing properly suited to remove this question now and for all time, to settle this question of the Territories on the basis of 36 deg. 30 min., and to remove this whole subject beyond the arena of politics. We first had Mr. Crittenden's amendment, but it was voted down; then we had Mr. Guthrie's proposition[17]—that was the Crittenden proposition with the backbone out of it—and Mr. Johnson's[18] amendment, which took out a few more bones, and destroyed its shape, and then Mr. Franklin's[19] amendment, which we may call a boned turkey—the whole thing being a sort of shapeless mass, without a bone in it—and that was presented and Missouri voted against it, I giving the casting vote myself, two of my colleagues voting one way and two another, none of the delegation, however, being in favor of it. I desired the amendment should contain an acknowledgment of the right in slave property and its ample protection, but not one word could we get into it in regard to master or slave, or protection, but all these things were stricken out, leaving it entirely to the judicial decisions; and therefore I preferred the Constitution of the United States as it stands now to any senseless interpretation to be decided hereafter. These judicial constructions are always for the strong and never for the weak, and if minorities are to be protected, it must be by specific enactment. Majorities can always find sufficient provisions in the Constitution to create Banks or a tariff, or destroy them, but at the same time not find authority for that protection to the institutions of a minority, which may be required. We desired these guaranties but they were rejected. In rejecting this proposition which was offered us, we did not necessarily say Missouri must go out of the Union. We said nothing except it was better to make up a patchwork about indefinite compromises. I desire to have nothing of that sort. If we are to have our rights, I desire to know it fully, entirely and expressly; but not to accept this proposition, and thereby be precluded from any other indemnity. I am not willing to take a dry bone. I voted against it, and I would do it again. These were the motives that governed us and our votes. We had but one object in view, and that was to remove this question entirely from the arena of politics, and give such guaranties to slaveholding States that are now in to remain, and induce the States that are now out eventually to come back. I believe, if Congress had passed such an amendment, and the North had acquiesced, the southern States would come in, not at the present, but in the course of time.

Source: *Proceedings of the Missouri State Convention Held at Jefferson City and St. Louis, March, 1861* (St. Louis: George Knapp & Co., Printers and Binders, 1861), 23–25.

John D. Coalter
March 5, 1861

John D. Coalter represented St. Louis at the Washington Peace Conference.

Coalter was not a major presence at the Peace Conference, his only substantive contribution was to suggest an amendment to the initial report of the General Committee on Proposals. He asked that the conference consider that "the term of all Presidents and Vice-Presidents of the United States, hereafter elected, shall be six years; and any person once elected to either of said offices, shall ever after be ineligible to the same office."[20] Following Doniphan's reflections on the Peace Conference, Coalter observed that the slave-state delegates were disadvantaged because of northern "hostility to slavery." The very issue that had "roused the Southern mind," he reported, "was the idea that they were *hostile* to us in *feeling*, and that this hostility could not be reconciled."

GEN. COALTER'S REMARKS

I thank you, Mr. President and gentlemen of the Convention, for the call which you have been pleased to make upon me. I came here with no expectation of addressing you, but deem it my duty to add a few remarks to the remarks of the gentleman who has just preceded me, and who has very properly given you a history of the proceedings of the Peace Conference. There is one point in which, according to my recollection, he does not speak exactly according to the record, and that is this: At the first ballot, the proposition of which he speaks, was rejected, Missouri voting in the negative. There was then a motion for reconsideration, which was carried, and on that reconsideration Missouri did not vote, as I understand. (To. Col. Doniphan)—I am correct in that, I am not?[21]

Mr. DONIPHAN. On the test vote as to whether Missouri would support that proposition or not, Missouri voted against it. On the motion to reconsider Missouri did not vote at all, according to my recollection. When the question came up a second time, Missouri having placed herself right on the record, was perfectly willing that this proposition should go to the country (not with her sanction) and therefore by the unanimous consent of her delegation she declined voting.

Mr. COALTER. That is true. If Missouri had voted against the propositions the second time, they would have been rejected. But we all thought that it was better that they should go before the country for what they were worth.

It was the best we could get there. The responsibility thereafter devolved upon Congress, who might accept or reject them or on the people who might pass upon them. So that there was no diversion of opinion in the Missouri Delegation, as would seem from the first statement of the gentleman. Upon the final vote Missouri was unanimous that the proposition should go before the people for what they were worth, not believing them to amount to anything, but still holding that it was the best they could get.

Gentlemen of the Convention: My colleague has very properly stated to you, that we felt how important was the occasion which had called us together, in Washington. We felt the condition of the country was such that peace was needed, in order to bring about any good and valuable results. We were met there by distinguished gentlemen from every part of the Union—twenty-one States in all—and we found one great difficulty in the beginning, and that was that gentlemen from the Northwest had come to the Convention, thinking themselves pledged to a particular platform and in other ways. They thought they had gained a great victory and they must reap the fruits of it. That seemed the prevailing sentiment. They said, "We are well satisfied to have peace, yet it must be peace on our own terms; and although we are willing for peace, yet we tell you at the same time that we abhor your institutions." Well, gentlemen, when any of us could get the floor, we defended our institutions with what ability was at our command. We told them: "This is a prejudice on your part. (And I must say that in this position we were sustained not only by the delegates from the South, but very ably, too, by some of the delegates from the North.) Your hostility to slavery has prejudiced you, and the sooner you get rid of that prejudice the better." We asked them moreover, the pregnant question. "If you abhor our institutions, how long a step will it be before you abhor *us*? If you abhor slavery, how long before you abhor *slaveholders*?" This, we represented to them, was the very point which had roused the Southern mind. It was the idea that they were *hostile* to us in *feeling*, and that this hostility could not be reconciled, but would show itself again and again, and produce perpetual dissension. We told them in submitting our propositions, it was not so much our object to gain anything valuable from them, as to see that the Northern mind could be reached upon them, that we wanted to go behind them to their constituents, that we wanted to have something upon which the Northern mind could vote, showing its readiness to acknowledge and guarantee the rights of the people of the South. We said: Do not let us, in view of this object, quarrel about little things; do not let us disagree on minor points; do not cavil with us upon the ninth part of the breadth of a hair, but show at once by your action that you do recognize the rights of the South. The people of the South, of which Missouri is a part, want to understand whether they can live in peace with you or not? If there is any settled hostility on the part of the North against the South, then we are two people inevitably; and God forbid we should be two people. We desire union; we desire this Union shall subsist, but we want to understand that you are not hostile to us, and therefore we ask you to come forward in the spirit of liberality of magnanimity, if you choose, (because you are the victorious party) and grant what is liberal, and grant it freely and frankly. Do not squabble with us about the ninth part of a breadth of a hair. Let us get at the minds of your people and let them vote on the propositions, and in that way let us see whether you will regard us as hostile or as friends!"

Gentlemen, in that spirit we were not met. They would cavil with us about everything; believing that we were trying all the time to take some advantage of them; insisting upon the great victory, and that they must reap the fruits of it, and they gave us nothing better than the resolution my colleague has spoken of.

I am sorry, gentlemen, that those resolutions, even such as they were, were not sanctioned by Congress. Congress did not choose to adopt them and what will now be adopted, God only knows. It is with you to say what course Missouri will take. I know the cause of Missouri is in good and able hands. Missouri will take her course for herself, not feeling herself bound to look to any other State, but looking to her own true interests. And, gentlemen, it has been well said by some philosopher, (Paley, I think,)[22] that nations do not act on notions of honor, but upon considerations of their true interest. I should say, however, that that rule is subject to another condition, and that is, that sometimes *the truest and best interest of a nation is to assert her honor.*

While I am upon this subject another idea suggests itself to me. It is this, that a great deal of the trouble now existing in the Northern mind is based on its blindness to the true nature of our institutions. The Northern people forget that this is not a consolidated government. They forget we are a Confederacy of sovereign, independent States; and, therefore, a man living in Massachusetts is apt to feel his conscience hurt from the fact that slavery is existing in Missouri or Arkansas. If they fully recognized and acted upon the true theory and principle of our Government as regards Southern institutions—if they were thoroughly imbued with the idea that each and every State is entirely sovereign, they would not be so sensitive with regard to those institutions. I do not understand that the Northern mind is very much troubled about the existence of slavery in Turkey, or Russia, or Cuba, but it is troubled about it in the United States, because they consider themselves partly responsible for its existence in the United States. Now let them fully recognize the true theory and principle of our Government, and they can no more be responsible for slavery in the United States than they can for slavery in Japan. We all, gentlemen, have been so much in the habit of looking to our General Government with pride and satisfaction, (and it was right that we should, because it has been a grand and glorious Government,) that we seem to forget that the greatness of our Union is not due to the circumstance that we are one great people, but that we are thirty-three great peoples. We are not one great people, but we are now thirty-four great peoples, and the greatness results from the fact that the General Government acts as the agent for *thirty-four peoples*. Let us fully recognize that fact—the fact that we are composed of sovereign peoples, each having its own control, and I think that our Government is destined to go on harmoniously to the end of time; and, gentlemen, if that principle were fully acted upon, I believe the Southern States would be satisfied, and we could ultimately hope to get them back. Those wise men who framed our institutions, knew that a consolidated government was not fit for a widely extended country, and by a wise division of power, placing in the hands of one Federal agency the administration of such duties as was necessary to be administered for the benefit of the whole, and leaving in the hands of the several States all those powers necessary for their independence and self-control—I say, they framed a system of government which alone is competent to extend and secure the blessings of freedom over a widely extended country. I can see only one hope of reconstructing the Government, and that is upon the basis of an acknowledgment of the true principles of our Government. I hope to see us come back to that yet. Otherwise there will always be danger of minorities being oppressed by majorities, and the strife between various sections of the country will never cease. I do not know that any good will result from the action of the Peace Congress. At any rate, however, we who met together freely interchanged our opinions and understood ourselves there. There were gentlemen of frankness and candor from every part of the Union, and they expressed themselves freely and frankly. They were no doubt extremely desirous of having this matter satisfactorily and amicably arranged. But there were also those who did not want to act promptly upon the matter. We were met by various abstract propositions, which we had to ward off, because they would have led to interminable discussions. One of these was that no State had a right to secede. We naturally asked, "What is the use of arguing such a question as that? Here we sit down in solemn conclave and consume hours and perhaps days in trying to arrive at a conclusion, and when we have finally arrived at a conclusion, we look around and find that seven States have already seceded. Then what do we gain by the discussion?" Other abstract propositions were offered to carry us off from the true purpose of our meeting.

Gentlemen of the Convention, I have thus hastily thrown before you a few suggestions which have occurred to me as the result of my experience in Washington City. I feel very thankful to you for the attention with which you have listened to me, and shall not trespass any more on your time at present. I may, at some future time, present my views in connection with the deliberations of the Peace Convention to the citizens of Missouri more fully in writing.

Source: *Proceedings of the Missouri State Convention Held at Jefferson City and St. Louis, March, 1861* (St. Louis: George Knapp & Co., Printers and Binders, 1861), 25–27.

Majority Report of the Committee on Federal Relations
March 9, 1861

On March 4, Hamilton R. Gamble proposed that a committee be formed to "consider and report on the relations now existing between the Government of the United States, the government of the people of the different States and the government of the people of this State." The following day, President Sterling Price appointed Gamble chair and announced the other members of the committee: John B. Henderson (Pike County), John T. Redd (Marion), William A. Hall (Randolph), Jacob T. Tindall (Grundy), Alexander W. Doniphan (Clay), Willard P. Hall (Buchanan), Nathaniel W. Watkins (Cape Girardeau), Harrison Hough (Mississippi), Samuel L. Sawyer (Lafayette), William Douglass (Cooper), John R. Chenault (Jasper), and William G. Pomeroy (Crawford).

Hamilton Rowan Gamble (1798–1864) was born in Winchester, Virginia, educated at Hampden-Sydney College, studied for and was admitted to the bar in 1817, and emigrated to St. Louis the following year. In 1824 he was appointed secretary of state by Governor Frederick Bates. Two years later he established his law practice in St. Louis. In 1846, he was elected to the Missouri legislature and in 1851 appointed to the Missouri Supreme Court. Gamble gained fame in 1852 when, as presiding judge of the court, he was the lone dissenter in the famous *Dred Scott* case.[23] A Whig who opposed the proslavery politics of Democrats, and the brother-in-law of Edward Bates who became President Lincoln's first attorney general, Gamble later served as provisional governor of Missouri for most of the war.

Gamble's committee report began with the pronouncement that the unrest in the country was due to the "anticipation of future evils, (rather than) in the pressure of any now actually endured." Furthermore, while the South had reasonable complaints against "many of their fellow-citizens of the North, it is equally true that heretofore there has been no complaint against

Majority Report of the Committee on Federal Relations, March 9

the action of the Federal Government." The committee went on to suggest that the courts would be a more appropriate course of action to "maintain the rights of Southern citizens." The report concluded with an endorsement of Senator John J. Crittenden's constitutional amendment, a desire that sectional disagreements be properly adjusted, a proposal for a national convention to suggest amendments to the Constitution, and a plea for the federal government as well as the Confederacy to "stay the arm of military power." Most significantly, the committee began with a resolution: "That at present there is no adequate cause to impel Missouri to dissolve her connection with the Federal Union." On March 19, the convention approved the proposal with only one dissenting vote from George Bast, a farmer from Montgomery County.

Mr. GAMBLE, from the Committee on Federal Relations, then made the following

REPORT.

The Committee on Federal Relations beg leave to report. On looking to the present condition of our late prosperous, happy and united country, we see seven of our sister States by the action of their conventions declaring themselves separated from the United States, and organizing for themselves a distinct national government; while others are in a disturbed condition, looking anxiously to the future, and uncertain about all that is to come.'

If, in our astonishment at the sudden disruption of our nation, we attempt to trace the causes that have produced the disastrous result, we find that the origin of the difficulty is rather in the alienated feelings existing between the Northern and Southern sections of the country, than in the actual injury suffered by either; rather in the anticipation of future evils, than in the pressure of any now actually endured.

It is true that the people of the Southern States have a right to complain of the incessant abuse poured upon their institutions by the press, the pulpit, and many of the people of the North. It is true that they have a right to complain of legislative enactments designed to interfere with the assertion of their constitutional rights. It is true that the hostile feelings to Southern institutions entertained by many at the North have manifested themselves in mob violence interfering with the execution of laws made to secure the rights of Southern citizens. It is true that in one instance this fanatical feeling has displayed itself in the actual invasion of a Southern State by a few madmen, who totally misunderstood the institution they came to subvert. It is true that a sectional political party has been organized at the North, based upon the idea that the institution of Southern slavery is not to be allowed to extend itself into the Territories of the United States, and that this party has for the present possessed itself of the power of the Government.

While it is true that the people of the South have well-grounded complaints against many of their fellow-citizens of the North, it is equally true that heretofore there has been no complaint against the action of the Federal Government in any of its departments, as designed to violate the rights of the Southern States.

By some incomprehensible delusion, many Northern people have come to believe that in some manner they are chargeable with complicity in what they are pleased to consider the sin of slavery, and for which, as existing in the Southern States, they are just as much responsible as they are for the same relation existing in the heart of Africa. This morbid sensitiveness has been ministered to by religious and political agitators for the purpose of increasing their own importance and advancing their own interests, and the natural consequences have followed: outbursts of mob violence and of political action against the owners of slaves.

While the prejudice thus existing in the Northern mind is latent, not exhibiting itself in action, we may lament its existence and the estrangement it produces; but we trust in such case, as in all others of similar character, that a better knowledge of the subject will remove the prejudice. Already the awakened attention of the Northern people gives promise that the miserable agitators will be stript of their power over the public mind, and that reason and a correct sense of duty and of justice will ultimately prevail and dispose our Northern fellow-citizens to fulfill all the duties they owe to us as citizens of the same country, living under the same Constitution, inheritors of the same blood, and sharers in the same destiny.

So far as the prejudice complained of has manifested itself in legislative action, the complaint is not merely that such action violates the Constitution of the United States, because our own State has passed acts which have been declared by our own judicial tribunals and by the Supreme Court of the United States to be violations of the Constitution of the United States; and those familiar with the judicial history of the country know that many, if not all the States of the Union, have at times passed laws which have been held to be inconsistent with that Constitution. Some of these acts related to land titles, some to contracts, some affected commerce with foreign nations and between the States; but all such laws as they were, not produced by any sectional feelings, were left to be decided upon by the tribunals of the country with an ultimate appeal to the Supreme Court of the United States, the final arbiter on all cases arising under the Constitution. Such cases produced no excitement in the public mind, and all confidence was reposed in that elevated tribunal that it would vindicate the supremacy of the Constitution.

Majority Report of the Committee on Federal Relations, March 9

There is no reason to apprehend that that tribunal would shrink from declaring the class of enactments of which we are now treating, which are aimed against the rights of slaveholders, repugnant to the Constitution and therefore void. There is, therefore, an obvious remedy for the grievance out of this unconstitutional legislation, and that, too, a remedy provided by the Constitution itself for an evil foreseen when it was made. Moreover, there are indications of a returning sense of justice in the Northern States, from which we may hope for the voluntary repeal of these obnoxious enactments.

Upon the subject of the violent interference by mobs with the execution of the fugitive slave law, and the forcible abduction of slaves when with their owners in the Northern States, it is proper to observe that there reigns throughout this land a spirit of insubordination to law that is probably unequalled in any other civilized country on the globe. While this is true, it is a fact of which we can still be proud that the judicial tribunals of the Federal Government have not failed in any case brought before them to maintain the rights of Southern citizens and to punish the violators of those rights.

When Southern soil is invaded by Northern madmen for the purpose of overthrowing the institution of slavery, they meet their death by the law, and that is the end of their scheme.

The fact that a sectional party avowing opposition to the admission of slavery into the Territories of the United States has been organized, and has for the present obtained possession of the Government, is to be deeply regretted, because it opens before us all the dangers against which the Father of his Country so earnestly warned us.

But the history of our country for a very few years back, instructs us in the truth that political parties, even when coming into power with over-whelming popularity, soon melt away under the influence of internal jealousies, and disappointments, and the attacks of vigilant opponents.

When a party comes into power upon the basis of a single question of policy, there is soon found the truth, that government cannot be administered upon a single idea, and its supporters become divided upon the questions which affect their own interests.

There is every reason to hope that the party which has just assumed the reins of government will feel that the vast interests intrusted to their management, are of much greater importance than the question, whether slaves shall or shall not be admitted into all the Territory that now belongs to the United States. There is reason to hope that when the masses of that party understand that the admission of slaves into a Territory does not increase the number of slaves in being, they will be prepared to make any arrangement with their Southern brethren that shall assure to them equal rights in the common Territories.

Under the state of facts now existing, it would seem almost needless to speak of the propriety of the state of Missouri in a revolution against the Federal

Government. Secession is the word commonly employed when the revolution now in progress is mentioned; but as the Constitution of the United States recognizes no power in any State to destroy the government, the word "secession," when used in this paper, is to be understood as equivalent to revolution.

To involve Missouri in revolution, under present circumstances, is certainly not demanded by the magnitude of the grievances of which we complain, nor by the certainty that they cannot be otherwise and more peacefully remedied, nor by the hope that they would be remedied or even diminished by such revolution.

The position of Missouri in relation to the adjacent States which would continue in the Union, would necessarily expose her, if she became a member of a new confederacy, to utter destruction whenever any rupture might take place between the different republics. In a military aspect, secession and a connection with a Southern Confederacy is annihilation for our State.

Many of our largest interests would perish under a system of free trade.

Emigration to the State must cease. No Southern man owning slaves would come to the frontier State; no Northern man would come to this foreign country avowedly hostile to his native land.

Our slave interest would be destroyed, because we would have no better right to recapture a slave found in a free State than we now have in Canada. The owners of slaves must either remove them to the South, or sell them, and so we would in a few years exhibit the spectacle of a State breaking up its most advantageous and important relations to the old Union, in order to enter into a slaveholding confederacy, and having itself no slaves.

The thought of revolution by Missouri, under present circumstances, is not, we believe, seriously entertained by any member of this Convention.

But what is now the true position for Missouri to assume? Evidently that of a State whose interests are bound up in the maintenance of the Union, and whose kind feelings and strong sympathies are with the people of the Southern States, with whom we are connected by ties of friendship and of blood. We want the peace and harmony of the country restored, and we want them with us. To go with them as they are now, to leave the government our fathers builded, to blot out the star of Missouri from the constellation of the Union, is to ruin ourselves without doing them any good. We cannot now follow them; we cannot now give up the Union; yet we will do all in our power to induce them to take their places with us in the family from which they have attempted to separate themselves. For this purpose we will not only recommend a compromise with which they ought to be satisfied, but we will unite in the endeavor to procure an assemblage of the whole family of States in order that in a General Convention such amendments to the Constitution may be agreed upon as shall permanently restore harmony to the whole nation.

Majority Report of the Committee on Federal Relations, March 9

While attempts are being made to heal the present divisions, it is a matter of the highest importance that there should occur no military conflict between the Federal Government and the government of any of the seceded States. Such conflict will certainly produce a high state of exasperation and very probably render abortive all attempts to adjust the matters of difference.

While it is admitted that every government must possess the power to execute its own laws, and that the Government of the United States is no exception to this necessary and universal rule, still, in a case such as that with which we are now dealing it is all important that those in authority should remember that such power is not given to be exercised for the destruction of the government, under the guise of maintaining its authority. The question of exercising such power is to be determined with a view to all existing circumstances, and while the power itself cannot be abandoned the greatest patience and forbearance may often be required in order to prevent evils in the highest degree dangerous to the peace of the nation.

Placed as Missouri is in the very centre of the confederacy, united to all its parts and interested in the prosperity of each part, she would speak to the Government of the United States and to the Governments of the seceding States, not in the language of menace but of kindness, not threatening but entreating; and with this feeling she would ask all concerned in the governments to avoid all military collisions which would without doubt produce uncontrollable excitement, and very probably ruinous civil war. Civil war among the American people, the citizens of the freest nation of the world, blest of God, envied of man, would be a spectacle at which humanity would shudder, over which freedom would weep, and from which Christianity affrighted would flee away.

If it be the glorious mission of Missouri to aid in arresting the progress of revolution and in restoring peace and prosperity to the country; if she shall be instrumental in binding together again the hearts of the American people, and thus restoring the union of affection as well as the union of political and individual interest, she will but occupy the position for which nature designed her by giving her a central position, and endowing her with all the elements of wealth and power. And why should she not?—she was brought forth in a storm and cradled in a compromise. She can resist the one and recommend the other.

In order to express her opinions and wishes, the following resolutions are submitted:

Resolved, That at present there is no adequate cause to impel Missouri to dissolve her connection with the Federal Union, but on the contrary she will labor for such an adjustment of existing troubles as will secure the peace as well as the rights and equality of all the States. {Approved March 19 (89-1); page 216}

Resolved, That the people of this State are devotedly attached to the institutions of our country and, earnestly desire that by a fair and amicable adjustment all the causes of disagreement that at present unfortunately distract us as a people may be removed, to the end that our Union may be preserved and perpetuated, and peace and harmony be restored between the North and the South. {Approved March 19 (90-0); 217}

Resolved, That the people of this State deem the amendments to the Constitution of the United States, proposed by the Hon. John J. Crittenden, of Kentucky, with the extension of the same to the Territory hereafter to be acquired by treaty or otherwise, a basis of adjustment which will successfully remove the causes of difference forever from the arena of national politics. {Approved March 19 (88-4); 233}

Resolved, That the people of Missouri believe the peace and quiet of the country will be promoted by a Convention to propose amendments to the Constitution of the United States, and this Convention therefore urges the Legislature of this State to take the proper steps for calling such a Convention in pursuance of the fifth article of the Constitution, and for providing by law for an election of one delegate to such Convention from each electoral district in this State. {Approved March 19 (85-9); 235}

Resolved, That, in the opinion of this Convention, the employment of military force by the Federal Government to coerce the submission of the seceding States, or the employment of military force by the seceding States to assail the Government of the United States, will inevitably plunge this country into civil war, and thereby entirely extinguish all hope of an amicable settlement of the fearful issues now pending before the country; we therefore earnestly entreat as well the Federal Government as the seceding States to withhold and stay the arm of military power, and on no pretense whatever bring upon the nation the horrors of civil war.

> {Amended to state: "And it is the opinion of this Convention that the cherished desire to preserve the country, and restore fraternal feelings would be promoted by the withdrawal of the Federal troops from such parts of the seceded States where there is danger of a collision between the Federal and State forces," 237; amended resolution approved March 19 (87-7); 245}

Resolved, That when this Convention adjourns its session in the city of St. Louis, it will adjourn to meet in the Hall of the House of Representatives at Jefferson City, on the third Monday of December, 1861. {Approved March 19 (78-19); 247}

Resolved, That a Committee of _____ {amended to state "seven delegates, one from each Congressional District} be elected by this Convention, a majority of which shall have power to call this Convention together at such time prior to the third Monday of December, and at such place as they may think the public exigencies require, and the survivors or the survivor of said Committee shall have power to fill any vacancies that may happen in said Committee by death, resignation, or otherwise, during the recess of this Convention. {Approved March 21 (93-3); 263}

GAMBLE, Chairmen.

Source: *Proceedings of the Missouri State Convention Held at Jefferson City and St. Louis, March, 1861* (St. Louis: George Knapp & Co., Printers and Binders, 1861), 55–58.

Minority Report of the Committee on Federal Relations
March 11, 1861

During the debate on the committee report, John Thomas Redd Jr., and Harrison Hough submitted a minority opinion. A native of Kentucky and a lawyer by profession, John T. Redd Jr. (1816–1884) represented Marion County in the state convention. Circuit Court Judge Harrison Hough (1811–1864) represented Mississippi County.

Delegates Redd and Hough dissented from the majority report believing it too passive, and that it did not describe sufficiently the threat the North posed to the slave-owning South. The northern antislavery party, they argued, was made up of "political demagogues" and "sensation preachers," and that they combined with the press in writing articles "misrepresenting and denouncing Southern institutions and Southern men." Redd and Hough believed a national convention, as called for in the majority report, would not yield results that would protect southern interests, but that a border state convention would. To that end, they recommended that Missouri delegates to said convention present the Crittenden resolutions as being "satisfactory to Missouri."

Mr. REDD, from the Committee on Federal Relations, presented the following

MINORITY REPORT.

The undersigned, members of the Committee on Federal Relations, being unable to agree to the report presented by the Committee, desire to present for the consideration of the Convention the views that they entertain and that they believe the people of Missouri entertain in relation to the causes that have led to the present alarming condition of our beloved Union, and the course that if pursued would most likely lead to an amicable adjustment of the issues involved in the present crisis, preserve the Union from further disintegration, and restore peace and harmony to our divided and distracted country.

Within the lifetime of many now living, our Federal Government, the best that the wisdom of man ever devised, was created and put in successful operation; its first President was inaugurated in March, 1789, and from that time through a long series of years it continued to increase in territory and population, in wealth and power, with a rapidity hitherto unparalleled in the history of nations, until twenty sovereign States were admitted as members of the Union, formed by the original thirteen; and until a comparatively recent period these States were all one people, one in sympathy, one in fraternal feeling, one in patriotic devotion to that common Union of which all were proud. How is it now? Fraternal feeling has fled; a spirit of bitter and determined hostility has taken its place; State stands arrayed against State, and section against section, arming for a deadly conflict; seven of the States have withdrawn from the Union that their fathers made, and made a Union of their own, and a Federal Government of their own; that Government with one of the most clearheaded and sagacious statesmen of the age at its head, is organized in full operation, exercising all the powers of sovereignty, and prepared to defend its sovereignty by military power.[24]

Other States, alarmed for the safety of their slave institutions, are preparing to follow their example; the din of preparation for civil strife is heard on every hand, and that once glorious Union, so dear to the heart of every American patriot, is now in the progress of its dissolution.

There is a cause for all this; a free people capable of self-government do not destroy institutions of which they were once so proud, and incur all the risks of civil strife, without some adequate cause; all experience demonstrates that mankind are more disposed to bear with great and pressing evils than to resort to revolution with all its attendant horrors.

It is our duty to examine into the causes that have environed the Union with perils and threatened its utter destruction, and, if possible, devise a plan to save it from further disintegration.—When we look back over the history of our country, we see arising in the Northern States an anti-slavery party, whose sole cohesive principle was a bitter hostility to the slave institutions of the Southern States. At first that party was weak, its members few, and scattered abroad, and considered by the Northern people themselves as mischievous fanatics; it continued gradually, but steadily, to increase, until political parties began to court its aid; from this time it progressed rapidly in numbers, and increased in its virulence and hatred to Southern slave institutions and to slave-holders. Political demagogues, to promote their own selfish ends, pandered to its prejudices from the political rostrum. Sensation preachers, to increase their own importance, Sabbath after Sabbath, proclaimed its incendiary doctrines from the pulpit, instead of preaching peace on earth and good will among men. It seized on the literature of the North, and corrupted it in all its channels.

Books written to inculcate its destructive heresies were introduced into its Sabbath schools, common schools and institutions of learning of higher grade.

A large portion of the Northern press, literary, religious and political, teemed with articles misrepresenting and denouncing Southern institutions and Southern men.

Nourished and fostered by these means, this anti-slavery party obtained the control of the governments in the free States, and as those States came under their control they violated the compact that united them to their sister States of the South. By that compact they had covenanted that a fugitive slave found within their borders should be delivered up upon demand of his master. They violated that compact.

1st, By failing to enact laws providing for his delivery;

2d, By refusing the master aid and permitting their lawless citizens to deprive him of his property by mob violence;

3d, When Congress interposed for his relief by the enactment of the Fugitive Slave Law, they trampled that law under foot, and nullified it by deliberate State legislation.

By the compact that united the Northern States to their Southern sisters, they covenanted that they, upon demand made, would deliver up for trial any fugitive from justice charged (by indictment) with treason, felony or other crime.

They have willfully and deliberately violated this covenant. They have (without passing laws to restrain them) permitted their citizens to invade the soil of Southern States, steal their slaves, and incite them to insurrection, and when the felon has been indicted and demanded, they have refused to give him up, and, to add insult to injury, they have justified the act by enunciating a proposition that strikes at the foundation of slave institutions, that as man cannot hold property in man, therefore slave stealing is no crime; and while there has been heretofore no just ground of complaint against the Federal Government, that Government has been powerless to remedy the evil.

This anti-slavery party, after having divided church organizations, and destroyed the noble old Whig and the gallant young American party, has upon their ruins erected (in disregard of the warning voice of the father of his country) a purely sectional party, called the Republican party.

We do not desire to do that party injustice. It should be judged as all other parties are judged, by its platform and the principles enunciated by its representative men, and upon the enunciation of which the party elevates them to power.

That party, through its chosen leader, proclaimed the dangerous and destructive heresies that our Federal Government cannot continue to exist as our fathers made it, part slave and part free; that in that condition it is a house divided against itself and cannot stand; that it must become all one or all the other; that an irrepressible conflict is progressing between freedom and slavery, and that it must continue until the public mind can rest satisfied in the belief that slavery is in the process of extinction; that hereafter the slave property of Southern men shall be taken from them by Congressional legislation, if they take it with them into the Territories, the common property of all the States.

The free States, deaf to the earnest remonstrances of their Southern sisters, regardless of the warning voice of a people jealous of their rights, indorsed the doctrine of that party and elevated its leader to the Presidential chair by large majorities in all the free States, except one, thus placing the Federal Government, to which the South had hitherto looked as its friend, in the hands of its enemies.[25]

These are the causes that have dissolved the Union, and have driven State after State beyond its pale; and these are the causes that will drive the remaining slave States out of the Union, unless these sectional issues can be settled upon some basis consistent with security to their slave institutions.

This Convention was called for no ordinary purpose, it has assembled upon no ordinary occasion; while the people of Missouri will never surrender their slave institutions at the bidding of any earthly power, they ardently desire the preservation of the Union and the preservation of their slave institutions in the Union; this is the high mission to which this Convention is called; this can be accomplished only by action, *prompt, decided* action. Delay is dangerous; we know not, no human sagacity can penetrate the dark vail [sic] that hides the future and tell us at what hour the country may be aroused from its repose by the clash of arms. The plan proposed by the committee is, that this Convention request the Legislature to pass an act calling on Congress to call a National Convention, to propose a basis of settlement in the shape of amendments to the Constitution, to be afterwards submitted to the States for ratification or rejection. This amounts to doing nothing, literally nothing; if the plan was practicable, it would require eighteen months to two years to carry it into effect. But is it practicable, is there a reasonable ground to hope that it would save the Union? Let us see: Congress can only act when called on by two-thirds of the States; Congress takes the position that the seceded States are yet in the Union. On this basis it would require the action of Legislatures of twenty-three States uniting in the call. Several of these Legislatures having already taken their position against any amendments, consequently would not unite in the call, and the plan would fall still-born.

But even if such a Convention should assemble, how would matters stand? Eight Slave States (if they remained in the Union, which is exceedingly doubtful) would go into Convention with nineteen Free States, and take such amendments as those States controlled by an anti-slavery party might be disposed to grant.

The preservation of the Union, in the opinion of the minority, should be the earnest desire not only of every American patriot, but also of every friend of civil liberty throughout the habitable globe; that this may be done is the earnest prayer of every American mother throughout this great republic; that it shall be preserved is the fixed determination of a large majority of the citizens of the Border Slave States whose citizens have ever been not only loyal to the Constitution and the Union, but also among the foremost in times past, when their country was in danger, to peril their lives to uphold her institutions. These States by assuming the position of mediators between the hostile sections, and taking a decided position, and proclaiming to those sectional parties who are now arming for fraternal strife, that they shall keep the peace.

These States, by meeting each other in convention, and agreeing on measures of compromise and adjustment founded on the principles of equal rights and justice to all, and by firmly, yet in a spirit of fraternal kindness, insisting on the compromises so agreed upon as the basis on which all irritating differences shall be settled, can, in the opinion of the undersigned, be the means of preserving the Union, reconstructing it upon a permanent basis, reconciling conflicting interests, and restoring peace and tranquility to the country.

Resolved, by the People of the State of Missouri, in Convention assembled:

1st. That the State of Missouri invites the States of Virginia, North Carolina, Maryland, Kentucky, Tennessee, Arkansas and Delaware, to send Commissioners to meet in Convention with Commissioners appointed by Missouri, at the city of Nashville, Tennessee, on the [__] day of [__]next, to agree upon a basis of settlement by way of constitutional amendments that will preserve the Union, and afford an adequate guarantee for the preservation of their slave institutions and the constitutional rights of their citizens, and to take such steps as they may deem necessary to have such amendments presented to the people of the free States for ratification or rejection.

2. That [__] be and they are hereby appointed Commissioners to represent the State of Missouri in said Convention.

3. That [__] is hereby appointed a Commissioner to the State of Virginia; [__] Commissioner to North Carolina; [__] Commissioner to Maryland; [__] Commissioner to Kentucky; [__] Commissioner to Tennessee; [__]

Commissioner to Arkansas; [___] Commissioner to Delaware; and said Commissioners are hereby authorized by the State of Missouri to present to the proper authorities of the said States, respectively, a copy of these resolutions, and to urge upon them the appointment of Commissioners to the Convention contemplated therein.

Resolved, That the Commissioners appointed to said Convention by Missouri are directed to present to said Convention for their consideration the resolutions commonly known as the Crittenden compromise measures, extending the provisions with reference to territory south of the line, to after-acquired territory, and to say, on behalf of Missouri, that those resolutions, or any other basis of settlement upon which the border slave States can agree, will be satisfactory to Missouri.

The people of the State of Missouri, being satisfied that the plan proposed in these resolutions (unless interrupted by civil strife) not only preserve the Union, but afford a fair prospect for a reconstruction by bringing back the seceded States; they, therefore, earnestly appeal to the General Government and the seceded States to stay the arm of military power and preserve the peace until the plan proposed can be fully tried. And, to enforce such appeal, they would state it as their settled conviction that an attempt at coercion, under any pretext, would result in civil strife, and forever destroy all hope for the preservation of the Union.

JOHN T. REDD,
H. HOUGH.

Source: *Proceedings of the Missouri State Convention Held at Jefferson City and St. Louis, March, 1861* (St. Louis: George Knapp & Co., Printers and Binders, 1861), 62–64.

Hamilton Rowan Gamble
March 11, 1861

Urged by his fellow delegates to explain the reasoning behind the majority report, Chairman Gamble began his remarks confessing a bit of awkwardness in defending his committee's report when the delegates had expressed no enmity toward the Union, had voiced "no expression antagonistic to the Union." He continued to submit that the federal government had supported the interests of Missouri in multiple ways since its admission as a state. Gamble spent the majority of his address rebutting the minority report's recommendation of a border state convention arguing that a national convention would be far more efficient. He concluded by warning against a civil war between the sections as such strife would "annihilate" both.

I am instructed, by those who are acquainted with parliamentary usage, that it is the duty of the chairman of the committee that has made a report on any subject to a deliberative body, to explain the principles upon which that report has been recommended, without going into any extended argument, at first, in support of the propositions submitted to the body, reserving to the chairman the conclusion of the debate, and the presentation of those views at the close of the debate. Simply stating at full length the propositions which have been submitted by the committee: The first proposition which has been submitted is, that at this time there is no adequate reason for Missouri to secede from the Union—that there is no adequate reason for her cutting the cords that bind her to her sister States, and that she entertains and will manifest a disposition to compromise all difficulties that now distract the country, and that she will employ all her power and influence to that end. In the beginning, Mr. President, I feel some embarrassment in speaking upon such a question as this, and to a body chosen by the State of Missouri, such as is now assembled. To speak in favor of the Union—of its importance—of the advantages which we derive from it, and of the glory which has been connected with it, to those who have been elected because they are friends of the Union, would seem to be entirely supererogatory. As far as my acquaintance with the gentlemen of this Convention extends, I know of no gentlemen who avow or insinuate, or in any manner admit that they entertain any unfriendly feeling to the Union. You may speak to any member of the Convention you please in reference to his position about the Union, and he will proclaim that he is in favor of the Union. How, then, in the introduction of this question before this body, shall I undertake to speak in favor of the Union, when there is a unanimity, an entire unanimity, among all its members upon the very view which I would endeavor to take and enforce. I should continually be under the necessity of repeating to gentlemen the very arguments which I am bound to suppose they used before their constituents, when they were candidates for election to this body. I am bound to suppose that, as they avow themselves friends to the Union, they entertain a deliberate purpose to do nothing that will in any degree endanger the continuance or the permanency of that Union or in any degree weaken the attachment of the people to the Union which is thus enshrined in their hearts. I am bound to suppose this, because I am bound to suppose that those who avow themselves in favor of the Union are sincere—as sincere as I am—as honest in the views they entertain and express as I am in the views I entertain and express, and therefore the difficulty is continually presenting itself to me, how to discuss a question in which the friends agree with entire unanimity.

If I speak to gentlemen of the Convention of the glories which cluster around that flag—if I speak to them of the pride that every American citizen in every quarter of the globe has in the American Union, I speak but what I am bound to suppose every gentleman fully understands and appreciates, when he says he is in favor of the Union. I speak the sentiments that I am bound to suppose were the sentiments uttered before the people by gentlemen who were candidates for election to this Convention. Therefore, I shall be but wasting time, when as I see, there is no expression antagonistic to the Union. I should be but wasting the time of the Convention if I should go through an enumeration of the blessings which we, as the people of Missouri, have derived from our connection with the common Government of our country. Sir, we are assembled here as the people of the State of Missouri. The position which we occupy, is a position in itself peculiar. We have our common history—we have the history of our connection with this great Government of which we are a part; we have been the recipients of its beneficent action; we have grown up under its protection, and we have received nothing but blessings from it. I was here before it was born as a State—when it was weak and feeble—when the Indians were on our Western borders, and from whom our extreme frontier settlements apprehended difficulties—and were we left to ourselves? were we left to protect ourselves against the savages who might desire to imbrue their hands in the blood of the wives and children of Missouri? No! The United States, at her own cost—under a National Government, for national purposes, and to carry out national obligations—maintained its own military forts, garrisoned by its own troops at its own expense, for our protection. Does our commerce meet with impediment or obstruction in its national outlets to the ocean? then the United States expends its means in endeavoring to remove those obstructions. She does not leave us to protect ourselves, but freely expends her money, that we may have all the facilities that we may require, in order that our resources may be more rapidly and advantageously developed. To come to our land system. Has she shown any niggardly spirit towards us, or any disinclination at all to foster our highest interests. When the poor man settles his quarter section of land in any portion of the country, and is unable to pay for it, even at a minimum price, reduced as it is to a mere fraction of the actual value of the property, what does she do in reference to persons in that condition? She lays her hand upon those who would take this property for their own advancement or speculation, and compels them to yield to the man who has selected a portion of the public domain, in order that he may establish thereon a domicil [sic] and rear his children. When we wish to engage in any enterprise to develop the commercial and agricultural interests of the country, and are unable to raise the money requisite to carry out such an enterprise, she says, "Here is a large domain we own within your territories; use it freely; we give millions in order to help you build your railroads," and so, gentlemen of this Convention, all the action that the United States Government has taken in relation to Missouri, and the relation we sustain towards the United States, have been such as to benefit ourselves. Nothing of aggression on the part of the United States, composed as the United States is, of all the States—nothing of a disposition to hamper or crush out the energies of Missouri; nothing of a disposition to leave us to ourselves to encounter difficulties that are liable to arise in every new and growing State; but, on the other hand, every disposition to foster our interests as a State.

Sir, I am bound to suppose that every member of this Convention, as he avows himself in favor of the Union, and as he has avowed himself before his constituents in favor of the Union, will do nothing to estrange the State from the General Government. How then shall I speak further, before a Convention that is unanimously in favor of the Union, in commendation of this fabric which our fathers have reared, and which was bequeathed to us from those who were peerless in wisdom as in valor. In opening, therefore, before the Convention the view which the committee present in reference to the impolicy of taking any steps to sever our connection with the General Government, I shall not detain the Convention in thus opening with any lengthy enumeration of the blessings which have flowed to us from our connection with the General Government. I shall not speak at length upon this subject, as there are others who can speak to the Convention and move the hearts of those who are true lovers of their country and in favor of the government under which we live. I shall expect to hear from members of this Convention, and if it becomes necessary to vindicate the propriety of the resolution we have presented, to wit: That we shall remain longer in the Union—I shall expect to hear that vindication coming from more eloquent lips and with greater power than I can employ before this body at this time.

Mr. President, it is true that there is discord now reigning in what was once, and very recently, a happy family of States. It is true that there has arisen an alienation of feeling, and it is true that that alienation is fast ripening into active hostility. But it is because there has been an entire misrepresentation of the relations that the States bear to each other—the interests in and responsibility for each other's institutions; and I am glad to believe that a returning sense of the true measure of responsibility that the inhabitants of each State owe to the General Government, and to the inhabitants of every other State—that a true sense of that responsibility is beginning to withdraw from the public mind all over the United States, and at the North particularly, that excitement that has been hurrying us on to ruin. I am glad to believe that in the Border States there is manifest a disposition sedulously to maintain the Union, in order that there may be ultimately and permanently effected an agreement between the extremes, which shall result in the restoration of harmony, and in the perpetuation of this glorious confederacy.

After having passed beyond the question of whether there exists at this time any reason for our severing our connection with the General Government, we come forward to make a declaration of our desire for a friendly and amicable adjustment of all difficulties between the sections who differ in their feelings and views of policy. It is proper that Missouri shall avow this. It is proper she shall entertain such views, and shall do all in her power to encourage those who are divided in their sentiments in regard to the subject of slavery, and some of whom have carried their action to the extent of attempting to sever their connection with the Government. That Missouri shall do all to restore harmony between the conflicting portions of our Union, and bring all back to amicable relations and national prosperity, a scheme has been recommended by the Committee with a view to this object, and that is the calling of a National Convention, in which there shall be assembled the representatives *of all the States* of the Union. You have recently read a proposition that would seem to be adverse to the holding of such a Convention, because it was likely to be futile. You have heard a proposition that looks to the holding of a Border slave States Convention. The question has been before the Committee, as you learn by the minority report which has just been read. It did not meet with the favor of the Committee because it was regarded as in itself unnecessary, and involved in the proposition of a National Convention. The National Convention which the Committee recommend, is an assemblage of the representatives of *all the States*, free and slave—all that are in the Union. They come together for the purpose of proposing amendments to the Constitution, and in the present case, inasmuch as amendments to the Constitution are demanded by the Border States, they come to consult upon these amendments and agree on their adoption. The Border States are the States that will demand the amendments—the *whole* are the States that pass upon the question whether that demand shall be granted or not. I say, therefore, that in the present condition of things, when the assembling of a National Convention is for the purpose of agreeing to the amendments that are demanded by the inhabitants of a particular section of the country, that Convention necessarily involves what is equivalent to a Border States Convention. Suppose the members from all the States of the Union assemble in such general Convention for the purpose as before indicated, what then will be the proposition? The proposition to the members of the Border States will be: "Agree among yourselves as to what you want and we will pass upon it." Is not that the natural result of a General Convention, called under the circumstances such as we are now placed in, and having for its object the amending of the Constitution upon subjects upon which there is now division and complaint? If such is the object of that Convention, the first proposition that must naturally arise in the mind of any man participating in it, would be: "You gentlemen who are from the Border States, agree upon any propositions that you wish to submit and then we will take them into consideration, and if we deem them reasonable, we will agree upon them." I say, therefore, that this General Convention involves the idea of a Border slave States Convention with this additional advantage: that there you have assembled the body that is at last to pass upon any proposed amendment and must agree to recommend or reject them. There they are, assembled from all the States, having the power under the Constitution of the United States to pass upon the question whether these proposed amendments shall be agreed to or not. On the contrary, the Border States' Convention is a body of men not known to law and the Constitution of the country, and it *can* do nothing but recommend; it can do nothing but agree upon amendments, which they may *afterwards* lay before a General Convention, for ratification by the whole country. It has no power to adopt amendments; it has no power to act upon any person or law; it has no power to do more than agree upon and recommend the amendments that they may suppose are needed by the Border States. Such being the case, we perceive that by calling a Border States Convention we double the machinery without deriving any new advantage. There is no power to render emphatic what the Border States agree upon. Now, I ask, is it not more wise, more statesmanlike, to agree upon calling together a body which, when it does meet, is recognized by the Constitution, and capable of acting under the Constitution? Is it not wiser and better to call a body whose action, when it goes forth before the people of the United States, shall carry with it a recommendation that no one can resist? Such is the view that has been entertained by the Committee in recommending a General Convention instead of a Border States Convention. We believe that we can better attain our end by consulting the whole people of the United States in a General Convention assembled, than by consulting only one section, and that there is now a disposition manifest all through this country to harmonize and settle existing difficulties, and restore peace and order to the community.

You will notice that the measure chiefly recommended in the minority report, is a Border States Convention. You will also notice that in several parts of that report contains the emphatic declaration of an attachment to the Union, and it would seem that the minority who presented it, chiefly bases its claim to be the consideration of the Convention on the ground that a Border States' Convention will be more likely to bring about a conciliation and the concerted action of all parties, than the adoption of the majority report. But I apprehend, gentlemen of the Convention, when you come to see the comparative operation of the two bodies; when you see that the one has power to recommend and the other to recommend and pass upon also; when you see that a General

Convention involves the idea of a Border States Convention besides offering other advantages—when you see the evils that may arise by an assembling of those who are only on one side, and take only a one-sided aspect, and the good which must result from the commingling of men from all parts of the Union, amicably and fraternally disposed, you will give the preference to the majority report.

The Committee have gone further, taking their position as that of a pacificator, desirous of intervening between parties in hostile array against each other. They have put forth their hands and said to each party; "Stay, be still until we can have an opportunity of settling the difficulty between you!" The Convention, we have taken it for granted, will look upon the policy of the employment of forces, the employment of arms of either one section or the whole government against a portion of the government, as an event greatly to be deplored, greatly involving in confusion and difficulty the differences which now exist between the different sections of the country, and rendering almost impossible the reconciliation of the different parties. It still is a question of policy, not a question of constitutional right, upon which the voice of each part of the United States ought to be heard and considered by each of the parties who now stand in hostile array to each other. Our interests as a State are bound up inseparably with the maintenance of this Union; our sympathies, our personal sympathies, in a large measure, are with the people of the South. Neither party ought to suppose that we would intentionally involve either of them in any compromise for arranging our difficulties that would touch its honor or materially injure its interests. They ought to know that the position which we occupy is one in which we can recognize the existence of any real fraternal feeling in every part of the country, and which enables us to speak the language of conciliation. They ought to trust us, as those who desire nothing but what is for their good. We therefore speak to both parties: "Shed not the blood of your brothers; come not into hostile collision; wake not up the furious passions that burn in the American heart at the sound of the trumpet of war! Wait, wait, until all peaceful means are exhausted; wait until you can assemble in cooler moments, and with all the passions of our being lulled, so that we can rationally consider, and honestly and justly do whatever may be necessary for the interest of any one of the States."

Gentlemen, there is not a more warlike people on the face of God's earth than this American people. Every man is a soldier; even white hairs do not prevent a man from being a soldier. [Applause in the lobby, checked by the President.] I say, therefore, that the strife between the different sections of the American people is a strife such as the world never saw and never will see again, because they will annihilate each other. I say, it is a time when every man who feels pulsating in his heart a love for the American brotherhood to which he belongs, ought to do all in his power to stay the hand of civil war, and it is with that impulse that the Committee here have, in the language of entreaty, not the language of menace, not raging on one side or the other, but in the language of a body who would be mediators between conflicting parties, said: Shed not each other's blood—let us interpose as mediators, standing between you and recommending what is for your interest and your honor; let us cast all our influence in the scale of justice and right, and we shall at last see harmony and unanimity in this country restored. It is a glorious mission, if we can accomplish such an object.

Gentlemen of the Convention, the proudest moment that ever anyone of you shall look back to in your future life, will be when you participated in any act or in any course of action which was calculated to bring back a feeling of brotherhood among the different parts of this American Republic, and when you can still feel that you are united to all its parts, in all its glory, in all its prosperity, and in all its happiness; when, after new glories and honors have clustered around the American flag, you will recollect that you have in any degree contributed to restore harmony among the American people in the past. It will be a feeling that will soothe you, in all cases of disaster, that will comfort and elevate you in all your walks of life.

Gentlemen, I consider that I have sufficiently explained the motives and objects of the committee in submitting the majority report. I apprehend that in relation to the question as to whether we should sever our connection with the Union or not, there will be a unanimous vote against any such course. Such unanimity would indeed be a great force and strength for all the purpose indicated in the report. I deem that I have now discharged the duty of opening the debate, as chairman of the committee, and shall close, reserving to myself the privilege of again addressing the Convention, should it become necessary in the course of the discussion.

Source: *Proceedings of the Missouri State Convention Held at Jefferson City and St. Louis, March, 1861* (St. Louis: George Knapp & Co., Printers and Binders, 1861), 64–68.

James Hugh Moss
March 11, 1861

A lawyer by profession, James H. Moss (1824–1873) represented Clay County in the state convention.

Following the conclusion of Gamble's address and a break for lunch, Delegate Moss offered support for a national convention and submitted a thoughtful endorsement of the Crittenden amendment. On the three points of contention argued by secessionists—protection of slavery in the States, return of fugitive slaves, and slavery in the territories—Moss asserted that the Crittenden resolutions would satisfy the demands of the South. After all, Moss argued, "we have never sought any protection [for slavery] at their hands that they [the North] did not grant." There was no immediate need to secede, and he was willing to wait "two years or five years," through the next several election cycles, to preserve the Union. The country was being beset by "unprincipled political tyrants," Moss concluded. "I have faith in the people of the South, but I have none in their political leaders. I have faith in the people of the North, but I have none in their political leaders."

AFTERNOON SESSION.

Convention re-assembled at 3 o'clock.

Mr. MOSS asked that his amendment to the majority report be read. It was read by the Secretary.

> {Offered earlier in the day, Delegate Moss's amendment read: "Amend the fifth resolution by adding, 'and further believing that the fate of Missouri depends upon the peaceable adjustment of our present difficulties, she will never countenance or aid a seceding State in making war on the General Government, nor will she furnish men and money for the purpose of aiding the General Government in any attempt to coerce a seceding State.'"}

Mr. MOSS. Gentlemen of the Convention: In offering this amendment to the majority report of the Committee on Federal Relations, I do not desire to be understood as occupying a position hostile to that report. On the contrary, I contend that the amendment which I offer is in entire harmony with the doctrine laid down in the Committee's resolutions. I duly appreciate the importance of having this report go forth to the people of Missouri, indorsed by an overwhelming majority of the members of this Convention; and my own opinion is, that the fewer amendments we offer to it, the better, provided we reach the points that are desired to be altered in the report.

As I remarked in the outset, I do not consider the amendment just offered as in conflict at all with the main propositions contained in that report. My understanding of that report is, that it places Missouri upon this position:

that she believes her fate depends upon the peaceful adjustment of the present difficulties; and this is in accordance with my own sentiments. Holding such sentiments, the resolution I have offered is not at all in conflict with them. We say to the two contending sections, we are standing between you. We believe that our fate depends upon the maintenance of the position we occupy. We stand like the rock in the ocean, rolling back from us the waves that come from the North and the South. We say to our natural allies, our Southern brethren, you must not imperil our condition. Whilst we are struggling to get additional guarantees for the protection of our rights, you are not to assail the General Government, thereby precipitating us into a revolution and ruining our cause. But whilst we speak to them in the solemn tone of remonstrance, we likewise say to the General Government, you shall not invade our Southern brethren. If you do, you can look for no aid from Missouri.

Gentlemen, it is urged by some of my friends—even those who occupy the same position in regard to this great question that I do—that it is enunciating the doctrine of nullification; but you should remember that we are in the midst of a revolution: that it is folly to attempt to conceal that idea from the people, and worst of all, it is folly to attempt to conceal that idea from yourselves. And now, I submit to every man in this assembly, of common sense, to tell me whether Missouri will ever furnish a regiment to invade a Southern State for the purpose of coercion. Never! Never! And gentlemen, Missouri expects this Convention to say so. When our friends in the Northern States—those gallant patriots who, surrounded by our enemies, and the enemies of our common country—have dared to say that they will never lend their aid to the General Government to coerce a Southern State—is Missouri to take a position lower than that? Never! I believe it to be the duty of Missouri to stand by the gallant men of Southern Illinois, who have passed resolutions that they will never suffer a Northern army to pass the southern boundary of Illinois for the purpose of invading a Southern State. I believe it to be the duty of Missouri to come to the rescue of, and back up such men as the gallant Stockton of New Jersey, who has had the daring courage to plant himself upon a like platform.[26] When I go home to my constituents—when I go home to meet the secessionists, I want to go with a weapon in my hand with which I can conquer, and lead the Union men on to triumph at the polls, when they come to indorse what this Convention has done. But, gentlemen, if you send me there empty handed—if you send me there with a document like that which has been given to us by President Lincoln,[27] about which there are forty different opinions, and leave it for an argument—a learned and ingenious argument—to settle its meaning, I tell you that our defeat will be certain, when we come to submit our doings to the people of Missouri.

But, gentlemen, it is not from motives of this sort, entirely, that I have introduced this amendment; but because I conscientiously *believe* that it is demanded. It does not pledge Missouri to go out of the Union—not at all. I would never dream of such a resolution as that. I do not believe it to be the will of Missouri; but I believe that if the Union is to be preserved, it cannot be preserved by the sword, but by a peaceable adjustment and fair and equitable compromises. And occupying that position, I say it is the duty of this Convention to plant Missouri between these two warring sections, and say to each, you cannot look to us for aid.

That is my position, gentlemen, in regard to that point. Now, so far as the preamble is concerned, which is attached to the resolutions which have been presented to this Convention, I suppose it to be a mere introduction, setting forth the reasons which have actuated the committee in submitting the resolutions, and not subject to any vote by the Convention. I hold that whatever may be our opinion in regard to the preamble, it is the resolutions, and not the preamble that we are to act on. Taking this view, I am indisposed to meddle with that preamble. It is a fine argument, and I agree with the sentiments enunciated therein, as great truths. I have some objections to the way in which they are stated, and do not agree to some of the particulars; but, taking it as a whole, I consider it a masterly exposition of the present state of affairs, and history of the commencement and growth of the troubles now upon us; I am disinclined to interfere with it in any way.

Mr. GAMBLE. The gentleman is right in saying that the preamble is not strictly before the Convention. It is to be looked upon merely as an introduction on the part of the Committee to the resolutions themselves.

Mr. MOSS. Then I am correct in my position, and I regard the statement of the gentleman who is Chairman of the Committee as a further evidence that this amendment which I offered is not only not in conflict with the report of the Committee, but in entire harmony with it. So much upon that point.

While I am up, gentlemen of the Convention, although perhaps it may not be strictly in order, yet I will briefly give my views in regard to this whole question. I do not know but what it is in order for me to do so. The majority report is now before the Convention, and I may be indulged in making my remarks, taking a wider range than is strictly included in my amendment. I will state that I have another amendment, which I shall offer at the proper time. But I will undertake to discuss it now, believing it to be in order.

The CHAIR. The gentleman will not discuss a resolution which has not been read by the Secretary.

Mr. MOSS. Well, I will not say anything about this amendment at present, but confine myself to the majority report. I agree with the position taken in that report—the position taken by my worthy friend who is before me, as the Chairman of the Committee. I believe, gentlemen, that the hopes of the people of Missouri—yea, of the Union, of the Border States as well as of the Northern States—I say, I believe that their only hope of salvation now is with the people; and the sooner we go to them the better. And for that reason I am opposed to all preliminary proceedings by bodies of men whose work, when it is finished, amounts to nothing. I tell you the people have got tired of such things. They are sick, and they want a physician who can heal them. They do not want to be compelled to swallow any more quack medicine.

It is urged by some of the friends of the Border State propositions, that it would be advantageous to decline, for the present, holding a National Convention. And why? They say, in order that we might present an unbroken front. They say, fix upon an ultimatum. Well, now, gentlemen, I disagree with my friends in that respect. I disagree with them for this reason: if I am dealing with an enemy—and for the sake of illustration, I will call those gentlemen who are advocating "irrepressible conflict" our enemies—and I propose to him to compromise, and I have four or five different plans of compromise; then, if I see that he indicates that he is in favor of a certain one of these plans, and that plan suits me to the letter, I believe that good policy is to meet him at once, and not waste my time discussing the advantages of the other propositions. If I see that he will give me all that I ask, then, gentlemen, I feel it to be my duty as well as my interest, and the dictates of common sense, to accede to it at once. Now, how do we stand in regard to this? Missouri says that she proposes the Crittenden resolutions as the proper basis for a settlement of the question. Do you doubt, that the Border States all indorse that proposition? I presume not. How is it in the North? Why, the Crittenden resolutions stand without a rival. Look at the memorials and petitions that have flooded our National Legislature.[28] What object have they been presented for? Look at the 14,000 names from the city of Boston praying for the adoption of those resolutions.

Now, my idea of the policy of Missouri is this: lead out in this great conciliatory movement. Tell your brothers of the Border States that, believing that a majority of the citizens of the United States are agreed that the Crittenden resolutions present a fair and equitable basis of settlement, Missouri plants herself upon that position, and calls upon the Border States to follow her. There is no doubt but the Northern States can be made to accede to them; and I tell you, gentlemen, we will go into that National Convention with four-fifths of her delegates instructed to occupy them as a basis. That is what we will do, and we will do it without holding a Border State Convention; and I believe, honestly, we will reach that point more successfully by Missouri's taking this ground right at the start, as she has a right to do, and determining that she is not going to hold any further consultation with sister States except in National Convention, and that she will instruct her delegates to the National Convention to stand upon that platform, and will call upon her sister Border

States to do likewise. Then gentlemen, I believe we will go into a National Convention—I mean the friends of compromise—I mean the delegates that come from the people, from whom we look for salvation, will go there as a unit, and I believe all will go virtually satisfied with the Crittenden compromise.

As I remarked before, the impatient people—they are in the habit of traveling by railroad and talking by telegraph, and they wish to see the great difficulty we have to contend with settled with dispatch. They are impatient. They have forgotten that it took eight long years of bloodshed, and suffering, and trial, to build up this magnificent edifice; and now, because they cannot stay its tottering walls, and re-instate it upon its ancient foundations in an hour, they get impatient and cry out for revolution. Gentlemen, the sooner we can get to the people the better.

If I thought that in advocating a National Convention, I should be instrumental in bringing about a conflict between delegates from the Border States and from Northern States, I would have different views about the matter. I should not advocate it; but I believe our delegates will go there, and the Northern delegates will go there, and a great majority of all will be instructed to vote for the Crittenden resolutions.

Although it may be a little tiresome for me now to discuss the merits of the Crittenden resolutions, much as they have been discussed, yet I hope I shall be indulged, for this reason: that we have these battles to fight over again with the people; and I know the skill and ingenuity and masterly management of our enemies in Missouri; (when I say our enemies, I mean the secessionists *per se*, these gentlemen who think that Missouri's salvation depends upon going out *now*.{)} I want the people of Missouri to understand the force of our position here. I know it will be contended by our enemies, when we have passed these resolutions, that we have done nothing—that what we have done amounts to nothing—and that Missouri has taken no position whatever; that we are submissionists, and all that sort of thing; and, recollecting these facts, recollecting the history of the canvas, and the fight made heretofore, I think it not inappropriate, in this connection, in a short way, to speak of the peculiar merits of the Crittenden resolutions as the basis of settlement.

In order to appreciate these merits, let us ask ourselves, in the first place, what are we seeking to remedy? What is it that has terrified the South in regard to the danger of her institutions? Is it the mere squabble about the Territories? Far from it. It is the announcement of the celebrated doctrine that Mr. Lincoln claims to be the father of the "irrepressible conflict." I know that Republicans interpret that one way, but the South—the men of the South—the men of the slave States—all interpret it another way, and I think their interpretation is right. How do they interpret it? They interpret it, gentlemen, to mean, not only the exclusion of Southern men from the Territories, and the hedging of slavery with a wall of fire, as has been remarked by some other gentleman. They may be wrong in this interpretation; but whether it be right or wrong, the general opinion entertained in the South is, that it means eternal and unceasing warfare upon the institution, and that, whilst the Republican party now, under our present Constitution, acknowledge that Congress has no power to invade a Southern State by legislation for the purpose of interfering with the institutions in the States, yet, when in some future time they have acquired sufficient strength, they will institute such interference. Whether that idea be erroneous or correct, is a matter I do not propose to investigate. Suffice it to say, that the great object in the outset of this conciliatory movement, is to give the Southern mind peace upon this great question. It is to satisfy them that they need no longer look with anxiety and dread to their Northern brethren.

Now, let us see whether the Crittenden resolutions reach that point. How does Mr. Crittenden propose to remedy the evil? How does he propose to give peace and safety to the South? He says we will amend the Constitution in a certain way, so as to deprive Congress of the power ever to interfere with the question of slavery in a State;[29] and for a further guarantee, we will make that provision in the Constitution like a law of the Medes and Persians, *unalterable*.[30]

Gentlemen, if there be any in this Convention, who are secessionists, (and I hope there are none;) if there is a man here with a true Southern heart in his bosom, who is honest and candid, I ask whether he would propose to offer amendment to that? Could we ask for a stronger guarantee than the one contained in the Crittenden resolutions reaching to that point? I believe, gentlemen, that no other statesman has offered an amendment to the Constitution that suits the people of the South better. We think it is as strong an amendment as we can get.

What is the next point? The next point, gentlemen, is to give protection to the four thousand millions of slave property in the States. You may talk about principles, your Territorial question, the theory of Government, and all that sort of thing, but I tell you the men who have labored for a lifetime to build up a little fortune, and have got half of it in slave property, will not rest satisfied for a moment without sufficient guarantees that they can lie down at night and sleep quietly and in safety, and know that no robber dare break in and take their property from them. They want protection for the four thousand millions of dollars of slave property. Now, how does Mr. Crittenden propose to reach that point? Is there any improvement which has ever been suggested upon his plan? What does he propose to do? Gentlemen, you are aware that we have upon our statute book, passed by our National Legislature, the Fugitive Slave Law. What has been the trouble in the South? It was, that when a Southern man undertook to pursue a slave into a free State a mob would arise and take his property from him, and he had no remedy—he was powerless. That needs rectifying. We need a stronger guarantee in regard to that point than we have had heretofore. How are we to get it? Mr. Crittenden proposes that the General Government shall come in with her strong arm and deal with the Northern robber who dares to violate the law. He does not leave the individual to struggle with the law; but he proposes that the General Government should pay the value of the stolen property to the owner, and that she shall undertake to deal with the offender according to his deserts.

Men of Missouri—slave holders—can you suggest an improvement on that? I believe none has ever been suggested that was more satisfactory to the South than that.

Then, gentlemen of the Convention, the two great points are now disposed of. Peace and quiet are restored to the South. They no longer look upon their Northern brethren as enemies, because they have not the *power* to do them injury.

All those startling fears upon which artful and designing men worked in order to carry themselves into power, without reference to the effect that it is to have upon the nation, and which have in a great measure led us to our present unfortunate condition, they are rid of. We put an impassible barrier between the enemies of slavery and the owners of slave property in the States. We deprive the Abolitionist of the power even to alter the American Constitution, so as to give Congress the power to invade a Southern State by legislation; and we give full and ample protection to the four thousand millions of dollars worth of property in the States.

Well, those two material points are satisfactorily disposed of. The next question, and, gentlemen, the only question remaining to be considered (for I believe that the people of the North agree that we are entitled, under the Constitution, to all those guarantees and to all the protection that we ask, so far as slavery is concerned in the States,) is that of the Territories. Well, what of the Territories? It is unnecessary for me to argue this question at length before this Convention; but, gentlemen, as that is the point upon which our enemies hang the fate of Missouri, I will argue it. That is the great weapon of war in the hands of our enemies. They say all is very well about the States, but the danger lies in the Territories. Well, now, this is not a question entirely of principle, but a question of fact—a question of practicability. You go on to demonstrate to them that the God of Nature has put his veto on the introduction of slavery north of 36 degrees 30 minutes. Yet they will argue with you a day, and say they don't care whether that is true or false—whether the laws of nature have placed impassible barriers between them and that Territory or not; they will maintain that the abstract principle is right, and that there should be no concession upon that point. They say the Revolution was fought on a preamble, and they talk about a *principle*. Well, I apprehend, whenever the people can understand this principle in a practical light, they will make but poor headway with that principle. They insist that they have the right of going into any Territory and occupying every foot of ground that the God of Nature will allow them to occupy, and that they are not willing to abandon that right in any instance whatever. That is the argument of the Secessionists.

Well, what does that amount to? It amounts to just this—our Northern brethren now, and I believe it sincerely, will give us the Crittenden Resolutions whenever we can get at the sense of the people in a National Convention; they will give us guarantees for the protection of slavery in the States; they will give us this impassible barrier to prevent men, hereafter, from carrying the war into Africa; they will give us protection for every foot of territory where you can take slavery according to the laws of Nature; but the Secessionists say we will surrender all these guarantees offered us, and for what? for the sake of asserting an abstract principle that is barren—a right that is a barren abstraction—and they say further, that they consider this compromise altogether on one side, that we give up every thing, and that we get nothing.—Why gentlemen, is that the manner in which the thing suggests itself to you; and right here, at the risk of being—as I remarked before—a little tedious, I will go slightly into the past political history of our country on the subject of slavery, and shall take, to some extent, the same line of argument pursued a day or two since by the gentleman from Clinton—Judge Birch.[31] Let us look to the national legislation of the past, and see whether or not this is not a compromise we are getting. It will be remembered, and I will pass very rapidly over the history, that in 1820, Missouri sought to come in as a slave State but was opposed, but at last she did come in with her significant domain. Time rolled on, and Texas with her magnificent empire sought to come into the Union. It was still opposed by men of the North, with the exception of those of our Northern friends who have always been willing to stand by our Constitutional rights, and they agreed to admit her. How? Texas has a territory of three hundred millions of acres of land. And what were the conditions prescribed by Texas? They were that she should be admitted with the right to divide her territory into four great States, and she has the right today if she is not out of the Union. It was part of the contract, as you will observe by reading the proceedings of Congress in 1845, and further, by reading WEBSTER'S great speech on the compromise measures of 1850, where he takes that ground and says: "Texas to-day has the right to divide her magnificent Territory into four slave States, and that it is a part of the contract under which she was admitted."[32] Well, gentlemen, time rolled on, and New Mexico and California sought to come in. The same enemies in the Northern States attempted to prevent the admission of those Territories, and what then took place? Why, the immortal Clay[33] came fortward [sic] and offered a resolution which embodied the celebrated doctrine of non-intervention, by means of which men of the slave States, with their property, could go into those territories and stand side by side the men of the free States. By and by our Southern brethren said to the North, this will not satisfy us. Your citizens have been encroaching upon us, and making war upon our institutions, and robbing us of our property, and we have no remedy. Give us the Fugitive Slave law. They did so. And while a Northern man {Millard Fillmore of New York} was in the Presidential chair they executed that law. That was not all. Time rolled on again, and in 1854, when Kansas and Nebraska sought to come in, what was done then? Our Southern brethren said this celebrated doctrine which was enunciated in the compromise measures of 1850, the doctrine of non-intervention, is cramped and trammeled in its full operation on account of the old Missouri Compromise, and we now ask you to do what by right and justice you should do to us. We ask you to remove the old Missouri restriction and give the people of the South the right to go into the common territory and say what institutions they shall have. Did they refuse? No, they gave it to us. What was done then? It was then sought to take the power of legislating on this subject of slavery in the Territories, as I before remarked, out of the hands of Congress. Our Southern brethren said: Take this away from Congress, and give us all a fair opportunity—Kentucky, Louisiana and Arkansas—and give us the opportunity to go there and take an equal chance with our Northern brethren, and let the people decide. We did go into Kansas Territory and passed laws for the protection of the slave, as we did in New Mexico, and which now stands on our statute book. That is the way the thing stands. I am now reciting this history for the purpose of showing that this is a compromise. I understand compromise to mean a yielding up on the part of both sides. Now, all this was right. I do not claim that the North has given us anything that we are not entitled to; but this Kansas-Nebraska bill was given to us upon our solicitation, and upon that platform we elected James Buchanan, a sworn friend of the South, by an overwhelming majority,[34] and the astonishing spectacle is now presented that notwithstanding all this seven of our Southern brethren have deserted us and gone out of the Union. I undertake to show you that the propositions contained in the Crittenden resolutions in reference to the territory are, in the truest sense of the word, a compromise, and I think I can demonstrate it. We have asked the fugitive slave law, and it was put upon our statute book. We asked that the power to regulate slavery in the territories be given to the people from Congress, and what do we find? We find that we cannot be protected in the territories—that the arm of the territorial legislature is too weak—that our Northern enemies, those who are really our Northern enemies, have three men to our one, and that they can fill the territories and rob us of our protection. Now, what do we ask? We ask that this power shall be placed back in Congress; that it shall once more be restored to the General Government that she by her strong arm shall give us protection. Suppose they do it, don't they give us something? Don't they yield us something? Certainly; and, I contend, just what we are entitled to. We now ask that we shall not be left to our enemies who get the power in the territories, but that the Government shall come to our rescue. Suppose they give it to us, is it nothing? But they tell us about the guarantees they gave us for slavery in the States. There is the Fugitive Slave Law, and all you can ask. We are not responsible for its execution. The President has the power to execute it, and we have done all we can. We say we admit that, and ask you to do more—to give us a remedy that will be of some practical utility to us. We ask you to let us go into this Territory with our slave property, and claim protection of the General Government.[35] I do not know what other men's ideas of compromise are, but that fills my idea exactly. And mind you, when I say all this, I don't mean to say that they yield one thing that we are not entitled to. We are entitled to it all, and we should take it in the spirit of compromise. I have deemed it proper, gentlemen of the Convention, to detain you thus long in the discussion of my views in regard to the Crittenden propositions. I have done so for the reasons that I suggested at the outset, that—

The CHAIR. I will say to the gentleman that he is out of order in discussing the Crittenden propositions, and has been to my full knowledge, but it has been my disposition to indulge him, and I hope the Convention will indulge him. He has cut off the whole merits of the subject by offering an amendment to a particular clause in the report. There being no objection, the gentleman will have leave to proceed.

No objection was made.

Mr. MOSS. I thank you, gentlemen, for the indulgence. I was aware of the fact, but as I stated at the outset that I did not contemplate again occupying the time of the Convention, I desired to say what I thought in regard to this whole question. Now, gentlemen, as I remarked in the outset—

[The speaker was here interrupted, by some one in the audience being seized with a fit. After the excitement had subsided he said:]

Gentlemen of the Convention, I take the position that I now occupy for the reason that I have intimated: I have faith in the Northern people. As I remarked a few minutes ago, and as my worthy friend from Clinton remarked, we have never sought any protection at their hands that they did not grant, and when I say this, I do not mean the Abolitionists of the North; I do not mean the men who avow no compromise and hostility to the institutions of the South, but I mean the noble patriots who have been willing to stand by the constitutional rights of the South in all times; but men now talk that they have no sympathy with Northern men; they are too apt to class all Northern men alike; they say our sympathies are altogether with the South. Do you know, gentlemen of the Convention, that in November, 1860, there was a quarter of a million more votes polled against Mr. LINCOLN in the North than in the

South?[36] Are these noble men who stand up in the midst of your enemies, to suffer martyrdom? Have they no claims on your sympathies? Have you no hope of the vindication of your rights, and of obtaining additional guarantees from those noble men who are now struggling for you in the free States. Turn to the past history of the country, to which I have referred, and remember that you have a stronger army fighting for you in the free States, than you have in the South. Such is the fact, and no man can deny it. Gentlemen who are without hope, and who have no confidence in the Northern people. I ask you to examine the result of the election of 1860, and see what a revolution you have got to produce. Take each State, and see how many votes you have got to take from the Republican party to add to the friends of your Constitutional Rights party, and see what a revolution you have got to work. Some time ago, while I was making a canvas in my District, I took the trouble to do that; and right here I will state my position in regard to our Southern brethren withdrawing from us. I know gentlemen on this floor will say it is no use now to talk about those things; but, gentlemen, I think it is. I think it is proper that the people of Missouri should understand this question, as how we stand and why we stand as we do. Our sisters of the South, without consultation with us, took the liberty of going out of the Union and inaugurating a revolution, and left us to our fate. I regret that. While I am disposed to complain of them for their arbitrary action, yet I am not disposed to abuse them. But I think a calm, dignified and firm action of the people of Missouri should be taken in regard to the circumstances that have led us to our present troubles. How did we stand upon the election of Lincoln? It was known that his hands were tied—that Congress was with us.[37] How did it stand in regard to adopting constitutional amendments? How would it stand to-day, in regard to the adoption of the Crittenden resolutions, if all our wandering sisters had staid in the Union? Gentlemen, I believe it would require but just eleven free States to give us a constitutional majority to adopt amendments to the Constitution. But they have gone out, and how do they leave us? They leave us so that we are now compelled to get fourteen of the Northern States, to get a majority of those left, and a still larger number to get the three-fourths of the original States in order to amend the Constitution. But look at the returns of the November election, and see the revolution necessary to be made, and you will be astonished; for you will remember that when you take from the Republican side, and add to our side, the thing counts double. You will perceive that in order to get three-fourths of the States, you would not have to make a revolution exceeding 10,000 votes in any State, except Pennsylvania and New York. Don't you believe that revolution has already taken place? I do, and it is for that reason that I would go with confidence into a National Convention; but I want the delegates to that Convention to come from the people; and I intend to offer a resolution, at the proper time, reaching that point—that we ask that to be done, and why? Because I don't want to go through a solemn farce like that which was enacted a short time since in the Peace Congress. I have no faith in delegates sent from Abolition Legislatures and Governors, who go to meet secession delegates from secession Governors and Legislatures, [applause;] and I, for one, have never staked my hopes of salvation in the hands of such men.

The CHAIR. The Sergeant-at-Arms will attend to his duties, and will clear the galleries, if there is any more cheering.

Mr. MOSS. The question was put to me on every stump, by every Secessionist, Will you not be willing to go out if this Congress fail? No, gentlemen, for I look for it to fail, and, as a distinguished member told us the other day, Northern men came there with the idea that they had to sustain the Chicago platform, without reference to any other question. I am opposed to Missouri going into a Convention composed of delegates that shall be sent by any Legislature now in existence. But, say the Secessionists, your hands are tied; these Legislatures that are now in existence won't send delegates to a National Convention. What are you going to do? Are you going to wait? Certainly I am. It took eight long years of blood and suffering to build this Government up, and I think it is worth twelve months delay or two years or five years to preserve it. And if these Legislatures refuse to send delegates there, and refuse to submit this question to the people; if members of Congress refuse to do their duty and refuse to give the people what is right, I am in favor of waiting; but I don't want Missouri to go out. I want her to wait until she can reach our Northern brethren at the ballot box. Then, when they turn their backs upon us and say they are no longer our brethren, then there will be time enough for Missouri to talk about going out of the Union. I am not inclined to break up this Government because a few unprincipled politicians have got into our legislative halls by swindling the people, or because they refuse to give us our rights. I will stay in it until we can reach the people, and never raise my voice for secession until our Northern brethren have declared at the ballot box that they will no longer live with us as brethren. Then there will be time enough for Missouri to talk of going out.

I know that political leaders of the South tell us that we cannot come together again, and my friends ask me if I have any hope? Yes, I have. I have faith in the people of the South, but I have none in their political leaders. I have faith in the people of the North, but I have none in their political leaders. And I have a hope it may be a sort of forlorn hope, a bitter hope, but it is this, that if these peaceable remedies fail, that at last the people, when they come to realize the fact that they have been trodden upon and oppressed by a set of unprincipled political tyrants, that they will rise up and trample these men down and upon this bloody ground plant the old national banner. This is my hope. I look to a reconstruction of this great Republic.

I had to-day a conversation with a very intelligent gentleman lately from the South, and a gentleman who is very warm in his attachment to the South, and he stated to me a fact that I have always believed, and that is that a large majority of the people of Louisiana, the day she went out of the Union, were against secession,[38] and I tell you, men of the border States, you form the great backbone, the vertebral column, to which are attached these Northern and Southern ribs—some of which have been broken off, but they will be reunited, I trust, despite the enemies of the country either North or South. I tell you, if you could get an adjustment of this question on what the Crittenden resolutions propose, we can once more be at peace. In spite of the agency of Orr,[39] Jeff. Davis or others, there will be found men at the South who will build up Union parties that will revolutionize the South, and they will come back. They will stand out just as long as they can stand, and then they will rise up and bury their oppressors. God grant the day may soon come!

Gentlemen, a reign of terror is prevailing there. No man dare open his lips in favor of the Union, and men who have shed their blood upon the battle field, statesmen who have contributed empires to our Southern States, have been denounced in the South as traitors, and I declare my blood ran cold when I read the denunciations of those noble patriots. Look at Sam Houston—a man who, by his military prowess and statesman ship, has added to the Southern galaxy that great empire, Texas—Sam Houston![40] Look at the traitor Wigfall—yea, I say traitor—talking about riding Sam Houston on a rail, and running him from a territory that he gave to us but a few years since.[41] San Houston! a man who has shed more patriotic blood on Southern soil, and in defense of Southern territory than ever flowed in the veins of all the traitor Wigfalls that ever lived. That is the way the thing stands at the South.—Noble men and patriots are denounced because they dare to love the Union. I tell you that reign of terror must have an end—it has had an end in all its past history. The history of the revolution in France, and of the world, point to a certainty that a revolution will overwhelm those who stand between the people and what they want. Gentlemen, I have occupied your time long enough. In conclusion, I only desire to state that I hail from a county where Lincoln did not get a vote, and where the secessionists got less than two hundred. My constituents are Union men, and they indorse my position, and they believe that all Missouri has is staked on the die—that she must have a peaceful settlement.—They do not want to go out of the Union, but they ask that their honor shall be safe in your hands. We occupy the middle ground, and we can extend to both sections a friendly hand, and say we want peace, and our salvation depends upon it. I hope the resolution will meet with a favorable reception.

Source: *Proceedings of the Missouri State Convention Held at Jefferson City and St. Louis, March, 1861* (St. Louis: George Knapp & Co., Printers and Binders, 1861), 68–75.

John Brooks Henderson
March 12, 1861

John B. Henderson (1824–1913) was born in Pittsylvania County, Virginia, and moved to Lincoln County, Missouri, with his family in 1832. He read for the law and began his law practice in Clarksville. Henderson served in the Missouri House of Representatives two terms (1848–1850, 1856–1858), and later was elected to the US Senate in 1862 to fill the seat of recently expelled Trusten Polk, and served until 1869.

Delegate Henderson's address offered a strong case for Union and a stronger one against disunion. Declaring secession "a damnable heresy," he logically asked his colleagues whether separation would resolve the fugitive slave issue. Could slave owners accomplish through treaties with a foreign nation what they could not under the United States Constitution? Regarding slavery in the territories, Henderson lectured, "There is not to-day a single law upon the statute books of the Federal Government denying the right of a citizen to enter into any territory belonging to the Union." Indeed, when Republicans came to control Congress following the secession of seven states, they organized three western territories without any restriction on the institution of slavery. Parties may be extreme in their views in the acquisition of power, he concluded, but in the administration of it "they have to confine themselves within the limits of the law, and when that is the case we need have no fear whatever."

Mr. HENDERSON—Mr. President and gentlemen of the Convention: It really seems to me that since the beginning of the deliberations of this Convention, we have been disposed to magnify and to give an undue importance to many of the apparent difficulties of the present time.—When we come to look at our condition it is not so bad as at first blush we might anticipate. Five months ago, we all thought that we were the happiest people on earth. I care not what party a man may have belonged to, or what set of political principles he was attempting to establish upon the policy of the country, yet it must be admitted that every man presumed that we had a Government the best that had been guaranteed to man, and that we enjoyed a prosperity never enjoyed by the people of any nation on the earth; and yet, by some strange delusion, by some unaccountable transformation of the human mind, we have come to the conclusion that we are just upon the verge of destruction. It is not so—not one word of it. There are loyal hearts in this country from one end to the other, that beat steadily and responsive in their loyalty to that flag and the Constitution of our fathers; and though for a short time party feeling may get the better of their judgment, though for a short time wild fanaticism may take possession of the better feelings of the human heart, yet the day of peace and regeneration is at hand. I witnessed this thing once before. I saw the very same States that have now seceded from Congress and from the Federal Government secede from a Convention.[42] I saw South Carolina secede. I then felt what must necessarily be the consequence. I saw Alabama leave, and Florida, and Mississippi, and Louisiana and Texas. I stood as I believed, the correct representative of the heart and feeling of my people. I said to them you may all secede, but I shall stand true to the State of Missouri. I let them go, and on returning I found that my State was unwilling to abandon me, and instead of so doing, stood true to the principles of the Constitution, firm for the Union and true to the conservative platform laid down by the Democracy of the Nation. Not having been intimidated then, but having been sustained and supported by an honest yeomanry, the free people of this State, I can witness their departure again, feeling conscious that nobody has been hurt except themselves. I would that they had never gone. I would that to-day a proper spirit and feeling animated their bosoms, that they might willingly and freely return back to the Union of our fathers. They must yet do it. Politicians of the Southern States—and I am going to talk plainly—the drunken demagogues of the present day, who unfortunately have possessed themselves of the power that ought to be in the hands of good and conservative men, have so far obtained the control in those States as to leave the people but little room for the expression of honest sentiments. Those that are interested in the character and perpetuity of the Union are in danger if they make known their sentiments of loyalty. I had supposed that in the march of our Government, from its infancy on towards its decline, as other governments have declined before us, the day might come when a Marius or a Scylla might figure.[43] I had supposed that when the nation should become degenerated and enfeebled by vice, in all probability there might be an American Cataline,[44] but I had not supposed that in the first eighty years of our existence, a Yancey,[45] with all the malignity of a Cataline, with a total disregard of all the blessings which now make us the happiest people on earth, would attempt to plunge the people into revolution, when the inevitable result must, in the course of a few years—even though they depart in peace from us to-day—be utter ruin and destruction to that people. Is not this so? And yet some gentlemen, even in Missouri, hesitate to say that a man is a traitor, even after he has proven himself to be a traitor. Gentlemen are afraid to say what they really think about this matter: they are afraid of the people—of that people who are to-day as true to the Union and the Constitution as any living people on earth. They seem to desire to engraft words of a certain meaning upon resolutions; they hesitate about marching up to the point that is now necessary to be reached to save the Government from ruin—and leave all in doubt and confusion. This will do us no good. This is no time for hesitancy. As some gentlemen refer to the political records, I say if I can make a record to save Missouri from impending ruin, I want no other record. No man in this proud State needs any other record than the record that he has contributed his mite to save us from the consequences that are now pressing upon us. New doctrines are being taught in the present day. A robber in one of the Northern States, following out the bent of his mind, seizes upon my property, takes it and appropriates it to his own use, and deprives me of it. I go in pursuit of my property, and meet a band of free negroes and contemptible white men who are associated together for the purpose of carrying out the original design of the robber and of depriving me of the use of my property. All these things occur, but as a remedy for it we are taught the new doctrine that all law must be repealed. Is that the true doctrine? Is our government to be preserved by a doctrine of that character? Surely not. I was once taught, and yet I believe it, that when the law is defective, when its execution is not properly enforced, we can make the law more stringent and provide better remedies for its true and proper enforcement. That is the true doctrine of the government, and when we depart from it ten thousand difficulties will environ Missouri and this Union, consecrated by the wisdom of an illustrious ancestry. Tell me not they made such a government—tell me not this is a new doctrine that is now being taught—tell me not that we owe our preservation so far and our prosperity, to the idea that we are thirty-four independent people, and not one people. It was supposed, when our institutions were founded, that in union there was strength. It was supposed that in union there was power to enforce the decrees of an honest judiciary. It was supposed, in the establishment of our Government that it would be perpetual, that it was to last not only to bless those who made it, but to bless future generations, and to open the door in our Government, and make it the asylum of the oppressed in all lands. But, as the great remedy for existing evils, the great remedy which is now advanced, is secession! Is this doctrine true? Some gentlemen are afraid of the people of Missouri. I am not. From my place here to-day I declare this doctrine of secession to be a damnable heresy! That expression is strong; but I declare my honest sentiments, and I am willing to trust an honest people to stand true to this declaration. It was never designed by our forefathers as a remedy for anything. It is but the destraction [sic] of the Government, unfortunately, and this must be accomplished, only to establish the fact that there is a spirit of insubordination and reckless folly—a spirit that disregards law and order—now prevailing from the Northern regions of our Republic to those of the South; a spirit that seems to delight in setting at defiance all that can tend to give us peace and prosperity, and we are looking upon that spirit of reckless disregard of law as a remedy for existing evils, and debating whether to plunge into this reckless disregard ourselves and offset one wrong against another. Is that the true doctrine? So long as we practice upon that—so long as we acknowledge it to be a truth in the government of the country, then the very evils we complain of impose upon us the necessity of revolution in order to redress our wrongs. What are our complaints? We complain that the fugitive slave law has been violated in the Northern States, and if we once admit the doctrine of secession to be true, then as an offset to an ordinance of secession, what is there to prevent the Northern States from at once passing laws that no slave owner shall recapture slaves? And this is a remedy, not for any evil, but to plunge hastily into a movement without looking at the consequences that must flow from such a course.

The people of Missouri expect us to act without fear. They expect an honest declaration of principles that will meet their views. What is the condition of our country? Seven stars of the constellation have shot madly from their orbits. What is the duty of Missouri? This is an important, a very important consideration, and when we look at the Constitution and the design of our institutions, there is but one answer left in the patriotic heart; there can be but one. I am told that they have gone to secure their rights in slave property. Having been brought up as a Democrat of the strictest sect, I too might have been led into this delusion, if I had not had an opportunity to know better. They never left this confederacy—I mean the politicians who have governed and controlled this movement—on account of any fear whatever as to their rights in negro property. It is a false idea of commercial greatness. They have, since 1832, inculcated a doctrine of a tariff upon imports is a mere burden upon exports; that their cities have languished under the revenue laws of the Government; that their fields have become barren under the oppressions and exactions of an unjust Government. The merchant of Charleston to-day, candidly and sincerely believes, in case his government can be established, that South Carolina can be separated from the Federal Union, Charleston in the course of ten years will become a New York. The merchants of Savannah have the same opinion, the merchants of Mobile and the merchants of New Orleans have the same opinion, and unfortunately I must say this delusion of the day is entertained by some of the merchants of the West. The great city of St. Louis to-day owes its greatness and prosperity alone to the Union. But this delusion has seized upon some men of sense in Missouri and in the city of St. Louis, and they have come to the conclusion that in case a Southern Confederacy is formed, Missouri must go with it and St. Louis will thereby become the great city upon this continent. This delusion upon the minds of some men of the South has caused this unfortunate state of affairs. But there is another thing and it is this:—in that country there are designing men, men who, in their estimation, have not been properly regarded with public favor in this country; men who have sought under the binding obligation of allegiance to oath-bound leagues, to go and take Cuba and subject its wealth to their rapacity; men who have formed organizations year after year, to go in the spirit of Cortez and Pizarro,[46] and seize upon the wealth of Central American States, and to carry on a war of pillage upon the commerce and wealth of their people.[47] There is a vast degree of feeling of that character, and these things combined with the idea that has been gravely inculcated on the Southern mind for a number of years, that the Government of the Union is oppressive: all these things have driven the people into a total disregard of their own interest and into that which must inevitably produce their ruin. This work has been done regardless of the consequences. The excuse that has been given for this movement is that which finds sympathy with the people of Missouri. We are left to believe that it is the fear of the great sectional and dominant party that has driven them to take this extraordinary step. Thousands of the very best Southern citizens have been driven out of the Union under the belief that the triumph of this sectional party was the real cause of their being thus driven out. Designing demagogues and politicians who to-day would rob them, if they could only conceal their plunder—and in the course of a few years they will be able to do it under the present state of affairs—have brought about this thing, and by and by they will be as secure as the soothsayers of Rome, who when they met each other, winked and laughed at the delusions practised in an unsuspecting people. This is the present condition of things in the Southern States, and we are called upon to follow them. The question, Mr. President, is whether we will recognize this as a constitutional right. I came here already sworn to support the Constitution of my country, and after I came I again renewed that fidelity and placed my hand upon the book and swore again that I would support it; and now, sir, I am ready to say that that instrument is the best instrument ever devised for the government of man. Sir, having been born in fidelity to it—having thus far enjoyed prosperity under it, such as I could not have enjoyed under any other government on earth—having thus far been protected in my rights, person and property—I love that government; I love its flag that has protected me and mine. I look forward with renewed hope to the brilliant prospects in the future, when I look to the hallowed associations of the past; and I now again renew my faith in the good of my country, and no act of mine, from this day on, shall ever tend to dissolve the union of Missouri with the Federal Government. My mind has been made up. I intend, sir, so far as I am concerned, that every right shall be guaranteed our Southern friends, and that every right shall be guaranteed our Northern friends, and everything that can be done shall be done upon my part to restore alienated feeling and bring back once more those erring sisters that have gone off in madness into the path of their own destruction. And, sir, looking at the best interests of Missouri—looking at my own fealty to the Constitution, I can never consent to follow.

Let us stand true. Do you want them back with you? Yes, says every man. How are you going to get them? By passing ordinances of secession—by passing anything that looks to their encouragement and support? Mr. President, no. There are two sides to this question. I detest the action of the Northern States that have passed laws interfering with the execution of the Fugitive Slave law; and, sir, to remedy that I would have passed by the next Congress a law by which every right of a citizen of the South shall be guaranteed to him. I would so amend that law that when a mob in the Northern States undertook to interfere with the execution of it, a penalty would be imposed such as would effectually prevent such interference.

> {After a break for lunch, Delegate Henderson resumed his repudiation of secession as a constitutional right. "If secession be true," he reasoned, any state could withdraw from the Union during a war with European powers, or refuse to pay its fair share of federal taxes. If secession be a constitutional right, then the Fugitive Slave Law could be "set at defiance by any Northern State."}

But aside from it as a Constitutional question, I propose, sir, to examine it as a question of expediency and propriety on the part of the people of this State. What is the difficulty now existing? It is, as I am told, the insecurity of slave property. Is that true? Then do you propose this Mississippi river, that rolls by your city, shall become the boundary line between Missouri and the Northern Confederacy, in order to protect slave property? *Can* this be urged with any degree of reason? I am told by gentlemen, and some of them in high quarters, (even the Governor of the State of Missouri, in my presence, the other evening, so said,) that treaties may secure, and will secure, that which country, good neighborhood, respect for the Constitution and laws of the land, that which common interest and common destiny will not grant to the people of the State.

How close are the ties that bind England and America. There is a common parentage—there is a common and mutual interest. There is everything based upon commercial relations or good neighborhood between two countries, to justify us in exacting from Great Britain the recognition to us of every right. Tell me, then, why is it that the fugitive slave in Canada is now secure. Why don't these gentlemen make treaties with Great Britain? Why is it, with our interests tied together as they are, that England, dependent as she is, in the language of our Southern sisters who have seceded, upon King Cotton, has never yet granted, and never will grant, the rendition of a fugitive slave? Standing upon the old doctrine of her statesmen and her poets, that whenever a man touches her consecrated soil his shackles fall, and he stands forth redeemed, regenerated and disenthralled, she tells the nations of the world that that is her only ultimatum in regard to questions of this character—that no matter how long a man may have been a slave—no matter how intimate the relations between Great Britain and the country from which the man has come, yet when he touches her consecrated soil, he becomes free as his master.[48] Is it true that it would be better to separate from our Northern friends, and erect a Southern Confederacy, and look to the protection of England, France and Russia, for those rights that are denied to us in this happy Government of ours? Is that true? If so, let me ask you, one moment, as to the probabilities, if you please, of securing treaties that will accomplish the ends that you design to accomplish. Are these men so hostile to slavery—are they so much arrayed in feeling and in principle against the institutions of the State of Missouri, that even now, with every inducement leading thereto, they will not render to us that which belongs to us? If so, when once you have dissolved the ties between North and South—(can any be dearer between independent nations than those which bind together England and America?)—can you expect to secure by a treaty a right that is now denied? I say no. Every gentleman upon this floor will say to himself that it is an utter impossibility that such a treaty can be made.

> {Henderson here argued that disunion will inevitably lead to a war that will not end until, "every material and social interest of this country has been buried beneath its ravages." Henderson believed that limits on slavery should only be placed by climate and soil. The people of Missouri voted in the last election for a compromise position (Stephen Douglas's) between the exclusion of slavery from the territories and the federal protection of slavery in the territories. As long as the policy of the federal government continued to honor popular sovereignty in the territories, the voters of Missouri "are satisfied to remain in this Confederacy."}

But another proposition suggests itself to me. There was another party in the State of Missouri, and I refer to these things in order to see how far the public mind has been driven from the position it occupied four or five months ago. In view of the disruption of the Democratic party at Charleston and Baltimore, I understand that the American party, as it was called, anticipated that some difficulty might arise in the affairs of the Government, that some obstacle would be presented to the enforcement of the laws, and they met together in Baltimore, and decided what? That they were in favor of the Union, the

Constitution and the enforcement of the laws. Where now is that American party? Does it yet live? That party that cast about an equal number of votes with the Douglas men in the State?[49]

Are they yet true and firm to the platform upon which they fought the canvas of last November? If so, I wish to know whether they can, upon this occasion, back out from the position they assumed, and which was inculcated upon the honest yeomanry of the country? I apprehend not. Sectionalism has taken possession of this country. That is the true theory of the anticipated difficulties now before us. It is not from wrongs that we are now suffering, is it? Surely not. As I understand it, the Democratic party and the American party of this country, but a few years ago, when in the majority in the Government adopted the doctrine contained in the compromise measures of 1850, in regard to the Territorial question. It is true, that the Republican party, during their canvas, advocated the right and duty of the Government to exclude slavery from the Territories. So soon as they come into power, however, they pass three territorial bills abjuring their own doctrine, and coming up to the doctrine laid down by Henry Clay in 1850—the same doctrine that was incorporated in the Kansas-Nebraska measure—leaving the people of the Territories to settle this difficult question for themselves. There is not to-day a single law upon the statute books of the Federal Government denying the right of a citizen to enter into any territory belonging to the Union. Then there is not a real grievance upon that question, but the anticipated grievance that may hereafter come.

Since the present Congress has met and in fact since the secession of a portion of the Southern States, if I am not incorrectly informed upon the subject, a proposition has been adopted by Northern States, by a majority of Republican members of both Houses of Congress, by which an amendment is to be engrafted upon the Federal Constitution, to the effect that that instrument shall never be so amended as to permit Congress to interfere with the institution of slavery in any State without the consent of every State in the Union.[50] If that be so, it is now in our power at least to close this difficult question for ever and ever. Then let our southern sisters come back into the Union. New York, New Jersey, Pennsylvania, yea, Rhode Island, Massachusetts and Maine, and even Vermont, will vote for the proposition, and let amity and that concord and that spirit of conciliation and harmony once more reign in this government that has been unnecessarily destroyed of late.

Now, Mr. President, one word in regard to this report and I am done. I am aware that men of all parties are in this Convention. It becomes our duty, sir, to do something to remove the apparent fears of the people. So far as I am concerned, I have no fear whatever that the dogmas of the Abolition party will ever find a place upon the statute books of this country. Never, sir, never! If it be their design to make the white and black races of this country equal, why, let me ask, are they not placed upon an equality in Massachusetts, Vermont and New Hampshire, to-day? Why is it, sir, where they have the power, that they do not put the negro upon an equality with the white man?[51] We all know that it is not so. My impression is, and I give it merely as my impression, that the combination of conservative Republicans, with the extreme and radical Abolitionists, has upon the present occasion worked out all the effects and consequences that it was ever intended to do. The object and design was to put out of power one party and put into power another. Parties are often radical in the acquisition of power; but when they come to administer the government, they will moderate their desires, and act not unlike Mr. {Millard} Fillmore, when he was appealed to by his friends to know whether he had not abandoned his views upon the negro question, when he said that the Fugitive Slave Law should be executed in the streets of Boston—though they ran red with human blood—and he answered that whilst he announced different opinions, he was a member of Congress from the Buffalo District, but he was now in power as President of the United States, and had sworn to support the Constitution and the laws passed in pursuance thereof, and that was all the answer he had to give.

Sir, parties may be extreme in their views in the acquisition of power, but in the administration of it they have to obey a written charter of right; they have to confine themselves within the limits of the law, and when that is the case we need have no fears whatever.

{Delegate Henderson brought his address to an end by observing that "we owe a duty to ourselves and to the country at large," to restore peace and quiet to the country and, if possible, arrest the revolution "that must inevitably engulf us in ruin unless it be speedily checked." He believed that the Crittenden amendment held the possibility of bringing a resolution to the slave question. He concluded on a personal note. "I, sir, in the spirit of love for the institutions of America—in the spirit of devotion and attachment to that flag that has given honored protection and character to the American citizen in every land and on every sea—would gladly lay down all that I have, and start anew in the world, could I thereby preserve the Union and perpetuate the best hopes of man."}

Source: *Proceedings of the Missouri State Convention Held at Jefferson City and St. Louis, March, 1861* (St. Louis: George Knapp & Co., Printers and Binders, 1861), 84–93.

John Thomas Redd, Jr.
March 14, 1861

Attorney John T. Redd Jr. (1816–1884) was born in Jefferson County, Kentucky, and represented Marion County in the convention.

Delegate Redd blamed the North and the Republican Party for unceasing attacks on slavery and at the same time, while he believed in the right of secession, condemned the departure of seven southern states as "hasty and unwise." Although he was convinced that the ultimate goal of the northern party was "the extinction of slavery everywhere," he stated that it did not propose immediate abolition. But, within "thirty years as certainly as the sun will rise to-morrow," there would be enough free states to approve an abolition amendment. Like many of his colleagues, Redd was concerned less about current antislavery threats than future dangers.

Mr. REDD. Mr. President and gentlemen of the Convention, it is well known to you that I entertain the view that a State, when its constitutional rights have been trampled under foot, and its institutions endangered, has the right to declare the compacts that unite it with its sister States at an end. I did not desire to discuss that question for the plain, palpable reason that under my view, that right does not spring up until a state of case exists under which every man who is not for unconditional submission would admit that the right of revolution exists. But while I would concur with a large majority of this Convention, and of my fellow citizens of Missouri in the existence of a right to defend the Constitution and maintain our institutions, if necessary, out of the Union, and by force of arms, I did not desire to enter into any controversy with them as to the name by which the right should be called. I was willing they should call it revolutionary right, because revolution has no terrors for me. I care not for a name. I did not intend to discuss this question at all; but I have heard Southern men and Southern States denounced as traitors to their country; I have seen the charges made by the New York Tribune, and papers of that character, and I have heard those charges reiterated and detailed here, and I deem it but an act of justice to *them* to discuss this question.

{Delegate Redd then expanded on his contention that the Constitution was a "compact" between the states. No state, he argued, could end its relationship with the federal government without just cause. He then stated that the northern states had violated the Constitution "again and again" by declaring that slave stealing was no crime and that "man cannot hold property in man." These constitutional transgressions were not done "by a few ultra Northern men, it has been the deliberate act of Northern States, speaking through their own chosen authorities."}

I will say here, in passing, that I have no complaint to make of the invasion of Virginia by John Brown. The Northern States are not chargeable with it. It is not right that they should be held accountable for it, unless they knew it beforehand, and failed to arrest him in his design. Therefore I have said nothing about him. But in regard to this subject, it is stated in the majority report that when a few mad men invaded the soil of a Southern State, and spilled the blood of Southern men, they were hanged, and that was the end of it. Now that, in my judgment, is not the voice of history. It is true that John Brown was hung. It is true many of his confederates were hung; but was that the end of it? No, they were canonized as martyrs to liberty and justice. Was that the end of it? No! for two of them escaped, one to the State of Ohio, the other to our sister State of Iowa. They were demanded by the governor of Virginia, but those States violated their compact by refusing to deliver them for trial. *That* was the end of it.

Now, by the third clause of the second section of the 4th article of the compact, the States agreed with each other that when a man bound to render service in one State escaped into another, first, that he should not be discharged from service by the law of that other State; secondly, that that State should deliver him up. This was a compact not between the North and the South, because they were then all slave States except one, and she (Massachusetts) held slaves within her limits. But it was emphatically a compact between all the States—a compact by which Missouri is bound as much as Illinois. For if a fugitive slave escapes from Kentucky into Missouri, Missouri is bound first not to attempt to set him free by her laws, and secondly, to deliver him up to his master. Now, have they complied with that compact? Here is something that they agree to do, and something that they agree not to do. The thing they agree to do is, that they will deliver him up. The thing they agree not to do is, that they will not attempt to set him free by their laws. I say they have violated that compact in both its branches. They have done it willfully, deliberately and repeatedly.

How have they done it? They covenanted that they would deliver him up. Did they make any law to carry that covenant into effect? Where is the State that made it? No, they violated that covenant. They neglected to do that which they covenanted they would do. How about the other branch? They covenanted they would not attempt to free him by their law. Have they not done it? Have they not passed their personal liberty bills, with the avowed object of making that slave free? They have. Aye, and they have gone further than that. Some of them have imposed heavy penalties upon the master, for daring to assert his constitutional rights to the possession of his slave within their limits. Now, if these States had lived up to their compact—if they had passed no law to set that slave free—if they had passed laws to secure his delivery to his master—there would have been no necessity for Congress to legislate upon the subject at all. But they violated that compact, and Congress, the common agent of all, that was created for the purpose of establishing justice, interposed and enacted the fugitive slave law. How did the Northern States treat that law? Did they respect it? Did they obey it? No. They treated it as they had treated the Constitution—they trampled it under foot—they nullified it, again and again, by deliberate State legislation; and they have done all this against the earnest entreaty of their sister States. They have done it against the repeated remonstrances of a united South.[52]

Again, gentlemen, the South has ever held that every citizen of the United States, without regard to where he was born or reared, has a right to go into any territory opened for settlement and take with him the members of his family and his property; that the Constitution of his country, that palladium of his rights, extends over him in that territory and protects him in his family and his property. I say that has ever been held by the South to be the doctrine of the Constitution—and it has been so held by the Supreme Court of the United States. I ask you, is it not right? There are members here of a party who have ever disputed that proposition. I ask them to throw aside if they can, the shackles of party prejudice, and pass upon that proposition, and tell me whether it is not right and just. Now, the North denied it. The Northern States, controlled by a feeling of anti-slavery and hostility to the slave institution, say to Southern men, you may go to the Territories, but you must leave behind members of your family—those who were born into your household—those to whom you have become attached next to your wife and your children—you must leave them behind. More than that—they have said, if you dare to take them, we will, by Congressional legislation, take them away. We will sever your family ties, and take from you your property, and make you no compensation. Is that right—is it just?

Now, a gentleman on this floor has said, have you any complaints to make against the General Government? Has the General Government ever violated the rights of the South? I say, yes, she has. Look at your Oregon bill. What do you find there? You find a clause excluding Southern men from that Territory, unless they leave behind them their slaves; or, if they take them there, the law takes them away. Then, I say, the General Government *did* violate that right in the passage of the Oregon bill. It also violated that right in the passage of the

Missouri Compromise bill. But I do not complain of the General Government on that ground. And why? Because Southern men, for the sake of peace and the Union that they love, consented to surrender a portion of their rights, thinking that, with that surrender they would appease this moloch of anti-slavery. But what is the condition of things now? How do we now stand? How *did* we stand when these States went out? A President was nominated upon principles that were destructive to the institutions of the South; a President was nominated who had enunciated the destructive error that our Government, as our fathers made it, partly slave and partly free, could not so continue to exist—that in that condition it was a house divided against itself, and must fall. It is true he said: "I do not anticipate that the house *will* fall—but the cause of division will be removed." Well, how removed? He tells you, "an irrepressible conflict is going on between freedom and slavery." He did not enunciate the exact truth there. It is a truth, but not the whole truth. He should have said that freedom, or this anti-slavery party, is waging an "irrepressible conflict" upon the slave institution of the South. If he had said that, he would have said the whole truth. But he tells you that that conflict cannot stop—that it must continue until slavery is in a process of extinction. That is how this cause of difficulty is to be removed. The Northern States indorsed these doctrines and purposes by large margins. Well, now, how is slavery to be extinguished? Gentlemen, while I do not admire the principles of this party, I must say this for them, I *do* admire their sagacity; I do admire the ability of the men who stand at the head of that party. If wisdom exists in adapting means to ends, then they are wise men and sages. Let us look at their plan. Their object is the extinction of slavery everywhere, or the establishment of the proposition that man cannot hold property in man. How is it to be done? We have fifteen slave States and eighteen free States. We have territory enough for fifty more States.[53] We are opening our Territories to the settlement of a foreign population, and that population is anti-slavery. Now, tell me, if you confine slavery to the limits of fifteen States; if this immense territory, extending across to the Pacific, is to be peopled and brought into the Union as States, and with a foreign emigration enough to people a State every year; how long would it be before the free States would have a majority of three-fourths of the States in the Confederacy? It would occur in the next thirty years as certainly as the sun will rise to-morrow. When it does occur, what is the result? Now, I will do this anti-slavery party the justice to say, that I have no doubt they are honest. I have no doubt they are acting up to the convictions of their own minds as to the duty that they owe to themselves and to their God. I judge men by their acts, and not by what they say. What is the leading principle of that party? It is this:—that slavery is a social, moral and political evil. What is the corollary of this position? It is this:—that it is our duty to get rid of that evil wherever we can reach it—hence we will abolish it in the Territories—hence we will abolish it in the District of Columbia—hence we will interfere with the inter-slave trade: contending, as they do, that under the Constitution they have the power to do this. But they do not propose, for the present, to interfere with it in the States, because they admit that the Constitution guards and guarantees it there. It is true, there is one element of that party I do not charge its acts upon the party, and they (are not responsible for it,) that takes even a broader position, namely, that slavery is an evil of a character that no law can guard, no constitution can sanctify; and that there is a higher law that nullifies the Constitution, and hence that element is for abolishing it in the States now. But, as I said before, I do not regard that to be the position of the Republican party.[54]

I honestly believe while the Constitution continues as it is, that the Republican party would not attempt by Federal legislation to abolish slavery in the States, for I believe that they are honest, but their principles would in the course of time necessarily lead them to that consummation. When thirty years have rolled on—when State after State has been brought into this Union, until the free States have the requisite majority of three-fourths—what will they do then? Then, for the first time in their history, the anti-slavery party controlling those States, will have power under the Constitution to abolish slavery in the States. Having the power, the moral responsibility, according to their views of slavery, rests upon them to do it, and as they are *honest* men, they will do it. And if that doctrine was established—I mean the doctrine of exclusion of slavery from the Territories—then the handwriting is upon the wall that announces the destruction of slavery, as certainly as it announced the destruction of Belshazzar.[55]

Now, in such a condition of things, our Southern brethren seeing that this Constitution had been violated—that it had been trampled under foot time and again—that a system of policy had been established that would inevitably result in the overthrow of their institutions, and that the time was rapidly approaching when that system of policy would be carried out—severed the tie that bound them to the Union, and under the law of nations declared the compact at an end, and took their fate into their own hands, as did the sires of 1776. While I admit that they had cause, yet I do not approve of the act. While I admit the right, I do not approve its exercise. I believe it was hasty and unwise that a portion of these fifteen States, those who seceded, having homogeneous institutions with the Border States—having the same constitutional rights to protect, ought, in good faith to have staid in the Union, and co-operated with us in endeavoring to settle the sectional issues upon some basis that would have secured our slave institutions and constitutional rights. That is what, in my judgment, they ought to have done. They have not done it. They had a right to judge for themselves.—But while I must condemn that act as hasty and unwise, I must say that they are not traitors, unless our sires in 1776 deserve that name. The States in the compact between them delegated certain specified powers enumerated in that instrument to the General Government created by them. There are certain other powers, such as to coin money, the enactment of an ex-post facto law, or a law impairing the obligation of contracts, &c., the exercise of which prohibited by that instrument to the States, and for fear that the Government they had created would usurp powers not delegated (a word that implies the power to take back) to the General Government by the Constitution, and not prohibited by it to the States, are reserved to the States or to the people. The power recognized by the law of nations to be in every sovereign State to declare any compact entered into by it with other States at an end when violated by the other parties to the compact not being one of the powers delegated to the General Government, nor one of the powers prohibited to the States, stands like the power to legislate on the subject of contracts, the descent of property, or the social relations of husband and wife, parent and child, guardian and ward, master and servant, as one of the powers expressly reserved to the States, and may lawfully be exercised when the occasion arises, without incurring the odium of treason.

Now, gentlemen, while I differ with the first resolution in this majority report, I would be willing to assent to it if the word "motive" was substituted for the word "cause." Can it be there is no cause, notwithstanding these repeated violations of the Constitution, notwithstanding the fact that our institutions are in danger—can it be that there is no cause for exercising the right of secession? I certainly admit the right, and that cause exists for its exercise; but I oppose its exercise, and I shall continue to oppose its exercise, so long as there is a hope of obtaining our rights in the Union. I oppose its exercise, not because I deny the right itself, but because I love the Union. I love it because our fathers made it. I love it because we have enjoyed under it unexampled prosperity. I love it because of the glorious memories that cluster around it; and it is my love for the Union, and no other motive, that makes me oppose secession, or revolution, and actuated by the same motive, I shall continue to oppose it so long as there is a hope of amicable settlement. But if the time should unfortunately come—God forbid that it should—when all hope is lost—when Missouri is driven to one of two alternatives, either to submit to the aggressions of this sectional party, and surrender her slave institutions at its bidding, or go out of the Union—I shall then, notwithstanding the committee organized upon this subject by this body, introduce upon this floor an ordinance of secession. The action of no such committees, and the threats of no party, have any terrors for me. But I never will do it until then. I believe that this Union, and our institutions in the Union, can be saved; for though the political firmament is covered by a dark and portentous cloud, within whose lurid bosom slumbers the whirlwind of desolation and civil strife, yet there are breaks in that cloud, through which we can see the glimmering of the sunlight of peace. But if the time arrives when these breaks shall close, and that cloud present but one aspect, and is ready to burst over our heads, and the border slave States shall have gone out, then my voice shall be raised for Missouri's standing up for her rights out of the Union—aye, unto the last dollar and to the last man.

I am opposed to this amendment.[56] With one alteration I could give it my hearty assent. If it is taken to mean Missouri while she remains in the Union will not aid a seceding State to make war upon the General Government, I give it my hearty assent, for Missouri will not do that—Missouri is for peace. But if it means that Missouri in *no* time to come, no matter what changes may occur, will not aid a seceding State in making war upon the General Government, I cannot give it my assent, because Missouri may be a seceding State herself. I hope she never will be. God forbid that she should! But she may be, and if this difficulty be not settled upon some basis that will guarantee her institutions, she will be. With one change, namely, that Missouri will not aid a seceding State, *while she is in the Union*, I will give my assent; but if she is driven out, and war is made upon her, and upon the other States, she *will* and *must* be prepared to resist the General Government.

Source: *Proceedings of the Missouri State Convention Held at Jefferson City and St. Louis, March, 1861* (St. Louis: George Knapp & Co., Printers and Binders, 1861), 129–36.

Thomas Tasker Gantt
March 14, 1861

Thomas T. Gantt (1814–1889) was born in Washington, DC. A lawyer, he represented St. Louis in the state convention. During the war he served as judge advocate, United States Volunteers.

Delegate Gantt spent his time on the floor in a spirited rebuttal of John T. Redd's address. While believing that the North's actions regarding slavery had been "aggressive in the first instance," the response of the South had "gone beyond the limits of a just defense." Gantt strongly rejected the compact theory of government labeling it "political heresy." He observed that since many of the northern states were reconsidering their personal liberty laws, the South should not use them as a reason for disunion. They were primarily enacted to protect their citizens against being kidnapped. In response to the northern objection to the extension of slavery into the territories, Gantt responded that since

1848 when slavery was prohibited in the Oregon Territory, Congress had excluded slavery from no territory. (The last time Congress organized a territory with a prohibition clause had been in 1849 with the organization of the Minnesota Territory, a result of the 1789 Northwest Ordinance.) Gantt decried the secession action of seven states and the "falsehoods" employed to energize the public by noting, "Nothing, indeed, is more striking in reviewing the history of this sad crisis than the degree to which political jugglers have deposed the people from their rightful supremacy, and impudently told them that they were stripped of power, and henceforth are to be merely subordinate."

Mr. GANTT. Mr. President, in entering upon this discussion, I shall first address myself to the proposition discussed by the gentleman {John T. Redd} who last engaged the attention of the house. He set out to prove that secession was a right that could be exercised without a violation of the Constitution, and then went on to show that while he contended for the right, he considered the action of our Southern sisters hasty and ill-judged, and would not recommend Missouri to follow their example. But in order that this might be one of the steps Missouri might take hereafter without guilt, and in order that she might understand distinctly what her rights were, he labored to show that *it was a right*, and might constitutionally be exercised. I have seldom, Mr. President, listened to an argument as to the nature of the Constitution which was so decidedly in the teeth of the canon against self-slaughter. He refers to the fact that the Constitution was ratified by the States, and that, until ratified by the States, it was not binding upon any of them—nay, that until it was ratified by nine States it was not binding upon the eight which had previously ratified it; he refers to that fact to show that it was nothing but a compact between the States, and that the framers of it commenced their work with a lie in their mouths. He admitted that the preamble used the words: "We, the people of the United States," &c., "in order to form a more perfect union"—a union more intimate and perfect than had been effected by the Articles of Confederation—but he said that the persons who thus sat in convention were *delegated* by the States, and that they merely had the office of *"scriveners,"* and that the instrument which was the work of their hands was nothing more than *proposition* until ratified by the States in their sovereign capacity. He committed the great mistake, as I conceive, of imagining that the Union of these States, and the Federal Government, which is the result of it, is nothing more than the confederacy which it replaced, or a compact between sovereign States, which may be dissolved at the pleasure of any one of them, and it is to that proposition that I shall proceed to address myself.

I say that in the course of his argument he was forced, in the first place, to admit that the recital of this Constitution declared that it was the work of the people of the States, and that they were welded together into a consolidated government by its terms. He went on to say that *because* the instrument which declares this thing had no validity until it was ratified by the States in their separate and sovereign capacities, therefore—and it was a monstrous *non sequitur*—therefore the instrument, being so ratified, operated not according to its tenor, but according to the idea which he had, I wont say the effrontery, but the hardihood to announce. Why, sir, does not every lawyer—and the gentleman is an able one, an ornament to the bar, and administrator of the laws on the bench—know that when an act of an agent is ratified by the superior authority, that ratification has relation to the inception of the instrument, and makes it good from the beginning, and that, when the act of an agent is thus ratified according to the terms and tenor of the act itself? How otherwise can it be? Would it not be the grossest contradiction in terms, to say that an instrument which is a certain declaration, or which declares there is a surrender by States previously sovereign of certain of their sovereign attributes; that these are for wise and patriotic purposes, vested in a central government, which is to administer them for the common good, and to save the country from those evils which have resulted from the imperfect Union which this perfect and perpetual Union was designed to replace—I say it is not a contradiction of terms, to say that when this solemn act is thus ratified by the competent parties, it is not to be as a ratification of the instrument upon its face, but the ratification of something entirely different? In the name of common sense, what does ratification mean? These States have the power to say whether this should or should not be the expression of their will. They declared that it was, and by virtue of that very sovereignty which he invokes, they had power to make good all that the preamble and the various sections of the Constitution declare; and one of those declarations is, that it is the act of the people, and makes us one people.

Mr. REDD. Is it not to be looked upon rather as an estoppel?[57]

Mr. GANTT. No, sir; it is not an estoppel, but a direct grant. Estoppels are odious. There is no occasion to invoke them, except when other rules of interpretation fail. Well, then, this being the plain import of the instrument, this reference to the simple meaning and working of the ratification, sufficiently disposes of the argument of the learned gentleman upon that subject. It is plain that this instrument is what it professes to be—that it makes us one people for the purpose of a General Government, though for the purposes of State governments we are thirty-four.

It has seemed to me, when the learned gentleman was arguing the right of secession, and when he made *that* dependent upon the supposed existence of a confederacy of States, or between sovereign States, and not upon one Central Government formed by the surrender of some of those sovereign attributes which were enjoyed by the States before this Central Government was formed,—it has seemed to me that he was wasting a good deal of time and trouble, unless he intended to say that this right so strongly contended for was one the exercise of which was essential at the present time. However, after he had, to his own satisfaction, (but I think by the aid only of a fallacy which has been sufficiently exposed,) maintained that this right existed, he went on to declare that its exercise would be unwise, and he proceeded further to say that the North had been guilty of great aggressions upon the South.

Well, here my friend and I are not so far apart as might at first sight appear. He is very much mistaken if he fancies that I stand here as the apologist of the Republican party. I am a Democrat of the strictest sect, and have nothing in common with the peculiar views of that party. There have been aggressions beyond number, and a spirit of meddlesomeness, a spirit, so to say, of Phariseeism,[58] has been displayed by portions of that party, in their conduct towards the South, which is intolerable to me as a Southern man, and it will not be endured. But, on the other hand, there have been acts committed on the part of the South, which are unfortunately almost as objectionable, perhaps quite as much so, as the provocation to which they owe their rise. The action of the North, upon the subject of slavery, has been, in my judgment, aggressive in the first instance; the acting of the South has been retaliatory, but it has gone beyond the limits of a just defense. But I am coming to that subject again, and merely wish to put myself right on this point, for when I speak of the offenses of which the North has been guilty, I am disposed to echo a good deal of what the gentleman has said.

I will not stop to consider what he said respecting the law of nations, as applicable to the Southern States, because I have shown that there was no such compact as he contends for. I have shown that there is an entirely different relation existing between the members of this Union, from that which exists by virtue of a compact between sovereign States.

The gentleman has said that if the South had seceded without cause, then the North has a right to coerce her, and not otherwise. Now, having shown that this Government is not a compact—that this Union is not a Confederacy, that it is something which has replaced the Confederacy, and which made it for all the purposes enumerated in its preamble an entirely different thing—I have disposed, I apprehend, of that *sacred* right of secession. But did not the gentleman see, when he admitted that *if* the Southern States have seceded without cause, the States of the North have the right to coerce them; that he was opening a door as wide to civil war as the bloodiest advocate of what is sometimes called coercion could possibly have done? Who is to be the judge of "good cause?" Is it to be the South? Is it to be the North? If there are so many independent States on one side, and so many on the other, differing in respect to that "good cause," and there is no common arbiter, what shall decide between them but the sword?

Sir, the position of those with whom I have the pleasure of acting here, is far more satisfactory, and looks to a pacific and complete solution of this troubled question, without a reference to that bloody arbitrament. We think that the General Government, whose laws, made in accordance with the Constitution, are the supreme laws of the land, is for all the purposes of a satisfactory settlement in contests between various States, the arbiter whose fiat will not only be decisive but peaceful. But to that matter I shall come a little further on.

The gentleman next proceeded with an enumeration of the grievances of which the South had to complain at the hands of the North. He spoke of the second clause of the second section of the fourth article of the Constitution, respecting the surrender of fugitives from justice, and claimed, as I understood him, that whereas this was a binding right—and this I have no inclination whatever to deny—and the North had in repeated instances refused to comply with its constitutional obligations, the South had never done anything of the kind. Now, it did so happen that during the past winter I heard a discussion upon that very point, and, fortunately for me, for it saved me a little trouble. One of those who were engaged in that discussion, in showing that the fault was not *entirely* on one side—as in what human controversy is it?—showed that amongst the earliest violations of the letter, at least, of that provision of the Constitution was a case occurring in Virginia. Now, I say, that no matter in what State, when or where, the violation occurs, if it does occur it is to be condemned.—I am satisfied that not one of this Convention hears me who does not echo this sentiment. The rights which that Constitution guarantees must be not only sacredly but punctiliously observed, if there is to be a continuance of that spirit of fraternal amity, without which our Union may indeed exist, but can never answer the purposes for which it was designed. So that it matters not to me whether Virginia or any other of the Southern States, or the Northern States have violated that provision. The fact only shows a diseased state of public morality, which must be cured on pain of death. In my judgment a greater number of violations of that sort have occurred upon the part of our Northern brethren. Whenever the subject of negro slavery has been the bone of contention, and a demand has been made upon a Northern Executive for the rendition of a fugitive from justice in which that fugitive was charged with some offense which derived its felonious character from the relation between master and slave, there has been in my judgment a failure to comply with the spirit of the Constitution upon that subject. For that, I say, I condemn the North. I call their attention to that violation, and I say that that wrong must be redressed, or worse will come of it. But what then? Is that a cause for secession?

I have just shown that the right of secession does not exist. But if the right did exist, I will say, is that a cause for secession? Could reason impel us to take that remedy for such a disease, a remedy which would aggravate tenfold the malady of which we make complaint? What compact, I pray you, was ever made—what Constitution—what code of laws has ever been made amongst mankind, and remained in force for twelve months without receiving some violation? Are we to throw away this fabric of government—are we to cast aside the blessings of which it is the minister, because there are bad men who need to be punished by the laws for which that Constitution makes provision.

The learned gentleman said further, that the South has been tried by the sentiments of Yancey and other extremists, and that this is not fair. It is not fair—he is right in saying so. It is not right to try the South by the sentiments of such men as Yancey, and Rhett, and Miles, and many others whom I might name.[59] I take it they are in a very small minority in the South. But on the other hand, is it fair to try the Republicans either by anything but their platform? The learned gentleman has referred to the sentiments which have been expressed by what he called an element of that party, meaning, I suppose, the Abolitionists, of whom Phillips, Garrison, and Tappan are the exponents.[60] Now, I recognize a distinction between the Republicans and the Abolitionists. I am glad to recognize that distinction, for if I supposed that the Republican party were animated by the same sentiments which those Abolitionists hold, I would be compelled to the conclusion that a large majority of the people of the North were in league with some of the worst men of the South, to put into actual practice this pestilent doctrine of secession, and overthrow, beyond remedy, all that makes us a nation. Those men, then, to whom he makes reference, are not to be taken as the exponents of the Republican party. We must look to the platform of that party; the platform upon which Mr. Lincoln was nominated; and I think we should also, in common fairness, look at the votes of the same party in Congress during the last session. It will be altogether a departure from the common rules by which reasonable men are guided, to try any party by the windy rhetoric or uncharitable speeches that fall from the lips of sensation orators, who, seeing their opponents applauded amongst a crowd for a sentiment which is all in one extreme, must needs outdo their rival in the other extreme, in order to gain the popular favor. It will not do to try a large party by the utterance of any such men, to say nothing of the fact that no one yet ever knew the *ins* and the *outs* to speak with the same caution. The *outs* are aggressive and bold; they have no responsibility upon them; but the *ins*, or those that get into office, feel the responsibility of their words—they must live up to the sentiments which they profess—and they are therefore careful not to say anything which they cannot maintain. Such too, has been the conduct of the Republican party. My friend was just enough to that party—for whom certainly I do not intend to be the apologist—to say that he believed them, as they now stood organized, to be sincere in their intention, indicated in one of the articles of their platform that they would not interfere with slavery in the States in which it existed by virtue of the municipal law.

He then proceeded to refer to the affair of John Brown. There, again, I found there was no difference of opinion between him and me. That act was viewed by me with the same abhorrence which I imagine it has excited in the minds of all right-minded men of the North and the South. That a number of persons who seemed to be utterly regardless of their duties as citizens—utterly reckless as to evil consequences of the most demoralizing sentiments, did speak of that old villain as if he were a saint and a martyr, is but too true, and I have no kind of doubt that the exasperating effect of such language as that has led, in a material manner, to the fomenting of the present troubles. Undoubtedly, no unjust or false word is said by any party, no injustice or wrong is done by any party, without bringing its bitter fruits—perhaps upon them alone, perhaps upon those who are innocent, and suffer with the guilty by a common fate. So that, upon that subject, there will not be much in the sentiments of my friend to which I am disposed to take issue.

He passed on to the third section of the fourth article, and said that this section had been systematically violated by the North.[61] Well, it is too true that it has been violated in a most nefarious manner; and if I did not believe that a returning sense of justice, that a condition of being appalled at the fearful consequences of their wickedness, was now seizing upon the minds of the North, I should do what I have never yet been able to do—*despair* of the Republic. But I say that now they have been brought face to face with the consequences, that now their most solid men have taken it upon themselves to examine and condemn the unconstitutional acts of their Legislatures, and that a sentence of condemnation has gone forth throughout the land—I refer you particularly to that which has been issued from the city of Boston, in which such men as Ex-Gov. Gov. [sic] Clifford, and the Ex-Chief Justice Shaw[62] declared, in the most solemn manner, that the personal liberty bill of Massachusetts could not remain upon the statute books without a violation of the oath which every member of the Massachusetts Assembly took to preserve the Constitution of the United States. Do we not see the fruits? In how many Northern States, for the last six months, have not those Personal Liberty bills either been repealed or so far advanced to repeal, that their end is easy to see. Does that give no comfort to my friend? Does he not see in that a peaceable, orderly redress of a wrong—a returning sense of justice on the part of those who have in a moment of madness inflicted that wrong?

Mr. REDD. I do, sir.

Mr. GANTT. I am glad that he agrees with me on that point, also. I think, then, that I may properly pass to another breach of the subject, for it is conceded that, although this is a wrong and a source of irritation, and a very great one, yet it furnishes no cause for the secession of which the Southern States have given us as an example.

The gentleman said that many of the States of the North had passed personal liberty bills with the avowed object of making slaves free. Now, I think he is wrong in that. I have looked into those statutes, and in no instance have I ever seen that purpose avowed. The gentleman will correct me, if mistaken in this statement. If he can furnish the name of the State, or the date of any statute in which such purpose is declared, I now ask him to inform me.

Mr. REDD. I do not recollect the date. When I spoke I alluded particularly to the statute of Maine, which not only declared the slave free, but provided a law whereby the master was punished as a felon for attempting to reclaim him. I think it was passed in 1858, but I am not certain.[63]

Mr. GANTT. I think my friend is mistaken. I think the style of the act indicates the purpose which was declared on its face. The *avowed* object was to protect their citizens against being kidnapped; but that, in my judgment, does not make the matter a great deal better, for I am quite satisfied in my mind that by reason of that avowal they only added the sin of hypocrisy to that of violating the Constitution. I am quite satisfied that it was the purpose of the framers of the laws to enable bad men to put in the way of the master who came to reclaim his slave every possible obstacle; to make it an expensive and dangerous business to him, and, in short, to make any one who was not most resolute, come to the conclusion that he had a great deal better acquiesce in the loss of, than attempt to recover, his property. I say that I will use the strongest language of which I am master in condemning such legislation—in denouncing such a spirit, and in declaring that if this Union is to be what it was in times past, that legislation and that conduct must cease. As to the particular statute of Maine, that can only be determined by reference to the statute book, and both my friend and myself are too much of lawyers, and too partial to the habits of accuracy, which the practice of our profession encourages, to be willing to discuss the import of an act without having the written letter before us. I will then say nothing more upon this subject until I have had an opportunity of examining that book.

The gentleman next passed on to say that the South has been excluded from the Territories. I asked myself when I heard that remark, "from which of them?" I know that in the Territories which have been most recently organized, no such exclusion has been found, and I really did not think that the Oregon bill was opposed by the votes of Southern men. David R. Atchison[64] is supposed to be rather sound upon this particular subject. Mr. Green[65] is supposed to be sound, upon *this* point at least; and it was such men as those in the two houses of Congress who voted for that bill, and Jas. K. Polk of Tennessee, approved it.[66] This bill was adduced by my friend as one measure of which the South had to complain; and after having done so, he said he did not complain of it because Southern men acquiesced in it. Then why enumerate it?

He also spoke of the Missouri compromise bill. That, too, was passed by Southern votes. And here let me say that one of the most serious misfortunes that ever happened {to} the South was that they could get Northern votes enough to co-operate with them in sweeping away that compromise, thereby violating that sound rule of statesmanship, which warns us *quieta non movere*,[67] that tells us that the true plan is not to disturb a settlement which has answered its purpose and been acquiesced in for a long time.

In all the territories which have been recently organized, we look in vain to see any of this exclusion of which the gentleman speaks; and if he means what the popular orators of the party have said upon the hustings, I must answer that I pay no more regard to the sentences of exclusion proceeding from such sources than I would to the whistlings of the idle wind.

Mr. REDD. I think the gentleman misapprehends me. I did not enumerate those acts as grievances. I said the question had been asked, and the propositions laid down on this floor, that the General Government had *never* violated the Constitution, but that in that proposition I could not acquiesce.

Mr. GANTT. Do you refer to the report?

Mr. REDD. No, sir, to the argument of speakers on this floor. I take the position that those bills *did* militate against the interests of the South, but that the South does not complain of them, because she acquiesced in them.

Mr. GANTT. I do not think it was said on this floor that the General Government had *never* violated the Constitution upon this subject. But it *was* said, and I think the assertion can be very well maintained, that the General Government has *never*, upon the subject, discriminated unconstitutionally against the rights of the South. If it passed the Missouri Compromise, at whose insistence was it passed? If it passed the Oregon bill, who asked for the passage of that bill and acquiesced in its passage? Will it be fair that a man, or community, or party, or section, shall first ask for the particular action of any body else, and then complain of that action? Certainly not. I think then, that part of the gentleman's argument is sufficiently answered.

But it was said that the natural consequences of the organization of the Territories and the exclusion of slaves therefrom, as contemplated by the Republican party, would be that at the end of thirty years the Northern States would have such a majority that they could alter the Constitution at their pleasure, and that they would use the power thus acquired for the overthrow of the peculiar institution of the South. So far the gentleman went in his statement. I did not directly understand, however, the conclusion that was deduced from the establishment of that proposition. I did not understand him to say that because he had some reason to fear that trouble would happen at the end of thirty years, *therefore* it was wise to precipitate *now* all the calamities which an active imagination might lead us to apprehend as possible after thirty years. But if he had said it, with all possible respect for him, I think that I may say that the position would have required no answer. If it be better to bear the ills we have than to fly to others that we know not of, how much more certain is it that it is a great deal better not to precipitate ourselves into certain calamity, because at the end of a long period it is *possible* that that same calamity may, peradventure, come upon us.

"The South has been rash and hasty in its action, but are not traitors, unless our sires in '76 were traitors;" he further proceeds to say. I must say that I object to that. I must say that I object to taking the names of those whom he must pardon me if I *will* call traitors—I now refer to Yancey, and others of the same stripe— he must pardon me if I say that I cannot endure to have their names taken in the same breath with those of the venerated men who lived in and adorned the former period of history. The men of '76 revolted against oppression. They rose to throw off a tyranny which was too great to be endured. They rose to throw off a degree of misgovernment which Heaven never intended that man should bear—which never, in particular, it was designed that the Anglo Saxon race should bear—the most jealous race on earth of its liberties and rights. They endured until endurance could no longer be, and then, in a religious, patriotic spirit, and in a calm, dignified manner, appealed to the god of battles. Has anything like that action distinguished the men of the present day in the South? I am afraid I should be out of order, if I should speak of them as I feel. So far from their having any real grievances to redress, for years past, sir, there has been an industrious manufacture of every pretense upon which discontent could be founded—the schemers! the pests!—by which the "Southern mind could be educated, the Southern heart fired, and an opportune moment seized to precipitate the cotton States into revolution." That base design has been impudently avowed, and I am sorry to say it has not met with *universal* condemnation; but, thank God, it is almost universal. What has been the course of the States in pursuance of the design of that architect of mischief, Mr. Yancey? Why, after South Carolina had seceded, after she had declared, through one of her Representatives, that if the whole North could sign a blank sheet of paper, and give it to South Carolina to write her conditions upon—the conditions on which she would be content to remain faithful to her obligations as a State in the Union— still that instrument would not suffice, still would not do; and South Carolina, in taking her position, virtually said this to the North: "We are going out; nothing can stop us, and no concessions, no modifications, no amendments of the Constitution, can prevail upon us to remain in the Union." I believe Georgia was the next in order. But how was the secession of Georgia brought about? Who that remembers that Georgia was one of the States of the Union, that her citizens are American citizens, that amongst them are those two illustrious men, Stephens and Hill[68]—and others, too, (but I can never mention the names of those two men without gratitude and reverence, and for their sakes I hesitate to speak otherwise than in the kindly spirit of Georgia,) can think without a blush of shame that the most infamous falsehoods were sent over the telegraph, in order to precipitate the passage of the act of secession by the Convention? It was reported through the telegraph, that the Federal Government had sent an army to Charleston: that operations were commenced by the bombardment of that city; that old men, helpless children and women were being slaughtered by the hundred; that the city was in flames—in short, all the horrors which attend upon the most bloody war, were declared to exist there, and by the act of a tyrannous Federal Executive, and under the influence of that lie—that infamous lie—the Convention of Georgia was induced to pass its ordinance of secession. It is not so very unnatural that, under such a monstrous misrepresentation, hasty and unjustifiable action might have been had. But what I do say is, that it is reprehensible that when those members who voted for that ordinance found they had done so under the influence of a villainous misrepresentation, they did not move for a reconsideration.

{The Journal here added a footnote which read: "NOTE.—Mr. GANTT desired [it] to be noted here that it has been suggested to him by a friend that these lying telegrams were put in use for the purpose of influencing the election of the convention, not the action of that body after it was elected.—Mr. GANTT spoke from the recollection of the matter, and stated in the newspaper at the time; and the matter may very well be, as indicated by the correction, for which he makes his acknowledgments."}

I believe, Mr. President, that whatever the *politicians* of the States of Georgia, Alabama, and others, have done, if the *people* of those States could have been properly consulted, different results would have appeared. I think the people have had a prodigiously small share in the acts of secession. Nothing, indeed, is more striking in reviewing the history of this sad crisis than the degree to which political jugglers have deposed the people from their rightful supremacy, and impudently told them that they were stripped of power, and henceforth are to be merely subordinate. Look at Alabama. At the election for delegates to the Convention which was to take into consideration the relations between Alabama and the Federal Government, less than one-third of the votes cast in November were cast, on both sides, for and against the members of the Convention. Of that one-third three-fifths were given to candidates in favor of secession, and two-fifths for Unionists or co-operationists, (for that is about the boldest name that even good and true men can take in this Southern reign of terror,) so that three-fifths of one third—equal to one-fifth of the whole popular vote—actually represents the proportion of the State of Alabama which was in favor of going out of the Union.

One of the gentlemen who preceded me, said that he looked confidently to the time when the people of those much injured Southern States would march back into the Union over the bodies of the traitors who had thus misrepresented the popular wishes. And I think that is literally true. The time will come, and I expect it will come before I am gray, when those States will come back, bringing, if necessary, the heads of those traitors with them, and offering them as a peace offering.

While the gentleman contended for the right of secession, he admitted that its exercise at the present time was not advisable; but, said, he, if the time ever should come when the people of Missouri would be deprived of their rights, and it would become necessary for the purpose of resisting intolerable oppression, to dissolve our connection with the General Government, he would offer an ordinance of secession. Well, it is impossible to find much fault with a proposition so carefully guarded. When that time comes, when the oppression of the Federal Government becomes intolerable, why, no doubt, we shall do many things—in short, when the sky falls, we shall catch larks! But, in the meantime, it is most unwise to speculate as to such action upon an hypothesis which never may happen; for the happening of which there is no political probability.

Now, I believe I have gone over the main points advanced by the gentleman, and given my reasons for what I regard as a political heresy, namely, the idea that this nation is a compact of States and not a Union.

As to the amendment now pending, I will say that it legitimately brings up all the topics which we can fairly consider in connection with the relation which Missouri occupies to the National Government.[69]

> {Delegate Gantt's speech against secession continued into the following day. At the same time that he expressed his opposition to secession, he also voiced his support for slavery stating that "I believe the negro race is blessed by the institution of African slavery, as it exists in these United States," and that "no where else is the African race so well cared for, as in the slave States of North America."}

Source: *Proceedings of the Missouri State Convention Held at Jefferson City and St. Louis, March, 1861* (St. Louis: George Knapp & Co., Printers and Binders, 1861), 136–48.

Abram Comingo
March 15, 1861

Abram Comingo (1820–1889) was born in Mercer County, Kentucky, graduated from Centre College in Danville, Kentucky, was admitted to the bar in 1847, and moved his practice the next year to Independence, Missouri. During the war he served as provost marshal of the sixth district of Missouri, and later in the US House of Representatives from 1871 to 1875. President Grant appointed him to a commission to arbitrate with the Sioux Tribe for the possession of lands in Dakota bordering on the Black Hills.

Delegate Comingo, in this brief address, expressed the belief that secession was heresy, and that if the Crittenden amendment had been passed, "slavery would never go north, and that it would not to any extent be established south of that line." The territorial issue according to Comingo, was a mere "abstraction," but one that if not dealt with satisfactorily would have grave consequences: "Civil war will ensue, as well as a total dissolution and disruption." He ended by favoring the adoption of the Moss amendment declaring complete neutrality because "its rejection will be fraught with evil."

Mr. COMINGO. When this discussion was commenced on the amendment offered by the gentleman from Clay, I did not intend to participate in the debate, but I have since changed my purpose, and determined to present a few views touching this matter. I have entertained the hope, until the last few days, that we were in the way of adjusting our difficulties; but that hope has been greatly depressed by the news I find in the morning papers. I have been fluctuating between hope and despair for many days, but this morning I feel greatly depressed. I feel that this nation is at this moment standing upon a treacherous crust of a fearful volcano.

I regret that the discussion of this subject has taken such a wide range. I could have wished the members had confined themselves more strictly to the amendment. It is very important that we should, in this matter, act with great deliberation; and we should be sure, before we act, that we are right. There has never been a time when such important questions have been presented for consideration; and I feel that we ought to ascertain what is our duty, and then discharge that duty, whatever it may be. What we are doing, Mr. President and gentlemen of the Convention, does not, and will not affect alone our interests, but will have an influence in all coming time. If we take steps which may involve the nation in civil war, we shall do that which in all future time we shall have cause to regret. Consequently, I say, that we ought to use the utmost deliberation before we attempt to do anything.

We are taught, by philosophy, that a small stone cast into the bosom of the Atlantic, produces a vibration that is felt upon its extreme verge, and if this is true in natural philosophy, how much more true is it in moral philosophy, and that every act we commit on this occasion will have a relation to all future time. I am not disposed to go into a history of the difficulties that now surround us. I do not conceive that it is important that we should discuss the history of Abolitionism or Republicanism. But we should deal with facts as they now exist. I do not conceive that history has anything to do with the subject. It seems to me to be about as wise for the planters of the Mississippi, in time of a crevasse, when the waters of the Mississippi are inundating their cotton fields, to stop and debate how much of that water came from the Ohio, how much from Lake Itasca, as it is for us to debate what have been the causes which have led to the present crisis in our affairs. Entertaining that view, I shall not attempt to trace the history of Republicanism, or trace any of our past history.

I am ready to use all my feeble efforts towards the preservation of our Union. I shall never cease my labors until the last ray of hope is extinguished. But while we are upon this subject, we should talk about it plainly—we should not attempt to conceal our view. So far as solving the present difficulties are concerned, I trust no gentlemen will feel disposed to occupy any equivocal ground. At the same time that we feel that our duty requires us to talk plainly in regard to our difficulties, we should speak in terms of the utmost kindness. I do not feel like casting censure upon any man at this time. This is no time for crimination. We should neither denounce a man for being a Secessionist, neither should we decry a man for being a Republican. But if we can do anything to save the country, I feel that our labors will have been sufficiently rewarded. I presume from what I have studied in regard to this matter that there is but one point upon which there is any difficulty, or upon which this Government is to be shipwrecked. It is well known to you all, I presume, that the Crittenden propositions received great favor, and would have been submitted to the people but for one of its clauses, that relating to the subject of slavery in the Territories. I shall not attempt to discuss the merits of that proposition, but call your attention to the fact that there would have been no difficulty in the way of adjusting our present troubles had it not been for that clause.[70] Now, gentlemen of the Convention, this difficulty which is exciting so much attention, is an abstraction, according to my opinion, although it is true there is a principle involved in it. It is maintained by some that slavery should be protected in every foot of Territory, and by others that slavery should not go into the

Territories, and this is the platform upon which Mr. Lincoln was elected. It is proposed by the Crittenden proposition that we shall divide this territory— that all north of a certain line shall be free and all south all slave. Our friends of the North say that they will not grant this privilege, and the tendency of their acts thus far has shown that they are willing to disrupt the nation and drench it in fraternal blood rather than concede this right. I maintain that if this line were drawn slavery would never go north, and that it would not to any extent be established south of that line. I think every man ought to concede this proposition and sacrifice so much of the principle as to permit us to take slavery south of that line. There is no use of disguising the fact that unless this question is adjusted in a satisfactory manner, civil war will ensue, as well as a total dissolution and disruption.

But what shall Missouri do at this time? Shall she secede at this time? No. I do not act here with that view. I do not propose that Missouri shall secede, but that she shall speak out to the border free and slave States, and to the whole Union, and tell them we want this Union preserved. We should tell them that we desire to settle difficulties, and we should indicate the plan of doing it. She should act as mediator; and therefore it is I favor the amendment of the gentleman from Clay {James H. Moss}. The resolution offered by the Committee on Federal Relations does not, I think, place Missouri in a proper position. Acting as she should in the capacity of mediator, I say the amendment is well calculated to place her in her true position. It has been said that it contains a threat and an ultimatum. I do not so regard it. I think it gives the people of both sections to understand what we require and what is the duty of the North and South. It is true we are part and parcel of the General Government, yet we tell them that as a part we will not aid in coercing seceding States. I say that we should not menace the South nor the General Government, and when we say we will not countenance the Southern Confederacy in a war, or the General Government in a war upon the Southern States, we are taking the proper position.

I do not think the resolution at all conflicts with our duty. We are dealing with the subject as it now presents itself. We say that as matters now stand, we believe that our line of duty lies here, and we will follow it. It is known that the very moment the General Government makes war upon one of the seceded States, all hope of adjustment is gone. There can be no adjustment if the General Government should attempt to supply Fort Sumter, or collect the revenue, or pass a law abolishing ports of entry. Any attempt of this kind, to cut off the supplies by means of the sword, would be coercion. I know that many differ with me in this respect, but I am opposed to the General Government moving one foot in coercing these States, in the manner which I have indicated. I am opposed to the reinforcement of Fort Sumter, or of supplying Fort Pickens, when such an attempt would involve the nation in such a manner as to place our difficulties beyond the hope of adjustment. And the moment that the first drop of blood is shed the last ray of hope vanishes, and then all the border slave States will go out. You cannot stop the tide of public feeling. I have as patriotic devotion for the Government as any man, but I cannot ignore the fact that when civil war is initiated then you must take a decided stand, and cannot be neutral. Then where shall we go? I think there cannot be any question about that.

What is the true position in regard to the seceding States. Now, I shall not discuss the Constitutional question of secession. I do not know that any gentleman will undertake to justify secession under the Constitution. I think secession is a heresy, and that no such term is applicable to the action of any State. The only term that can be used is revolution. Then I say that South Carolina and the other six States have revolutionized, and that the revolution is complete, and they are this day, although their independence has not been acknowledged by the United States, an independent government. This revolution has been bloodless, but it is complete. There was a time when this revolution could have been arrested and its leaders hung for treason. But I ask, gentlemen, whether that state of case now exists. They have formed a constitution. Mr. Buchanan never attempted to arrest the tide which has taken them out of the Union, and now they can never be brought back, except by treaty or stipulation. Do you suppose that if Lincoln marched an army to the South, and captured Jeff. Davis, the articles of war would not be observed, and that Jefferson Davis would be treated otherwise than as a prisoner of war? Those who are now living under that government are subject to it. They have taken an oath of allegiance to it, and now their action cannot be considered treason. You will find that action of that character is not so regarded by the best authorities. I say then, the course indicated by the amendment to the resolution under consideration, is the true one. I am unwilling to forego hope that peace may be restored. I hope this amendment will be adopted, because its rejection will be fraught with evil.

Source: *Proceedings of the Missouri State Convention Held at Jefferson City and St. Louis, March, 1861* (St. Louis: George Knapp & Co., Printers and Binders, 1861), 148–50.

Dr. Moses Lewis Linton
March 16, 1861

Moses L. Linton (1808–1872) was born in Logan County, Kentucky, received his medical training at Transylvania University in Lexington, Kentucky, and moved to St. Louis to join the faculty of the St. Louis University Medical School.

Dr. Linton began his short speech by objecting to James Moss's amendment on neutrality. It was superfluous, "it is nullification, it is revolutionary, for it asserts that Missouri will not do what the President, by constitutional power, can require her to do." Linton approved of the majority report of the Committee on Federal Relations. Believing that there existed no cause to prompt the secession of seven states, he contended that slavery was secure throughout the South because of the Republican platform and the constitutional amendment agreed to by the Committee of Thirty-Three in Congress that prohibited the federal government from interfering with slavery in the states. The territorial issue was not relevant because slavery had already spread to "all the Territory that slavery claims." He further observed that the Republican Party did not prohibit the institution in recently organized territories north of the 36°30′ line. To guarantee slavery in future acquisitions of land, as the Crittenden resolution held, was to Linton, "wanton wickedness." He also dismissed the personal liberty laws of northern states because "it is very well known that the General Government pays no attention to them." For Linton, Thomas Corwin's proposed amendment prohibiting the federal government from interfering with slavery in the states was the most he could want. "Those who will not be satisfied with that, will not be satisfied with anything."

Mr. LINTON, I propose, Mr. President, to occupy the attention of the Convention for about five minutes. I object to the amendment of the good gentleman from Clay, for two very good reasons: First, that it is supererogatory; and second, that it is revolutionary. It is supererogatory, because Lincoln has already said that he does not intend to invade any State, and that he does not intend war. What is the use, then, of passing a resolution that he shall not do it. I say for that reason, it is supererogatory. But, in addition to this, it is nullification, it is revolutionary, for it asserts that Missouri will not do what the President, by constitutional power, can require her to do. If it be constitutional for the President to call upon us for aid, then the passage of the resolve declaring that the State will not extend such aid, would be a wanton act of nullification. So far as principle is concerned, I should like to know what difference there would be between Missouri saying to the General Government, we will resist your civil demands, and South Carolina declaring that the General Government shall not collect the imposts at Charleston? I say, then, it is secession in disguise—it is an ultimatum and nullification. Although I do not believe that gentleman intended it, yet it is so, and, to use a sort of illustration, with which I am familiar, and which I borrow from the gentleman from Greene, (Mr. Orr,)[71] it does not matter what you meant when you gave strychnine, if you gave enough to kill, it will kill, although you may have given it to cure.

I do not say, Mr. President, that I do not wish this amendment to be sanctioned by the Convention, because I know it will not be. I do say, however, that I hope it will not get a dozen votes. I know I have taken the right view of it, and that it is useless and wanton, and that it is nullification and secession. So much for the amendment.

I wish merely to say, as the debate has taken a wide range, a few words upon the majority report. I approve it. As others have said, however, it is not exactly such an one as I would have gotten up, although it is a much better one probably than I could have devised. I regard it as the ablest document which has been elicited by the present troubles of the country. For myself, I could take less than it asks, and for the sake of the Union, I would ask even more than it asks.

I feel very differently, now, Mr. President, from what I did three weeks ago, when I first met you in Jefferson City. I felt nervous, then, and alarmed; but I do not feel so to-day—I feel that it is all right with Missouri. When I got to Jefferson City, and heard nothing but the Marsellaise and Dixey, in place of the Star Spangled Banner, I felt uneasy enough. And when I heard Governor Jackson speak, I felt badly—and when I heard the Commissioner from Georgia, I felt uneasy.

I recollect, with my colleague, Mr. Broadhead,[72] hearing Dixey played on the streets, and that we stepped up to the leader of the band and asked him to play the Star Spangled Banner. He said, (being a foreigner) "Oh me 'fraid to play that." We assured him there was no danger, and he played one stanza of the Star Spangled Banner, but immediately went off into Dixey, and of course we went off in disgust. But we need have no fears of Missouri now or hereafter.

Mr. President, there never has been any adequate cause why any State should secede. There never has been even a respectable pretext. What have any of them suffered? Have armies been quartered amongst them in time of peace? Have hordes of officers been sent among them to eat out their substance? Have they been taxed without the liberty of being represented? Have they been denied trial by jury? Have they suffered any of those wrongs declared by Jefferson in the Declaration of Independence? Not at all. What outrage has any State suffered? I answer nothing that would in any degree justify secession. They cannot complain that slavery will be interfered with in any of the States, for the Chicago platform repudiates that doctrine—the Committee of Thirty-Three has set that matter forever at rest. They have taken it out of the power of Congress to interfere with slavery in any of the slave States.[73] Slavery already exists in all the Territory that slavery claims. The only Territory that the Crittenden Compromise claims—and there is no Wilmot Proviso to prevent it from going into the territories of the North. But the territory hereafter to be acquired is what the Crittenden Compromise provides for. Mr. President, I think it is a wanton wickedness to interfere and endeavor to raise a quarrel about property which we may never have. I say it is wickedness to endeavor to raise a quarrel of that sort. And I say more, that I hope we may never have another foot, if it be used as an element of strife.

As to the personal liberty bills, it is very well known that the General Government pays no attention to them; that it executes the fugitive slave law in spite of them. I have read that one fugitive slave returned in one instance cost $40,000. What do we care for their bills if the General Government carries its laws into effect in spite of those bills? Have any of these seceding States ever lost a slave by any of those bills? No, they have not. But Southern orators say that, like a scorpion girt by fire, slavery will sting itself to death, if bounded. It is obliged to be bounded by the Crittenden Compromise, and, if it is so dangerous, it will have to sting itself to death, even if the Crittenden Compromise is adopted. If it is the scorpion it appears to be, we had better get rid of it in Africa than extend it through our territories. At any rate, we cannot blame people for being afraid of the scorpion. For myself, I want nothing better than the Corwin Compromise reported by the Committee of Thirty-three. Those who will not be satisfied with that, will not be satisfied with anything. South Carolina will not be satisfied with anything, and in this connection I beg leave to read an extract from a letter from a gentleman who is well known, was a Bell Everett man recently and a good Union man more recently and always. He says "the amendment of the Committee of Thirty-three which has been submitted by them to Congress for ratification, will put that question forever at rest, and all reasonable and patriotic Southern citizens ought to be satisfied. But I fear it will not be enough for the seceding States. Their whole course has been unpatriotic, selfish, and unmanly to other States and especially to the border States. There is no patriotism in the secession movement, and no patriotic State should give momentum to it by uniting in defense of it, and in my estimation Missouri should be the last of the border States to do so. Laying aside every patriotic consideration, her interest is opposed to such a step—1st. her expenses must greatly exceed what they now are; and 2nd, her geographical position is such that if she should go into a Southern Confederacy, in five years she would be a free State; and that, however much you might wish it otherwise, she would present the strange fact of being nominally a slave State without having any slaves, and of being hitched on to an aggressive Southern aristocracy without any sympathy with it."

A VOICE. Who is that letter from?

Mr. LINTON. From Judge Booker of Ky. Mr. President, it is sad to see a great nation destroyed for no other reason than a mere punctilio. The South desires to be permitted to do what she would not do if permitted, namely, to carry slavery into Territories unfitted for it. What a cause to fight for and to bleed for—a war for the extension of slavery where it could not exist! Surely, there must be some great advantage in secession, when the people rush into it without a cause. No, there is not. It will only intensify the evils complained of—it will make a Canada of every Northern State, and the North will be a bourne from which no slave traveller will return. Disunion is a terrible remedy for a slight and trivial disease. It is like cutting off an arm to cure a wart—it is like jumping out of the frying pan into the fire. But, sir, Missouri is saved—I am satisfied so far. I think the people of the seceded States will be brought back, and that the names of their betrayers will be placed in the same catalogue as those of Burr and Arnold.[74] I do not like to use the word traitor, especially as gentlemen here object to it, but, sir, I must say that many of these men of the South are what I used to think was meant by the word traitor; and if I do not apply it to them, I must erase it from my vocabulary. I am certain they are traitors according to the dictionary of Henry Clay, and according to Webster's dictionary. The country, sir, is not doomed to disunion—its flag is not to be torn to tatters—it will yet wave over every sea and be recognized in every land—its constellation is better known than the stars of heaven, for it is familiar to millions on whom the stars of the North never shone—to millions who never beheld the Southern cross. Glorious FLAG! next to the emblem of man's salvation, I revere the glorious UNION! next to the church of the Loving God—thou hast my homage.

Source: *Proceedings of the Missouri State Convention Held at Jefferson City and St. Louis, March, 1861* (St. Louis: George Knapp & Co., Printers and Binders, 1861), 167–69.

Emilius Kitchell Sayre
March 16, 1861

Emilius K. Sayre (1810–1899) was born in Morris County, New Jersey. A farmer by profession, he represented Lewis County in the state convention.

Delegate Sayre began his address by stating that he objected to the Moss amendment because it essentially declared that "we will not give assistance to the one party or to the other, under any circumstances, reserving to ourselves a neutral position, where we can stand pusillanimously by, in a place of safety, while our brethren are fighting this great quarrel." "I think it would be sufficient to say," he continued, "that any act of hostility on either side, while we are in negotiation, would be regarded as unfriendly and offensive." He then moved on to note that the concerns of the people of the South are "nothing more than the apprehension of these future aggressions." To support this idea Sayre provided a long analysis of offensive comments said and claimed (but not enacted) by Republicans—including that "the white man and the black man had equal rights"! They (Republicans) did not intend to abolish slavery immediately, but gradually. At the same time, Sayre considered the people of the seven seceded states "patriots" for anticipating the eventual demise of slavery in Republican administrations. Their concerns were real: "It is not necessary to say that slavery can not continue at all under these perversions of the Constitution; nor is it necessary to say that the entire South must be rendered desolate if slavery is abolished." His solution was to support Delegate John T. Redd's proposal of conferring with the remaining slave states and recommending amendments to the Constitution that would protect slave property.

Gentlemen have undertaken to argue upon this amendment the whole questions which have divided the North and the South. It is a proper occasion, therefore, and a duty imposed upon me, to bear my testimony as to what the voice of the people with whom I am acquainted declares upon this subject. With that object I wish to make a comment or two upon the positions which have been taken here, in regard to the action we should take. I was sent here to attempt to provide guarantees for our rights—rights that have not only been invaded and trespassed upon, but much more; rights that have been and are threatened to a more serious extent. What we have suffered, and now, in point of fact, are suffering, is set forth clearly and honestly, so far as it goes, in the majority report. But there is more than this—there are the threats of future aggressions, and so far as I am concerned, and so far as the great mass of the people of the South are concerned, the cause of the action they have taken, is nothing more nor less than the apprehension of these future aggressions. I know it is thought to be an imaginary apprehension, but I stand here to declare, in my place that these apprehensions are based upon facts, real, solid, and dangerous.—Why! how could it be otherwise? Here are millions of people of our own race, and no one will say that the great mass of them are cowards or fools, who, because of this apprehension, have sacrificed the ties which bind them to their country. They are patriots, and they have shown their love for their country to be as sincere and devoted as the love of country ever shown by any other people. They have parted with all the glorious memories of the past, and with all the bright hopes of the future, as connected with our Government. They have imposed upon themselves enormous burdens, they have run the risk of individual ruin, of having their rights wrested from them, and their property, by an aggrarian [sic] distribution, thrown into new hands. They have been, and they are the most conservative of all people upon this whole globe, yet they have broken up their government and incurred these great dangers. Would they have done this without a cause? Never. What then was the cause? We have seen, that for nearly thirty years past, the minds of the Northern people have been poisoned, and their consciences perverted, by being taught, from the school room to the desk of the minister, in the forum, on the bench, in the Court House, in the Lyceum, in the literature of the country, in the nursery, and even in the prayers of the family alter, that slavery was a sin, and that it was incumbent on them to wage war upon it. The people of the south have repeatedly, and in all possible ways, declared to the people of the north, that the opinions you are inculcating, are dangerous to our peace and destructive of the security of the Government, and if persisted in, must necessarily result in separation. They were answered with fresh aggressions and additional insults. The contest has continued from the time of the anti-slavery societies of 1815 and 1825, to the more active abolition societies of 1830 and 1835, until it at last resulted in the great Republican party, and the nomination of a candidate in the Presidential canvas in which Buchanan was elected, upon a platform containing a set of principles, which were not the least changed in substance and effect in the platform adopted at Chicago. Thus these views have been continually on the increase, and the party has grown in power in spite of the warnings of the South, until in consequence of these views hostile to the institutions with which their existence is entwined, the South has been compelled to separate. Does any one deny the existence of such a party, whose sole idea is hostility to slavery? It cannot be denied. For what other purpose does the party exist? and what is the ultimate purpose of this great party? They do not expect to accomplish it on the instant, but by a course of legislation, perhaps judicial legislation, which shall place the institution of slavery gradually and inevitably in their power, until at last it shall be done away with. They declare that the Northern mind will never rest satisfied until slavery is put in the course of ultimate extinction. No man can deny that this is their main object; that while they may be compelled to bear with it temporarily in the States where it exists, yet their policy is to effect the obliteration of the evil. We have heard it said from this stand that the people of the South do not suffer, that they have no cause to complain, but that the people of the border States suffer; that our slaves are taken by mobs, and carried away; that the whole South has not suffered one-hundredth part as much as the State of Missouri.—I do not wish to contradict it. But what will be the case if this great party succeeds and abolishes the system of slavery? What will be the situation of our brethren in the South where the slaves outnumber the whites as four to three?[75] They are more interested than we are, are necessarily more sensitive, and forsee [sic] the approaching evils from a greater distance. What is to become of them when the tie which binds the slave to the master is unloosed and the system is abolished?

Do you not know Mr. President, that their hillsides are exhausted? that the rice fields, the sea islands, and the cotton fields, where the strangers' fever prevails, cannot be cultivated by the white man? When slavery is abolished what is to be their situation? The horrors of St. Domingo are but peace in comparison to what must befal [sic] that afflicted country, the moment that the tie which binds the slave to the master is severed.[76] Better far that the waters of the Atlantic, and of the Gulf envelop them in a common ruin. They have constantly warned the Northern people to cease this war upon them. The Northern people have been regardless of this warning. The people of the South now see that the North is in a condition to carry its threats into execution, and that, though the object may not be accomplished in their day, it may be in the day of their children and grandchildren, who may be compelled to live perhaps on an equality with the negroes, perhaps obey them as masters. Is it wonderful that these people resist? Is it to be expected that they shall be less sensitive on their children's account than on their own? Why will not gentlemen look these facts in the face, as the real cause which has compelled the Southern people to take their decided step. I have waited in vain for other gentlemen, who understand these things better than I do, to give voice as to the real causes which have led to these troubles. It is because of real and well grounded apprehensions of terrible and intolerable dangers. It would not be difficult to give the doctrines and platforms of the party which has been inculcating this anti-slavery idea for more than a generation, but it is sufficient to take up the last—that formed at Chicago. The more especially, as objection has been made to their being judged except by their platform.—What is the testimony of this platform as to the intentions of this party? They have clothed their nefarious purposes, and on that account all the more offensively to us, in a pretended devotion to the Declaration of Independence, and the Constitution of their country. But the exposition of their meaning, and construction of the Declaration of Independence and of the Constitution is well known over the whole land. We know how these planks of the Chicago platform were offered one day in the Wigwam to propitiate Mr. Giddings[77] and the radical abolitionists, and after debate and full consideration, they were voted down. We know how then Mr. Giddings left, scraping the dust from his feet. How then the action of the Wigwam was reconsidered and those planks adopted, and Mr. Giddings then was willing to occupy a position among them.[78] Their construction of those planks in the platform are pregnant with the utmost significance. They place particular stress upon the clause which declares that all men are created equal. Was it not natural that the South should be alive to the danger, when this great party, numbering over eighteen hundred and sixty thousand voters,[79] elected their President to carry into effect this great truth. They expressed what was meant, and gave a significant meaning to it,—that the white man and the black man had equal rights! Sir, a President has been elected upon that platform, who, though he avowed in some of his speeches in the Senatorial canvas with Mr. Douglas, that he was not in favor of giving the right of suffrage to the negro in Illinois, that he was not in favor of repealing the so called Black laws there, yet afterwards repeatedly scouted the distinction of colors and races as to the equality of rights. He has said in his triumphal passage from his home to the Presidency, that he would yield no inch of his platform, and at Independence Hall, on the very birth-day of the father of his country, that he would like to save the country, if he could do so consistently, with this principle. But if he could not do so it would be awful. Rather than yield it, he was about to say, he had rather be assassinated on the spot, giving full assurance that he intends to press the principle till he sees the burthen lifted from the shoulders of all men. The men whom he has selected for his Cabinet, share his sentiments. If there is one man whom we dread more than any other, it is CHASE of Ohio.[80] How long is it since he declared his approbation of the practice of amalgamation. Mr. SEWARD is his principle adviser.[81] He did more, perhaps, for his election than any other man, and again and again has expressed the same sentiments. It is these things that have compelled the South to take their present course. I was pleased with the address of the gentleman from St. Louis, (Mr. GANTT)[82] yesterday, in which he held up to merited scorn and contempt, the action of the Northern Legislatures, which, adding the sin of hypocrisy to the guilt of violating the Constitution of their country, have attempted to obstruct the rendition of fugitive slaves. But I regretted to hear him place as a full set off, against their continued persistent and systematic violations of Southern rights, the inhospitable treatment, as he called it, of Mr. SAM'L HOAR and his daughter, in 1835, in South Carolina.[83] Mr. HOAR went there as an emissary of the anti-Slavery Societies of the North, clothed with authority from Massachusetts, to contend for and secure negroes' rights in South Carolina. It was a regular part of the warfare on the South to do away with slavery. It was one step in the progress to their one great end. They talk about people of the South being upon a volcano—in a house filled with combustibles. They abound with all such figures of speech, which are calculated to strike terror into the hearts of those who choose to listen to such nonsense. If these things were so, Judge HOAR went there with a lighted flambeau in his hand, to set fire to the institutions of the South—not in a manly manner, but meanly sheltered by the presence of his daughter, whom he brought to protect him from the indignation of an outraged people. For their treatment of him they cannot be accused of a want of chivalrous feeling. They desired him to return home with his daughter. They were not willing that she should shield him while making war upon them. I do not think the sending home of Judge HOAR and his daughter from South Carolina is a full answer and "counterpoise" to the encroachments of the North. Their action was in self-defence, and as it turned out afterwards, in accordance with the law. There has since been a decision made upon the right of the black man to citizenship.[84] This decision denies the right. More than this, the South have considered, and still consider it, not only an outrage but an insult to question their title to their slaves.

In another part of the constitution, freedom of the press and freedom of speech are provided for. It is known that the North construe that to mean that they have the right to send emissaries and inflammatory handbills to the south to incite the slaves to insurrection.

In another part of the Constitution, Congress has power to regulate commerce. Under this power, the North claim the power to interdict the inter-state slave trade, to prevent a citizen of of [sic] Kentucky from moving to Missouri with his servants.

In another part of the Constitution, the citizens of one state are guaranteed the privileges and immunities of citizens of the several States. Under this power, the North claims that a free negro of New York or Massachusetts, has a right to move to Missouri, and enjoy the privileges of citizenship.

In another part of the Constitution is secured to Congress the power to pass all needful rules and regulations respecting the territories and other property of the United States. Under this power they claim the authority to abolish slavery in the territories, in the forts, dock-yards, and in other posts of the United States, as well as in the District of Columbia; that thus, where our common government has jurisdiction, shall be found an asylum for runaway slaves. It is well known, that they claim under the power over the territories and other property, that they have the right to prohibit slavery; and under the Fremont platform they declare it their duty to do it where they had the power. Though this is left out, in plain words the substance is retained in a more offensive shape in the Chicago platform. By some strange delusion they have come to the conclusion, that they are as responsible as the South is for slavery in the South. We claim that we have under the Constitution, the same right to be protected in our property, that they have in theirs. For our allegiance, we are entitled to protection; that allegiance and protection are correlative; They [sic] limit and deny our right to protection to our slave property, and declare that all our remedies for securing and re-taking it, shall be taken away from us whenever they have the power; that the laws of God may be vindicated in accordance with their perverted views of the lessons of history, and the laws of progress and civilization. All their acts declare that slavery is of purely local and not of general character as to its remedies; and that we have a right to have it protected only in the places where our State laws have jurisdiction; and if our slaves are found in the forts, arsenals, or other property of the government, they can and should withhold from us our right to recover them. They declared so, four years ago, that it was their right and duty to wield the policy and patronage of the government in hostility to our institutions. That particular language was left out of the Chicago platform; not because of any change of views, but because their purpose was sufficiently palpable without it.

These, then, are the purposes of the Republican party of the North, and by putting demagogue judges upon the bench of the Supreme Court, they can easily, and in a short time, be carried into full effect, by judicial legislation, without going to Congress for new enactments. Seven States believing thus for most abundant reasons, that these are the intentions of the Northern people, and perceiving that they have sufficient power to execute them, have separated themselves for their protection. It is not necessary to say that slavery can not continue at all under these perversions of the Constitution; nor is it necessary to say that the entire South must be rendered desolate if slavery is abolished. What, then, is our duty? We complain of the South because they have taken their mode of redress without consulting us. They have taken, to say the least of it, a rash remedy. They have deserted us when we were sharing their dangers, and worse than all, have left us behind with diminished numbers and strength to fight their battles for them. It is natural that they should be more sensitive to these great evils than we are. It is a matter of life and death with them. Our slaves may be taken away from us, but still, Missouri, degraded and dishonored, PERHAPS, can exist. But with them it is a question of life or annihilation. From the speeches of gentlemen, it might be supposed that our troubles and complaints were for the few slaves stolen from us; but that is nothing in comparison. Our great trouble is the war that is made on us by the North, without cause. They make this war upon us, though they continue to use rice, cotton, sugar, tobacco and hemp; to buy and sell, and trade, and grow rich upon the products of slave labor. We sympathise [sic] with our Southern brethren; but we regret that they should have attempted to take their remedy into their own hands, without consulting us. They should not have done it. We should not, and we cannot now go with them. I think the course which they should have taken, is the course proper for us to take now. We should confer with the remaining slave States in a Convention, and set forth in clear, and firm, and moderate terms, our claims for guarantees by amendments to the Constitution, and should urge the North and the South to assist in having them adopted. When the Committee on Federal Relations made their first report, I was not satisfied with it; but now, since they have made their amended or supplemental report, recommending the Convention of the remaining slave States for conference and consultation, I can cheerfully give it my support, as a mode well calculated to secure the guarantees we need. By this Convention, and a subsequent Convention of all the States, I indulge now strong hopes of working out a remedy for our troubles.

{Delegate Sayre concluded his remarks on a hopeful note: "I can not believe that if sufficient and proper guarantees are accorded, they [the seven states that had seceded] would hesitate long before returning to us; until the redress which they and we desire is obtained, it does not become us to take any steps for their destruction."}

I will now offer my substitute.
The amendment was then read as follows:
Amend by adding, "that the commencement of hostilities by either must necessarily be regarded by Missouri as unfriendly and offensive."
Mr. WRIGHT. Is that to be added to the original resolution?
The CHAIR. It is an amendment to the fifth resolution, instead of the amendment offered by the gentleman from Clay.

Source: *Proceedings of the Missouri State Convention Held at Jefferson City and St. Louis, March, 1861* (St. Louis: George Knapp & Co., Printers and Binders, 1861), 169–73.

Uriel Sebree Wright
March 18, 1861

Uriel S. Wright (1804–1869) was born in Madison County, Virginia, briefly attended the United States Military Academy, studied for the bar in Judge Henry Tucker's law school in Winchester, Virginia, and began his practice in his home county. In 1833, he moved to Marion County, Missouri, and three years later was elected to the Missouri House of Representatives (1836-1837). Following his term in Jefferson City, he relocated to St. Louis where he established himself as an attorney of note. Wright disagreed with the removal from office of Governor Jackson and, although a Unionist, served throughout the war as judge advocate for the Confederate Army in Richmond.[85]

In this robust defense of Unionism, Delegate Wright directly confronted John T. Redd's address given four days earlier opining that "his ordinarily clear and logical mind has been lost in the transcendentalism of secession metaphysics." Wright lectured his colleagues on the divided sovereignty created by the United States Constitution and observed that "if secession is right, there can never be any government on earth." Spending much of his time analyzing the Republican position of nonextension of slavery into the western territories, he observed that the Republican-controlled Congress had (only two weeks before) organized three western territories without attaching the Wilmot Proviso's prohibition clause. "Is that not," he concluded, "patriotic evidence of a disposition on their part to meet the issue in the spirit of kindness?" Like other southern Unionists, Wright also emphasized the fact that if the seceding states had remained, the Lincoln administration would have been powerless. "Two departments of the Government would have been against the Administration—Congress and the Judicial department. The Senate would have been against him, the House would have been against him, and the Supreme court would have been against him. What, then, could he do under our form of Government? Where was the source of any actual danger?"

Mr. WRIGHT. Mr. President, the first resolution reported by the majority of the committee declares that at present "there is no adequate cause to impel Missouri to dissolve her connection with the Federal Union, but on the contrary we will labor for such an adjustment of existing difficulties as will secure the peace, as well as the rights and equality of all the States." This resolution, Mr. President, involves a wide and important inquiry. I was astonished to hear from some members in this body, that it was not profitable under our present exigencies, to determine the nature and character of the Government under which we live—that all theories touching the form and nature of government, are not practical in this exigency, and that all mind or genius spent in that direction is a waste of intellect. If I thought so, Mr. President, I should not rise in this body to make a speech at all. But on the contrary, I hold, sir, that this resolution makes such an inquiry as that, the most pertinent of all interrogatories: how can we determine whether we ought to break it up or hold out, unless we appreciate its nature. Is it a military government? Is it a constitutional government? Is it a national government? Is it any government at all? Or is it a thing that can be dissolved at the whim and caprice and pleasure of any of the actual or supposed parties to it. The birthright of an American citizen, what is it, Mr. President? Is it an estate at all? We—you and I, sir—have been proud of it from the first moment that we had conscious thought on the question of liberty. It gratified us in our youth? [sic] And it has been the admiration of our manhood. What is this birthright of an American citizen, not the question of your right to live in Missouri as your home, or in Virginia or Tennessee, but the right to hold that other, and that broader, and that larger title, the title to be an American citizen, whose home and country is not the State in which he lives, but who can rightfully and proudly claim that his empire stretches to the widest and utmost verge of our boundary—bounded by two oceans—reaching to the cold regions of the North, and going South to the semi-tropical clime.

> {Wright here continued to muse on the nature of the federal government. He argued that the national government was neither a consolidated, nor a military government, but a benevolent one characterized by "its appeal to the calm, reasoning, and Godlike, lofty, noble qualities with which man has been endowed by his Maker."}

In these days and this wild reign, not of terror I will not say of *terror*—I will drop the t—in this wild reign of *error*, it is very fit that we discuss this question of right, the constitutional right of a State to dissolve this Union. From what sources do those who are for this proposition derive the power?— First it is said that the States who made it were independent, sovereign States. Well. *Secondly*, that they have reserved powers to themselves. Grant it, also. Thirdly, that being sovereign and independent States, they can resume their sovereignty whenever they choose. So that, according to this argument, the right of peaceable, constitutional secession, springs out of the nature of our Government, out of the character of the parties who formed it, and the inherent, inalienable and untransferable power of sovereignty which originally belonged to the parties who entered into this compact.

Now let us practically test this thing by the Constitution itself. I would say to the gentleman from Marion, (Mr. Redd,) that his ordinary clear and logical mind, has been lost in the transcendentalism of secession metaphysics. I would ask him if he thought that when this Government bought Florida, not for the value of its soil, not for anything but a military reason, in order that this Government might hold the key to the Gulf of Mexico—I will ask him whether, if she was in her territorial form, she could take the step she has taken? I imagine that the intellect and candor of the gentleman would answer *no*. Why? Because, he would say, she is not a sovereign—she is a mere dependency; her people live by such organic acts as the Government of the United States may think proper to spread over her Territory; she is a pigmy now, and there is no such thing as a power resident in her to break up this Government—but by and by she will be a giant, and when she is clothed with this immaculate power of sovereignty, why, of course, she may go back and occupy the identical position of Virginia on the day that she helped to make this Government, and may resume the inherent powers with which she is now clothed, and the moment she takes her place fully, freely and perfectly as a State in this Union, may then claim it as an independent and constitutional right to break it up.

I have read the speech which seems to have furished [sic] the staple for some of the arguments in the convention, (the speech of Mr. Benjamin, of Louisiana,)[86] a speech which I find circulated broadcast throughout this land, and it has fallen with tremendous power on our Capitol and the men in it, and especially those who rule in it. It says: "Read, Missourians! and be prepared to defend your rights by argument as well as by arms, the great speech of Hon. J. P. Benjamin." Mr. Benjamin' speech itself is nothing more than a rehash of old arguments furnished in the troubles of 1833.

He has not advanced one new idea in that argument, but he has revamped and ressurected [sic] ideas in favor of this heresy, and spread them abroad, and they have obtained currency through the epidemic passions of the hour. Because the States were sovereign and had reserved rights, and especially because, as the gentleman said, they delegated power and did did [sic] not grant any; therefore, the resumption of this power is a logical inference, and each State that entered into this Union at the very moment of making it reserved to itself the power to break it when she thought proper. It is true Mr. Benjamin says that she has only the right to do it in a clear and palpable case of violation of the Constitution.

Mr. REDD. I desire to say that I do not know what Mr. Benjamin's position is, but my position is that by the law of nations, when a compact is entered into each Government has the right to dissolve its connection with that Government when that compact is violated by the one party—that the injured party has the right to declare the compact, in so far as that party is concerned, broken.

Mr. WRIGHT. That is precisely Mr. Benjamin's position, that by the law of nations and by the hand of sovereignty, and by the fact that the powers were delegated and not surrendered, a State can dissolve her connections with the General Government at pleasure; but, he says, a State can dissolve the Union by the exercise of its Constitutional right, and is not driven to the necessity of revolution in a *clear and palpable case* of violation of the Constitution. The trouble about that argument is—who is to judge whether it is palpable or not. Where is the power to determine? If a State can do it, how do you impose the limitation upon the power. The logical mind of the gentleman from Marion must see at a glance, that the power Constitutionally to secede from the Union, under any limitations—which are limitations only from the power that secedes, is a power without any limitations at all. Mr. Benjamin in his speech, quoting the provisions of our Constitution, italicises, as my friend from Marion did, the word delegated, the point upon which the whole thing hangs, according to my friend from Marion. If it had been "granted," or "surrendered," it would have been different—but it is only the "delegation" of the power. Now Mr. Benjamin had to read in the context that whole proposition of the Constitution, and it is short, and I ask the gentleman from Marion, or any other gentleman about whose mind hang the cobwebs which fetter its reason—and I would almost say defferentially [sic] and respectfully, fetter its patriotism—I ask his attention to the whole of this provision of the Constitution. It reads "the powers not delegated by the States, nor prohibited to the States, are reserved to the States themselves, or to the people."[87] What is his error? In the first place is a delegated power reserved? A power delegated. Is that reserved? Is a prohibited power reserved? Every man knows that no reserved power can take away a granted one, and it is equally manifest that no reservation can take away a power expressly prohibited. So that a reservation is what? A reservation is what is left after taking out the powers *delegated*, and the powers *prohibited* to the States, and then the residuum is the reservation, and that residuum is distributed in some cases to the States, and in some cases to the people.

Mr. President, the framers of the Constitution were men who matched words well to thoughts; they understood the character of the government they were making, and this, their sentence in the fundamental law, throws a flood of light upon the whole instrument. It is the key by which you unlock all its mysteries. It presents the only government on earth with such a distribution of power. In other words, it is the invention of the American mind, brought into living action by a great crisis, in so far as we can look upon their action as an independent and spontaneous movement of the human mind. I do not believe we say the whole truth when we say it was the genius of America; it was the profound sagacity of our fathers, met in council, that made that instrument. I believe as firmly as I stand before you this day, that they were helped to it, that there was a Providence that shaped their work, the same Providence which raised up Washington, and which discovered this continent at the right hour and time—the same Providence which not only went with us to battle but sat by us in council, and stilled the waves of passion which might rise in that body, and at last produced such a result as the world has never seen. The people, the source of power—not the divine right of kings—distributing the power in the first place to the States, and reserving to themselves the powers which they did not grant, then distributing powers affirmatively to the Federal Government—next prohibiting power to the States and ever so distributing it as to make power beneficial everywhere, and hurtful nowhere. That is by distributing power in no such wise as to make any sovereign anywhere. They held the residuum in their own hands. We talk familiarly about the sovereign State of Missouri; the sovereign State of South Carolina; the sovereign State of Louisiana; the sovereign States of Texas and Florida. I deny it. There is not a roving tribe of Indians between this and the smooth sea, nor a band of Bedouins in the Arabian desert, that, in the sense of publicists and the jurists, are not more sovereign than any State in this Union. Mr. Benjamin says—that a sovereign State, according to his notion, that a government itself, under whatever form soever, without dependence on any foreign power, is a sovereign State. Let me suppose a case. These publicists have never written about our plan of government. The misery of this word sovereignty is this, that lawyers and statesmen read the books of Europe—Grotius, Puffendorff, Vattel[88]—and they talk about governments unlike our own—and we get the idea of sovereignty from them, and we attempt to apply it for want of better terms, to our own Government. But let me ask the gentleman from Marion, (Mr. Redd,) and I select him because I respect his intellect, because I know he is blest with large powers from above, and because, therefore, I have more interest in his error than if he were a stranger. Suppose there had risen up in Europe a government contemplated by Vattel, Grotius and Puffendorff and other publicists of the world, there is no place to locate it because there is no such government in Europe. But, suppose there were one in Europe and having no power to make war or to conclude peace—no right to coin money, nor any authority to regulate commerce. Suppose it could not grant letters of marque and reprisal, that it could not send any ambassador to any court in the world, that it could not collect tonnage duties without the lawful consent of another government, and that after obtaining consent it would have to take the proceeds and put them in the Treasury of that other government. Suppose, in addition to that, every citizen in that country, or every subject, was bound by an oath of allegiance to another government, a superior and paramount allegiance, and suppose every one of its officers before they could act in that state, would have to swear to support that other government, and swear that when a conflict took place between the powers of that other government and its own, that it should side with a foreign power. Suppose it was a State that could not use uniform weights and measures; could not pass any bill of attainder. Would Vattel say that was a sovereign nation or an independent nation? I judge not.—Now, this imaginary nation I have spoken of in the old world, is identical with the nature of every State of this Union under the Federal Constitution. It would be a power incapable of maintaining itself in a conflict with nations. Would she be a sovereign State in any sense, and have the right of international law? She would not, but yet she would have power. Well, let us cast our eyes to another government. Suppose there were a government in Europe that could declare war and conclude peace; that could send ambassadors to a foreign court; that could coin money; that could establish a standard of weights and measures, and emit bills of credit, that could establish post-roads, although it would be doubtful whether it could make any other road having no power of eminent domain. Suppose it were a government that had the power of taxation—that could levy duties on imports and excises—and suppose it was a government that could not settle a landed estate—not having jurisdiction of the soil—that it could not determine an action of ejectment[89]—or could not pass any statutes of distribution, what would they say of that government? I am describing the Constitution of the United States and the Federal Government. What would these publicists say of that sort of government? They would say this: It is limited in the most important matters—it has no municipal power and no police power. They would say of such a government: It is anomalous—it comes up to no standard of sovereignty in the minds of publicists. In the sense of the word the Federal Government itself is not a sovereign government. It is supreme in its sphere of action, but then its sphere of action is limited, and an obstruction upon sovereignty. But are these governments less valuable, less efficacious as instruments of good and preservers and bulwarks, because shorn of this sovereignty. No, their precise value lies in the very difficulties of obstruction. Have we got no sovereignty anywhere in this country, will say the gentlemen from Marion. Strictly speaking, no. The people are the source of power, and the people in it are the government, and are not an Athenian Democracy or mob. What can the people do? The people of America, the source and original foundation of an eternal living power—what can they do? Can they act as sovereign—collect taxes or make war—conclude peace or pass laws? No, they cannot do that. The sovereign people of the State of Missouri can change our form of government as it stands provided they take a republican form, and provided they do not hurt the Constitution of the United States. But, the people cannot levy taxes—they cannot raise armies—they cannot make laws; the source of their power speaks only through a legitimate superstructure so beautifully erected as to perform all its appropriate functions in a healthy and becoming manner. It flourishes, because sovereignty in this sense does not exist. It is a grand invention of the American mind, calculated to make liberty more secure. Away, then, with this sentiment of the publicists; away with this doctrine of secession that springs from the idea that a State can resume its sovereignty, not only by taking away a granted power, but can go a step farther, and take away a prohibited power. Do you believe the wise men who made this Government, ever designed to so construct the instrument as to leave to any party the power to dissolve it at pleasure. My objection to secession is not only that it hurts our Government, but I go still deeper than that, for the argument reaches below it. I object to it, because if secession is right, there can never be any government on earth. Our Government will be the last, if secession be right.

> {Wright continued in his discourse on secession by suggesting disunion threatened the free navigation of the Mississippi, that

Maryland might want to reclaim the land it donated for the District of Columbia, and that the Utah Territory, being "occupied by aliens—men, scarcely any of whom have sworn allegiance to the country," might be a candidate for secession. Secessionists, he lectured, "cannot escape the ignominy and contempt which will be sure to follow."}

Mt. President, I, for one, shall take no hand in this national suicide. I will not be false to my country, false to humanity and false to my allegiance. Now let me consider this resolution.

"*Resolved*, That at present there is no adequate cause to impel Missouri to dissolve her connection with the General Government; but, on the contrary, she will labor for such an adjustment of existing troubles, as will secure peace as well as the rights and equality of all the States."

There is no adequate cause, says the resolution; I grant it. But still we have a cause to complain. There must be some cause, real or imaginary, to have produced the effects which are now visible all through these States. Such public disorders have never presented themselves before. We have had critical periods before, but no trouble like the present, and one of the greatest difficulties about these troubles is their intangibility of character. Our sentiment of honor is assailed; our rights are invaded; not by law, but by declared purposes, and our equality is practically denied. Our sentiments of honor are wounded; our sentiments are hurt, and there are dogmas and constitutional propositions rife in the land, which, if ripened into action would materially disturb us. The main cause, but not *the* only cause is this African question. That African question itself, has been exasperated, and intensified by other considerations which are not glanced at, except very incidentally in the report, and they have not been illustrated by any member who has arisen on this floor. The agitation of this slavery question is the most prominent cause of our public disorders; but behind that and cooperating with it is another cause, and that is the party spirit in this land; and that has arisen out of the immense patronage at the Federal head—a fruitful source of corruption, dividing and destroying the independence of our public men, and getting up a condition in political organizations which will seize, in all quarters, North and South, every element of fanaticism which may be valuable as a political power in the political condition of the day. We know enough of party among us—we need not go out of the State of Missouri to be assured of that fact; that parties, especially in times of excitement, will avail themselves of every attainable element around them—whether fanaticism or anything else—party will avail itself of everything around it that can be converted into political capital. What is the result? One section of the country will be arrayed against the other, so that there is a positive emulation in parties in this country, and has been for twenty-five years, and between organizations in this country, to see who can be the most successful in controlling that element which will enable men to mount up those steeps [sic] that statesmen climb.

I do not propose to go into the anti-slavery agitation, but I have some views in regard to the question which, not having been submitted by others, I will endeavor to present. It is said by the Abolitionists of the North, that slavery is not only a sin, but it is a crime—that it is the sum and substance of all other crimes in the decalogue. These are men who have representatives in such characters as Phillips and Garrison.[90] They say the Constitution of the United States is a covenant with hell, and that there is no provision in it which recognizes the relation of master and slave—that it is against the Divine law, and therefore they are for the destruction of the present Constitution. The Republican party of the North say, we stand between you and the Abolitionists; we rise up as an intermediate party; we do not claim to interfere with slavery in the States. The Abolitionists say it is a crime everywhere, that it is the crime of the age—that it is a human iniquity everywhere, and must be destroyed. The Republican party say no, we will not touch it in the States; we have nothing to do with it in the States. It is surrounded by constitutional guarantees in the States, and more than that, we have that provision which makes the Fugitive Slave Law obligatory upon every man; but in regard to slavery in the Territories, they say that cannot be. Why? Now, just here we find the Abolitionists and the radical Republicans meet. The Republican does not say the Constitution of the United States is a covenant with hell and against the divine law. He does not think the institutions of the South are absolutely wicked, but when they come to the argument why it shall not go into the Territories, then they take up the line of argument furnished by the Abolitionists, and they say it is a curse and a blot upon the country. Take the view that was given by senator Baker[91]—and I was sorry to see it, for he is my friend—because I looked upon that man as possessed of genius, and looked to his future rise—take his view as given in the Senate of the United States, and he says it is a black spot upon America. So when you come to argue with the Republicans why slavery should not be extended there, they take up the position of the Abolitionists, and declare it is immoral, a blight, a curse and a black spot on our institutions, and, although we won't trouble it or attempt to wipe it out within the boundaries of the States, it shall not extend beyond the boundaries.[92] Well, now, in the best and most fraternal spirit, under the promptings of fraternal regard, under a state of mind which will enable me to pardon much where I see it associated with patriotism—in a fraternal spirit I would say to the people of the North, I will be conscious of your virtues and a very little blind to your faults, and in that spirit let me suggest to you some of the improprieties of that argument. You do not deny that the relation of master and slave is recognized by the Constitution. You say it is a constitutional right that the master should take back his fugitive from service. Now, if we were founding a government this day, we should have the element of the African among us and the element of the Indian—we should have to determine among ourselves what (if any) part of the rights should be conferred on the black man, in the distribution of power in the government that we were going to make. In the formation of this government you could, if you thought so, take the ground that the relation of master and slave is void. But when living under the Constitution of the United States, supporting the Constitution itself—that fundamental charter by which all our actions must be measured—tell me what right you have to say that slavery is a sin? Tell me what right you have to say that slavery is immoral? Tell me by what right you say it is a curse? Tell me by what right you say, as a member of the American Confederacy, a supporter of the Constitution of the United States—what right have you to say it is a black spot on our institutions? Whatever is constitutional must be right. The political right of governments is not a system of ethics—it is not a code of morals—nor is it an elaboration upon the virtues, and charities, and benevolence of the human soul. Of all practical things in the world government is the most practical. The Constitution of the United States is not an essay upon the rights of man; it is not an essay upon ethical doctrine, but it is practically laying down a government which is designed to secure the rights of every man and every citizen. Of all practical things in this world, I repeat, government is the most practical. It is nothing more than an actual scheme by which the greatest benefit is to be brought about to the greatest number of people. The object is to secure certain rights—life, liberty and property. If you want any other sort of government you have to go to the Utopian dreams of Plato.[93] You might find in the Constitution which John Locke[94] puzzled his understanding over—you might find some Utopian scheme in regard to government. But the men who framed our Constitution were not Platos nor Lockes. They were practical, sensible gentlemen, and knew how to sacrifice a theory and make out of it some practical good. Don't you see, if you say slavery is a sin, that you charge that document itself with being a corrupt and immoral document? If slavery be a sin and recognized by the Constitution, the Constitution itself is a sinful and immoral document. Do you mean that, or have you only availed yourself of it in party strife, that you might fire the fanaticism around you, and beat the Democracy, and elevate yourselves? If you take that ground, you cannot do it without imputing immorality to the instrument which came from our fathers, an everlasting work, I trust—you impute to them dishonor—you say within itself it is corrupt. I do not know what you think of it on careful reflection, but it seems to me you must lose in some degree your allegiance to the instrument itself, when by your argument you impute to it the character of an immoral and sinful document. Such an argument is offensive. It is an assumption of superiority you have no right to claim. You may be more learned than the framers of the Constitution, but you impute to them necessarily dishonor, and you offend our private character and you wound our self-respect in doing it.—I was uttering just such words as these, (being a Black Republican, and especially showing my principles by battling against Lincoln during the last canvass,) in the Military Garden of New York, when a gentleman in the crowd said: "Sir, you seem to be a fair man, and you tell me this territorial question is only important in one respect, and that is that the dogma of Republicanism makes it offensive. Sir, I am a candid man, and I think you are so, and I would like to have you tell me how I have been offensive in wanting slavery prohibited in the territories. I do not mean to do anything offensive. I like the people of the South, and I respect them." "Sir," I replied, "I think it is offensive. Do you not see practically that there are fifteen slave States, but you will have no more such; you tolerate such as have slavery, but you will not have any more such. You say practically in regard to the common territory—you say practically in regard to the Government, that the people can go there just as well as we can; but you say when a man South comes into the territory he must put himself in quarantine until he rids himself of a disease and gets cured of a black plague, and then he can come in and not before. Now, sir, that is offensive." Said the man in reply, "I believe it is; and I tell you candidly, I never looked at it in that light before; I looked upon it as a political arrangement—a mere question of political economy; according to my views, it being better that the South should have no slaves in the territories, I thought I was exercising a power for the benefit of that people. I thought I was taking from them a burden to their intelligence and safe progress.{"} That is precisely the position the Republican party occupy, or numbers of them now in the great crisis of the country.

> {The inexhaustible Wright continued here for some length speaking of the formation of the Constitution and the nature of the Black man "who lives only by subjection and the will of a superior race." After a break for lunch, he persisted in arguing that he was against secession and believed that an "adjustment with our Republican brethren at the North," was ever possible.}

Now, the Chicago Platform says that the Congress has the power to prohibit slavery in the Territories. Let us be fair and just. I once entertained that opinion myself; I entertained it for twenty years; I learned it from such men as Clay and Webster. I learned it from every great man who figured in our annals for the last thirty years. They all affirmed the power, but all of them denied the propriety of its exercise. The Chicago Platform says that the power exists in Congress. Mr Webster[95] took the extraordinary ground upon this proposition—and when he took it I began to fear I was not right in my opinion—and he was not alone in it—that the Territories were never governed by the Constitution at all; that from the earliest moment of acquisition up to the period in which he spoke, Congress had *never* governed the Territories according to the Constitution. I was startled at the result of that opinion, because it brought me to this idea. Here is a Government of limited power, supreme within its sphere of action, that has the exercise of a power without bound. I therefore thought there was something wrong. I studied the antagonistic ideas of Mr. Calhoun,[96] whose subtlety of intellect always puzzled mine, and sometimes did much more, I think, that is, deceived itself. But the result of my own investigations upon the subject—and as a lawyer, studying the thorny pathways which carry men over the conflicts of individuals with the Government, it being my duty to understand something about the nature of our Government—was that there was a power in the General Government to prohibit slavery in the Territories. But I never thought it was a power which should be exercised, and when the Dred Scott decision came, I had to be a convert to the views delivered by Justice Taney. But I was a convert, and I was a sincere convert. He satisfied me of my error, and he has made an argument that I think cannot be overthrown. He has settled the power in the General Government to regulate the Territories.[97] That far I always went. But as to the quality of that power, he has shown the error of the teachings of Mr. Webster. It had to receive the limitations in the Constitution itself, it was not to be a vagrant power turned loose careering [sic] where it may, and doing what it choose—but a power capable of doing what it says, and to be fenced in, and limited, and restricted, like all the other powers of that instrument, and by the terms of that instrument; so that I am perfectly satisfied that the General Government has no power to prohibit slavery in the Territories.[98] I am satisfied beyond all question that it has the power to regulate the Territories, and to give them government, but that it has no power under the limitations of the Constitution to deprive a man either life, liberty or property, without the judgment of his peers or the law of the land, and therefore there is no power in that Government to confiscate any property, or disturb any legal relations, existing in the States, whether it be that of husband and wife, parent and child, master and apprentice, or owner and slave.

But while these are my convictions, I am perfectly willing to admit that a man may be honest and patriotic also, who entertains an antagonistic idea, because the question is one about which not only *may* the human mind honestly differ, but touching which the greatest statesmen and jurists of the country have differed, and have differed for forty years, and in any adjustment that I will offer to make with our Northern brethren, and with the Republican party—for I speak of the Republican party, giving them prominence, not with any view to impugn them, but because they are a party who constitute a large portion of the people with whom we have to make this adjustment. I shall not ask a surrender of the pride of opinion, I shall not ask anything that is inconsistent with the honor of a Republican, or any Northern man. A great many men in this country, and especially men who are clamorous for the preservation of the Union, declare they love their rights, but I do not know any of them that are not willing to surrender two-thirds of them at a jump. They must have their rights, they say. Therefore they go for the Crittenden resolutions. Well, what are your rights? The Dred Scott decision says you have the right to carry slavery into all the Territories. And now you are perfectly willing to surrender, to a prohibition that will cover two-thirds of the Territories. But you will have your rights.

I wonder what these gentlemen thought about, the time that Oregon was organized. We are discussing now the abstract question of power. Can Congress prohibit slavery in the Territories? Congress never did it but once, and that was when Oregon was organized.[99] That was our Territory. It was the right of every Southern man, South Carolinian, Floridian, Mississippian, Alabamian, Louisianian and Texan, to carry slaves into Oregon. But yet here is Congress, both in the Lower House and Senate, passing the bill, and with the sanction of the President, they organized one of our Territories, with the Wilmot Proviso, declaring that slavery shall never exist in that Territory. What is the reason we did not secede then? What is the reason there was not a clamor for our rights then? If this thing be one of principle, why did we not make a clamor about it? Why did we not secede, and take the United States forts and arsenals, &c.? Why didn't we seduce the allegiance of an officer of the army?

In looking over this broad, wonderful country of ours, there are some spots that excite a painful emotion in my mind. Somewhere in Texas there is a place, small in geographical position, that is called the Alamo.[100] I know it by its history as the scene of a bloody, inhuman, uncivilized, savage massacre, in which individual heroism was slaughtered by brutal, ferocious and reckless power; and now, as if Providence determined that such a place should never be forgotten, however insignificant in point of form, it is the precise place at which the laurels that were growing green upon one of the Hoary veterans of this country, all turned to ashes in an hour, every twig and branch fading.

But why was it that when Oregon organized, the South did not rise in indignation? Why was the principle violated if that *is* our right? I will tell you why, and I only mention it because it furnishes the solution of our remedy in this case, a remedy consistent with the honor of every man in this land, whether of the North or of the South. We made no quarrel about Oregon, because we knew that, practically, no man would ever carry a slave to Oregon, and therefore the parchment on which the Wilmot Proviso was written, was not worth the material that had to be used in writing it. And so now I hold in regard to our Territories, whenever there is any Territory in which slavery won't go, practically by natural laws, it is idle to make a quarrel about it, and it is worse than idle to attempt to break up a government, in regard to the question whether there shall be a Wilmot Proviso or not. And one of the madnesses of the madness of the times, in the South as well as the North, is, that there are dogmatic opinions in connection with this question. There is a party, in the North, who insist upon the Wilmot Proviso upon our Territories, where a Wilmot Proviso can never practically accomplish anything; and there are mad men in the South who insist upon the dogma of protection where there can never be a slave to be protected.

Why, we have other rights besides the right to carry slavery into the regions where no sensible man would ever think of carrying one. I think we have a right, the Constitutional right of all men South to cultivate the sugar cane upon the highest glacier of the Rocky Mountains; I do not doubt it—and do it by slave labor, too, if we can. I think if our territory is extended to the equinoctial line, we should have the Constitutional right to gather icicles upon the equator. There is not a political doubt about our Constitutional right. But, then, may I go and destroy our Government because I maintain this right and some man denies it? And yet, Mr. President, I would rather break up the Government upon a point such as that than upon the territorial question. I would rather break up this Government, in so far as any agency of mine is concerned, upon the abstract right to cultivate sugar cane upon the Rocky Mountains, or gather icicles upon the equator, than upon this territorial question, because I would know that if posterity thought of one so humble as I, they would say, instead of having a right to speak with any potent voice in favor of my country, I ought to have been under lock and key of a lunatic asylum, so that I would stand vindicated to posterity from my action on the ground that I was not *responsible* for what I did.

> {Delegate Wright reiterated his plea for an honorable "adjustment" of the crisis. Neither side was at fault; both sides were at fault. "Heaven knows there are enough wrongs, both North and South to be corrected." Speaking to those who feared slave insurrections, Wright observed that there should be less fear of slave revolts than in the past. Under the hand of benign "masters," slaves, he posited, were being turned into "civilized" men: "In proportion as you reduce his savage traits, you make him subject to the will of a superior race, as in wild animals subjected to the taming process—in proportion as there is moral and Christian culture in this barbarian, just in that proportion is he dominated over peacefully by the will of a superior race."

He begged the assembled to invoke the spirit of Henry Clay, the "great pacificator," who repeatedly sought and found compromise during politically turbulent times: "He never failed. No man can ever fail who comes in this (Clay's) spirit, and uses such agencies and instrumentalities of power. More than that, no man ever *can* succeed who does not."}

What are our prospects for a compromise? What hopes are before us? You have seen the stand taken by Arkansas. You know what North Carolina has done. She has decided against a Convention. North Carolina and Arkansas have said, the mad waves of secession shall not overwhelm us.[101] We stay this tide. We are struggling for our rights in the Union, and we will stand by the border States. But there is a sectional President in power. Have we any hopes of him? He is a Republican. He has a divided Cabinet. Some are conservative men, some are radical. What are the the [sic] prospects before us? Well, now, first let me say, that, although suicide is getting to be epidemic I have no idea at all that this Administration is going to commit suicide. I have no idea the Republican party intend to destroy themselves. But I give it credit for great shrewdness and tact. There is one man in that Cabinet that sees all these struggles in their actual practical import. I think there are one or two men in it who have not the remotest idea at all of the actual condition of public affairs. There is no reliance to be placed upon them. But, as I said, there is one man in the Cabinet who sees, with the vision of entire coolness, the whole landscape of our political horizon, and knows what the actual condition of this country at this hour is, and that man is Seward. He is not going to destroy himself. He, in common with the Republican party, want to perpetuate themselves. They do not wish to be mere ephemerals that live an hour or a day, but they want to perpetuate themselves and establish a Republican dynasty, after the fashion, at least in duration, of the defunct Democratic dynasty that has gone by the board. Well, how can they do so if the Union is broken. If the border States go out what becomes of the Republican party? It dies instanter, for the very moment that the border States leave this Union there is no longer any distinctive characteristic belonging to the Republican party, at least on the slavery question, and they have to take their chances with the people of the North in a new confederacy, and get up issues leaving out the element of slavery agitation.

In any aspect, therefore, in which you can view this question, it appears to me manifest that this Administration is not going to commit suicide. They are going to preserve this Union, and they can only do it by making an adjustment with the border States. And when such an adjustment is made, satisfactory to the honor and interest of these States, *all* men will be without excuse if they do not join.

But let us see what has been the practical operation of the Republican party in the last Congress. This, you will say, is a speculation of mine. But let me point your attention, especially, my very clear-headed, and, if you permit me to say so, my very eloquent friend from Lewis.[102] Permit me, since you are under a lively apprehension touching the action of the Republican party, and since, especially, you dread their dogma, the Wilmot Proviso, to call your attention to the actual conduct of this Republican party in Congress, since the period when they have had all the power. When our Southern brethren abandoned us, and left us alone to fight their battles on the strongholds of the Constitution, what result did they bring upon us? If they had stayed, this Administration would have been powerless. Two departments of the Government would have been against the Administration—Congress and the Judicial department. The Senate would have been against him, the House would have been against him, and the Supreme Court would have been against him. What, then, could he do under our form of Government? Where was the source of any actual danger? Is any gentleman afraid? What is he afraid of? What are our remedies? Can we guard against danger which may be threatened to bring upon us? Yes, no law can be passed that is hurtful to us. If an unconstitutional law were to pass, the Supreme Court would denounce it. He was elected by an accident—he was elected by the blunders of his adversaries—by the erroneous manner in which the campaign was fought against him. We made his victory easy, although he was a minority President. He took advantage of our error, and he got into power, and now there he is powerless. He cannot make a Cabinet minister unless you elect him. He cannot make an appointment to any office of high grade without your say-so. If the Southern States had not gone out, *all* the States that opposed his election might have conferred with each other as to what were the *actual* evils to complain of. They might have met in a body through their commissioners, and set out in writing what they thought were their grievances, and what they held to be the proper means of redressing them. Had there been such counsel as that, no such complication would have arisen as when Georgia sent her ambassador here.[103] I struggled then, because I wanted to receive him, to get this Convention to adopt a resolution which would have enabled every man in this body to have listened to him with pleasure, and to practice towards him all the courtesies due to the representative of a sister State. I wanted them to adopt a resolution that this sister of ours, whether she thought so or not, was our sister still; and, being one of the family, she had a right to talk, and talk to all the family. But it was determined under the genius of precipitancy and hot haste, to do otherwise.

I hear a great deal said about coercion. Undoubtedly, we are against coercion. It is not right that the Federal Government should force a State into submission.[104] But do gentlemen consider the coercion which is used against us? The only *real* coercion that has been used in these troubles has been used by the South against us. I will say nothing now about those acts of war of which some of the Southern States have been guilty and which, if committed by an independent foreign nation, would have fired this nation from one end to the other: of the firing on our flag; the seizing of our forts; of the capture of our treasury; of taking the jurisdiction of the Mississippi. All these are really acts of war against the Government of the United States; and yet that Government, with a forbearance that is parental and benign, and worthy of all commendation, has said nothing in return, but has used the magnanimity which can be rightly used by a great Government towards its citizens—has been doing what Edmund Burke asked of Lord North, in the time of George the Third, to do towards these colonies.[105] This Government has thus far acted in the spirit of conciliation. It has forborne; it has not undertaken to resist force by force, because I suppose there is no doubt of it in the world that every act committed by our Southern brethren, and especially the act of organizing a government, and taking jurisdiction of the Mississippi river, and seizing the forts, are all acts of war, which would not be tolerated by this Government if practiced by any nation upon the face of the earth. But it was not of that particularly that I wish to speak. I wish to speak of another sort of coercion that has been practiced towards us, and I fear it was intended—I mean the coercion arising from holding such views as these:

"Well, now, it is idle to dispute about secession, or the right of secession.—The fact is, South Carolina has gone; and then Alabama says, the fact is, South Carolina has gone, and we may as well go also. And little Florida said she would go too, and so of the rest. All these are *facts*, and must be treated as *facts*." Well, what is the meaning of that? Why, the logical sequence is, that the fact is to operate on us to determine *our* action. In other words, we are to do now what we would not have done, or thought of doing, unless these examples had gone before us. I say that is practical coercion. Then, again, their resolves in regard to the international slave trade, cutting it off and not letting us carry our negroes among them. That is coercion likewise, and it is unfriendly coercion, it is unsisterly. But let it pass. I dismiss the whole subject of coercion upon the ground that we live in a Government in which no great results can ever be brought about by the exercise of power.

Now, after the South abandoned, us leaving the Federal Government in the possession of the Republican party, what has that party done? My friend from Lewis said it had not abandoned the Chicago platform. He ought to take that back, because it is not just. You remember that, at the last session of Congress, there was a little sprinkling of slavery in New Mexico, created there by Territorial Legislation for the especial benefit of the efforts of the army, who wishing body servants to go with them when they were ordered into the Territory, and had no power to refuse, desired them to clean their boots, brush their clothes, and attend to other work of that sort, and they took their slaves, and as some of them had been sued for taking slaves where the laws had prohibited slavery, the Territorial Legislature recognized slavery for the special accommodation of those officers.[106] Now, one of the parties in the Lower House of Congress, in accordance with the platform made in Chicago, moved to repeal that law, and they did repeal it. The Senate rejected the measure. This was before the Presidential victory had been achieved. But since that victory, seeing that they have the whole power of the Government in their hands, they have organized three Territories, two of them south of Oregon, and yet no man of the Republican party has risen in that body, either in the Senate or the Lower House to attach a Wilmot Proviso to an act of organization. What does that prove? Is not that a surrender of the party platform? Is not that a patriotic evidence of a disposition on their part to meet the issue in the spirit of kindness? They had the power, why didn't they use it? If you say that the action of the South probably has scared them; very well I do not care what is the cause. If you put it down to the ignoble sentiment of fear and not of patriotic inspiration, be it so. But the fact is nevertheless that, with the power in their own hands, they have organized three Territories, and they have just done it, and two of them are south of Oregon, and no Republican in the Senate, not even Wade, nor Hale, nor the radical Sumner, nor the clear-sighted, far-seeing Seward, nor Lovejoy in the Lower House—whom, by the by, I don't regard as a Republican at all, but as belonging to the school of Wendell Phillips and Lloyd Garrison—has risen to ask that a Wilmot Proviso be attached to the Act.[107] I think it is a clear and unmistakable evidence of a disposition on their part to surrender dogmas to the welfare and the peace of their country.

> {Delegate Wright continued his address at length during the next day's proceedings reiterating his opinion that the right of secession was "not only heresy, but that it furnishes no remedy for our ills." He also argued for the necessity of slavery because White men are "not going to cultivate cotton . . . wherever we find the geological formation that will admit the growth of cotton, we find that it will be an impossibility that it shall be grown by anybody but an inferior race under the domination of a superior race."}

Source: *Proceedings of the Missouri State Convention Held at Jefferson City and St. Louis, March, 1861* (St. Louis: George Knapp & Co., Printers and Binders, 1861), 186–207.

George Youse Bast Sr.
March 19, 1861

George Y. Bast Sr., (1812–1879) was born in Fayette County, Kentucky. A farmer by profession, he represented Montgomery County in the state convention.

Following the lengthy address by Uriel Wright, Delegate Bast wanted his colleagues to know that causes did exist to cause Missourians to consider disunion. The Republican Party planned to "extinguish" the institution of slavery and if that eventuality were to come, southern hopes for the present and future would also be extinguished. The cultivation of southern soil, he continued, "cannot be cultivated by any other labor than slave labor." At the same time, Bast pronounced that he was not a secessionist, and did "not represent a secession constituency." He thought Senator Crittenden's proposed amendment was appropriate and would be "acceptable to a majority of this Convention." He concluded that even though there was ample cause for Missouri to secede, he did "not wish it to be understood that I advocate the doctrine of secession."

Mr. BAST. Now, sir, at first sight it occurred to me that there could be no argument against a resolution of that description. (The first of the series reported by the Committee on Federal Relations.) We all admit that we are now in trouble. No one doubts it. Every argument that has been produced in this Convention has been made in reference to this matter, that we are in trouble. What are these troubles? Is our commerce and progress the same as heretofore? Is the peace and quiet of the country as it has been heretofore? Are the minds of this immense number of people in as quiet and tranquil a condition as before the present agitation was commenced? I think there are many causes to operate upon the minds of the people, which causes are weighed differently by different individuals, as illustrated by the members of this Convention, and the people through the country. If we have any cause, what is that cause? Have the Southern people of this confederacy, who have withdrawn from the present Union, any cause for doing so. Are they not contending for their own just rights—their families and their firesides? They are well aware from the aggressions of the North as they understand them, that in the event of the entire success of its own opinions, it is the intention of the Republican party to extinguish the institution of slavery, and by extinguishing it do they not at once extinguish all their hopes for the present and the future. Their very sustenance depends upon the maintenance of the slave institutions of the South. Upon the slave property of the South depends the cultivation of the soil which, on account of the warm climate of the South, cannot be cultivated by any other labor than slave labor. Who can make cotton? Can white labor be performed in that country so as to make it profitable? Great Britain has tried various plans to run in opposition to the slavery of the South, but without success. Cotton can be supplied more cheaply from the Southern States, than from anywhere else. I say, then, this is a question of life and death to Southern interests. We are exempt from that cause to a great extent. Our institutions are like theirs, and though we might live without slavery, yet our interests are identical with them, and I think we can, with strict justice to ourselves, say to the Southern people that they have not at least done very wrong in taking the course they have. I may be considered and pointed out as a secessionist, but I say such is not the case. I am no secessionist. I do not represent a secession constituency. I represent as honorable a constituency, as high-minded and patriotic a constituency as any representative on this floor. They are not secessionists. They are men who are in favor of their just and independent rights, and they would say to any person opposed to their interest, we demand our rights; we do not intend to come with suppliant knee and petition for our rights, but we come boldly and say we demand our rights, and nothing more; we want nothing more than strict, honest, just and constitutional rights, but being a magnanimous people, and taking into consideration the present excited condition of the public mind, we are willing to say we will compromise and take what our sister border States are willing to accept. Under these circumstances, we are ready to say, if you will not continue your aggressive acts, we will remain with you; but if you continue to persevere in those acts, we must then fall back on our reserved rights. Mr. President, I don't think it is necessary, and neither would I undertake to discuss this question in relation to the formation of our government. I conceive it to be irrelevant to the question at issue. We are called here for a certain purpose; our country is in trouble, and we are called here to bring about some means of reconciliation if we can do so. What has the foundation of the government to do with the reconciliation of these difficulties. The facts are before us; our country is dismembered; commerce is trammelled; we are fettered in many ways, and is it not indisputably necessary that we should set all irrelevant questions aside, and say at once to the country at large, what we think should be done? Now the Crittenden plan of adjustment has been proposed. I believe it is acceptable to a majority of this Convention, and to a majority of the people of Missouri. The Crittenden amendment extends to Territories hereafter to be acquired. I do not think there can be any serious objection to the adoption of a proposition of that kind. But we know that in accepting that, we are not getting the full extent of our rights; but, as a magnanimous people, and for the sake of compromise, we say we are willing to accept a little less than our rights, and compromise these difficulties.

If the difficulties under which we are laboring—if I can consider in relation to the difficulties and troubles that caused our Southern brethren to secede, if they are operating upon us—if these troubles have caused seven States to secede, and most of the other slave States to call Conventions, and take into consideration these difficulties, is it not necessary that we should pause and reflect before we say there is no cause why Missouri should separate or change her form of government. I think there is ample cause. There is at present—and I am speaking to an intelligent audience—there is, I say, ample cause why Missouri should secede. But I do not wish it to be understood that I advocate the doctrine of secession. I say, however, we have cause to secede, but good sound policy requires us as a magnanimous people to act in co-operation with our sister States, and bring about a reconciliation, and bring back the government to its pristine purity, if such a thing can be brought about. It would be the happiest act of my life if I could in any degree bring about that desirable end.—When I came to this Convention there were other subjects on which I expected to speak, but as, we have the privilege of speaking to each of these resolutions, I will not occupy any more time. I wish, however, to say in conclusion, to the latter part of this resolution, that it is the duty and for the interest and welfare of Missouri, under all circumstances, to exert herself so as to secure the rights and equalities of the States.

> {Following Delegate Bast's address, J. S. Allen from Harrison County briefly amended an earlier speech he had given remarking that if an adjustment could be reached that would bring the seceded states back, he would act as the father of the prodigal son and "it would be the ladies I would be in favor of kissing." John T. Redd then offered an amendment to the resolution suggesting that "cause" be replaced with "motive."}

The vote was then taken and the {Redd's} amendment was lost. The original resolution was then adopted—ayes 89, noes 1, Mr Bast voting in the negative.

> {The first resolution recommended by the Committee on Federal Relations read: "*Resolved*, That at present there is no adequate cause to impel Missouri to dissolve her connections with the General Government; but, on the contrary, she will labor for such an adjustment of existing troubles, as will secure peace as well as the rights and equality of all the States."}

Source: *Proceedings of the Missouri State Convention Held at Jefferson City and St. Louis, March, 1861* (St. Louis: George Knapp & Co., Printers and Binders, 1861), 215–16.

Committee Response to Commissioner Glenn
March 21, 1861

The day after Commissioner Glenn delivered his address, John Henderson, representing Pike County, offered a resolution "that a committee of five members be appointed by the President, to whom shall be referred the communications made to the Convention by the Hon. Luther J. Glenn, Commissioner from the State of Georgia, and that they report to the Convention such action as they may deem a respectful and suitable response thereto on the part of this State." As appointed by President Sterling Price, the committee included, in addition to John B. Henderson as chair, James H. Birch (Clinton County), William J. Howell (Monroe), Robert M. Stewart (Buchanan), Uriel Wright (St. Louis), Asa C. Marvin (Henry), and James Proctor Knott (Cole).

Committee chair John Brooks Henderson (1824–1913) was born in Pittsylvania County, Virginia, and relocated to Lincoln County, Missouri, with his family in 1832. He passed the bar in 1836 and established his law office in Clarksville and served two terms in the Missouri General Assembly in the late 1840s and again in the late 1850s. He represented Pike County in the Missouri state convention. Upon the expulsion of Senator Trusten Polk in 1862, Lieutenant Governor Willard Preble Hall appointed Henderson to complete his term. Henderson was reelected in 1863 and served until 1869.

In a response twice as long as Glenn's address, the committee methodically and logically refuted his main points of argument. It invoked the Chicago Platform to discredit the charge that Republicans intended to abolish slavery in the states. As proof of their intent, the committee cited the Corwin amendment which had been approved by Congress on March 4. The committee invalidated the commissioner's claim that Republicans would prevent southern slave owners from settling the western territories by referring to Congress's recent organization of the Dakota, Colorado, and Nevada territories, which included no restrictions on slavery. "No Federal legislation," the report asserted, "discriminating against the institution [of slavery], has ever been imposed upon the South by the sectional power of the North." From every point of view, the report concluded, "in which we have been able to examine the communication soliciting our withdrawal from the Union, whether as viewed as a Constitutional right, a remedy for existing evils, or a preventive of anticipated wrongs, we find it in conflict with our allegiance to a good government, and wholly inefficient to accomplish the ends designed."

Mr. HENDERSON, from the committee to whom was referred the communication from the Georgia Commissioner, presented the following

REPORT.

Mr. PRESIDENT: Your committee, to whom was referred the communication of the Honorable Luther J. Glenn, who appeared before the Convention as a Commissioner from Georgia, and having presented the ordinance of secession adopted by said State, was pleased to "invite the cooperation of Missouri with Georgia and the other seceding States in the formation of a Southern Confederacy," have had the same under consideration, and beg leave to report as follows:

The Committee sincerely regret that the commission under which Mr. Glenn was accredited to our State, was limited in its scope to a mere invitation to withdraw from the Government of our fathers and form a distinct confederacy with the Gulf States. His mission seems to contemplate no plan for reconciliation—no measure of redress for alleged grievances, which, being adopted, would prove satisfactory to Georgia. Having chosen secession as the only remedy for existing ills, Georgia, through her Commissioner, supposes that similar interests, connected with the exigency precipitated upon us by the action of the cotton States, will impel Missouri to withdraw from the Union and cast her lot with them.

The reasons assigned by Mr. Glenn for this action on the part of his State are: First, that the laws of Congress imposing duties on imports have been so framed as to discriminate very injuriously against Southern interests;[108] Second, that a great sectional party, chiefly confined to the Northern States of the Union, whose leading idea is animosity to the institution of negro slavery, has gradually become so strong as to obtain the chief executive power of the nation, which is regarded as a present insult to the South; and, Third, that the ultimate object of this party is the total extinction of slavery in the States where it now exists by law, and the placing upon them terms of *political* equality, at least, the white and black races; and to prevent evils of such magnitude, as well as to preserve the honor and safety of the South, Georgia and some of her sister

States have deliberately resolved to withdraw from the Union, never to return.

Your Committee trust that they duly appreciate the gravity of the communication thus made to the people of Missouri.

Missouri entered the Union at the close of an angry contest on the subject of slavery. Her geographical position, the variety of the branches of industry to which her resources point, her past growth and future prospects, combine to demand that all her counsels be taken in the spirit of sobriety and conciliation.

Your Committee waive for the moment the consideration of the moral aspect of what they consider to be the heresy of secession, because if they entered, in the first instance, upon this examination, its results would preclude any inquiry into the material consequences of the action to which Missouri is solicited.

The peculiar institution of our State is different from that of Georgia, or any other of the cotton-growing States. If it be true, as represented, that the revenue laws of the country operate oppressively upon them—and this objection is now heard for the first time after an interval of nearly thirty years—it cannot be pretended that any part of this particular grievance touches Missouri.

Acknowledging as we do the power of Congress to impose such duties for revenue purposes at least, and trusting to the wisdom and justice of the body for impartial legislation, we are unwilling to seek, in a step promising nothing but the most unequivocal calamities, a refuge from imaginary evils.

In reference to the more important matter presented as a reason for the action of Georgia, your committee would say, that Missouri has watched, with painful anxiety, the progress of a great sectional party in the North, based upon the exclusion of slavery from the Territories, which are the common property of the whole Union. Doing the Republican party the justice to believe that it means to carry out the articles of its political creed, as stated in its platform and indicated by its recent votes in Congress, we deem it incorrect to declare that it cherishes any present intention to interfere with slavery in the States of the Union. Any such attempt would justly arouse the highest exasperation in every slaveholding State; but it is considered unwise to go out of our way to denounce hypothetically a design which, so far from being threatened, is disavowed by that party.

We are aware that individual members of the Republican party have at times enunciated most dangerous heresies, and that some of its extremists have, with apparent deliberation, embodied in the form of resolutions, and published to the world, sentiments which would fully authorize, if regarded as the views of the whole organization, the condemnation due to principles at war with the security of rights of property in nearly half the States of the Union; but we must guard ourselves against the double error of imagining that all the bad rhetoric and uncharitable speech of orators whose highest aim is to produce a sensation, are to be taken as the true exponent of the sober views of their party, and that language recklessly used by a party seeking to obtain power is a faithful index of the conduct it will pursue when power has been once obtained.

In support of these views, your Committee may instance the adoption of a constitutional amendment by the requisite two-thirds vote of each branch of the last Congress, after the Representatives from seven Southern States had withdrawn, providing against all interference by Congress with the institution of slavery, as it may exist in any State of the Union—a provision irrevocable without the consent of every State.[109] From this it may be seen that the extremists attached to the Republican party have so far been unable to control it.

In proof of the proposition that parties are more radical in the acquisition than in the exercise of power, we may refer to the recent organization of three territorial governments,[110] upon the principles contained in the compromise measures of 1850—and afterwards applied upon demand of the South, to the provisional governments of Kansas and Nebraska.

But not withstanding these evidences denoting thus far a proper appreciation of the rights and wishes of the people of the South, the Honorable Commissioner was pleased to assure us that Georgia had lost all confidence in the North. Such, Mr. President, is not the sentiment of Missouri. That many of the citizens of the North, including the turbulent demagogues, who incite to treason, and their deluded followers who execute their teachings by invading other States, with a view of inaugurating revolution or setting at defiance, by forcible resistance, the Federal laws, on their own soil, have forfeited our confidence, will not be denied. But to denounce the innocent with the guilty and charge whole communities with the crimes or bad faith of a few, does not accord with the moral or political ethics of Missourians.

It is true that some of the Northern States have enacted laws, the provisions of which seem designed to impede the prompt and faithful execution of the Fugitive Slave Law, but such enactments are void. They disgrace the statute books on which they appear, and serve no other purpose than to weaken the fraternal ties that should bind together the people of different sections of the Union. These enactments are fast disappearing; and the hope may be indulged that, in the course of a few months, this source of irritation will be permanently removed.

So far then from having lost all confidence in the North, Missouri is assured, by the history of the past, that every right she may constitutionally claim will be accorded to her. Let the passions of the day, engendered by political conflict, subside and the ultra dogmas of party leaders will be discarded. Let the American mind once more be directed to the importance of perpetuating the blessings of a good government, instead of indulging vain hopes of establishing a better one, at the close of the most dangerous and criminal revolutions, and then the peace of the country will have been restored.

We are not advised that concessions demanded by the Southern people, on the subject of slavery, have heretofore been refused by those of the North. No Federal legislation, discriminating against the institution, has ever been imposed upon the South by the sectional power of the North. The ordinance of 1787, prohibiting slavery in the Northwest territory, ceded to the General Government by the State of Virginia, was proposed and advocated by one of the most distinguished sons of the "Old Dominion."[111] The proposition was seconded and supported by Southern men, and, though the result of the measure was the exclusion of slavery from the soil of five large States of the Union, yet the South should not be so unjust as now to complain of the deed.

The Missouri compromise was agreed upon by the representatives of both sections of the country, and neither should now reproach the other. It was proposed by a Southern man,[112] received the assent of the South, and acquiesced in by the people of the nation.

And though, it may be said, the compact was made in ignorance of the law, as recently declared by the Supreme Court, the people of the South will scarcely now sacrifice their high sense of honor, so long claimed as a leading characteristic, in eager and unnatural desire to find causes of quarrel with their brethren of the North.

At a subsequent period the South demanded a repeal of the Missouri Compromise line, and the adoption of the principle of non-intervention upon the subject of slavery in the territories. The demand was acceded to, and territorial governments established in accordance with their wishes.[113] That portion of the territory, once covered by the restriction of 1820, was thus opened to the introduction of slavery, and now, for the first time since the organization of the Federal Government has slavery become lawful upon every part of the public domain. Georgia and Missouri united in this appeal to the patriotism and justice of the North.

The concession was made, and Missouri would be false to every principle of honor should she find in the act a pretext for the charge of broken faith.

The operation of this principle having become distasteful to some of our Southern friends, it was thought by them advisable to make yet another demand upon the people of the North. The doctrine of Congressional protection of slavery in the territories was urged as a substitute for that of popular sovereignty, so recently adopted at their own instance and request. The demand, however, is only made in a political convention, and admitted, by the parties urging it, to be an unnecessary and impracticable abstraction. When attempted to be engrafted upon the legislation of the country, it is repudiated by nearly the entire South, and even by Georgia itself. Your committee are by no means satisfied that even this request would be refused by a large proportion of the Northern people, were it necessary to preserve the Union, or secure the rights of their brethren. But, until it shall be acknowledged as a vital and living principle by the South, and refused by the North, Missouri will be slow even to complain of injustice, much less to enter into any schemes for the destruction of the Government.

Missouri is not yet ready to abandon the experiment of free government. She has not lost all confidence in the people of any section of the nation, because the past furnishes assurance to the contrary; the present is cheered by her unshaken faith in the capacity of man to govern himself—and the future invites to peace and continued Union, for the prosperity of all.

If evils exist under the Constitution and laws, as they are, let the proper appeal be addressed to the American heart, both North and South, and these evils will be removed. If, in the heat of partizan rancor, the expressions or deeds of the vicious shall point to future aggressions, the patriotism of the masses needs only to be invoked for new guarantees against anticipated wrong.

From what has been already said, it will be seen that the views of Georgia, as expressed by her Commissioner and those of your Committee, in reference to the policy to be pursued by the Southern States in the present emergency, are essentially different. We believe that Missouri yet relies upon the justice of the American people, whilst Georgia seems to despair. The one recognizes friends in the North, whose lives, if necessary, will be devoted to her defence; the other, regarding them as unworthy of her confidence, spurns their friendship, and defies their enmity. Missouri looks to the Federal Constitution to protect the rights of her citizens, whilst Georgia unnecessarily rushes into revolution and hazards all upon a single issue. Georgia, seeming to regard the Union as the source of imaginary ills, adopts secession as a remedy; Missouri, feeling that she is indebted to the Union for the prosperity of her citizens, her power and wealth as a State, yet clings to it with the patriotic devotion of earlier days.

Your committee, so far, have confined themselves to an examination of the causes alleged for the revolution in the Southern States, and the apparent want of necessity for so extraordinary a movement at the present time. Indeed, so rapid and ill-advised has this action been, that it seems rather the execution of meditated conspiracy against the Government by restless and uneasy demagogues, than the slow and determined movement of a reflecting people. We see many of the dangerous men who controlled the nullification plot in South Carolina in 1832, the prominent actors in the present desperate experiment against the peace and happiness of the country. Feeling, as we do, the total inadequacy of the causes presented for this ruinous policy, your committee will be excused in the expression of some doubt as to the deliberation and wisdom with which the honorable Commissioner was pleased to assure us

Georgia had acted in the premises. And in this connection we will be further excused for commending to the serious consideration of the good citizens of Georgia, and other seceding States who may for the moment have been seduced from the paths of safety by the artful schemes of bad men, the following memorable words from one whose patriotism will not be doubted, and whose unerring sagacity is being daily verified in the history of the Republic.

"WASHINGTON, May 1, 1833.

"MY DEAR SIR: ****** I have had a laborious task here; but nullification is dead, and its actors and courtiers will only be remembered by the people to be execrated for their wicked designs to sever and destroy the only good Government on the globe, and that prosperity and happiness we enjoy over every portion of the world. Haman's gallows[114] ought to be the fate of all such ambitious men, who would involve their country in civil war, and all the evils in its train, that they might reign, and ride on its whirlwind and direct the storm. The free people of these United States have spoken, and consigned these wicked demagogues to their proper doom. Take care of your nullifiers; you have them among you; let them meet with the indignant frowns of every man who loves his country. The tariff, it is *now* known, was a mere pretext. *The next pretext will be the negro or slavery question.*[115]

"ANDREW JACKSON.
"Rev. ANDREW J. CRAWFORD."[116]

The Commissioner was pleased to invoke the identity of interests and feeling between the people of Georgia and Missouri, as a reason that we should abandon the Government of our fathers and take our position with the seceding States. It will be borne in mind that this proposition was urged, not with a view of securing such guaranties as might ultimately lead to a reunion of the States, and the establishment of fraternal peace, but for the purpose of constructing permanently a separate and distinct confederacy.

If the union of these two great States, under the same government—and we admit the fact—be so desirable to Georgia, we will be pardoned in the expression of astonishment that she saw fit to dissolve that connection, which had been peaceful and happy for the last forty years, without consulting the interests or wishes of Missouri. It may not be intended, but the inference is forced upon us, that longer to enjoy the beneficial results to flow from union with our revolting sisters, we must surrender our own convictions of duty and follow the imperative behests of others. Missouri must resign her place in the present galaxy of States, where the lustre and brilliancy of each but add harmony and beauty to the whole, and accept such position as may be assigned her in the new constellation, whose light, we fear, may never penetrate beyond the southern skies.

The importance of the accession of Missouri to any confederacy formed upon the ruins of the present Union will be readily granted; but, before accepting any such invitation without any guaranty for the future, it behooves us now to examine the character of the remedy proposed, and also its inevitable consequences upon the people of Missouri. Should the government become destructive of the ends for which it was instituted, and oppression become the established rule of its action, we presume that none will deny the revolutionary right of redress. This, however, is a remedy outside of the provisions of the Federal Constitution and one that must necessarily address itself to the moral sense of the civilized world. It depends for its success upon deep convictions of wrong by citizens of the revolting district, claiming, when justifiable, the encouragement and sympathy of other nations. It is the last remedy of injured man to obtain in violence and bloodshed, if need be, the establishment of an incontestible [sic] right. It presumes the total inefficiency of his government to redress his wrongs. It supposes that all the efforts of peace have been exhausted, and that present evils are beyond endurance.

If it be true "that governments long established should not be changed for light and transient causes,"[117] it occurs to your Committee that a proper appreciation of this truth will at once dispel all ideas of present revolution.

Secession, on the other hand, is claimed as a right resulting from the nature of our Government; that the Constitution is a mere compact between the States, not subject even to the ordinary rules governing contracts; that it is a confederation of States, not a government of the people.

It will be observed that no attempt of a serious character has ever been made to overthrow the Government without adopting this theory as the best means to accomplish the end. The reason is obvious; for although it is declared in the instrument itself that "this Constitution and the laws of the United States which shall be made in pursuance thereof, and all treaties made under the authority of the United States, shall be the supreme law of the land; and the Judges in every State shall be bound thereby, anything in the Constitution or laws of any State to the contrary notwithstanding," this doctrine interposes State authority between the rebellious citizen and the consequences of his crime. Hence the delegates from the five New England States who met at Hartford, Connecticut, in 1814,[118] in response to the call of the Massachusetts Legislature, saying "it was expedient to lay the foundation for a radical reform in the National compact, and devise some mode of defense suitable to those States, the affinities of whose interests are closest, and whose intercourse are more frequent," after enumerating their grievances against the Government, declare that "in cases of deliberate, dangerous and palpable infractions of the Constitution, affecting the sovereignty of a State and the liberties of the people, it is not only the right but the duty of such a State to interpose its authority for protection, in the manner best calculated to secure that end. When emergencies occur, which are either beyond the reach of the judicial tribunals, or too pressing to admit of the delay incident to their forms, States which have no common umpire *must be their own judges* and execute their own decisions."

Looking forward to the ultimate dissolution of the Union and the erection of a Northern Confederacy, as one of the means to secure that end, they recommended amendments to the Constitution, which they must have known would not be adopted. Their rejection, it was hoped, no doubt, would "fire the Northern mind and precipitate" the New England States "into a revolution." Seeing the enormity of their proceedings and that merited punishment would likely be visited upon them by the Government, they, too, entered their solemn protest against coercion, and declared "if the Union be destined to dissolution by reason of the multiplied abuses of bad administration, it should be, if possible, the work of peaceable times and deliberate consent," and that "a separation by *equitable arrangement* will be preferable to an alliance by constraint among nominal friends but real enemies."

We pause but to remark that the amendments to the Constitution proposed by this sectional convention were never adopted, the New England States remained in the Union, peace and prosperity again blessed the land, and the conspirators, abhorred and shunned by men, silently passed along to the grave of infamy.

At a subsequent period a movement somewhat similar in its nature was inaugurated in some of the Southern States, and your Committee hope that the allusion will give no offense to Georgia. The grievance complained of was the tariff act of 1828. South Carolina took the incipient step and declared the Constitution to be a compact between States as independent sovereignties, and not a government of the people—that the Federal Government was responsible to the State Legislatures, when it assumed powers not conferred—that notwithstanding a tribunal was appointed under the Constitution to decide controversies where the United States was a party, there were some questions that must occur between the Government and the States, which it would be unsafe to submit to any judicial tribunal, and finally, that the State had a right to judge for itself as to infractions of the Constitution.

Alabama, Virginia and Georgia having yielded assent to this exposition of the principles of the Government, a Convention was assembled in South Carolina, which at once declared the obnoxious law to be null and void, and of no binding force upon the citizens of that State. It was further resolved, that in case of an attempt by the General Government to enforce the tariff laws of 1828 or 1832, the Union was to be dissolved, and a Convention called to form an independent government of that State; and in order that the nullification might be thorough and complete, it was provided, that no appeal should be permitted to the Supreme Court of the United States, in any question concerning the validity of the ordinance or of the laws that might be passed by the Legislature to give it effect. In pursuance of this scheme, the Governor was authorized by the Legislature, to call on the militia of the State to resist the enforcement of the Federal laws; arms and munitions of war were placed at his disposal, and the State judiciary was to be exonerated from their oaths to support the Federal Constitution. Treason to the Union became sanctified with the name of patriotism, and its hideous deformity was attempted to be shielded by the mantle of State Sovereignty.

At this juncture appeared the proclamation of Jackson, explaining the nature of the American Government, denying the pretended right of sovereignty and claiming the supremacy of the Federal Constitution. A military force was ordered to assemble at Charleston, and a sloop-of-war was dispatched to the same point, to protect the Federal officers in the discharge of their duties. False theories were exploded; the tide of revolution that threatened to engulf the entire South was checked; the passions of the moment subsided; the public mind that had been maddened by the unlicensed declamation of the demagogue, was remitted to calm reflection, and soon the whole country responded to the patriotic sentiment of the iron-nerved statesman: "Our Federal Union—it must be preserved."

We pause but to remark, that the revenues were collected, peace was preserved, the country was saved, and a new batch of restless men consigned to oblivion by an indignant people. Other instances might be given in which false constructions of the Constitution have been urged, with the obvious intention ultimately to destroy it; but your Committee feel assured that the instrument itself, when viewed in connection with the history of its adoption, cannot be so tortured as to sanction the right of secession. It is an instrument of delegated powers, granted by "the people of the United States, in order to form a more perfect Union, establish justice, insure domestic tranquility, provide for the common defense, promote the general welfare, and secure the blessings of liberty to themselves and their posterity."

All legislative powers granted in the Constitution are vested in a Congress, composed of a Senate and House of Representatives. After an express enumeration of grants of power that may be exercised by that body, it is further provided, that Congress shall have power "to make all laws which shall be necessary and proper for carrying into execution the foregoing powers, and all other powers vested by this Constitution in the Government of the United States or in any department or officer thereof."

It is then provided, that "the laws of the United States, which shall be made in pursuance" of these grants of power, "shall be the supreme law of the land,

and the Judge in every State," in their administration of justice, "shall be bound thereby," notwithstanding the Constitution and laws of their own State may be to the contrary.

"The powers not delegated to the United States by the Constitution, nor prohibited by it to the States, are reserved to the States respectively, or to the people." If the framers of the Constitution had stopped at this point and furnished us no tribunal, before which the humblest citizen may obtain redress, when the limitations of the instrument shall be exceeded by the lawmaking power, the pretext for the assumed right would be infinitely more plausible. But such is not the case. The powers delegated, having been granted by the people for purposes of permanent and perpetual government, cannot be withdrawn by any State or any number of States, except in the mode indicated in the Constitution itself. These grants of power were at the time supposed to be essential to the common good; that being of a general nature, it were best to confer their exercise upon a National Government.

This having been done, the several States cannot be regarded as perfect sovereignties. The people of the whole Union having surrendered to the General Government a portion of their powers—which are material attributes of sovereignty—and having declared that government to be the supreme law of the land, it cannot be seriously urged that any number of the people organizing a State government, may confer upon it powers with which they have already parted.

But, in order to protect the people of each and every State against encroachment by the Federal authority; to prevent interference by the States with powers delegated to the Federal Government, and to preserve to each its appropriate rights for all time to come, a wise provision was made, which so far, it must be admitted, has answered all the ends for which it was adopted.

Controversies must necessarily spring up in the administration of governments so complicated in their nature, for each may be said to be sovereign within its appropriate sphere, and in order that a peaceable solution may be had in every possible case that can arise, our forefathers provided an arbiter in the Judiciary department of the Government; its power extending "to all cases in law and equity arising under this Constitution, the laws of the United States, and treaties made, or which shall be made, under their authority;" "to controversies to which the United States shall be a party; to controversies between two or more States; between a State and citizens of another State; between citizens of different States; between citizens of the same State, claiming lands under grants of different States, and between a State or citizens thereof and foreign States, citizens or subjects."[119]

This, in connection with other provisions of the Constitution referred to renders our Government, in the judgment of your Committee, the best ever established by man. Whether Georgia and other seceding States may be able to devise a better, the future alone can determine.

If we are disposed further to demonstrate the heterodoxy of secession as a right deducible from the Constitution, we might refer to other plain provisions of that instrument, and ask pertinent questions as to the reason of their adoption, and the consequences flowing from an admission of the right.

Why grant the power "to borrow money on the credit of the United States," if the State, perhaps receiving the benefit of the fund, can withdraw and absolve her citizens from all obligation to pay? Why the power "to lay and collect taxes, duties, imposts, and excises, to pay the debts and provide for the common defense and general welfare of the United States," if a simple ordinance of secession excuses the citizen and nullifies the provision for calling "forth the militia to execute the laws of the Union?" Why the power "to declare war," if, in the midst of hostilities, the State whose representatives may have voted for the declaration, but now wearied of its calamities, may seek peace in secession, and leave the Government to struggle with its dangers and its burdens? Why declare that "no State shall enter into any treaty, alliance or confederation;" that "no State shall enter into any agreement or compact with another State, or with a foreign power," if all these things can be done in perfect accordance with the Constitution?[120]

We might also refer to the acquisition of Florida, the purchase of Louisiana, the payment of the Texas debt, and the boasted "indemnity for the past and security for the future," supposed to be realized at the close of the war with Mexico, all of which were mere "promises to the ear," if the doctrine of secession be true.

But were your Committee disposed to abandon the dictates of patriotism and forget for the moment their loyalty to the Constitution of the nation, a proper regard for the local interests of our own State would demand at our hands an examination of the probable consequences of the action proposed. We are told by the Commissioner that Georgia acted for herself and adopted such course as she deemed best calculated to protect her honor and secure the welfare of her citizens.

If it be true that each State possesses the right to judge for itself, and its own peculiar interests should control its policy, in emergencies like the present, and that Georgia, in the exercise of that right, has acted with an eye single to her own welfare, it may be well doubted whether a similar instinct of self-preservation on our part should be influenced by the conduct of others.

It is urged that the Northern mind has become so corrupted by the anti-slavery mania of the day, as to render this species of property insecure. If secession could remove our State beyond the reach of this morbid sentiment, or build mountains and seas upon our borders, to arrest the operation of its influence, the remedy proposed might at least be regarded in a more favorable light. Our State is surrounded by territory which, in the event of separation, will pass under the jurisdiction of a foreign government; and if it be once admitted that fraternal regard and a sense of mutual dependence, cemented by the associations of the past and the hopes of the future, are now insufficient to check the insubordinate citizens of adjacent States, what limit to outrage may be anticipated when these restraints are removed.

Mr. WELCH.[121] I move to dispense with the further reading of the report, and that it be made the special order for the third Monday in December, 1861, and on that motion I call the ayes and noes.

Mr. BRECKINRIDGE.[122] It strikes me that would hardly be an act of courtesy to the gentleman from Pike, (Mr. Henderson.) I trust he may be allowed at least to finish the reading of his report.

Mr. SHEELEY.[123] Is the question susceptible of division? I desire as an act of courtesy that the report be read through, but I am in favor of postponing until the third Monday in December.

Mr. WELCH. At the request of Gentlemen, I defer my motion until the report has been read.

Mr. HENDERSON then continued:

Supposing that a peaceable separation could be accomplished, new and important questions would be precipitated upon us. The present elements of our prosperity as one people would become the sources of bitter strife. What gives power as a nation would bring about conflicts between its different societies, as independent sovereignties, that must soon terminate in the destruction of the weaker and the comparative ruin of the stronger. The great rivers of our country, now floating the commerce of a happy people, would daily present questions for angry controversy, between rival Republics. There being no common arbiter for the adjustment of these exciting differences, an appeal to the sword will be made to settle them. Treaties will likely fail to secure what now is claimed as a constitutional right. In this view of the case, Missouri having withdrawn from the Union, to obtain greater security in negro property, would suddenly find herself surrounded by territory affording for the fugitive slave an asylum as safe as the Canadian provinces. Secession does not commend itself to Missouri as a proper solution of the problem involved in political strife upon the territorial question.

It has been already remarked that the idea of excluding slavery from the Territories, as entertained by the Republican party, is in conflict with an unreversed decision of the Supreme Court of the United States, and was wholly abandoned by that party in the recent organization of territorial governments. The right to carry slaves into all the public domain is to-day clear and undisputed, and if the soil and climate be such as to forbid the permanent existence of the institution therein, secession will scarcely be regarded by Missouri as a remedy for the supposed grievance.

Again we may ask if the Southern States withdraw from the government, will it not be argued that they have abandoned all interest in the public property? We waive the questions of right, for evidently it resolves itself into one power, and it is at least certain that such will be the view of those from whom we may have separated. This of itself will inaugurate a contest of the most violent character, and whether the institution of slavery may be safely planted upon any soil in the midst of hostilities, originating from these causes, is a question deserving our serious consideration.

In conclusion, Mr. President, your Committee desire to express the hope that the errors of the day, both North and South, will soon be abandoned, that fraternal love will be restored by adjustment, honorable alike to every section, and that Georgia and Missouri may continue in the Union of our fathers, to bless and be blessed, in the great family of States.

In every point of view in which we have been able to examine the communication soliciting our withdrawal from the Union, whether viewed as a Constitutional right, a remedy for existing evils, or a preventive of anticipated wrongs, we find it in conflict with our allegiance to a good Government, and wholly inefficient to accomplish the ends designed.

We therefore recommend to the Convention the adoption of the following resolutions:

1st. That the communication made to the Convention by the Hon. Luther J. Glenn, as a Commissioner from the State of Georgia, so far as it asserts the constitutional right of secession meets with our disapproval.

2d. That whilst we reprobate, in common with Georgia, the violation of constitutional duty by Northern fanatics, we cannot approve the secession of Georgia and her sister States, as a measure likely to prove beneficial either to us or to themselves.

3d. That in our opinion the dissolution of the Union would be ruinous to the best interests of Missouri, hence no effects should be spared on her part to secure its continued blessings to her people, and she will labor for an adjustment of all existing differences, on such a basis as will be compatible with the interest and the honor of all the States.

4th. That this Convention exhorts Georgia and the other seceding States to desist from the revolutionary measures commenced by them, and unite their voice with ours in restoring peace and cementing the union of our fathers.

5th. *Resolved,* That the President of this Convention transmit a copy of these resolutions, together with a copy of those concerning our Federal Relations adopted by the Convention, to the President of the Convention of Georgia, or if the Convention shall have adjourned, then to the Governor of said State.

Mr. BIRCH (of the same committee.) It is due to myself to state, that in view of the delicate and important duties of the Committee, I moved at an early day of the session that it (as well as the Committee on Federal Relations) should have leave to sit during the sessions of the Convention. I design to cast no reproach upon the Chairman of the Committee, but to state, as a reason why I have not myself prepared a somewhat different (though, of course, a less able) report, that although I had personally called the attention of the Chairman to the propriety of a more early meeting of his Committee, its first session was held last night, and even then the meeting was not a full one. I will add no more except that the resolutions which I read to the Convention are all I have had leisure to properly prepare in behalf of the minority of the Committee, and in consonance with the views I have more fully indicated in my speech during the first week of the session. These resolutions I will offer, at a proper time, as substitute for those of the majority of the committee.

Mr. BIRCH then read his resolutions, as follows:

Resolved, That whilst denying the legal right of a State to secede from the Union, (as assumed in the communication which has been made to this State by the Commissioner from the State of Georgia,) we recognize in lieu thereof the right of revolution, should sufficient reason arise therefor.

2. That whilst in common with the State of Georgia, we deplore and reprobate the sectional disregard of duty and fraternity so forcibly presented by her Commissioner, we are nevertheless undespairing of future justice; nor *will* we despair until our complaints shall have been specifically and unavailingly submitted to the Northern PEOPLE.

3. That we concur with the Commissioner of the State of Georgia, that the possession of slave property is a constitutional right, and as such ought to continue to be recognized by the Federal Government; that, if it shall invade or impair that right, the slaveholding States should be found united in its defense; and that in such events as may legitimately follow, this State will share the danger and the destiny of her sister slave States.

4. That, relying upon the restoration of fraternal relations on the basis of adjustment thus and otherwise denoted in the action of this Convention, the President is requested to communicate to each of the seceding States a copy of its resolves, and to invoke for them the same earnest and respectful consideration in which they are submitted, and which restrains this Convention from any further criticism upon the mode or manner, the motives or the influences for the action of the seceding States—than to add, that it has elicited our unfeigned regret.

Source: *Proceedings of the Missouri State Convention Held at Jefferson City and St. Louis, March, 1861* (St. Louis: George Knapp & Co., Printers and Binders, 1861), 248–55.

CHAPTER 5

AFTERWARD

May–October 1861

News of Governor Jackson's refusal to supply the requested troops to put down the southern rebellion brought the secession crisis in Missouri to a head. The state's secessionists and Unionists became more vocal and active. Jackson ordered the militia to establish a camp in St. Louis (appropriately named Camp Jackson) to counter the federal presence in the city. The resulting military encounter between General Lyon and state troops set in motion events that would result in the political confrontation between a secessionist governor and the Unionist commander of the St. Louis Arsenal. Presuming federal authority, Lyon marched on Jefferson City, as Jackson and secessionist members of the legislature abandoned the capital and relocated to the southwest corner of the state. The state convention reconvened, stepping into a political vacuum, and would manage the state's affairs throughout most of the ensuing war.

Claiborne Fox Jackson's Address to the General Assembly

May 3, 1861

On April 22, 1861, following the Confederate bombardment of Ft. Sumter and President Lincoln's April 15 call for 75,000 state troops, Governor Jackson requested the general assembly to reconvene on May 2. In his opening message, Jackson blamed the "progress of fanaticism, sectionalism and cupidity in the Northern States for the present crisis." Without mentioning the attack on the federal fort in Charleston Harbor, he intoned that the Lincoln administration intended to "practically convert the government of the United States into an overshadowing consolidated despotism." Jackson announced he had denied Washington its four regiments and, with the hope of recusing Missouri from the war "about to be inaugurated," had called for the militia law to be revised to prepare for the state's defense. On May 7, the general assembly authorized Jackson to recruit for a period of one year, "five companies of infantry of one hundred men each, to be armed and equipped at the expense of the State, for the protection of the public property."

Gentlemen of the Senate and of the House of Representatives:

I had no reason to anticipate, when you adjourned, that circumstances would so soon arise, which would render it my imperative duty to call you together again. It is deeply to be regretted that such a step has to be taken at a season of the year when time is so precious, and the loss of it, in your private affairs, must occasion such serious inconvenience. I am confident, however, that you have not reluctantly responded to the call, and that the objects for which you have assembled can be promptly and unanimously accomplished in a very few days. Since your adjournment, events affecting the peace and safety of the country, have been transpiring almost with the rapidity of thought, and of a nature well calculated to awaken, in the bosom of every patriot, the most gloomy apprehensions. Manifestations from every quarter, and of a character neither to be overlooked or disregarded, indicate but too plainly that our whole country, its Constitution and laws, are in imminent danger of disorder and destruction.

Our Federal Constitution, the bond of union of a once united and happy people, was framed by the delegates of distinct and separate States, and severally ratified by them in their sovereign capacity as States. This Constitution emanated from men who were guided by intelligence and patriotism, and taught by the lessons of experience and history, and whose minds were illuminated by the lights of philosophy and wisdom. Its object was to establish equality and justice between the States, and to insure domestic tranquility within them. Had the same spirit of justice and patriotism, which animated the men who devised it, guided the people of the free States in the proper observance of its obligations to the present hour, we would now have a united, prosperous and happy Union, instead of a distracted and broken Confederacy. There has been no necessary conflict of interests between the North and the South, the East and the West. Varieties of climate, locality and products involved, it is true, contrasting, but not conflicting organizations of labor, and social structures, animated by different but not adverse principles. But the progress of fanaticism, sectionalism and cupidity in the Northern States, for the last quarter of a century, has, with accumulating force, culminated in the triumph of a purely sectional faction, which under the forms, but in violation of the principles of the Constitution, threatens to destroy the sovereignty of the States, and practically convert the government of the United States into an overshadowing consolidated despotism. The present Executive of the United States seems to regard the States, in their relation to the Federal Government, as similar to those which counties bear to State sovereignties. A perversion so monstrous and so dangerous, all wise and reflecting men foresaw must end in a dissolution of the Confederacy, and that result has not taken us by surprise. Prior to the inauguration of President Lincoln seven States had seceded; they united with each other under a new Constitution; elected their officers, organized armies, instituted judicial tribunals, and asserted all the powers rightfully belonging to sovereign States. To this they were impelled by well founded apprehensions of imminent danger to all their vital interests, and by a consciousness that every thing dear to them was directly menaced by the predominance of a faction avowedly hostile to their very existence as communities. For calamities so deplorable the people of Missouri cannot be reproached. They have preserved with scrupulous fidelity their attachment to the Constitution and the Union. They have asked for nothing which was not their right. They have done nothing in derogation of the rights of others. They have patiently submitted to many and great injuries for the sake of peace. They have ever counseled concord and fraternity. Their statute books have not been defaced by enactments in contravention of the Constitution, and the laws made in pursuance thereof. They have been slow to believe that designs destructive of their rights and interests could be entertained by the Administration of Mr. Lincoln. They refused to see in his inaugural any purpose of introducing the horrors of civil war. They have cordially united in every effort of the people of the Border States to effect such a compromise as would secure the rights and honor of all, restore fraternal feeling, reconstitute the Union, and impart new vigor to the Constitution. Their counsels and their rights have been alike unheeded. The old Confederacy is broken; a new one has been organized by a portion of the States; and President Lincoln, by his proclamation calling out a force of seventy-five thousand men to subdue the seceded States, has threatened a destructive war between the States.

On the 15th day of April, I received a dispatch from the Secretary of War, calling on me to furnish the government at Washington with four regiments to aid in the prosecution of the civil war about to be inaugurated. I am sure I but gave utterance to the universal heart of our people when I replied, that Missouri would not furnish one man to assist in such a war. The action of the

President is evidently unconstitutional and illegal, and will only tend to still further alienate the people of the free and slaveholding States in their opinions and sentiments. In confirmation of this opinion it is sufficient to say that the power to coerce a State, by the Federal Union, was proposed in the Convention that framed the Constitution in several different forms, and rejected; and it is an insult to the common sense of the people to assert, that a war upon individuals, acting under the authority of a State, and by virtue of its commission, or in obedience to its government, is not a war upon the State. The President, it appears, has not only discovered the power in the *government* to make war on the States, but has assumed that the *Executive Department* can initiate that war. Neither Washington, nor Jefferson, nor Jackson ever for one moment imagined that they were clothed with such a despotic power as this. On the contrary, we have been taught by the following language in the farewell address of General Jackson, that the harmony and permanency of the Union could only be perpetuated by such a policy as would command the love and confidence of the people of the several States. He said: "But the constition [sic] cannot be maintained, nor the Union preserved, in opposition to public feeling, by the mere exertion of the coercive powers confided to the government. The foundations must be laid in the affections of the people; in the security it gives to life, liberty, character and property *in every quarter of the country*; and in the fraternal attachments which the citizens of the several States bear to one another, as members of one political family, mutually contributing to promote the happiness of each other."[1] We have also been warned by John Quincy Adams,[2] that the permanency of the Union rested not in the coercive powers of the Federal Government, but in the love and affections of the people. His opinions were expressed in regard to the perpetuity of the government, following strong and truthful language: "The indissoluble link of Union between the people of the several States of the Confederate nation, is, after all, not in the *right*, but in the *heart*. If the day should ever come, (may heaven avert it,) when the affections of the people of these States shall be alienated from each other; when the fraternal spirit shall give way to cold indifference, or collisions of interest shall fester into hatred, the bands of political association will not long hold together parties no longer attached by the magnetism of conciliated interests and kindly sympathies; and far better will it be for the people of the *disunited* States to part in friendship from each other, than to be held together by constraint."[3]

But the lessons of wisdom taught by the older and purer statesmen of the country seem to be unheeded by the present Administration. Its policy is rapidly tending to revolution; and, unless speedily arrested, will end in ruin and disaster to the hitherto prosperous and happy people of the American Continent. The great and patriotic State of Virginia, after having failed in all her efforts to re-adjust the Union, has at last yielded in despair, and seceded from the old Federal Union.[4] North Carolina, Tennessee and Arkansas, it is believed, will rapidly follow in the footsteps of Virginia; and Kentucky is profoundly moved in this great question.[5] Our interests and our sympathies are identical with those of the slaveholding States, and necessarily unite our destiny with theirs. The similarity of our social and political institutions; our industrial interests; our sympathies, habits and tastes; our common origin and territorial contiguity, all concur in pointing out our duty in regard to the separation which is now taking place between the States of the old Federal Union. In the meantime, it is, in my judgment, indispensable to our safety that we should emulate the policy of all the other States in arming our people, and placing the State in a proper attitude for defense. The Militia Law should be revised and rendered more efficient. A good system of drill and discipline should also be adopted, in order to place ourselves in a position where our rights can be defended by strong arms and willing hearts.

Missouri has, at this time, no war to prosecute. It is not her policy to make aggressions on any State or people; but in the present state of the country, she would be faithless to her honor, and recreant in her duty, were she to hesitate a moment in making the most ample preparation for the protection of her people against the aggression of all assailants.

I, therefore, respectfully recommend the appropriation of a sufficient sum of money to place the State, at the earliest practicable moment, in a complete state of defense.

In conclusion, permit me to appeal to you, and through you, to the whole people of the State, to whom we are responsible, to do nothing imprudently or precipitately. We, gentlemen, have a most solemn duty to perform. Let us, then, calmly reason one with another; avoid all passion and all tendency to tumult and disorder; obey implicitly the law and the constituted authorities, and endeavor, ultimately, to unite all our citizens in cordial co-operation, for the preservation of our honor, the security of our property, and the performance of all those high duties imposed upon us by our obligations to our families, our country, and our God.

Respectfully,
C. F. JACKSON.

Source: *Journal of the House of Representatives of the State of Missouri, at the Called Session of the Twenty-First General Assembly* (Jefferson City: J. P. Ament, Public Printer, 1861), 13–16.

Afterward

Claiborne Fox Jackson's "To the People of Missouri"

June 12, 1861

Following the breakup of the meeting between Governor Jackson and Lyon on June 11, Jackson directed his aide, Thomas L. Snead, to draft a proclamation that would clearly present the federal government as the aggressor and the governor as the defender of the rights of Missouri's citizens. In its condemnation of the government of the United States and General Lyon specifically for rejecting Jackson's peace offering, the pronouncement served as a rallying cry for Missourians to cast off the "military occupiers of your State." "Rise, then," it announced, "and drive out ignominiously the invaders who have dared to desecrate the soil which your labors have made fruitful, and which is consecrated by your homes!"

TO THE PEOPLE OF MISSOURI
June 14, 1861

From the Missouri Republican, June 14, 1861

To the People of Missouri:
A series of unprovoked unparalleled outrages have been inflicted upon the peace and dignity of this commonwealth and upon the rights and liberties of its people, by wicked and unprincipled men professing to act under the authority of the United States Government; the solemn enactments of your Legislature have been nullified; your volunteer soldiers have been taken prisoners; your commerce with your sister States has been suspended; your trade with your own fellow citizens, has been, and is, subjected to the harassing control of an armed soldiery; peaceful citizens have been imprisoned without warrant of law; unoffending and defenseless men, women and children have been ruthlessly shot down and murdered; and other unbearable indignities have been heaped upon your State and yourselves.

To all of these outrages and indignities you have submitted with a patriotic forbearance, which has only encouraged the perpetrators of these grievous wrongs to attempt still bolder and more daring usurpations.

It has been my earnest endeavor under all these embarrassing circumstances to maintain the peace of the State, and to avert, if possible, from our borders the desolating effects of a civil war. With that object in view I authorized Major

General Price[6] several weeks ago, to arrange with General Harney,[7] commanding the Federal troops in this State, the terms of an agreement by which the peace of the State might be preserved. They came, on the 21st of May, to an understanding, which was made public. The State authorities have faithfully labored to carry out the terms of that agreement. The Federal Government on the other hand not only manifested its strong disapprobation of it, by the instant dismissal of the distinguished officer who, on its part, entered into it; but it at once began, and has unintermittingly carried out, a system of hostile operations, in utter contempt of that agreement and in reckless disregard of its own plighted faith. These acts have latterly portended revolution and civil war so unmistakably, that I resolve to make one further effort to avert these dangers from you. I therefore solicited an interview with Brig. Gen. Lyon, commanding the Federal army in Missouri.[8] It was granted, and on the 10th inst., waiving all questions of personal and official dignity, I went to St. Louis, accompanied by Major-General Price.

We had an interview on the 11th inst., with Gen. Lyon and Colonel F. P. Blair, Jr.,[9] at which {time} I submitted to them the proposition: That I would disband the State Guard, and break up its organization; that I would disarm all the companies which had been armed by the State; that I would pledge myself not to attempt to organize the militia under the Military Bill; that no arms or munitions of war should be brought into the State; that I would protect all citizens equally in all their rights, regardless of their political opinions; that I would repress all insurrectionary movements within the State; that I would repel all attempts to invade it, from whatever quarter, and by whomsoever made; and that I would thus maintain a strict neutrality in the present unhappy contest, and preserve the peace of the State. And I further proposed that I would, if necessary, invoke the assistance of the United States troops to carry out these pledges. All this I proposed to do upon condition that the Federal Government would undertake to disarm the Home Guards which it has illegally organized and armed throughout the State, and pledge itself not to occupy with its troops any localities in the State, not occupied by them at this time.

Nothing but the most earnest desire to avert the horrors of civil war from our beloved State, could have tempted me to propose those humiliating terms. They were rejected by the Federal officers.

They demanded not only the disorganization and disarming of the State militia, and the nullification of the Military Bill, but they refused to disarm their own Home Guards and insisted that the Federal Government should enjoy an unrestricted right to move and *station* its troops throughout the State, whenever and wherever they might, *in the opinion of its officers*, be necessary, either for the protection of the "loyal subjects" of the Federal Government, or for the repelling of the invasion; and they plainly announced that it was the intention of the Administration to take military occupation, under these pretexts, of the whole State, and to reduce it, as avowed by General Lyon himself, to the "exact conditions of Maryland."

The acceptance by me of these degrading terms would not only have sullied the honor of Missouri, but would have aroused the indignation of every brave citizen, and precipitated the very conflict which it has been my aim to prevent.—We refuse to accede to them and the conference was broken up.

Fellow-citizens: All our efforts toward conciliation have failed. We can hope nothing from the justice or moderation of the agents of the Federal Government in this State. They are energetically hastening the execution of their bloody and revolutionary schemes for the inauguration of civil war in their midst, and for the military occupation of your State by the armed bands of lawless invaders, for the overthrow of your State Government, and for the subversion of those liberties which that Government has always sought to protect; and they intend to exert their whole power to subjugate you, if possible, to the military despotism which has usurped the powers of the Federal Government.

Now, THEREFORE, I, C. F. JACKSON, Governor of the State of Missouri, do, in view of the foregoing facts, and by virtue of the powers vested in me by the Constitution and laws of this Commonwealth, issue this, my proclamation, calling the militia of the State, to the number of *fifty thousand*, into active service of this State, for the purpose of repelling said invasion, and for the protection of the lives, liberty, and property of the citizens of this State. And I earnestly exhort all good citizens of Missouri to rally under the flag of their State for the protection of their endangered homes and firesides, and for the defense of their most sacred rights and dearest liberties.

In issuing this Proclamation, I hold it to be my solemn duty to remind you that Missouri is still one of the United States; that the Executive Department of the State Government does not arrogate to itself the power to disturb that relation; that that power has been wisely invested in a Convention, which will, at the proper time, express your sovereign will; and that meanwhile it is your duty to obey all the *constitutional* requirements of the Federal Government. But it is equally my duty to advise you that your first allegiance is one to your own State; and that you are under no obligation, whatever, to obey the *Unconstitutional* edicts of the military despotism which has enthroned itself at Washington, nor to submit to the infamous and degrading sway of its wicked millions in this State. No brave and true-hearted Missourian will obey the one, or submit to the other. Rise, then, and drive out ignominiously the invaders who have dared to desecrate the soil which your labors have made fruitful, and which is consecrated by your homes!

Given under my hand as Governor, and under the great seal of the State of Missouri, at Jefferson City this twelfth day of June, 1861

By the Governor: CLAIBORNE F. JACKSON
B. F. MASSEY[10]
Secretary of State.

Source: Buel Leopard and Floyd C. Shoemaker, eds., *The Messages and Proclamations of the Governors of the State of Missouri*, vol. III (Columbia: State Historical Society of Missouri, 1922), 385–89.

Missouri State Convention's Committee of Eight Report
July 29, 1861

Only days after Governor Jackson and some members of the general assembly fled the capital on June 13, Nathaniel Lyon entered Jefferson City. On July 6, with the state government in retreat to the southwest, delegates of the state convention called the gathering back into session to begin on July 22. The convention quickly appointed a Committee of Seven (later Eight) to report on "what action is necessary to be taken by this Convention in the present condition of public affairs in Missouri." The committee included James O. Broadhead (St. Louis County) as chair, John B. Henderson (Pike), William A. Hall (Randolph), Willard P. Hall (Buchanan), William Douglass (Cooper), Littleberry Hendrick (Greene), Joseph Bogy (St. Genevieve), and later, Hamilton R. Gamble (St. Louis).

James Overton Broadhead (1819–1898) was born in Charlottesville, Virginia; studied one year at the University of Virginia, before moving to St. Charles County, Missouri, in 1837. He was admitted to the bar in 1842 having been tutored by Edward Bates a prominent attorney in St. Louis who later became President Lincoln's attorney general. Broadhead served in the Missouri House of Representatives (1846–1847) and in the Missouri Senate (1850–1853).

Mr. BROADHEAD, Chairman of the Committee of Eight, presented the following amended Report:

Mr. PRESIDENT—The Committee of Eight, to whom was recommended the report concerning the necessary action to be taken by the Convention, has instructed me to report the following as a substitute for the former report, and recommend its adoption.

AN ORDINANCE PROVIDING FOR CERTAIN AMENDMENTS TO THE CONSTITUTION

The People of the State of Missouri, by their Delegates in Convention assembled, do ordain as follows:

First. That the offices of Governor, Lieutenant Governor, Secretary of State, and members of the General Assembly, be and the same are hereby vacated.

Second. A Governor, Lieutenant Governor, and Secretary of State, shall be appointed by this Convention, to discharge the duties and exercise the powers which pertain to their respective offices by the existing laws of the State, and to continue in office until the first Monday of November, 1861, and until their successors are elected and qualified, or until the qualified voters, as hereinafter provided, disapprove the action of this convention.

Third. On the first Monday of November, 1861, a Governor, Lieutenant Governor, and Secretary of State, and members of the General Assembly, shall be elected by the qualified voters of this State, to hold their offices during the term for which the present incumbents of said offices were elected.

Fourth. The elections provided to be held by this ordinance on the first Monday of November, 1861, shall be conducted in the same manner in all respects as is now provided by the election laws of this State now in force, and shall be held by the qualified voters of the State, at the same place in the election precincts now established by law where the elections were held for delegates to this Convention on the 18th day of February last; and in case any clerk shall fail to make out the proper poll books, or in case any sheriff shall fail to deliver the same to the judges of election, then the clerks of the election may proceed to make out such poll books.

Fifth. In case the Clerks of the several Courts, whose duty it is, as now provided by law, {fail} to certify and send up to the Secretary of State an abstract of the votes given at such election, or in case there should be a failure to receive such returns at the seat of Government within twenty days after the first Monday in November, 1861, the Secretary of State shall dispatch a messenger to the county not returned, with directions to bring up the poll-books authorized to be retained by the judges of election, and the Secretary of State, in the presence of the Governor, shall proceed to cast up the votes given at such election, and shall thereupon proceed to issue commissions to the candidates having the highest number of votes.

Sixth. Be it further ordained, That the returns of the election for Governor, Lieutenant Governor, and Secretary of State, provided for by this ordinance, shall be made to the office of the Secretary of State, as now provided by law; and the Secretary of State, within forty days after the first Monday of November, 1861, or sooner if the returns shall have been made, shall, in the presence of the Governor, proceed to cast up the votes given at said election for Governor, Lieutenant Governor, and Secretary of State; and shall give to the persons having the highest number of votes for these officers, respectively, certificates of their election; and the persons so elected shall immediately thereafter be qualified and enter upon the discharge of the duties of their respective offices.

Your Committee would also recommend that the following Ordinance be adoptedby the Convention, to-wit:

AN ORDINANCE CONCERNING THE REPEAL AND ABROGATION OF CERTAIN LAWS, AND FOR OTHER PURPOSES.

WHEREAS, the General Assembly of the State of Missouri did, in secret session, contrary to the known wishes of their constituents, in violation of the Constitution and the dearest rights and interests of the people, and for the purpose of dissolving the political relations of this State to the Government of the United States, and subverting the institutions of this State, enact certain odious laws hereinafter enumerated; therefore,

1. *Be it ordained by the People of Missouri in Convention assembled,* That an act entitled "An act to provide for the organization , government and support of the military forces of the State of Missouri," approved May 14th, 1861; also, an act to create a military fund for the State, entitled "An act to raise money to arm the State, repel an invasion, and protect the lives and property of the people of Missouri," approved May 11th, 1861; also an act entitled "An act to authorize the appointment of one Major General for the Missouri Militia," approved May 15th, 1861; also a "Joint Resolution to suspend the apportionment of the State School Money for the year 1861," approved May 11th, 1861; also an act entitled "An act to perpetuate friendly relations with the Indian tribes," approved May 11th, 1861, be and the same are hereby repealed and declared of no effect or validity whatever.

2. That all commissions issued or appointments made under the authority of the above recited acts or any of them, be and the same are hereby annulled; and all soldiers and other persons serving or employed under any of said acts are hereby disbanded and discharged from such service or employment.

3. *And be it further ordained,* That for the purpose of providing for the organization of the militia of the State, the following act, to-wit, an act entitled "An act to govern and regulate the Volunteer Militia of the State," approved December 31st, 1859, be and the same is hereby revived and declared to be in full force and effect.

Also, the following ordinance, to-wit:

AN ORDINANCE FOR SUBMITTING THE ACTION OF THIS CONVENTION TO A VOTE OF THE PEOPLE OF MISSOURI.

Be it ordained, that at the election provided to be held on the first Monday of November, 1861, for the election of Governor, Lieutenant Governor, and Secretary of State, and members of the General Assembly, the several Clerks of the County Courts in making the poll-books for the election shall provide two columns—one headed "For the action of the Convention," and the other "Against the action of the Convention;" and if a majority of the legal votes upon the action of the Convention be for the same, then the officers elected shall hold their offices as provided by the ordinance for their election; but if a majority of the votes cast as aforesaid be against the action of the Convention, then said election shall be null and void, and the persons so chosen shall not enter upon the discharge of the duties of their offices; the officers chosen by this Convention shall go out of office, and the ordinance of this Convention, providing for the abrogation of certain acts of the Legislature, shall thereafter be of no force or effect whatever. The returns of the votes so cast on the action of the Convention shall be made to the office of the Secretary of State in the same manner as is provided by ordinance of this Convention in regard to the offices of Governor, Lieutenant Governor, and Secretary of State, and the votes shall be cast up by the same officer; and when the result thereof shall be ascertained, the Governor appointed by this Convention shall, by public proclamation, announce the same, which proclamation shall be filed in the office of the Secretary of State.

Source: *Journal of the Missouri State Convention, Held at Jefferson City, July, 1861* (St. Louis: George Knapp & Co., Printers and Binders, 1861), 17–18.

Missouri State Convention's "To the People of the State of Missouri"

July 31, 1861

Believing that their actions required an explanation and justification, the delegates prepared an address to the people of Missouri. After listing the endeavors of the General Assembly in secret session to align Missouri with the Confederacy, which to the committee had "produced evils and dangers of vast magnitude," the address announced that "your delegates in Convention have addressed themselves to the important and delicate duty of attempting to free the State from these evils." The pronouncement concluded by stating that the delegates hoped that their efforts would bring "peace and security to all her citizens." If those efforts failed to restore peace, however, "your delegates will find consolation in the fact that they have done what they could."

The Committee who was appointed to prepare an address to the people of the State through their Chairman Hon. Hamilton R. Gamble, presented the following:

TO THE PEOPLE OF THE STATE OF MISSOURI.

Your delegates assembled in Convention propose to address you upon the present condition of affairs within our State.

Since the adjournment of this Convention in March last, the most startling events have rushed upon us with such rapidity that the nation stands astonished at the condition of anarchy and strife to which in so brief a period it has been reduced. When the Convention adjourned, although the muttering of the storm was heard, it seemed to be distant, and it was hoped that some quiet but powerful force might be applied by the beneficent Providence to avert its fury and preserve our country from threatened ruin. That hope has not been realized. The storm in all its fury has burst upon the country, the armed hosts of different sections have met each other in bloody conflict, and the grave has already received the remains of thousands of slaughtered citizens. Passion, inflamed to madness, demands that the stream of blood shall flow broader and deeper, and the whole energies of a people, but a few months since prosperous and happy, are now directed to the collection of larger hosts, and the preparation of increased and more destructive enginery of death.

Your delegates enjoy the satisfaction of knowing that, neither by their action, nor their failure to act, have they in any degree contributed to the ferocious war spirit which now prevails so generally over the whole land. We have sought peace, we have entreated those who were about to engage in war to withhold their hands from the strife, and in this course we know that we but expressed the wishes and feelings of the State. Our entreaties have been unheeded; and now, while war is raging in other parts of our common country,[11] we have felt that our first and highest duty is to preserve, if possible, our own State from its ravages. The danger is imminent, and demands prompt and decisive measures of prevention.

We have assembled in Jefferson under circumstances widely different from those that existed when the Convention adjourned its session at St. Louis.

We find high offices of the State Government engaged in actual hostilities with the forces of the United States, and blood has been shed upon the soil of Missouri. Many of our citizens have yielded obedience to an ill-judged call of the Governor and have assembled in arms for the purpose of "repelling the invasion of the State by armed bands of lawless invaders," as the troops of the

United States are designated by the Governor in his proclamation of the 12th day of June last.

We find that troops from the State of Arkansas have come into Missouri for the purpose of sustaining the action of our Governor in his contest with the United States, and this at the request of our Executive.

We find no person present, or likely soon to be present, at the seat of government to exercise the ordinary functions of the Executive department or to maintain the internal peace of the State.

We find that throughout the State there is imminent danger of civil war in its worst form, in which neighbor shall seek the life of neighbor, the bonds of society shall be dissolved, and universal anarchy shall reign.

If it be possible to find a remedy for existing evils and to avert the threatened horrors of anarchy it is manifestly the duty of your delegates assembled in Convention to provide such remedy. And in order to determine upon the remedy, it is necessary to trace very briefly the origin and progress of the evils that now afflict the State.

It is not necessary that any lengthy reference should be made to the action of those States which have seceded from the Union. We cannot remedy or recall that secession. They have acted for themselves, and must abide the consequences of their own action. So far as you have expressed your wishes, you have declared your determination not to leave the Union, and your wishes have been expressed by this Convention.

Any action of any officer of the State in conflict with your will thus expressed, is an action in plain opposition to the principles of our Government which recognizes the people as the source of political power, and their will as the rule of conduct for all their officers. It would have been but a reasonable compliance with your will, that after you had, through this convention, expressed your determination to remain in the Union, your Executive and Legislative officers should not only have refrained from any opposition to your will, but should have exerted all their powers to carry your will into effect.

We have been enabled to ascertain by some correspondence of different public officers, accidentally made public, that several of those officers not only entertained and expressed opinions and wishes against the continuance of Missouri in the Union, but actually engaged in schemes to withdraw her from the Union, contrary to your known wishes.

After the adjournment of your convention in March, which had expressed your purpose to remain in the Union, Governor Claiborne F. Jackson, in a letter addressed to David Walker, President of the Arkansas Convention, dated April 19, 1861, says: "From the beginning my own conviction has been that the interest, duty and honor of every slave-holding State demands their separation from the Northern or non-slaveholding States." Again, he says: "I have been from the beginning in favor of decided and prompt action on the part of the Southern States, but the majority of the people of Missouri, up to the present time, have differed with me." Here we have the declaration of his opinion and wishes, and the open confession that a majority of the people did not agree with him. But he proceeds: "What their future action (meaning the future action of the people) may be, no man, with certainty, can predict or foretell; but my impression is, judging from the indications hourly occuring [sic], *that Missouri will be ready for secession in less than thirty days, and will secede if Arkansas will only get out of the way and give her a free passage.*[12]

It will presently be seen by an extract from another letter what the Governor means by being "ready for secession," but it is very remarkable that he should undertake not only to say that she would be ready to secede in thirty days; but further, that *"she will secede,"* when in fact your convention at that time stood adjourned to the third Monday of December next. His declaration, that the State would secede, is made, doubtless, upon some plan of his own, independent of the Convention.

Nine days after this letter to the President of the Arkansas Convention, he wrote another addressed to J. W. Tucker, Esq., the editor of a secession newspaper in St. Louis.[13] This letter is dated April 28, 1861.[14] The writer says:

"I do not think Missouri should secede today or to-morrow, but I do not think it good policy that I should so openly declare. *I want a little time to arm the State,* and I am assuming every responsibility to do it with all possible dispatch."

Again, he says, "*We should keep our own counsels.* Everybody in the State is in favor of arming the State; then let it be done. All are opposed to furnishing Mr. Lincoln with soldiers. *Time will settle the balance. Nothing should be said about the time or the manner in which Missouri should go out.* That she ought to go and will go at the proper time I have no doubt. She ought to have gone last winter, *when she could have seized the public arms and public property and defended herself.*" Here we have the fixed mind and purpose of the Governor that Missouri shall leave the Union. He wants time—a little time to arm the State. He thinks secrecy should be preserved by the parties with whom he acts in keeping their counsels. He suggests that nothing should be said about the time or the manner in which Missouri should go out, manifestly implying that the time and manner of going out which he and those with whom he acted proposed to adopt, was some other time and manner than such as was to be fixed by the people through their Convention. It was no doubt to be a time and manner to be fixed by the Governor and the General Assembly, or by the Governor and a military body to be provided with arms during the "little time" needed by the Governor for that purpose. There has been no specific disclosure made to the public of the details of this plan, but the Governor expresses his strong conviction that at the *proper time* the State will go out.

Afterward

This correspondence of the Governor occurred at a time when there was no interference by soldiers of the United States with any of the citizens or with the peace of the State. The event which produced exasperation through the State—the capture of Camp Jackson—did not take place until the 10th of May. Yet the evidence is conclusive that there was at the time of this correspondence a secret plan for taking Missouri out of the Union without any assent of the people through their Convention.

An address to the people of Missouri was issued by Thomas C. Reynolds, the Lieutenant Governor,[15] in which he declares that "in Arkansas, Tennessee, and Virginia, his efforts have now been directed increasingly to the best of his limited ability to the promotion of our interests, indissolubly connected with the vindication of our liberties, and our speedy union with the Confederate States." Here is the second Executive officer of Missouri avowedly engaged in traveling through the States, which he must regard while Missouri continues in the Union as foreign States, and in those States endeavoring, as he says, to promote the interests of our State. The mode of promoting our interests is disclosed in another passage of the address, in which he gives the people assurance "that the people of the confederate States, though engaged in a war with a powerful foe, would not hesitate still farther to tax their energies and resources at the proper time, and on a proper occasion, in aid of Missouri." The mode of promoting our interests, then, was by obtaining military aid, and this while Missouri continued in the Union.

The result of the joint action of the first and second Executive officers of the State has been, that a body of the military forces of Arkansas has actually invaded Missouri, to carry out the schemes of your own officers, who ought to have conformed to your will as you had made it known at elections, and had expressed it by your delegates in Convention.

Still farther to execute the purpose of severing the connexion of Missouri with the United States, the General Assembly was called, and when assembled sat in secret session, and enacted laws which had for their object the placing in the hands of the Governor large sums of money to be expended in his discretion for military purposes, and a law for the organization of a military force which was to be sustained by extraordinary taxation, and to be absolutely subject to the orders of the Governor to act against all opposers, including the United States. By these acts, schools are closed, and the demands of humanity for the support of lunatics are denied, that the money raised for the purposes of education and benevolence may swell the fund to be expended in war.

Without referring more particularly to the provisions of these several acts, which are most extraordinary and extremely dangerous as precedents, it is sufficient to say that they display the same purpose to engage in a conflict with the General Government, and to break the connection of Missouri with the United States, which had before been manifested by the Governor.

The conduct of these officers of the legislative and executive departments has produced evils and dangers of vast magnitude, and your delegates in Convention have addressed themselves to the important and delicate duty of attempting to free the State from these evils.

The high executive officers have fled from the seat of Government and from the State, leaving us without the officers to discharge the ordinary and necessary executive functions. But, more than this, they are actually engaged in carrying on a war within the State, supported by troops from States in the Southern Confederacy; so that the State, whilst earnestly desiring to keep out of the war, has become the scene of conflict without any action of the people assuming such position of hostility.

Any remedy for our present evils, to be adequate, must be one which shall vacate the offices held by the officers who have thus brought our troubles upon us.

Your delegates desire that you shall by election fill these offices by persons of your own choice, and for this purpose they have directed, by ordinance, that an election shall be held on the first Monday in November. This time, rather than one nearer at hand, was selected so as to conform to the spirit of the provision in the Constitution, which requires three months' notice to be given of an election to fill a vacancy in the office of the Governor. But, in the meantime, much damage might happen to the State by keeping the present incumbents in office, not only by leaving necessary Executive duties unperformed, while they prosecute their war measures, but by continuing and increasing the internal social strife which threatens the peace of the whole State. Your delegates judged it necessary that in order to preserve the peace, and in order to arrest invasions of the State, that these Executive offices should be vacated at once, and be filled by persons selected by your delegates until you could fill them by election. They have, therefore, made such selection as they trust will be found to be judicious in preserving the peace of the State.

The office of Secretary of State has not been mentioned before, and it is sufficient to say, that Benjamin F. Massey,[16] the present incumbent, has abandoned the seat of Government, and has followed the fortunes of the Governor, taking with him the seal of State. As an instrument of evil he may be employed by the Governor in action deeply injurious to the State; and he has been dealt with by your delegates in the same manner as the Governor and Lieutenant Governor.

In regard to the members of the General Assembly, it is only necessary to say that, by the enactment of the law called the military bill, which violates the Constitution and places the entire military strength of the State at the almost unlimited control of the Executive, and imposes onerous burdens upon the citizens for the support of an army, and by the passage of general appropriation acts which give to the Executive the command of large funds to be expended at his discretion for military purposes, thus uniting the control of the purse and the sword in the same hands, they have displayed their willingness to sustain the war policy of the Executive, and place the destinies of the State in the hands of the Governor.

The offices of the members of the General Assembly have therefore been vacated and a new election ordered, so that you may have an opportunity of choosing such legislative representatives as may carry out your own views of policy.

In order that the schemes of those who seek to take Missouri out of the Union may not farther be aided by the late secret legislation of the General Assembly, your delegates have by ordinance annulled the military law, and such other acts as were doubtless passed for the purpose of disturbing the relations of the State with the Federal Government.

These are the measures adopted by your delegates in Convention for the purpose of restoring peace to our disturbed State, and enabling you to select officers for yourselves to declare and carry into effect your views of the true policy of the State. They are measures which seem to be imperatively demanded by the present alarming condition of public affairs, and your delegates have determined to submit them to you for your approval or disapproval, that they may have the authority of your sanction, if you find them to be adapted to secure the peace and welfare of the State.

There are some who question the power of the Convention to adopt these measures. A very brief examination of this question of power will show that the power exists beyond doubt.

It is one of the fundamental principles of our government that all political power resides in the people, and it is established beyond question, that a Convention of delegates of the people, when regularly called and assembled, possess all the political power which the people themselves possess, and stands in the place of the assemblage of all the people in one vast mass. If there be no limitation upon the power of the Convention, made in the call of the body, then the body is possessed of unlimited political power. If it be a State Convention, then there is a limitation upon it, imposed by the Constitution of the United States.

If we state the position of the opponents of the powers now exercised by this Convention in the strongest form, it is this: The Convention was called by an act of the General Assembly for specific purposes declared in the act, and therefore the people in electing delegates under that act intended to limit the Convention to the subjects therein specified, and the action taken by the Convention in vacating state offices is not within the scope of the subjects thus submitted to the Convention.

It is very well understood by all that a Convention of the people does not derive any power from any act of the Legislature. All its power is directly the power of the people, and is not dependent upon any act of the ordinary functionaries of the State. It cannot be claimed, in the present case, that we are to look at the act of Assembly referred to for any other purpose than to find whether there is any limitation imposed by the people upon the powers of the Convention, by electing the Convention under the act. If it be examined with that view, and if it be conceded that any of its provisions were designed to limit the powers of the Convention, it will be seen that all the Convention has done comes clearly within the scope of the powers designed to be exercised.

The fifth section of the act provides that the Convention, when assembled, "shall proceed to consider the then existing relations between the Government of the United States, the people and the governments of the different States, and the government and people of the State of Missouri, *and to adopt such measures for vindicating the sovereignty of the State and the protection of its institutions as shall appear to them to be demanded.*"[17] The measures to be adopted are to be such as the Convention shall judge to be demanded in order to vindicate the sovereignty of the State and protect its institutions. Those measures are left to the judgment of the Convention, and may reach any officer or any class of persons.

Let us take the case, then, of an armed invasion of the State by troops from Arkansas, either invited or headed by the Governor of Missouri. The vindication of the sovereignty of the State may demand that such invasion be repelled by force, and every person can see that while the forces of Missouri may be employed in repelling the invasion, it is perfectly obvious that the vindication of our sovereignty requires that the Governor, who is by the Constitution the Commander-in-Chief of the army of the State, must be removed from that office when he is actually engaged in leading or inciting the invasion. To consider the relations existing between the people and Government of Arkansas and the people and Government of Missouri, and to adopt measures to vindicate our sovereignty, imperatively demands in the case supposed, and which actually exists, that the Commander-in-Chief of Missouri be removed from his office.

This case is stated merely as an illustration of the principles upon which the Convention has felt itself bound to act. Other cases equally strong, and equally demanding the interposition of the Constitution, might be stated as actually existing, but that now stated is sufficient to put you in possession of the principle upon which the action of the Convention rests. It is clearly an action demanded by the duty of vindicating the sovereignty of the State, and it applies to the other persons removed from office by the Convention upon the ground that they are all involved in the same scheme for assailing the sovereignty of the State.

In relation to the members of the General Assembly, the convention are aware that all the members did not participate in the action which is regarded as an attempt to destroy the institutions of the State by destroying her connexion with the Union and thus overturning the institutions which she has as one of the United States. But no distinction could be made among the members on account of their individual opinions. The body was necessarily treated collectively.

And now having stated the necessity for the action of the Convention, and the principles which have governed its action, your delegates submit the whole for your consideration and calm judgment. They have felt their own position and that of the State to be peculiar. They have looked over Missouri and beheld the dangers that threaten her. They desire to avert them. They desire to restore peace to all her citizens. They have adopted the measures which in their judgment gave the highest promise of peace and security to all her citizens. If the measures adopted should have the desired effect, your delegates will feel that gratification which always attends the success of well intended effort. If the measures should fail to restore peace, your delegates will find consolation in the fact that they have done what they could.

The question being on agreeing to the address, the same was adopted by the Convention.

Mr. BIRCH presented the following:

Resolved, That fifty thousand copies of the address just read, together with the ordinances adopted by this Convention, be printed and distributed by George Knapp & Co., in equal portions, to the address of the members of this body,—the expense thereof to be audited and paid for at the same rates and charges that the proceedings and debates of the previous session of this Convention were.

Source: *Journal of the Missouri State Convention, Held at Jefferson City, July, 1861* (St. Louis: George Knapp & Co., Printers and Binders, 1861), 27–32.

Hamilton Rowan Gamble's Inaugural Address
July 31, 1861

By 1861, Gamble, having resigned from the state Supreme Court in 1854, was living in Pennsylvania. At the urging of friends, he returned to St. Louis to become a candidate for the state convention. As a member of that body he played an active role chairing the Committee on Federal Relations. During the second session of the convention, on July 31, the delegates unanimously elected Gamble to the position of provisional governor.

Speaking only hours after being elected, Governor Gamble admitted he had not made any "elaborate" preparations for his inaugural address. He expressed apprehension for the future of the state which may devolve into a "condition of anarchy." The convention, however, to his mind had done its best under difficult circumstances to "pacify this community and restore peace and harmony to the State."

The hour of performing the inauguration ceremonies having arrived, the committee entered with the Hon. H. R. Gamble, and conducted him to a seat at the right of the Chair.

Mr. Gamble was then introduced to the Convention by the President,[18] and acknowledged his election as follows:

Mr. President and gentlemen of the Convention:

I feel greatly oppressed by the circumstances under which I now stand before you. After a life spent in labor I had hoped that I would be permitted to pass its evening in retirement. I have never coveted public office, never desired public station. I have been content to discharge my duties as a private citizen, and I hoped such would be my lot during the remainder of my life. Circumstances seemed to make it a duty for me when this Convention was first elected, to agree to serve as one of its members, because the condition of the State and country at large seemed to demand that every citizen of the State should throw aside his own preferences, choice, and even his own scheme of life, if necessary, in order to serve the country. In accordance with what I regarded as the obligation every citizen owes to the community of which he is a member, I allowed myself to be chosen as a member of this body. I came here and endeavored, so far as I could, to serve the best interests of the State, and you now have chosen to put upon me a still more onerous and still more distasteful duty—a duty from which I shrink. Nothing but the manner in which it has been pressed upon me, ever would have induced me to yield my personal objection to it. The members of this body, in the present distracted state of the country, have come to me since it was clearly manifested that the office of Provisional Governor would be made, and have urged that I should allow myself to fill that position. Nor was it the action of any political party—men of all parties have united in it. Those who have belonged to the parties that have all departed in the midst of the present difficulties and trials of the country, have united in making this application to me. They have represented that my long residence in the State and the familiar acquaintance of the people with me, would insure a higher degree of confidence, and better secure the interests, the peace and order in the community, than would be consequent on the selection of any other person. I resisted. God knows, there is nothing now that I would not give, within the limits of anything reasonable, in order to escape being appointed. But when it was said to me, by those representing the people of the State, that I could contribute, by assuming this public trust, to secure the peace of Missouri, in which I have lived for more than forty years; that I might secure the peace of those who are the children of fathers with whom I was intimate, I thought it my duty to serve.

It is, therefore, an entire yielding up. It is the yielding of all my own schemes, of all my own individual wishes and purposes, when I undertake to assume this office. I could give you, gentlemen of the Convention, no better idea of my devotion, to what I believe to be the interest of the State, than I do now, if you could only understand the reluctance with which I accept the election with which you were pleased to honor me. But yet, gentlemen, with all that has been said of the good result to be accomplished by me, it is utterly impossible that any one man can pacify the troubled waters of the State; that any one man can still the commotion now running throughout our borders. No man can do it. You, as you go forth to mingle with your fellow citizens throughout the land, look back upon this election as an experiment that is about to be tried to endeavor to pacify this community and restore peace and harmony to the State. It is an experiment by those whose interests are with your interests, and who are bound to do all in their power to effect this pacification of the State. It may be we have not adopted the best plan or the best mode of securing the object which we desire, but we have done what seemed to us in our maturest judgment best calculated to accomplish it. And now, gentlemen, when you go forth to mingle with your fellow citizens, it must depend upon you what shall be the result of this experiment. If you desire the peace of the State—if you earnestly desire it, then give this experiment a fair trial—give it a full opportunity of developing all its powers of restoring peace. I ask you—I have a right to ask of every member of this Convention—that he and I should so act together as will redound to the common good of our State. I feel I have a right to ask that when you have by your voice placed me in such a position, that you shall unite with me your efforts and voice, instead of endeavoring to prevent the result we all desire. Unite all your efforts so that the good which is desired may be accomplished; and with the blessings of that Providence which rules over all affairs, public and private, we may accomplish this end for which we have labored and which shall cause all the inhabitants of the State to rejoice.

Gentlemen of the Convention, what is it that we are now threatened with? We apprehend that we may soon be in that condition of anarchy in which a man when he goes to bed with his family at night, does not know whether he shall ever rise again, or whether his house shall remain intact until morning. That is the kind of danger; not merely a war between different divisions of the State, but a war between neighbors, so that when a man meets those with whom he has associated from childhood, he begins to feel that they are his enemies. We must avoid that. It is terrible. The scenes of the French revolution[19] may be enacted in every quarter of our State if we do not succeed in avoiding that kind of war. We can do it if we are in earnest, and endeavor with all our power. So far as I am concerned, I assure you that it shall be the very highest object—the sole aim of every official act of mine—to make sure that the people of the State of Missouri can worship their God together, each feeling that the man who sits in the same pew with him, because he differs with him on political questions, is not his enemy, that they may attend the same communion and go to the same Heaven. I wish for every citizen of the State of Missouri, that when he meets his fellow man confidence in him may be restored, and confidence in the whole society restored, and that there shall be conversations upon other subjects than those of blood and slaughter; that there shall be something better than this endeavor to encourage hostility between persons who entertain different political opinions, and something more and better than a desire to produce injury to those who may differ from them.

Gentlemen, if you will unite with me, and carry home this purpose to carry it out faithfully, much can be accomplished, much good can be done; and I am persuaded that each one of you will feel that it is his duty, his individual duty, for in this case it is the duty of every American citizen to do all he can for the welfare of the State. I have made no elaborate preparations for an address to you on this occasion, but I have come now to express to you my earnest desire that we shall be found co-operating for that same common good in which each one of us is equally interested; that, although differing as to modes and schemes, we shall be found united in the great work of pacification.

Source: *Proceedings of the Missouri State Convention, Held at Jefferson City, July, 1861* (St. Louis: George Knapp & Co., Printers and Binders, 1861), 134–35.

Claiborne Fox Jackson Convening the Rebel General Assembly
September 26, 1861

Following his abandonment of Jefferson City in mid-June, Jackson traveled first to Memphis and then to Richmond, Virginia, to meet with Jefferson Davis. In offices still being organized after the recent move from Montgomery, Alabama, Jackson and former US senator David Rice Atchison solicited support from the Confederate president. Upon gaining Davis's support, Jackson returned to Memphis and then moved on to Springfield and Lexington.[20]

In his call for the general assembly to reassemble late in the next month, Jackson selected Neosho in the extreme southwest corner of the state. He began by castigating federal authorities for "murdering our citizens, destroying our property, and as far as in their power, desolating our land." War now existed, he announced, between Missouri and the United States. To determine whether the time had arrived for Missouri to "dissolve" its relationship with the federal government, Jackson summoned the legislature to assemble at the Masonic Hall in Neosho.

On motion of Mr. Goodlett, Mr. Vernon was called to the chair, who called the Senate to order.[21]

The President then ordered the following proclamation to be read:

To the members of the Senate and House of Representatives of the General Assembly of the State of Missouri:

The Constitution of the State of Missouri vests in me the power to convene by proclamation the General Assembly on extraordinary occasions, and requires me to state to them the purposes for which they are convened.

The present condition of the State makes it eminently proper that I should now exercise this power. The Federal authorities have for months past, in violation of the Constitution of the United States, waged a ruthless war upon the people of the State of Missouri, murdering our citizens, destroying our property, and as far as in their power, desolating our land. I have in vain endeavored to secure your constitutional rights by peaceful means, and have only resorted to war when it becomes necessary to repel the most cruel and long continued aggressions. War now exists between the State of Missouri and the Federal Government, and a state of war is incompatible with the continuance of our union with that government.

Therefore, for the purpose of giving to the representatives of the people of Missouri an opportunity of determining whether it be proper now to dissolve the constitutional bond, which binds us to the Government of the United States, when all other bonds between us are broken, I, Claiborne F. Jackson, Governor of the State of Missouri, by authority in me vested, do proclaim that the members of the Senate and House of Representatives of the State of Missouri, shall convene at the Masonic Hall,[22] in town of Neosho, in the County of Newton, on the twenty-first day of October, 1861.

CLAIBORNE F. JACKSON,
Governor of the State of Missouri.
DATED LEXINGTON, MO., Sept. 26, 1861.

Source: *Journal of the Senate, Extra Session of The Rebel Legislature, Called Together by a Proclamation of C. F. Jackson. Begun and Held at the Town of Neosho, Newton County,*

Missouri, on the Twenty-First Day of October, Eighteen Hundred and Sixty-One (Jefferson City: Emory S. Foster, Public Printer, 1865-6), 3–4.

Claiborne Fox Jackson's Address to the Rebel General Assembly
October 22, 1861

Jackson's opening address to the remnants of the general assembly in exile in Neosho was given before a body lacking a quorum. He spoke again of the unconstitutional aggressions Missouri had suffered at the hands of the federal government. Formally articulating his predisposition in favor of secession, Jackson asked the rump gathering to dissolve the political connection with the United States, join the Confederate States of America, approve an election for representatives to the Confederate Congress, and authorize the raising of bonds to support the war.

Mr. Goodlett, from the joint committee appointed to wait upon the Governor, laid before the Senate the following communication from the Governor:

Gentlemen of the Senate and House of Representatives of the General Assembly of the State of Missouri:

In pursuance of a power vested in me by the Constitution of the State of Missouri, I have convened you for the purpose of deliberating upon the relations of this State to the government of the United States. About the close of your last session the authorities of the United States government had manifested plainly, by a series of outrageous acts, that they had lost all proper appreciation of the principles of free government, and were determined, regardless of the most sacred obligations, to trample upon our liberties, to violate our dearest constitutional rights, and, in every manner known to tyrants, to insult, injure and afflict our people. The spectacle was for the first time presented of a government whose boast had been its free institutions, and the attachment of its citizens to the constitution and the laws, plunging at one bound from the most exalted eminence among the nations into the deepest abyss of despotic and arbitrary power. Men, women and children, in open day and in the public thoroughfares, shot down and murdered by a brutal soldiery, with the connivance of government officers. Our citizen soldiers were arrested and imprisoned. State property was seized and confiscated without warrant of law; private citizens were insecure in their persons and property; the writ of habeas corpus had been nullified, and the brave judges who had attempted to protect by it the liberties of the citizens had been insulted and threatened, and a tyrant

President, reveling in unbound powers, had crowned all these acts of unconditional aggression by declaring war against a number of the States composing the former Union. Since your adjournment these wrongs and injuries have ripened into a war against our people, waged with unusual and unrelenting ferocity, and on the largest scale.

It is in vain to hope for a restoration of amicable relations between Missouri and the other United States of America under the same government, and it is not desirable if it could be accomplished.

It is idle to speak of preserving the mere paper bonds of union with a government whose licentious rulers have cut to shreds all other bonds between us. While insult and injury have been heaped upon us by the United States Government until they were no longer endurable, it gives me pleasure to call your attention to the sympathy manifested towards us by the Confederate States of America in the act of their Congress, a copy of which I herewith submit, and in the aid in men, arms and munitions of war supplied by their President to the citizens of Missouri, struggling for their liberties. In view of these facts, I beg leave to recommend to you the passage

1st. Of an ordinance dissolving all political connection between the State of Missouri and the United States of America.

2d. Of an act of provisional union with the Confederate States of America.

3d. The appointment of three commissioners to the Provisional Congress of the Confederate States of America.

4th. The passage of a law authorizing the Executive of the State to cause an election to be held for the election of Senators and Representatives to the Confederate States of America, as early as practicable after the State of Missouri shall be admitted as a member of said Confederate States, and providing in said law the mode and manner that the citizens of the State who may, at the time of such election, belong to the army, can cast their votes for Representatives.

5th. The passage of an act empowering your Executive to cause to be engraved, and from time to time issue, over his signature as Governor, bonds of the State of Missouri, not exceeding——dollars, in such sums and of such denominations as the public welfare may require.

Before closing this communication, gentlemen, I cannot refrain from congratulating you and the people of our State upon the glorious victories which have crowned our arms since your last adjournment. At Carthage, at Springfield, at Fort Scott and at Lexington, the brave soldiers of Missouri, led on by gallant generals, met the well appointed, well armed hordes of the enemy, and gained signal victories.[23]

Their deeds have crowned them with imperishable renown. No soldiers upon this continent rank above them.

With such soldiers and a just cause we cannot fail of achieving our liberties.

In referring to our victories it is due to the brave men and gallant leaders of the Confederate and Arkansas army, to express our grateful acknowledgment of their gallant and efficient aid at the battle of Springfield.

No troops ever fought more gallantly, or with better success.

God's protecting providence has been over us in all our past struggles. Let us devoutly return thanks for his protection and fervently implore its continuance.

C. F. JACKSON, Governor.

On leave, Mr. Goodlett introduced a bill entitled

An act to dissolve the political connection of the State of Missouri with the United States of America;

Which was read a first time, rule suspended, read a second and third time and passed. All the Senators voting in the affirmative except Mr. Hardin.[24]

NOTE: This *Extra Session of the Rebel Legislature* contained the following explanatory statement: "The proceedings of C. F. Jackson/s Senate, together with other papers and documents contained in the appendix, were captured by the 49th Missouri Volunteers, in the State of Alabama, forwarded to this Department, and ordered printed by the House of Representatives of the Twenty-third General Assembly."

FRANCIS RODMAN, Secretary of State.[25]

Source: *Journal of the Senate, Extra Session of The Rebel Legislature, Called Together by a Proclamation of C. F. Jackson. Begun and Held at the Town of Neosho, Newton County, Missouri, on the Twenty-First Day of October, Eighteen Hundred and Sixty-One* (Jefferson City: Emory S. Foster, Public Printer, 1865-6), 7–8.

Ordinance of Secession
October 28, 1861

At the same time the rump general assembly approved the ordinance of secession, it also elected senators and representatives to the Confederate Congress without providing for the popular election called for by Jackson. The former governor's desire to have Missouri join the Confederacy was satisfied on November 28, 1861, when the Confederate Congress admitted Missouri as a "full and equal member."[26]

AN ACT declaring the political ties heretofore existing between the State of Missouri and the United States of America dissolved.

WHEREAS, The government of the United States, in the possession and under the control of a sectional party, has wantonly violated the compact originally made between said government and the State of Missouri, by invading with hostile armies the soil of the State, attacking and making prisoners of the militia whilst legally assembled under the State laws, forcibly occupying the State capital, and attempting, through the instrumentality of domestic traitors, to usurp the State government, seizing and destroying private property, and murdering with fiendish malignity peaceable citizens, men, women and children, together with other acts of atrocity indicating a deep settled hostility towards the people of Missouri and their institutions, and,

WHEREAS, The present administration of the government of the United States has utterly ignored the Constitution, subverted the government as constructed and intended by its makers, and established a despotic and arbitrary power instead thereof; now, therefore,

Be it enacted by the General Assembly of the State of Missouri, as follows:

That all political ties of every character now existing between the government of the United States of America, and the people and government of the State of Missouri, are hereby dissolved, and the State of Missouri, resuming the sovereignty granted by compact to the said United States upon the admission of said State into the Federal Union, does again take its place as a free and independent republic amongst the nations of the earth.

This act to take effect and be in force from and after its passage.

Read first and second time and amended. Read third time and passed, October 28, 1861.

John T. Crisp, *Secretary Senate.*

Source: *Journal of the Senate, Extra Session of The Rebel Legislature, Called Together by a Proclamation of C. F. Jackson. Begun and Held at the Town of Neosho, Newton County, Missouri, on the Twenty-First Day of October, Eighteen Hundred and Sixty-One* (Jefferson City: Emory S. Foster, Public Printer, 1865–66), 39.

APPENDIX I

STATE CONVENTION DELEGATES

Name	Nativity	Age	Profession	County	Office
Sterling Price	VA	51	Bank Commissioner	Chariton	President
Samuel A. Lowe	MD	41	Clerk of Courts	Pettis	Secretary
R. A. Campbell	MO	26	Lawyer	Pike	Assistant Secretary
C. P. Anderson	TN	42	Editor	Moniteau	Door Keeper
Benjamin Whiteman Grover	OH	49	Farmer	Johnson	Sergeant at Arms
Andrew Monroe	VA	68	Minister	Fayette	Chaplain
John S. Allen	TN	46	Merchant	Harrison	
Orson Bartlett	VA	51	Merchant	Stoddard	
Eli Everett Bass	TN	54	Farmer	Boone	
George Youse Bast, Sr.	KY	48	Farmer	Montgomery	
James Harvey Birch	VA	57	Lawyer	Clinton	
Joseph Bogy	MO	54	Farmer	Saint Genevieve	
Samuel Miller Breckinridge	KY	32	Judge	St. Louis	
James Overton Broadhead	VA	41	Lawyer	St. Louis	
Hudson Erastus Bridge	NH	50	Merchant	St. Louis	
Robert A. Brown	TN	51	Farmer	Cass	
Isidor Bush	Austria	39	Merchant	St. Louis	
Robert Calhoun	Ireland	57	Farmer	Callaway	

Appendix 1

Name	Nativity	Age	Profession	County	Office
Milton Pleasant Cayce, Sr.	VA	56	Merchant	St. Francis	
John R. Chenault	KY	51	Judge	Jasper	
Samuel C. Collier	MO	35	Lawyer	Madison	
Abram Comingo	KY	41	Lawyer	Independence	
Robert W. Crawford	VA	49	Lawyer	Lawrence	
Alexander William Doniphan	KY	52	Lawyer	Clay	
Robert Washington Donnell	NC	42	Merchant & Banker	St. Joseph	
William Douglass	VA	32	Lawyer	Cooper	
Charles Drake	KY	32	Lawyer	Moniteau	
George W. Dunn	KY	45	Judge	Richmond	
Charles Dietrich Eitzen	Bremen, Ger.	41	Merchant	Hermann	
Robert B. Frayser	VA	55	Farmer	St. Charles	
Joseph Flood	KY	48	Farmer	Callaway	
John D. Foster	KY	40	Lawyer	Adair	
Hamilton Rowan Gamble	VA	62	Lawyer	St. Louis	
Thomas Tasker Gantt	DC	46	Lawyer	St. Louis	
N. F. Givens	KY	52	Lawyer	Clark	
Henry M. Gorin	KY	48	Merchant	Scotland	
Joseph Jackson Gravely	VA	32	Farmer	Cedar	
Willard Preble Hall	VA	40	Lawyer	Buchanan	
William A. Hall	ME	45	Judge	Randolph	
A. S. Harbin	NC	60	Farmer	Barry	
Robert Anthony Hatcher	VA	42	Lawyer	New Madrid	
John Brooks Henderson	VA	34	Lawyer	Pike	
Littleberry Hendrick	VA	61	Lawyer	Greene	
Vanderver Berry Hill	KY	32	Lawyer	Pulaski	
Henry Hitchcock	AL	31	Lawyer	St. Louis	
Robert Holmes	PA	45	Lumber Dealer	St. Louis	
John Holt	KY	66	Farmer	Dent	
Harrison Hough	KY	49	Judge	Mississippi	
John How	PA	50	Tanner	St. Louis	
William J. Howell	KY	47	Lawyer	Monroe	

State Convention Delegates

Name	Nativity	Age	Profession	County	Office
Prince L. Hudgins	KY	49	Lawyer	Andrew	
Joseph M. Irwin	VA	42	Lawyer	Shelby	
Zachariah Isbell	VA	48	Farmer	Osage	
William Jackson	TN	38	Farmer	Putnam	
Robert W. Jamison	KY	49	Farmer	Webster	
James W. Johnson	VA	49	Farmer	Bolivar	
Christopher Garland Kidd	KY	40	Lawyer	Henry	
James Proctor Knott	KY	30	Lawyer	Cole	
William Thomas Leeper	TN	38	Farmer	Wayne	
Moses Lewis Linton	KY	52	Physician	St. Louis	
John F. Long	MO	44	Civil Engineer	St. Louis	
Vincent Marmaduke	MO	28	Farmer	Saline	
Asa C. Marvin	NH	46	Farmer	Henry	
James T. Matson	MO	39	Physician	Ralls	
Amos W. Maupin	MO	33	Blacksmith	Franklin	
Joseph Washington McClurg	MO	43	Merchant	Linn	
James Robinson McCormack	MO	36	Physician	Perry	
Nelson McDowell	IL	59	Farmer	Dade	
James McFerran	MD	41	Judge	Daviess	
Ferdinand Meyer	Prussia	34	Leather Dealer	St. Louis	
William L. Morrow, Sr.	TN	43	Merchant	Dallas	
James Hugh Moss	MO	35	Lawyer	Clay	
James C. Noell	VA	29	Lawyer	Bollinger	
Elijah Hise Norton	KY	39	Lawyer	Platte	
Sample Orr	TN	44	Lawyer	Greene	
John Finis Phillips	MO	26	Lawyer	Pettis	
Phillip Pipkin	TN	46	Lawyer	Iron	
William G. Pomeroy	NY	46	Lawyer	Crawford	
Charles G. Rankin	MO	53	Merchant	Jefferson	
Robert D. Ray	KY	44	Lawyer	Carrollton	
John Thomas Redd	KY	44	Lawyer	Marion	
Mathew H. Ritchey	TN	49	Farmer	Newton	
James M. Ross	MD	48	Lawyer	Morgan	
Frederick Rowland	NC	56	Farmer	Macon	

Appendix 1

Name	Nativity	Age	Profession	County	Office
Samuel L. Sawyer	NH	46	Lawyer	Lafayette	
Emilius Kitchell Sayre	NJ	51	Farmer	Lewis	
Thomas Scott	KY	44	Farmer	Tuscumbia	
Thomas Shackelford	MO	39	Lawyer	Howard	
John T. Shackelford	KY	57	Farmer	St. Louis	
James K. Sheeley	KY	46	Judge	Jackson	
Jacob Smith	KY	44	Lawyer	Linn	
Sol Smith	NY	59	Lawyer	St. Louis	
Robert Marcellus Stewart	NY	43	Lawyer	Buchanan	
Jacob T. Tindall	NY	34	Lawyer	Grundy	
W. W. Turner	IL	24	Lawyer	Laclede	
Joseph G. Waller	VA	58	Farmer	Warren	
Nathaniel Wilson Watkins, Sr.	KY	65	Lawyer	Cape Girardeau	
Aikman Welch	MO	33	Lawyer	Johnson	
Robert Wilson	VA	58	Lawyer	Buchanan	
Warren Woodson	VA	64	Farmer	Boone	
Alexander M. Woolfolk	KY	25	Lawyer	Livingston	
Uriel Sebree Wright	VA	55	Lawyer	St. Louis	
Ellzey Vanbuskirk	OH	39	Circuit Clerk	Holt	
George W. Zimmerman	VA	67	Farmer	Lincoln	

Source: *Journal and Proceedings of the Missouri State Convention, Held at Jefferson City and St. Louis, March, 1861* (St. Louis: George Knapp & Co., Printers and Binders, 1861), 5–7.

APPENDIX 2

QUESTIONS FOR DISCUSSION

1. Governors Robert M. Stewart and Claiborne F. Jackson held differing views on January 3, 1861, regarding the state of the Union and Missouri's future. Some of those differences were bold, others rather subtle. How would you characterize those differences? Did you find one address more compelling than the other? Why?

2. Senator Trusten Polk proposed a constitutional amendment as a compromise measure to guarantee Southern rights. What does his amendment tell you about the important issues roiling the country? Polk claimed that his suggested changes to the Constitution were "in perfect concord with both its provisions and spirit." Do you agree?

3. While not in the form of a constitutional amendment, Representative Thomas L. Anderson listed a set of demands that would preserve the Union, reunite the four seceded states, and allow the nation to "march on to further attainments in greatness and renown." How does his list of issues that needed resolution compare with Senator Polk's proposed constitutional amendment? Which, to your mind, would have better served the country? Why?

4. Representative John B. Clark suggested that secession from the federal government was warranted only when "their grievances are too heavy to be borne." Given the grievances listed by Representative Clark and other Missouri officials, did Missouri's choice to stay in the Union accord with Clark's measure? Put differently, to what degree was the federal government responsible for grievances articulated by Missouri's elected officials?

5. Representative John R. Barret's address suggests several interesting questions. Given that his remarks were designed for public consumption, how do think his listeners processed his negative characterization

of abolitionists and Republicans, and his emphatic conclusion that the "cotton States should have remained in the Union"? Barret erroneously pronounced that the Republican Party had "gained possession of the Government," and intended to "abolish slavery in the States." Can his deliberate falsehoods be compared to those of contemporary politicians? With the public's access to multiple sources of information today, is political misinformation more or less threatening to civil discourse?

6. Delegate Sample Orr objected strongly to the convention permitting secession commissioner Luther J. Glenn to address the gathering. If you had been a member of the convention, would you have agreed with Orr or disagreed? Why?

7. On the same day that Abraham Lincoln was being inaugurated in Washington, DC, Georgian Luther J. Glenn addressed the delegates of the state convention. Six weeks earlier secession commissioner Daniel R. Russell had addressed Missouri's General Assembly. Which speech did you find more convincing? Why? Commissioner Glenn spoke of the 1860 Republican platform and its opposition to the extension of slavery into the western territories. He concluded that such a policy would lead to the ultimate extinction of slavery in the states, and "that there was no hope in the future" that that Republican goal would be thwarted. Given that the Democratic Party would control both houses of Congress for the first two years of the Lincoln administration, was his appeal in favor of secession logical?

8. Several weeks after Glenn's address, the convention presented a formal response to his comments. This lengthy report was designed to refute, point by point, Commissioner Glenn's rationalization in favor of secession. If you had been a member of the convention, would you have agreed with the committee's report? Why? Why not? Would you have preferred Delegate Birch's resolutions?

9. Five days after the inauguration of President Lincoln, future governor Hamilton R. Gamble presented the Majority Report of the Committee on Federal Relations. Two days later, Delegates John T. Redd and Harrison Hough offered a minority opinion. What were the major differences between the two? Given Missouri's position as a border state, which report do you believe was the more appropriate? Why?

10. The convention delegates debated the majority and minority reports by the Committee on Federal Relations for a little over a week. Among other topics discussed, the delegates argued over the nature of the federal government itself: Was it based on an assumption that the government

would be perpetual? Was it based on the compact theory that maintained that individual states could voluntarily secede? Delegate John T. Redd presented and defended the compact theory defense of secession while Delegate Uriel S. Wright took the opposite approach suggesting that John Redd, who ordinarily maintained a "clear and logical mind, has been lost in the transcendentalism of secession metaphysics." Which argument did you find more persuasive? On what issues did they agree?

11. The delegates also debated the causes of southern grievances against northern states and the Republican Party—northern personal liberty laws and the Republican Party's official position opposing the extension of slavery into the western territories drawing the most attention. Missouri ultimately voted against secession although eleven other slave-owning states seceded based precisely on those two grievances. Why did Missouri come to a different answer to the secession crisis?

12. On June 12, 1861, Governor Fox issued a proclamation to the citizens of the state. Six weeks later, the state convention produced a different proclamation, "To the People of the State of Missouri." If you were a resident of Missouri in 1861, which one would you have found more reasonable or truthful?

13. Missouri's elected officials, like elected officials of other southern states, often pronounced falsehoods in their list of grievances, such as the Republican Party had taken over the government when in fact, for the first two years of the Lincoln administration, Democrats would have controlled both houses of Congress. Or that Republicans were going to abolish slavery in the states when the 1860 Republican platform specifically afforded states the exclusive right to accept or reject slavery. Thinking about political discourse today, are fabrications like these injurious to democratic norms, or are they simply a part of benign political gamesmanship?

NOTES

Introduction

1. For a close look at St. Louis politics on the eve of the war, see Louis S. Gerteis, *Civil War St. Louis* (Lawrence: University Press of Kansas, 2001), 37–87.
2. The Old Courthouse has been managed since 1954 by the National Park Service as a part of the Jefferson National Expansion Memorial.
3. Robert Pierce Forbes, *The Missouri Compromise and Its Aftermath: Slavery and the Meaning of America* (Chapel Hill: University of North Carolina Press, 2007), 109–18.
4. For a detailed analysis of the 1850s, see Elizabeth R. Varon, *Disunion: The Coming of the American Civil War, 1789–1859* (Chapel Hill: University of North Carolina Press, 2008), 199–342.
5. Michael F. Holt, *The Election of 1860: "A Campaign Fraught with Consequences"* (Lawrence: University Press of Kansas, 2017).
6. William E. Parrish, *Turbulent Partnership: Missouri and the Union, 1861–1865* (Columbia: University of Missouri Press, 1963), 1–6.
7. Christopher Phillips, *Missouri's Confederate: Claiborne Fox Jackson and the Creation of Southern Identity in the Border West* (Columbia: University of Missouri Press, 2000), 228.
8. *Journal of the House of Representatives of the State of Missouri, at the First Session of the Twenty-First General Assembly* (Jefferson City: W. G. Cheeny, Public Printer, 1861), 18–26.
9. In January 1861, the entire strength of the United States Army totaled 16,367 scattered throughout the country from Maryland to California. On April 17, 1861, Virginia's militia was reported to total 18,400. Clayton R. Newell, *The Regular Army Before the Civil War, 1845–1860* (Washington, D.C.: Center of Military History, 2014), 50; George H. Reese, ed., *Proceedings of the Virginia State Convention of 1861, February 13– May 1* (Richmond: Virginia State Library, 1965), IV: 91–92.
10. Article V of the Constitution provides for amendments to be proposed by Congress with two-thirds of both houses approving, or by a national convention called by the legislatures of two-thirds of the states.
11. *Journal of the House of Representatives of the State of Missouri, at the First Session of the Twenty-First General Assembly*, 45–51; Phillips, *Missouri's Confederate*, 236. It was Missouri's identification with the South as a slave state

12. For an analysis of the commissioners and their messages, see Charles B. Dew, *Apostles of Disunion: Southern Secession Commissioners and the Causes of the Civil War* (Charlottesville: University of Virginia Press, 2001).
13. St. Louis *Daily Missouri Democrat*, January 21, 1861.
14. *Congressional Globe*, 36th Cong., 2nd Sess., 112–14 (Joint Resolution No. 50.) See also Dwight T. Pitcaithley, *Kentucky and the Secession Crisis: A Documentary History* (Knoxville: University of Tennessee Press, 2022), 39–138.
15. See Dwight T. Pitcaithley, *The U.S. Constitution and Secession: A Documentary Anthology of Slavery and White Supremacy* (Lawrence: University Press of Kansas, 2018), 161–275. Since the publication of that volume, two additional proposed amendments have been identified.
16. *Congressional Globe*, 36th Cong., 2nd Sess., 355–60.
17. *Congressional Globe*, 36th Cong., 2nd Sess., 355–60.
18. *Congressional Globe*, 36th Cong., 2nd Sess., 855.
19. Senator Polk did vote in favor of the Corwin Amendment. *Congressional Globe*, 36th Cong., 2nd Sess., March 4, 1861, 1403.
20. *Congressional Globe*, 36th Cong., 2nd Sess., 865–69.
21. *Congressional Globe*, 36th Cong., 2nd Sess., 710.
22. Seymour V. Connor, *Texas: A History* (New York: Thomas Y. Crowell Company, 1971), 154.
23. *Congressional Globe*, 36th Cong., 2nd Sess., 397–401
24. 36th Cong., 2nd Sess., Senate Report 288, 3.
25. Charles Robert Lee, Jr., *The Confederate Constitutions* (Chapel Hill: University of North Carolina Press, 1963), 171–98. Interestingly, the constitution retained the three-fifths clause dealing with representatives to the Confederate Congress. While clearly classifying slaves as property, the delegates in Montgomery (perhaps inadvertently), also recognized them as persons for the purposes of representation.
26. Northern Black men were allowed to vote in Maine, New Hampshire, Vermont, Massachusetts, and Rhode Island. James Oliver Horton and Lois E. Horton, *In Hope of Liberty: Culture, Community, and Protest Among Northern Free Blacks, 1700–1860* (New York: Oxford University Press, 1997), 169.
27. *Congressional Globe*, 36th Cong., 2nd Sess., January 26, 1861, 577–80.
28. The leading historian of southern history during the early years of the twentieth century argued that retention of white supremacy was the central theme of southern history. See Ulrich B. Phillips, "The Central Theme of Southern History," *American Historical Review* 34, no. 1 (October 1928): 30–43. For a more recent in-depth analysis of white supremacy and its political and cul-

tural use throughout the nineteenth century, see Alexander Saxton, *The Rise and Fall of the White Republic: Class Politics and Mass Culture in Nineteenth Century America* (New York: Verso, 1990).

29. *Congressional Globe*, 36th Cong., 2nd Sess., Appendix, 246–50. See also Nicholas W. Sacco, "Searching for Compromise: Missouri Congressman John Richard Barret's Fight to Save the Union," *The Confluence* (Fall/Winter 2018–2019): 5–32.

30. *Congressional Globe*, 36th Cong., 2nd Sess., 249; *Journal of the House of Representatives of the State of Missouri*, 22. See also *Journal and Proceedings of the Missouri State Convention, Held at Jefferson City and St. Louis, March 1861* (St. Louis: George Knapp & Co., Printers and Binders, 1861), 57, 69, 149.

31. *Journal and Proceedings of the Missouri State Convention*, 3–4.

32. Phillips, *Missouri's Confederate*, 238–39.

33. Phillips, *Missouri's Confederate*, 239; *Proceedings of the Missouri State Convention*, 193, 216.

34. Built in 1854, the St. Louis Mercantile Library was in many ways the cultural center of the city. Located at the corner of Broadway and Locust streets, it contained a 2,000 seat auditorium. Missouri's first senator Thomas Hart Benton lay in state there following his death on April 10, 1858

35. *Proceedings of the Missouri State Convention*, 14–15.

36. *Proceedings of the Missouri State Convention*, 17–20.

37. *Proceedings of the Missouri State Convention*, 21, 23.

38. For a short analysis of Republican ideology and the organization of those territories see David M. Potter, *Lincoln and His Party in the Secession Crisis* (Baton Rouge: Louisiana University Press, 1995; first published in 1942), 277–78; Allan Nevins, *The Emergence of Lincoln: Prologue to Civil War, 1859–1861* (New York: Charles Scribner's Sons, 1950), 448.

39. *Proceedings of the Missouri State Convention*, 248–55.

40. One week after his failed raid on Harpers Ferry, Virginia, John Brown was arraigned in a county court in nearby Charles Town. A week later he was found guilty of conspiracy to incite a slave rebellion, treason against the State of Virginia, and first-degree murder. On December 2, 1859, Brown was hanged on a gallows erected on Rebecca Hunter's farm on the south end of Charles Town. David S, Reynolds, *John Brown, Abolitionist: The Man Who Killed Slavery, Sparked the Civil War, and Seeded Civil Rights* (New York: Vintage Books, 2005), 348–47, 392–98

41. *Proceedings of the Missouri State Convention*, 55–58.

42. *Proceedings of the Missouri State Convention*, 62–64.

43. Moss's amendment was eventually rejected by the delegates on March 16 by a vote of 61 to 30. *Proceedings of the Missouri State Convention*, 61, 184.

44. *Proceedings of the Missouri State Convention*, 64–68.

45. *Proceedings of the Missouri State Convention*, 84–93.
46. For a concise analysis of the compact theory of government as employed in 1860–1861, see David M. Potter, *The Impending Crisis: 1848–1861* (New York: Harper & Row, Publishers, 1976), 479–84. Constitutional scholars have largely discredited this interpretation of the Constitution calling it "open to very serious objections on historical, theoretical, and practical grounds." Alfred H. Kelly and Winfred A. Harbison, *The American Constitution: Its Origins and Development* (New York: W. W. Norton & Company, 1970), 306–11. In his message to the First Session of the Thirty-Seventh Congress, President Lincoln termed the idea "an ingenious sophism." The notion that a state possessed the right to leave the Union of its own accord was absurd: "The principle itself is one of disintegration, and upon which no Government can possibly endure." *Congressional Globe*, 37th Cong., 1st Sess., July 4, 1861, 1–4. A recent study of Secession Winter affirms the compact theory and holds that secession was constitutional; see Peter Radan, *Creating a More Perfect Slaveholders' Union: Slavery and the Constitution, and Secession in Antebellum America* (Lawrence: University Press of Kansas, 2023).
47. While Delegate Redd could not have known the number of states that would be carved from the western territories, Congress admitted fourteen additional states between 1861 and 1912. If the fifteen slave states had voted as a block, an amendment abolishing slavery would have fallen far short of the three-fourths required for ratification.
48. *Proceedings of the Missouri State Convention*, 129–36.
49. *Proceedings of the Missouri State Convention*, 136–48.
50. The idea of who would decide whether secession was justifiable occurred to at least five elected officials over Secession Winter. New York Representative Daniel E. Sickles, Pennsylvania Representative Thomas B. Florence, Ohio Representative Clement L. Vallandigham, Connecticut Representative Orris S. Ferry, and Wisconsin Senator James R. Doolittle all proposed constitutional amendments that established secession protocols. See Pitcaithley, *The U.S. Constitution and Secession*, 177–78, 215–17, 227–31, 254–55.
51. For an excellent explanation of sovereignty and the United States Constitution, see Daniel Farber, *Lincoln's Constitution* (Chicago: University of Chicago Press, 2003), 26–44.
52. During the 1846 debate in Congress over funding the war with Mexico, David Wilmot of Pennsylvania proposed that if any land was acquired as a result of the war, slavery would be prohibited there. The so-called Wilmot Proviso never passed both houses of Congress.
53. *Proceedings of the Missouri State Convention*, 186–207.
54. Phillips, *Missouri's Confederate*, 241–44.

55. For a close assessment of St. Louis' German citizens during this period, see Adam Arenson, *The Great Heart of the Republic: St. Louis and the Cultural Civil War* (Columbia: University of Missouri Press), 107–30.
56. Ezra J. Warner, *Generals in Blue: Lives of the Union Commanders* (Baton Rouge: Louisiana State University Press, 1964), 208–9, 627.
57. Phillips, *Missouri's Confederate*, 245.
58. Phillips, *Missouri's Confederate*, 246–49. Arkansas's state convention voted to secede from the United States on May 6.
59. Christopher Phillips, *Damned Yankee: The Life of General Nathaniel Lyon* (Columbia: University of Missouri Press, 1990), 164–66.
60. Phillips, *Damned Yankee*, 166–67. See also Parrish, *Turbulent Partnership*, 19.
61. *Journal of the House of Representatives of the State of Missouri, at the Called Session of the Twenty-First General Assembly*
62. Phillips, *Damned Yankee*, 185–92; Gerteis, *Civil War St. Louis*, 96–115.
63. Captain Ulysses S. Grant happened to be in St. Louis during the Camp Jackson affair and noted the change in the political atmosphere. "As soon as the news of the capture of Camp Jackson reached the city the condition of affairs was changed. Union men became rampant, aggressive, and if you will, intolerant. They proclaimed their sentiments boldly, and were impatient at anything like disrespect for the Union. The secessionists became quiet but were filled with suppressed rage. They had been playing the bully. The Union men ordered the rebel flag taken down from the building on Pine Street. [Disunionists in St. Louis had a headquarters building in the Berthold mansion at Fifth and Pine Street.] The command was given in tones of authority and it was taken down, never to be raised again in St. Louis." Ulysses S. Grant, *Personal Memoirs of U. S. Grant* (New York: Konecy & Konecky, n.d.), 141.
64. Phillips, *Damned Yankee*, 194; Phillips, *Missouri's Confederate*, 252–54; Robert E. Shalhope, *Sterling Price: Portrait of a Southerner* (Columbia: University of Missouri Press, 1971), 158; William E. Parrish, *Frank Blair: Lincoln's Conservative* (Columbia: University of Missouri Press, 1998), 103–6.
65. Phillips, *Missouri's Confederate*, 254–55; Shalhope, *Sterling Price*, 160–62; Phillips, *Damned Yankee*, 204–6; Parrish, *Frank Blair*, 105–6. The expansion of secessionist fervor in Missouri was noticed by Iowa's governor Samuel J. Kirkwood. During his address on May 16 to a specially called session of that state's legislature, he noted that Iowa was exposed to attack on its southern border "by reckless men from Missouri," and that "Missouri is unfortunately strongly infected with the heresy of Secession which is hurrying so many of our Southern States to ruin." *Journal of the House of Representatives at the Extra Session of the Eighth General Assembly of the State of Iowa, Which Convened at the Capitol in Des Moines, on Wednesday, the 15th Day of May, 1861* (Des Moines: F. W. Palmer, State Printer, 1861), 11.

66. Harney had a history of being relieved of commands. See Warner, *Generals in Blue*, 208–9.
67. Parrish, *Frank Blair*, 106–7.
68. Parrish, *Frank Blair*, 107–8; Phillips, *Missouri's Confederate*, 257; Phillips, *Damned Yankee*, 211.
69. One narrative of the meeting has Lyon ending it by exclaiming, "this means war." The only source for this, however, was Thomas Snead's 1886 account of the gathering. An insightful analysis of the comment can be found in Joan Stack, "The Rise and Fall of General Nathaniel Lyon in the Missouri State Capitol," *Gateway* 33 (2013): 60–67. See also Phillips, *Damned Yankee*, 211–14; Gerteis, *Civil War St. Louis*, 123–25.
70. Buel Leopard and Floyd C. Shoemaker, eds., *The Messages and Proclamations of the Governors of the State of Missouri*, vol. 3 (Columbia: State Historical Society of Missouri, 1922), 385–89; Phillips, *Missouri's Confederate*, 257–60.
71. Phillips, *Missouri's Confederate*, 260–63; Phillips, *Damned Yankee*, 215–56; Shalhope, *Sterling Price*, 166–78.
72. *Journal of the Missouri State Convention, Held at Jefferson City, July, 1861* (St. Louis: George Knapp & Co., Printers and Binders, 1861), 3. The five delegates were Robert Wilson (St. Joseph County), Jacob T. Tindall (Grundy), J. W. McClurg (Linn Creek), James R. McCormack (Perry), and Thomas T. Gantt (St. Louis).
73. *Journal of the Missouri State Convention, Held at Jefferson City, July, 1861*, 5.
74. *Journal of the Missouri State Convention, Held at Jefferson City, July, 1861*, 10.
75. *Journal of the Missouri State Convention, Held at Jefferson City, July, 1861*, 17–18.
76. *Journal of the Missouri State Convention, Held at Jefferson City, July, 1861*, 25.
77. *Journal of the Missouri State Convention, Held at Jefferson City, July, 1861*, 27–31.
78. *Proceedings of the State of the Missouri State Convention, Held at Jefferson City, July, 1861* (St. Louis: George Knapp & Co., Printers and Binders, 1861), 134–35.
79. Dennis K. Boman, *Lincoln's Resolute Unionist: Hamilton Gamble, Dred Scott Dissenter and Missouri's Civil War Governor* (Baton Rouge: Louisiana State University Press, 2006), 184–86.
80. *Journal of the Senate of Missouri, at the First Session of the Twenty-Second General Assembly* (Jefferson City: n.p., 1863), 13–25. In his annual address to Congress on December 1, 1862, President Lincoln devoted almost a fourth of his speech to the subject of compensated emancipation. Believing that "without slavery the rebellion could never have existed; without slavery it could not continue," the president proposed a constitutional amendment that would allow the federal government to compensate slave owners in every state that abolished the institution before January 1, 1900. *Congressional Globe*, 37th Cong., 3rd Sess., 1–5.

81. Parrish, *Turbulent Partnership*, 200–201.
82. Phillips, *Missouri's Confederate*, 262–66; *Journal of the Senate, Extra Session of the Rebel Legislature, Called Together by a Proclamation of C. F. Jackson. Begun and Held at the Town of Neosho, Newton County, Missouri, on the Twenty-First Day of October, Eighteen Hundred and Sixty-One* (Jefferson City: Emory S. Foster, Public Printer, 1865–1866), 3–4.
83. Phillips, *Missouri's Confederate*, 267–68.
84. Phillips, *Missouri's Confederate*, 268; *Journal of the Senate, Extra Session*, 7–8.
85. *Journal of the Senate, Extra Session*, 39.
86. *Journal of the House of Representatives of the State of Missouri, at the First Session of the Twenty-first General Assembly*, 49.

1. Missouri General Assembly

1. Leopard and Shoemaker, eds., *The Messages and Proclamations of the Governors of the State of Missouri*, 3:53–58; Lawrence O. Christensen, William E. Foley, Gary R. Kremer and Kenneth H. Winn, eds., *Dictionary of Missouri Biography* (Columbia: University of Missouri Press, 1999), 720.
2. Published in 1852, Harriet Beecher Stowe's anti-slavery novel, Uncle Tom's Cabin, quickly became a theatrical mainstay in the North. It is estimated that many more northerners attended a performance of the play than read the book. Born to actors, Lynne Townsend (the editor's mother) first took to the stage at age five in the role of Little Eva, the daughter of the novel's New Orleans slave-owner, Augustine St. Clare.
3. For an insightful analysis of connections between slavery and northern industry, see Martin H. Blatt and David R. Roediger, eds., *The Meaning of Slavery in the North* (New York: Routledge, 1998).
4. The importation of slaves from Africa, or any other country, had been banned in the United States since 1809.
5. Lincoln received a total of 26,388 votes from the slave states of Delaware, Kentucky, Maryland, Missouri, and Virginia. He was not included on the 1860 ballot in the states of the Deep South. See Holt, *The Election of 1860*, 195.
6. The 1860 census listed numbers of manumitted and fugitive slaves, but not those that had been kidnapped. In that year, Missouri reported 99 fugitive slaves (from a total slave population of 114,931), fourth in the South behind Kentucky, Virginia, and Maryland. Kennedy, *Preliminary Report on the Eighth Census*, 137.
7. It is unclear how Stewart came by these figures. In 1860, Missouri was second only to Virginia in population among the slave states, but lagged behind in general wealth. Its real estate and personal property ranked seventh in the South behind Virginia, Kentucky, Georgia, Mississippi, Louisiana, and South Carolina. In capital represented by banks, however, it stood last

among the slave states reporting $1.2 million compared to its sister border states of Kentucky ($7.5 million), Maryland ($8.1 Million), and Delaware ($1.3 million). Kennedy, *Preliminary Report on the Eighth Census*, 2, 195, 192.

8. Of the 803 fugitive slaves reported in the 1860 census, 345 (43%) were recorded from the border states of Missouri, Kentucky, Maryland, and Delaware. Kennedy, *Preliminary Report on the Eighth Census*, 137.

9. Leopard and Shoemaker, eds., *The Messages and Proclamations of the Governors of the State of Missouri*, 3:317–27; Christensen, Foley, Kremer and Winn, eds., *Dictionary of Missouri Biography*, 423–26. Jackson had become quite wealthy working in partnership with Dr. John S. Sappington (1776–1856), a pioneer and physician in Saline County, whose three daughters (Jane, Louisa, and Elizabeth) Jackson married successively.

10. A reference to Thomas Jefferson's reaction to the passage of the Missouri Compromise on March 3, 1820. In a letter dated April 22, 1820, to a congressman from Massachusetts, he wrote, "But this momentous question, like a fire-bell in the night, awakened and filled me with terror. I considered it at once as the knell of the Union. It is hushed, indeed, for the moment. But this is a reprieve only, not a final sentence." Jefferson continued to write, "But as it is, we have the wolf (slavery) by the ears, and we can neither hold him, nor safely let him go. Justice is in one scale, and self-preservation in the other." Merrill D. Peterson, ed., *The Portable Thomas Jefferson* (New York: Penguin Books, 1975), 568.

11. A 1975 study of nineteenth century wealth in the United States determined that the total value of southern slaves was $3.6 billion. Lee Soltow, *Men and Wealth in the United States, 1850–1870* (New Haven: Yale University Press, 1975), 182.

12. Revolutionary War notables Francis Marion (1732–1795), Thomas Sumter (1734–1832), William Jasper (1750–1779), William Moultrie (1730–1805), Henry Laurens (1724–1792), Pierce Butler (1744–1822). Butler was a signer of the US Constitution, as was Charles Pinckney (1757–1824) and Charles Cotesworth Pinckney (1746–1825); Edward Rutledge (1749–1800), signer of the Declaration of Independence; Henry Middleton (1717–1784), attendant of the First Continental Congress; William Jones Lowndes (1782–1822), US representative; George McDuffie (1790–1851), US senator; Paul Hamilton (1762–1816), Secretary of the Navy; Robert Young Hayne (1791–1839), US senator; Hugh Swinton Legaré (1797–1843), US attorney general; John Smith Preston (1809–1881), secession commissioner to Virginia; Pierce Mason Butler (1798–1847), South Carolina governor (1836–1838).

13. US senator from Massachusetts Daniel Webster (1782–1852), and US senator from Kentucky Henry Clay (1777–1852).

14. The 1860 census listed Missouri's slave population at 87,422. If the average

value of a slave was $900, the total value of the state's slaves was $78,679,800. See Soltow, *Men and Wealth in the United States, 1850–1870*) 182.

15. Russell was one of fifty-two commissioners dispatched to other slave states to promote the secession message to governors, legislatures, and state conventions. See Dew, *Apostles of Disunion*, 19.
16. *Hudibras* is a satirical poem, written in a mock-heroic style by Samuel Butler (1613–1680).
17. John McAfee of Shelby County had been elected speaker of the House on January 2, 1861.
18. Thomas Caute Reynolds (1821–1887) served as lieutenant governor from January 3, 1861, until July 31 when he joined Claiborne F. Jackson in Missouri's government in exile.
19. John Dunlap Stevenson (1821–1897) later joined the US Army and served as colonel of the 7th Missouri Volunteer Infantry Regiment. He later commanded the "Irish Brigade" during the siege of Vicksburg, Mississippi, and remained in the Army until 1870.
20. William Henry Seward (1801–1872), governor of New York (1838–1842), US senator (1849–1861), and secretary of state (1861–1869).
21. John Letcher (1813–1884) served as Virginia's governor from January 1860 until January 1864. In his annual address to Virginia's general assembly on January 7, 1861, Letcher complained that South Carolina had seceded without "consultation with any one of her slaveholding sister States." See *Journal of the Senate of the Commonwealth of Virginia: Begun and Held at the Capitol in the City of Richmond, on Monday, the Seventh of January, 1861, in the Year One Thousand Eight Hundred and Sixty-One—Being the Eighty-Fifth Year of the Commonwealth, Extra Session* (Richmond: James E. Goode, Senate Printer, 1861), 9–27.
22. A reference to John Brown's raid on Harpers Ferry, Virginia, in October 1859; and John Montgomery, a Kansas abolitionist known for murdering slave owners and freeing slaves.
23. On January 9, 1861, South Carolina troops on Morris Island and Fort Moultrie at the entrance to Charleston Harbor, fired upon and turned away the *Star of the West*, a US government resupply ship headed to Ft. Sumter.

2. United States Senate

1. Benjamin Franklin Wade (1800–1878) served in the Senate from 1851 until 1869, first as a Whig and later a Republican. On December 17, 1860, Representative Wade argued that while Republicans opposed the extension of slavery into the western territories, they had no intention of interfering with the institution in the states. Not only was there no reason for the southern

states to secede (South Carolina would do so on December 20), there was no authority for secession in the US Constitution. *Congressional Globe*, 36th Cong., 2nd Sess., 99–104.

2. Proverbs 22:3.
3. On August 14, 1848, Congress created the Oregon Territory excluding slavery in the same manner that the institution had been excluded from the Northwest Territory in 1789. Missouri Senator Thomas Hart Benton voted in the affirmative. See Potter, *The Impending Crisis*, 64–76.
4. The Missouri Compromise of 1820 barred slavery north of the 36°30′ parallel only in territory then owned by the United States. At that time, California was a province of Mexico.
5. Jacob Collamer (1791–1865), a Republican senator who served in the US Senate from 1855 until his death in Woodstock, Vermont, on November 9, 1865.
6. The census of 1860 spent considerable time analyzing the number of fugitive slaves. Noting that the total number of runaways declined from 1,011 in 1850 to 803 in 1860, the percentage of slaves involved dropped from .0315 to .0203 over the decade. "Small and inconsiderable" as those numbers appear, the report continued, "the fact becomes evident that the escape of this class of persons, while rapidly decreasing in ratio in the border slave States, occurs independent of proximity to a free population, being in the nature of things incident to the relation of master and slave." Kennedy, *Preliminary Report on the Eighth Census, 1860*, 11–12.
7. James Rood Doolittle (1815–1897), a Republican who served in the US Senate from 1857 until 1869.
8. In 1854, Sherman Booth was convicted in a district federal court of violating the 1850 Fugitive Slave Law. The Wisconsin state supreme court freed Booth holding that his conviction was illegal and the Fugitive Slave Law unconstitutional. Chief Justice Roger B. Taney's 1859 decision in *Ableman v. Booth* denied the right of state judiciary to interfere in federal cases, upheld the supremacy of the federal Constitution, and defended the role of the federal judiciary to decide constitutional issues. See Michael J. C. Taylor, "'A More Perfect Union': *Ableman v. Booth* and the Culmination of Federal Sovereignty," *Journal of Supreme Court History* 28, no. 2 (July 2003), 101–15; Paul Finkelman, *An Imperfect Union: Slavery, Federalism, and Comity* (Chapel Hill: University of North Carolina Press, 1981), 336–37.
9. In 1860, Missouri ranked fourth in fugitive slaves behind Kentucky, Virginia, and Maryland. Using Soltow's estimate of $900 per slave, Kentucky's 119 fugitive slaves would have been valued at $107,100, while Missouri's 99 fugitives would have been valued at $89,100. See Kennedy, *Preliminary Report on the Eighth Census*, 137.
10. A variation on eighteenth-century English poet William Congreve's quote

"Heaven has no rage like love to hatred turned, nor hell a fury like a woman scorned."

11. The concept of an "irrepressible conflict" is attributed to Senator William H. Seward from a speech he delivered in Rochester, October 25, 1858. Seward warned that a collision between the free-labor and slave-labor systems in the United States, "an irrepressible conflict," meant that the "United States must and will . . . become either entirely a slave-holding nation, or entirely a free-labor nation." Four months earlier, Abraham Lincoln had delivered his "House Divided" campaign speech in Springfield, Illinois, in which he offered the same analysis of the arguments over slavery, but did not employ the term "irrepressible conflict." Lincoln's phrasing was: "Either the *opponents* of slavery, will arrest the further spread of it, and place it where the public mind shall rest in the belief that it is in course of ultimate extinction; or its *advocates* will push it forward, till it shall become alike lawful in *all* the States, old as well and *new—North* as well as *South*."

12. George Ellis Pugh (1822–1876) served in the US Senate from 1855 until 1861 as a Democrat.

13. William Henry Seward (1801–1871) served as governor of New York (1838–1842) and later in the US Senate from 1849 until 1861, first as a Whig and later as a Republican. He served presidents Abraham Lincoln and Andrew Johnson as secretary of state (1861–1869).

14. Although gaining compensation for slaves carried off by the British during the American Revolution was one of John Jay's goals, Jay's Treaty of 1794 included no mention of such compensation.

15. Signed on Christmas Eve 1814, the Treaty of Ghent settled issues caused by the War of 1812 with Great Britain. It provided that "All territory, places, and possessions whatsoever taken by either party from the other during the war, . . . shall be restored without delay" including "any Slaves or other private property." Return, but not indemnification.

16. Article III of the Louisiana Purchase agreement stipulated that the "inhabitants of the ceded territory shall be incorporated in the Union of the United States and admitted as soon as possible according to the principles of the federal Constitution to the enjoyment of all these rights, advantages and immunities of citizens of the United States, and in the mean time they shall be maintained and protected in the free enjoyment of their liberty, property and the Religion which they profess."

17. From James Buchanan's annual address to Congress. *Congressional Globe*, 36th Cong., 2nd Sess., December 3, 1860, Appendix, 1–7.

18. Psalms 91:5–6.

19. One of the grievances espoused by southerners stemmed from the Lemmon Slave Case. In 1852, eight slaves owned by Virginian Juliet Lemon were

taken from her in New York City in the discharge of an 1841 state law that freed slaves brought into New York by their owners. Virginia appealed the case, lost both in the New York Supreme Court and the New York Court of Appeals, but was not, for reasons not fully understood, placed before the US Supreme Court. The local press and the courts changed the case from *Lemon* to *Lemmon*. See Marie Tyler-McGraw and Dwight T. Pitcaithley, "The Lemmon Slave Case: Courtroom Drama, Constitutional Crisis and the Southern Quest to Nationalize Slavery," *Commonplace: The Journal of Early American Life*, https://commonplace.online/article/lemmon-slave-case/, accessed May 27, 2024.

20. Edmund Burke's speech "On The Nabob Of Arcot's Debts" delivered on February 28, 1785, described Hyder Ali's destruction of the south Indian province of Carnatic in 1780.
21. John Caldwell Calhoun (1782–1850) was a statesman and political theorist who became the leading proponent of states' rights and limited government.
22. Preston King (1806–1865), Republican senator from New York.
23. For Virginia's long deliberations before seceding, see Dwight T. Pitcaithley, *Virginia Secedes: A Documentary History* (Knoxville: University of Tennessee Press, 2024).
24. The resolution, introduced by Republican George William Palmer of New York read: "*Resolved*, that neither the Federal Government, nor the people or governments of the non-slaveholding States, have a purpose or a constitutional right to legislate upon or interfere with slavery in any of the States of the Union. *Resolved*, That those persons in the North who do not subscribe to the foregoing propositions are too insignificant in numbers or influence to excite the serious attention or alarm of any portion of the people of the Republic, and that the increase in their numbers and influence does not keep pace with the increase of the aggregate population of the Union." The resolution was approved by a vote of 116 to 4. Those voting against were Missouri Representatives John Smith Phelps (Democrat) and Samuel Hughes Woodson (American Party), New York Representative Thomas Jefferson Barr (Independent Democrat), and Charles Lewis Scott (Democrat) from California. *Congressional Globe*, 36th Cong., 2nd Sess., February 11, 1861, 855.
25. William Henry Seward (1801–1872), Republican from New York.
26. Henry Bowen Anthony (1815–1884), Republican from Rhode Island.
27. Jesse David Bright (1812–1875), Democrat from Indiana.
28. Graham Newell Fitch (1808–1892), Democrat from Indiana.
29. Kansas became the thirty-fourth state on January 29, 1861.
30. James Murray Mason (1798–1871), Democrat from Virginia.

3. United States House of Representatives

1. See Pitcaithley, *The U.S. Constitution and Secession*, 227–31, 166, 206, 260–62.
2. Connor, *Texas: A History*, 154.
3. The "relic of barbarism" phrase was used by the Republican Party in its 1856 platform, but not in the 1860 platform.
4. For more on the issue of repealing Pennsylvania's personal liberty law of 1847, see Thomas D. Morris, *Free Men All: The Personal Liberty Laws of the North, 1780–1861* (Baltimore: Johns Hopkins University Press, 1974), 216–18.
5. Missouri's population in 1860 totaled 1,182,012, second only to Virginia's which numbered 1,596,318.
6. John J. Crittenden.
7. In 1860, Missouri reported ninety-nine fugitive slaves. Those reported from the five states bordering the Gulf of Mexico totaled 177. Kennedy, *Preliminary Report on the Eighth Census*, 137.
8. The 1860 census listed a total of 803 fugitive slaves for the year (300 fewer than in 1850). The Cotton states reported 223 fugitives, the Upper South states 235, while the four border states reported 345. Kennedy, *Preliminary Report on the Eighth Census*, 137.
9. 36th Cong., 2nd Sess., House of Representatives, January 29, 1861, Report No. 31.
10. By January 26, South Carolina, Mississippi, Florida, Alabama, and Georgia had seceded. Louisiana would secede that very day.
11. Republican John Sherman (1823–1900) later served as secretary of the treasury in the Rutherford B. Hayes administration and secretary of state under President William McKinley. His older brother was William Tecumseh Sherman (1820–1891), US general who helped defeat the Confederacy with his march through Georgia in 1864.
12. Republican John Franklin Farnsworth (1820–1897).
13. According to Lincoln scholar Eric Foner, Lincoln opposed Black suffrage until late in his administration when he became open to limited, or conditional, voting by Black men. Eric Foner, *The Fiery Trial: Abraham Lincoln and American Slavery* (New York: W. W. Norton & Company, 2010), 139, 141, 335.
14. Republican Benjamin Stanton (1809–1872) from Ohio.
15. Republican Charles Brooks Hoard (1805–1886) of New York.
16. Republican David Kilgore (1804–1879) of Indiana.
17. Opposition Party member John Adams Gilmer (1805–1868) of North Carolina.
18. The Jackson-Napton Resolutions (named for Claiborne Fox Jackson and William Barklay Napton) were passed with large majorities in both houses of the Missouri General Assembly. Introduced by Jackson on January 15,

1849, but written by Napton, a justice of the Missouri Supreme Court, the resolutions held that Congress had no authority to legislate on slavery in the territories, only the settlers had that right, that the Missouri Compromise could be applied to future territories, but that any attempt by Congress to interfere with slavery south of the 36°30' line would impel Missouri to cooperate with the slaveholding states for mutual protection. Phillips, *Missouri's Confederate*, 169–72.

19. See Sacco, "Searching for Compromise: Missouri Congressman John Richard Barret's Fight to Save the Union," 5–32.
20. George Washington's Circular Letter to the States, June 8, 1783.
21. George Washington's Farewell Address, September 17, 1796.
22. Thomas Jefferson (1743–1826).
23. President James Monroe (1758–1831).
24. John Adams (1735–1826).
25. Gilbert du Motier, Marquis de Lafayette (1757–1834), French supporter during the American Revolution.
26. John Holmes (1773–1843), former US representative from Massachusetts. It was in that same letter that Jefferson supported the idea of "general emancipation and *expatriation* . . . gradually, and with due sacrifices." "But as it is," he continued, "we have the wolf (slavery) by the ears, and we can neither hold him, nor safely let him go. Justice is in one scale, and self-preservation in the other." Peterson, *The Portable Thomas Jefferson*, 567–69.
27. David Kilgore (1804–1878), representative from Indiana.
28. William Shakespeare, *Othello*, 2.3; *Henry V*, 2.2; and *Henry VIII*, 2.4. References are to act and scene. Barret cleverly used this reference to the racism evident in *Othello* as introduction to his antipathy for Negro equality. Early in the play, Brabantio, a senator, expresses his distaste for racial equality and intermarriage. If Desdemona (his daughter) and Othello were to marry and have children, he observes, "Bond-slaves and pagans shall our statesmen be." Likewise, Barret set up his "hell in their wicked hearts" attack by quoting Queen Katherine in *Henry VIII*. In the line that follows, "With meekness and humility," Katherine rebukes Cardinal Wolsey, as Barret rebuked abolitionists, with the reproach, "but your heart is cramm'd with arrogancy, spleen, and pride." For more on references to Shakespeare over Secession Winter, see John Andrews and Dwight T. Pitcaithley, "Cry Havoc," *New York Times*, February 19, 2011, https://opinionator.blogs.nytimes.com/2011/02/19/cry-havoc/.
29. Joshua Reed Giddings (1795–1864), a leading abolitionist and a founding member of the Republican Party.
30. Probably George William Curtis (1824–1892), a founding member of the Republican Party.

31. From the Lincoln-Douglas debate in Galesburg, Illinois, October 7, 1858.
32. To that extent.
33. Lincoln immediately followed this statement with: "Let it not be said that I am contending for the establishment of political and social equality between whites and blacks. I have already said the contrary. I am not now combating the argument of NECESSITY, arising from the fact that blacks are already amongst us; but I am combating what is set up as MORAL argument for allowing them to be taken where they never yet been—arguing against the EXTENSION of a bad thing, which where it already exists, we must of necessity, manage as best we can." Roy P. Basler, *The Collected Works of Abraham Lincoln*, 9 vols. (New Brunswick: Rutgers University Press, 1953), 2:266.
34. Carl Shurz (1829–1906), a German American political leader, journalist, dedicated reformer, and secretary of the interior from 1877 until 1881.
35. Speech delivered by Shurz in Springfield, Massachusetts, on January 4, 1860.
36. Charles Sumner (1811–1874), senator from Massachusetts.
37. In 1857, North Carolinian Hinton Rowan Helper (1829–1909) published *The Impending Crisis of the South: How to Meet It*, an antislavery polemic that detailed how slavery impeded the South's economic and cultural development. An 1860 revised and renamed version (*Compendium of the Impending Crisis of the South*) was endorsed by a number of leading Republicans including William H. Seward, Charles Sumner, Salmon P. Chase, Frank P. Blair, Thomas Corwin, Ralph Waldo Emerson, and Harriet Beecher Stowe. Helper believed that White non-slave-owning southerners should overthrow the slave-owning oligarchy and relocate the slave population to Africa. At no point in his critique of southern slavery did he propose or endorse slave rebellions. David Brown, *Southern Outcast: Hinton Rowan Helper and The Impending Crisis of the South* (Baton Rouge: Louisiana State University Press, 2006).
38. A reference to the massacre in 1572 of French Calvinist Protestants by extreme Catholics during the French wars of religion. Modern estimates for the number of dead across France vary widely from 5,000 to 30,000.
39. All quotes are from the 1857 edition, *The Impending Crisis of the South: How to Meet It*.
40. Henry Clay (1777–1852), US senator from Kentucky.
41. Clay's speech, titled "Abolition Petitions," detailed the various groups of abolitionists and explained why abolishing slavery was impossible. While claiming he was "no friend of slavery," Clay contended, "The liberty of the descendants of Africa in the United States is incompatible with the safety and liberty of the European descendants." He also took pains to distance abolitionists from either the Whig or Democratic parties: "Mr. President, it is not true, and I rejoice that it is not true, that either of the two great parties

in this country has any designs or aims at abolition." "But I am far," he continued, "from being disposed to accuse our adversaries of being Abolitionists." *Congressional Globe*, 25th Cong., 3rd Sess., February 7, 1839, Appendix, 354–59.

42. Historian William W. Freehling estimates that no more than two percent of the northern voting population self-identified as abolitionists. William W. Freehling, *The Road to Disunion*, vol. 2, *Secessionists Triumphant* (New York: Oxford University Press, 2007), 12.
43. Helper never encouraged slave revolts. Abolition, by his lights, should be effected by nonslaveholding Whites rejecting all support for slave owners. He developed an eleven-point plan whereby slavery would be ended and none of his ideas favored or supported slave rebellions. Brown, *Southern Outcast*, 117–18.
44. Theodore Parker (1810–1860), a theologian, author, and abolitionist was a member of the secret committee that supported John Brown's raid on Harpers Ferry, Virginia, in 1859.
45. From *Metamorphoses*, book 7, *The Story of Medea and Jason* by the Roman poet Ovid (Publius Ovidius Naso).
46. While the Republican Party won control of the Executive Branch as a result of the election of 1860, the Democratic Party won majorities in both houses of Congress, and the proslavery Chief Justice Roger B. Taney still commanded the US Supreme Court.
47. John Quincy Adams died on February 23, 1848.
48. Henry Wilson (1812–1875). In December 1861, Senator Wilson introduced a bill designed to abolish slavery in the District of Columbia. He later served as President Grant's second vice president from 1873 until 1877.
49. Anson Burlingame (1820–1870) from Massachusetts.
50. Of these assumed goals of the Lincoln administration only the abolition of slavery in the District of Columbia was attempted or achieved. Lincoln signed into law the D.C. emancipation measure on April 16, 1862. By the time Barret addressed his colleagues, both houses of Congress had approved the organization of the Colorado Territory without any restrictions on slavery. The bill passed the House of Representatives on February 18 on a vote of 90 to 44. Representative Barret voted nay. By March 1, the Republican-controlled Congress would organize the Dakota and Nevada Territories also without invoking the Wilmot Proviso.
51. Michael Holt's analysis of the election of 1860 produced similar numbers: 1,574,864 in the North and 1,247,840 in the South against Lincoln, and 1,839,205 in the North and 26,388 in the South for Lincoln. See Holt, *The Election of Lincoln*, 194–95.
52. In the Compromise of 1850, Congress organized the New Mexico Territory without any prohibition on slavery, thus allowing the settlers therein to

decide the future of the institution. In 1859, the territorial legislature passed a detailed bill protecting slavery throughout the territory which it later repealed on December 10, 1861. For an excellent analysis of the law see, John P. Hays, "The Curious Case of New Mexico's Pre-Civil War Slave Code," *New Mexico Historical Review* 92, no. 3 (Summer 2017):251–83. Within months after New Mexico passed the code Congress debated and attempted, but failed, to repeal it. See 36th Cong., 1st Sess., May 10, 1860, House Report 508.

53. Edward Bates (1793–1869), attorney and politician, served as Missouri's attorney general (1820–1821) and later as US attorney general in the Lincoln administration (1861–1864). For Bates as Republican contender in 1860, see Nevins, *The Emergence of Lincoln*, 237–60.
54. Henry Winter Davis (1817–1865), served in the US House of Representatives (American Party) from 1855 until 1861 and again from 1863 to 1865 as an Unconditional Unionist.
55. In 1752, Benjamin Franklin invented a lightning rod conductor, popularly called a Franklin rod.
56. While Barret focused his attention on the second plank of the 1860 Republican platform, he ignored the fourth plank which read: "That the maintenance inviolate of the rights of the states, and especially the right of each state to order and control its own domestic institutions, according to its own judgment exclusively, is essential to that balance of power on which the perfection and endurance of our political fabric depend."
57. On January 9, 1861, shore batteries in Charleston Harbor repulsed the *Star of the West*, a ship sent by President James Buchanan to resupply Ft. Sumter.

4. Missouri State Convention

1. *Journal and Proceedings of the Missouri State Convention, Held at Jefferson City and St. Louis, March, 1861*, 3–4.
2. Probably George Graham Vest (1830–1903), member of the Missouri House of Representatives (1860–1861), of both houses of the Confederate Congress (1862–1865), and US senator from 1879 until 1903.
3. See Dew, *Apostles of Disunion*.
4. James Osgood Andrew (1794–1871) was bishop of the Methodist Episcopal Church from 1832 until 1844. His ownership of slaves in Georgia, as a result of his several marriages, caused the rupture of the northern and southern factions of the church. After the split, he remained bishop of the Methodist Episcopal Church, South until 1866.
5. Henry Clay of Kentucky.
6. John Charles Fremont (1813–1890).
7. James Buchanan (1791–1868) won the election with 45.3 percent of the popular vote. He bested the Republican candidate, Fremont, who received 33.1

percent; and former president Millard Fillmore, nominee of the Whig/Know Nothing Party, with 21.5 percent.

8. Henry Wilson (1812–1875) was a US senator from Massachusetts from 1855 until 1873 when he became Ulysses S. Grant's second vice president.

9. Georgia's state convention approved its ordinance of secession on January 19, dissolving its connection with the United States. Ten days later, the convention explained its action in a declaration of causes. Georgia seceded because of the Republican Party's "prohibition of slavery in the territories, hostility to it [slavery] everywhere, [support for] the equality of the black and white races" and the refusal of northern states to return fugitive slaves. Georgia chose secession because of the Republican Party's avowed purpose to "subvert our society, and subject us, not only to the loss of our property but the destruction of ourselves, our wives and our children, and the desolation of our homes, our altars, and our firesides." Pitcaithley, *The U.S. Constitution and Secession*, 101–9.

10. See Roger D. Launius, *Alexander William Doniphan: Portrait of a Missouri Moderate* (Columbia: University of Missouri Press, 1997).

11. Lucius E. Chittenden, *A Report of the Debates and Proceedings in the Secret Sessions of the Conference Convention, for Proposing Amendments to the Constitution of the United States, Held at Washington, D. C., in February, A. D. 1861* (New York: D. Appleton & Company, 1864), 312, 378.

12. The entire report of the delegates to the Washington Peace Conference can be found in *Journal of the Senate of Missouri, at the First Session of the Twenty-First General Assembly* (Jefferson City: W. G. Cheeney, Public Printer, 1861), Appendix, 569–75.

13. Harrison Hough had been elected to the Missouri House of Representatives in 1844 from Scott County.

14. John D. Coalter had represented St. Louis in the Washington Peace Conference.

15. Henry C. Spalding & Co. manufactured "Spalding's Celebrated Prepared Glue" in the 1850s and 1860s as a product to mend household items.

16. In folklore, a Javanese tree alleged to poison its surroundings and said to be fatal to approach.

17. James Guthrie (1792–1869) had been secretary of the treasury in the Franklin Pierce administration and served as chair of the Washington Peace Conference's General Committee on Proposals. The committee's final proposed amendment regarding the territories was similar to Senator Crittenden's amendment with the exception that it did not protect slavery in future acquisitions of territory south of the 36°30' north parallel. For Guthrie's comparison of the two amendments see Pitcaithley, *Kentucky and the Secession Crisis*, 176–83.

18. On February 16, Reverdy Johnson from Maryland proposed defining territory more clearly by prefacing it with the word "present." Chittenden, *A Report of the Debates and Proceedings*, 73.
19. Thomas Emlen Franklin (1810–1884) was a delegate from Pennsylvania. On February 22, he proposed an alternative to the article dealing with slavery in the territories. The primary difference was that Franklin exempted Cherokee treaty lands from the prohibition of slavery north of the 36°30' line. Chittenden, *A Report of the Debates and Proceedings*, 291.
20. Chittenden, *A Report of the Debates and Proceedings*, 209.
21. Coalter was correct; Missouri did not vote on the final version of Article 1 on February 27. Chittenden, *A Report of the Debates and Proceedings*, 441.
22. William Paley (1743–1805), Anglican priest, philosopher, and author of books on Christianity, ethics, and science. Perhaps Coalter was thinking of Paley's *The Principles of Moral and Political Philosophy* (1794).
23. Don E. Fehrenbacher, *The Dred Scott Case: Its Significance in American Law and Politics* (New York: Oxford University Press, 1978), 262–65. For the St. Louis perspective on *Dred Scott's* litigation and its aftermath, see Arenson, *The Great Heart of the Republic*, 82–106.
24. For a detailed analysis of Jefferson Davis as president of the Confederacy, see James M. McPherson, *Embattled Rebel: Jefferson Davis as Commander in Chief* (New York: Penguin Press, 2014).
25. Abraham Lincoln won popular majorities in all the non-slave states except for California where he gained only 32 percent, Oregon (38 percent), and New Jersey (48 percent). See Holt, *The Election of 1860*, 194.
26. Likely Robert Field Stockton (1795–1866), a Democratic delegate to the Washington Peace Conference who, on February 19, spoke at length against the idea of the federal government attempting to "coerce" the seceding states. Chittenden, *A Report of the Debates and Proceedings*, 113–20.
27. A reference to Lincoln's March 4 Inaugural Address.
28. For a sampling of those memorials and petitions see Pitcaithley, *Kentucky and the Secession Crisis*, 151–66.
29. Senator Crittenden's sixth article proposed that "no amendment shall be made to the Constitution which shall authorize or give to Congress any power to abolish or interfere with slavery in any of the States by whose laws it is, or may be, allowed or permitted." Representative Thomas Corwin's amendment which stipulated that "No Amendment shall be made to the Constitution which will authorize or give to Congress the power to abolish or interfere, within any State, with the domestic institutions thereof, including that of persons held to labor or service by the laws of the said State," was approved by the US House of Representatives on February 18, and by the Senate on March 4.

30. From Daniel 6:8. A reference to an unalterable law or decree.
31. Attorney James H. Birch represented Clinton County.
32. A reference to Massachusetts Senator Daniel Webster's Seventh of March speech in support of the Compromise of 1850.
33. Kentucky Senator Henry Clay designed the Compromise of 1850 that employed the concept of popular sovereignty into the organization of the Kansas and Nebraska Territories.
34. While Buchanan won easily in the Electoral College, he amassed only 45.3 percent of the popular vote (1,832,955) to Fremont's 1,340,537, and Fillmore's 871,731. Holt, *The Election of 1860*, 11.
35. With the 1820 Missouri Compromise line being overturned by the Kansas-Nebraska Act and the theory of popular sovereignty becoming unsatisfactory to the South after the 1858 failure of Kansas's proslavery Lecompton Constitution, attention increasingly turned to federal protection of slavery in the territories. On May 25, 1860, the Senate overwhelmingly approved a resolution earlier proposed by Senator Jefferson Davis which held that "if experience should at any time prove that the judicial and executive authority do not possess means to insure adequate protection to constitutional rights in a Territory, and if the territorial government should fail or refuse to provide the necessary remedies for that purpose, it will be the duty of Congress to supply such deficiency." *Congressional Globe*, 36th Cong., 1st Sess., 2344, 2350.
36. In the Election of 1860, Lincoln received 1,839,205 votes in the North while only 26,388 in the South due to the Republican not being on the ballot in ten southern states. The final tally of northern votes against Lincoln in the North was 1,574,864 and in the South 1,247,840. See Holt, *The Election of 1860*, 194–95.
37. As a result of the 1860 congressional election, Democrats would have controlled both houses of the Thirty-Seventh Congress for the first two years of the Lincoln administration.
38. On January 26, 1861, immediately before voting in favor of an ordinance of secession, delegates to Louisiana's state convention voted against (by a vote of 84 to 43) a resolution that would have allowed the White male voters of the state to ratify the convention's decision. *Official Journal of the Proceedings of the Convention of the State of Louisiana* (New Orleans: J. O. Nixon, Printer to the State Convention, 1861), 16–17.
39. James Lawrence Orr (1822–1873) of South Carolina. Orr served in the US Congress from 1849 until 1859; during the Thirty-Fifth Congress as speaker of the House. A leading secessionist during the summer of 1860, he was quoted as saying that Lincoln's election would "require prompt secession." Quoted in Freehling, *The Road to Disunion*, 377.
40. Texas Governor Sam Houston, a staunch Unionist, opposed secession and attempted to block the movement in the state legislature and in the state

convention. Ultimately, the convention vacated the office of the governor, not unlike in Missouri, and handed the governorship to Lieutenant Governor Edward Clark. Connor, *Texas: A History*, 192–95; James L Haley, *Sam Houston* (Norman: University of Oklahoma Press, 2002), 390.

41. Louis Trezevant Wigfall (1816–1874), secessionist senator from Texas, remained in the US Senate after the secession of Texas until expelled by that body on July 11, 1861. *Congressional Globe*, 37th Cong., 1st Sess., 62–64.
42. A reference to the fractured 1860 Democratic nominating convention in Charleston when South Carolina and other Deep South states withdrew in protest over a platform that did not contain national protections for slavery. See Holt, *The Election of 1860*, 50–66.
43. Gaius Marius (157–86 BCE) and Lucius Cornelius Sulla (138–79 BCE) were Roman military commanders and politicians who ruthlessly competed against each other for control of Rome.
44. A reference to Lucius Sergius Catilina, an aristocrat who turned demagogue and made an unsuccessful attempt to overthrow the late Roman Republic.
45. William Lowndes Yancey (1814–1863) was a politician and orator and leader of the Southern secession movement. At the 1860 Democratic National Convention, he led the Alabama delegation and was instrumental in splitting the party into northern and southern factions. For his role over Secession Winter see William C. Davis, *"A Government of Our Own:" The Making of the Confederacy* (Baton Rouge: Louisiana State University Press, 1994), 20–27.
46. Hérnan Cortéz (1485–1547), a Spanish conquistador who invaded Mexico and toppled the Aztec Empire (1519–1521). Francisco Pizarro (1478–1541), a Spanish conquistador who conquered the Inca Empire in Peru in 1532.
47. During the 1850s as southerners envisioned slavery being circumscribed north of the 36°30' parallel there was increased interest in the expansion of slavery into the tropics. Numerous extralegal "filibustering" expeditions attempted to expand slavery's domain into Mexico, Cuba, and Central America. See Robert E. May, *The Southern Dream of a Caribbean Empire, 1854–1861* (Gainesville: University Press of Florida, 2002; first published in 1973); Matthew Karp, *This Vast Southern Empire: Slaveholders at the Helm of American Foreign Policy* (Cambridge: Harvard University Press, 2016).
48. Henderson referenced here the British case of *Somerset v. Stewart* (1772) wherein the Chief Justice of the Court of the King's Bench ruled that a slave brought to England could not be compelled to leave the realm. Paul Finkelman, *An Imperfect Union*, 38–40.
49. During the 1860 campaign, the American Party melded into the Constitutional Union Party and nominated John Bell of Tennessee. While Northern Democratic candidate Stephen A. Douglas of Illinois garnered all nine of

Missouri's electoral votes, the popular vote was extremely close: 58,502 for Douglas, 58,362 for Bell. See Holt, *The Election of 1860*, 198.
50. A reference to the Corwin amendment passed by Congress only a week earlier.
51. In 1860, Black men could vote without restriction in Massachusetts, Vermont, and New Hampshire (and Maine and Rhode Island). They had the right to vote with some restrictions in New York, Ohio, and Michigan. Horton and Horton, *In Hope of Liberty*, 169.
52. The personal liberty laws enacted by northern states stretched back to the early years of the nineteenth century primarily to prevent the kidnapping of free Black citizens. A 1974 study of those laws determined that only those of Massachusetts and Wisconsin were "unconstitutional beyond question." Morris, *Free Men All*, 208. The 803 fugitives reported in the 1860 census represented .0203 percent of the South's slave population. The 99 fugitives reported by Missouri that year represented .0860 percent of that state's slave population. Kennedy, *Preliminary Report of the Eighth Census*, 137.
53. Congress ultimately carved the remaining western territories into fourteen additional states. With a total of forty-eight states (and later fifty), if the fifteen slave states voted as a block, they could have prevented passage of a constitutional amendment abolishing slavery.
54. Historian William Freehling has estimated that only 2 percent of the northern voting population self-identified as abolitionists. Freehling, *The Road to Disunion*, 12.
55. In Daniel 5:1–31, Belshazzar threw a feast for thousands during which words written on a wall foretold the end of his kingdom. Belshazzar read the words and was slain later that night.
56. On March 11, James H. Moss introduced an amendment proposing that Missouri aid neither the Confederacy nor the federal government. *Proceedings of the Missouri State Convention*, 61.
57. A bar or impediment which precludes allegation of a certain fact in consequence of a previous allegation or denial or conduct or admission. A classically convoluted and contorted legal principle, estoppel was a concept more prevalent in the nineteenth century than today.
58. The behavior of a sanctimonious or self-righteous person.
59. Along with William L. Yancey, Robert Barnwell Rhett (1800–1876) and William Porcher Miles (1822–1899), both from South Carolina, were among the foremost proponents of secession.
60. Wendell Phillips (1811–1884), William Lloyd Garrison (1805–1879), and Arthur Tappan (1786–1865) were all abolitionists from Massachusetts.
61. Henderson undoubtedly was referring to the second section of the fourth

article of the Constitution which read: "No person held to Service or Labour in one State, under the Laws thereof, escaping into another, shall, in Consequence of any Law or Regulation therein, be discharged from such Service or Labour, but shall be delivered up on Claim of the Party to whom such Service or Labour may be due."

62. John Henry Clifford (1809–1876), governor of Massachusetts (1853–1854); Lemuel Shaw (1781–1861) served as chief justice of the Massachusetts Supreme Court from 1830 until 1860. In December 1860, Shaw signed a petition that recommended "the unconditional repeal of the state's Personal Liberty Laws to demonstrate to the South the state's disposition to abide by the Constitution." Although the legislature changed the law, it was not repealed. Morris, *Free Men All*, 208–13. Shaw's daughter, Elizabeth, married the author Herman Melville. In 1847, Melville dedicated his novel *Typee* to his father-in-law.

63. Redd may have been referring to an 1857 law enacted by Maine's legislature that freed all slaves brought into the state by their owners. This law, however, did not apply to fugitive slaves, but only those accompanying their owners into Maine. A similar law passed by New York in 1841 resulted in the famous Lemmon Slave Case noted elsewhere in this book. See Morris, *Free Men All*, 219.

64. David Rice Atchison (1807–1886). As a US senator from Missouri, Atchison requested that Senator Stephen Douglas of Illinois introduce the Kansas-Nebraska Act in 1854.

65. James Stephen Green (1817–1870), Democratic senator from Missouri.

66. James Knox Polk (1795–1849). As president from 1845 until 1849, Polk, from Tennessee, signed the bill organizing the Oregon Territory with the slavery prohibition.

67. Meaning "do not disturb what is settled."

68. In November 1860, Alexander Stephens (1812–1883) and Benjamin Harvey Hill (1823–1882) had offered strong Unionist speeches to the Georgia legislature. During the war, Stephens served as vice president of the Confederacy, and Hill as a Confederate senator. See William W. Freehling and Craig M. Simpson, eds., *Secession Debated: Georgia's Showdown in 1860* (New York: Oxford University Press, 1992), 51–79, 80–104.

69. Gantt here referred to Delegate Moss's amendment that precluded Missouri from supporting either the Confederacy or the United States in coercing the other.

70. Crittenden's amendment proposed protecting slavery in all territory "now held, or hereafter acquired" south of the 36°30′ parallel. Opposed by Republicans and northern Democrats, the clause was not included in the amendment approved by the Washington Peace Conference. The stipulation was

designed to avoid another slavery debate if the United States acquired Cuba or parts of Mexico as many southern Democrats desired.
71. Sample Orr.
72. Attorney James O. Broadhead from St. Louis.
73. The Corwin amendment which prohibited the federal government from interfering with slavery in the states passed Congress on March 4, 1861. Representative Corwin chaired the Committee of Thirty-Three.
74. While sitting as vice president, Aaron Burr (1756–1836) killed Alexander Hamilton in a duel in 1804. He was later charged with treason for violating the Neutrality Act of 1794, but acquitted. Benedict Arnold (1741–1801) committed treason during the American Revolution and was forced to flee to British lines.
75. In 1860, slaves outnumbered Whites in only two southern states: Mississippi (436,631 to 353,901) and South Carolina (402,406 to 291,388). In Missouri, Whites outnumbered slaves 1,063,509 to 114,931. Kennedy, *Preliminary Report on The Eighth Census*, 131.
76. A reference to the slave rebellion in the French West Indies colony of Saint-Domingue that lasted from 1791 until 1804 and resulted in Haitian independence. Southerners often referenced the rebellion as evidence of the horrors that can result from abolition. May, *The Southern Dream of a Caribbean Empire*, 33–34; see also Michel-Rolph Trouillot, *Silencing the Past: Power and the Production of History* (Boston: Beacon Press, 1995).
77. The Wigwam was a convention center and meeting hall in Chicago and site of the 1860 Republican Convention. Joshua Reed Giddings was one of the founders of the Republican Party.
78. For the actions of Joshua Giddings during the Chicago convention, see James Brewer Stewart, *Joshua R. Giddings and the Tactics of Radical Politics* (Cleveland: Press of Case Western Reserve University, 1970), 271–73; Holt, *The Election of 1860*, 105, 113.
79. The number of votes for Lincoln totaled 1,865,593; 26,388 of them being cast in the slave states of Delaware, Kentucky, Maryland, Missouri, and Virginia, the only southern states where Lincoln was on the ballot. The total number of votes against Lincoln, North and South totaled 2,822,704. Holt, *The Election of 1860*, 194–95.
80. Salmon Portland Chase (1808–1873), former US senator (1849–1855), founder of the Free-Soil Party, and later secretary of the treasury in the Lincoln administration.
81. William H. Seward would become Lincoln's secretary of state.
82. Attorney Thomas T. Gantt.
83. Samuel Hoar (1778–1856), former US representative from Massachusetts; sent by the state legislature to South Carolina to test the constitutionality of

acts prohibiting free Negroes from coming into the State. Upon his arrival in December 1844, the legislature of South Carolina passed resolutions expelling him from the city of Charleston. For Hoar's account of his adventure see, "Samuel Hoar's Expulsion from Charleston," *Old South Leaflets* vi, no. 140, 313–32.

84. In his 1857 decision in *Dred Scott v. Sandford*, Chief Justice Roger B. Taney determined that free Blacks could never be citizens of the United States.

85. Marshall Hier, *Famous and Infamous Lawyers in St. Louis History* (St. Louis: Bar Association of Metropolitan St. Louis, 2014), 133–35. See also, Gerteis, *Civil War St. Louis*, 129–31.

86. On December 31, 1860, Judah Philip Benjamin (1811–1884), senator from Louisiana delivered a speech to Congress defending the constitutional right of secession. Jon L. Wakelyn, ed., *Southern Pamphlets on Secession, November 1860-April 1861* (Chapel Hill: University of North Carolina Press, 1996), 101–14. During the war, Benjamin served as Confederate attorney general, secretary of war, and secretary of state. Avoiding capture after the fall of Richmond, he fled to England were he established a career as a barrister until 1883. He died in Paris the following year and is buried in Paris's largest and most historic cemetery, Pere Lachaise among other European and American notables including the singer-songwriter Jim Morrison.

87. The actual wording of the Tenth Amendment is "The powers not delegated to the United States by the Constitution, nor prohibited by it to the States, are reserved to the States respectively, or to the people."

88. Hugo Grotius (1583–1645), Dutch jurist; Samuel Freiherr von Pufendorf (1632–1694), German political philosopher; Emer de Vattel (1714–1767), Prussian international lawyer best known for *The Law of Nations: Or, Principles of the Law of Nature Applied to the Conduct and Affairs of Nations and Sovereigns* (1758).

89. An action to eject a defendant from certain property (and recover ownership of said property) on the grounds that the defendant had no legal right to be there.

90. Abolitionists Wendell Phillips and William Lloyd Garrison.

91. Born in London, Edward Dickinson Baker (1811–1861) served as a Republican from Oregon. Baker introduced Abraham Lincoln at his Inaugural on March 4. He was killed in the Battle of Balls Bluff, Virginia, October 21, 1861.

92. As Wright acknowledged later in his address, just two weeks before he took the floor, Congress had organized three western territories without prohibiting slavery.

93. Plato (429?–347 BCE). The "Utopian dreams of Plato" are found in Plato's *Republic*, a treatise on the ideal government. Purportedly a utopia, Plato's government was, in reality, a totalitarian society governed by philosopher

kings who maintained order by promoting lies such as that social classes exist by nature.

94. John Locke (1632–1704), an English philosopher whose contributions to classical republicanism and liberal theory are reflected in the Declaration of Independence.

95. A likely reference to Massachusetts Senator Daniel Webster (1782–1852) and his Seventh of March (1850) speech in which he argued it was pointless to argue over the extension of slavery into land unsuitable for plantation agriculture. *Congressional Globe*, 31st Cong., 1st Sess., March 7, 1850, Appendix, 269–76.

96. Senator John C. Calhoun (1782–1850), defender of slavery and proponent of states' rights and nullification.

97. For differing views on the *Dred Scott* case, see Don E. Fehrenbacher, *The Dred Scott Case: Its Significance in American Law and Politics* (New York: Oxford University Press, 1978) and Mark A. Graber, *Dred Scott and the Problem of Constitutional Evil* (New York: Cambridge University Press, 2006).

98. To this point, Article IV, Section 3 of the US Constitution directs that "The Congress shall have Power to dispose of and make all needful Rules and Regulations respecting the Territory or other Property belonging to the United States; and nothing in this Constitution shall be so construed as to Prejudice any Claims of the United States, or of any particular State."

99. Congress prohibited slavery from the Northwest Territory (1789), the northern part of the Louisiana Territory (1820), the Iowa Territory (1838), the Oregon Territory (1848), and the Minnesota Territory in 1849.

100. On March 6, 1836, Mexican General Antonio López de Santa Anna defeated a group of defenders including William Travis, James Bowie, and David Crockett at the Alamo, a Spanish mission in San Antonio, Texas. Just days before, Texas had declared its independence from Mexico beginning its decade-long period as a republic.

101. North Carolina's general assembly called for a state convention on May 1, 1861; on February 18 the White male voters of Arkansas voted in favor of a state convention to convene on March 4. North Carolina seceded on May 20 and Arkansas on May 6.

102. Emilius Kitchell Sayre.

103. Secession commissioner Luther J. Glenn.

104. Prior to President Lincoln's call for troops after the Confederate bombardment of Fort Sumter, the strength of the United States Army totaled 16,367 men. See Newell, *The Regular Army Before the Civil War*, 50.

105. British statesman, Edmund Burke (1729–1797). As a member of Parliament, Burke implored Prime Minister Lord North in 1774 and 1775 to rescind the taxes imposed on the American colonists without their consent.

106. On February 3, 1859, the New Mexico territorial legislature passed "An act to provide for the protection of property in Slaves in the Territory." The law did not limit slave ownership to the military. See *Laws of the Territory of New Mexico Passed by the Legislative Assembly, Session of 1859–60* (Santa Fe: O. P. Hovey, Public Printer, 1860), 64–80; Hays, "The Curious Case of New Mexico's Pre-Civil War Slave Code," 251–83; *Slavery in the Territory of New Mexico*, 36th Cong., 1st Sess., House of Representatives, Report No. 508.
107. Republican senator from Ohio Benjamin Franklin Wade (1800–1878); Republican senator from New Hampshire John Parker Hale (1806–1873); Republican senator from Massachusetts Charles Sumner (1811–1874); Republican senator from New York William Henry Seward (1801–1872); and Republican representative from Ohio Owen Lovejoy (1811–1864).
108. While Commissioner Glenn may have mentioned tariffs as being detrimental to southern interests to informal gatherings in St. Louis, he did not include the subject of imposts in his formal address to the convention.
109. The referenced amendment was introduced by Republican Representative Thomas Corwin of Ohio on February 27, passed by the House the next day, and by the Senate on March 4. It specified that "no amendment shall be made to the Constitution which will authorize or give to Congress the power to abolish or interfere, within any State, with the domestic institutions thereof, including that of persons held to labor or service by the laws of said State." Corwin adopted the exact language used by Republican Senator William H. Seward in his proposed amendment of December 24, 1860. Pitcaithley, *The U.S. Constitution and Secession*, 183, 250–51. For a detailed examination of the Corwin amendment see, Daniel W. Crofts, *Lincoln and the Politics of Slavery: The Other Thirteenth Amendment and the Struggle to Save the Union* (Chapel Hill: University of North Carolina Press, 2016).
110. By March 1, 1861, following the departure of southern congressmen after the secession of the Deep South states, the Republican-controlled Congress organized the territories of Colorado, Dakota, and Nevada without any restrictions on slavery.
111. Thomas Jefferson.
112. Henry Clay.
113. A reference to the 1854 Kansas-Nebraska Act.
114. In the Book of Ester, Haman, an official in the court of the Persian King Ahasuerus, had built a gallows to hang one of the king's servants for not paying him (Haman) due respect. Because the servant, Mordechai, was a Jew, Haman convinced the king to have all the Jews in the empire killed. Ahasuerus's wife, Queen Ester, herself a Jew, informed the king that Haman's plot would also require killing her. King Ahasuerus had Haman killed instead using the gallows erected by Haman.

115. Regarding connections between the nullification crisis of the 1830s and the rise of a secessionist ideology following Lincoln's election, see William W. Freehling, *Prelude to Civil War: The Nullification Controversy in South Carolina, 1816–1836* (New York: Harper & Row, 1968; first published in 1965).
116. Andrew Jackson Crawford (1798–1866) was a second cousin to Andrew Jackson and served under Jackson in the Battle of New Orleans during the War of 1812.
117. From the introduction of the Declaration of Independence.
118. Delegates to the Hartford Convention met from December 15, 1814, until January 5, 1815, to protest President James Madison and his economic policies which had led to the War of 1812. The convention's threat of secession ended with Andrew Jackson's victory against the British in New Orleans on January 8.
119. US Constitution, Article III, Section 2.
120. US Constitution, Article I, Section 8, and Section 10.
121. Attorney Aikman Welch represented Johnson County.
122. Circuit Court Judge Samuel M. Breckinridge represented St. Louis.
123. Judge of the Common Pleas Court, James K. Sheeley represented Independence County.

5. Afterward

1. President Andrew Jackson's farewell address upon leaving office on March 4, 1837.
2. President from 1825 until 1829.
3. From an address given by Adams in New York City on April 30, 1839, titled "The Jubilee of the Constitution," commemorating George Washington's inauguration.
4. Virginia's state convention voted to secede on April 17, 1861. The convention provided, however, that the decision must be approved by a vote of the electorate. The White male voters of the state voted to secede 86 percent to 14 percent on May 23. See Dwight T. Pitcaithley, *Virginia Secedes: A Documentary History* (Knoxville: University of Tennessee Press, 2024).
5. North Carolina's state convention unanimously voted to secede on the first day of the gathering, May 20, 1861; Tennessee's legislature approved an ordinance of secession on May 6 with the requirement that the public approve the separation in a vote scheduled for June 8. The White male electorate endorsed the convention's decision 69 percent to 31 percent. Arkansas's state convention voted for disunion also on May 6, approving the ordinance by a vote of 99 percent to 1 percent.
6. Sterling Price (1809–1867). Rather than surrender at the end of the war, Price emigrated to Mexico where he and many other former Confederates founded

the town of Carlota near Vera Cruz. The brainchild of Confederate Navy Commander Matthew F. Maury, Carlota lasted only a year or two before it was abandoned. Notable among its colonists were former Tennessee governor Isham G. Harris; former US senator from Missouri Trusten Polk; Missouri General Joseph Orville Shelby; former US representative from Arkansas Thomas C. Hindman; and former Confederate general from Florida, Edmund Kirby Smith. See Carl Coke Rister, "Carlota: A Confederate Colony in Mexico," *Journal of Southern History* 11, no. 1 (February 1945): 33–50; Shalhope, *Sterling Price: Portrait of a Southerner*, 281–88.

7. William Selby Harney (1800–1889). The Maj. Gen. William S. Harney Summer Home in Sullivan, Crawford County, Missouri, is privately owned by the Harney Mansion Foundation.
8. Nathaniel Lyon (1818–1861), later killed on August 10, 1861, at the Battle of Wilson's Creek.
9. Francis Preston Blair Jr. (1821–1875).
10. Benjamin Franklin Massey (1811–1879) served as secretary of state from 1856 until 1861 when he joined Governor Jackson's government in exile.
11. The battle of Bull Run (Manassas) outside of Washington, DC, the first major battle of the war, had taken place just ten days earlier on July 21.
12. For an analysis of Jackson's letter to Walker, see Phillips, *Missouri's Confederate*, 248–49.
13. Joseph W. Tucker.
14. Recent scholarship has cast doubt on the origins of this letter. See Phillips, *Missouri's Confederate*, 249n10.
15. Thomas Caute Reynolds (1821–1887) succeeded Jackson as governor in exile upon Jackson's death on December 6, 1862.
16. Benjamin Franklin Massey (1811–1879).
17. The full text of the General Assembly's January 21, 1861, act calling for the state convention can be found in *Journal and Proceedings of the Missouri State Convention*, 3–4.
18. Attorney Robert Wilson represented St. Joseph County.
19. The French Revolution marked a decade of radical political and societal change from 1789 until 1799. While inordinately violent, its motto of "liberty, equality, and fraternity" created a vision for future advances in broadly defined individual freedoms.
20. Phillips, *Missouri's Confederate*, 261–66.
21. M. C. Goodlett from Johnson County and Miles Vernon from Laclede County.
22. A two-story frame building, Neosho's Masonic Hall stood at the corner of Washington and Spring Streets.
23. The Battle of Carthage took place on July 5, 1861. Wilson's Creek (near

Springfield) was fought on August 10 during which General Nathaniel Lyon was killed; the site has been administered by the National Park Service since 1960. The Battle of Dry Wood Creek (near Fort Scott) took place on September 2. The siege and battle of Lexington occurred between September 13 and 20; the battlefield has been designated a state historic site and is managed by the Missouri Department of Natural Resources.

24. Charles Henry Hardin (1820–1892), the only senator to vote against the ordinance of secession, later served as the governor of Missouri between 1875 and 1877.
25. Francis Rodman (1829–1888) was Missouri secretary of state from 1865 until 1871.
26. Phillips, *Missouri's Confederate*, 269.

BIBLIOGRAPHY

Primary Sources

Chittenden, Lucius E., ed. *A Report of the Debates and Proceedings in the Secret Sessions of the Conference Convention, for Proposing Amendments to the Constitution of the United States, Held at Washington, D. C. In February, A. D. 1861.* New York: D. Appleton & Company, 1864.

Journal and Proceedings of the Missouri State Convention, Held at Jefferson City and St. Louis, March, 1861. St. Louis: George Knapp & Co., Printers and Binders, 1861.

Journal of the House of Representatives of the State of Missouri, at the Called Session of the Twenty-First General Assembly. Jefferson City: J. P. Ament, Public Printer, 1861.

Journal of the House of Representatives of the State of Missouri, at the First Session of the Twenty-First General Assembly. Jefferson City: W. G. Cheeney, Public Printers, 1861.

Journal of the Missouri State Convention, Held at Jefferson City, July, 1861. St. Louis: George Knapp & Co., Printers and Binders, 1861.

Journal of the Senate, Extra Session of the Rebel Legislature, Called Together by a Proclamation of C. F. Jackson, Begun and Held at the Town of Neosho, Newton County, Missouri, on the Twenty-First Day of October, Eighteen Hundred and Sixty-One. Jefferson City: Emory S. Foster, Public Printer, 1865–1866.

Journal of the Senate of Missouri, at the First Session of the Twenty-First General Assembly. Jefferson City: W. G. Cheeney, Public Printer, 1861.

Leopard, Buel, and Floyd C. Shoemaker, eds. *The Messages and Proclamations of the Governors of the State of Missouri.* Vol. 3. Columbia: State Historical Society of Missouri, 1922.

Proceedings of the Missouri State Convention, Held at Jefferson City, July, 1861 St. Louis: George Knapp & Co., Printers and Binders, 1861.

Siddali, Silvana R., ed. *Missouri's War: The Civil War in Documents.* Athens: Ohio University Press, 2009.

United States Congress. *Congressional Globe*, 36th Cong., 2nd Sess., December 1860–March 1861. https://webarchive.loc.gov/all/20211110153216/https://memory.loc.gov/ammem/amlaw/lwcglink.html#anchor36

Wakelyn, Jon L., ed. *Southern Pamphlets on Secession, November 1860–April 1861.* Chapel Hill: University of North Carolina Press, 1996.

Bibliography

Suggestions for Further Reading

Arenson, Adam. *The Great Heart of the Republic: St. Louis and the Cultural Civil War*. Columbia: University of Missouri Press, 2011.

Boman, Dennis K. *Lincoln and Citizens' Rights in Civil War Missouri: Balancing Freedom and Security*. Baton Rouge: Louisiana State University, 2011.

———. *Lincoln's Resolute Unionist: Hamilton Gamble, Dred Scott Dissenter and Missouri's Civil War Governor*. Baton Rouge: Louisiana State University Press, 2006.

Crofts, Daniel W. *Lincoln and the Politics of Slavery: The Other Thirteenth Amendment and the Struggle to Save the Union*. Chapel Hill: University of North Carolina Press, 2016.

Dew, Charles B. *Apostles of Disunion: Southern Secession Commissioners and the Causes of the Civil War*. Charlottesville: University Press of Virginia, 2001.

Fehrenbacher, Don E. *The Dred Scott Case: Its Significance in American Law and Politics*. New York: Oxford University Press, 1978.

Fluker, Amy Laurel. *Commonwealth of Compromise: Civil War Commemoration in Missouri*. Columbia: University of Missouri Press, 2020.

Forbes, Robert Pierce. *The Missouri Compromise and Its Aftermath: Slavery and the Meaning of America*. Chapel Hill: University of North Carolina Press, 2007.

Freehling, William W. *The Road to Disunion: Secessionists Triumphant*. Vol. 2. New York: Oxford University Press, 2007.

Geiger, Mark W. *Financial Fraud and Guerrilla Violence in Missouri's Civil War, 1861–1865*. New Haven: Yale University Press, 2010.

Gerteis, Louis S. *Civil War St. Louis*. Lawrence: University Press of Kansas, 2001.

Graber, Mark A. *Dred Scott and the Problem of Constitutional Evil*. New York: Cambridge University Press, 2006.

Holt, Michael F. *The Election of 1860: "A Campaign Fraught with Consequences."* Lawrence: University Press of Kansas, 2017.

Launius, Roger D. *Alexander William Doniphan: Portrait of a Missouri Moderate*. Columbia: University of Missouri Press, 1997.

Lee, Charles Robert, Jr., *The Confederate Constitutions*. Chapel Hill: University of North Carolina Press, 1963.

Morris, Thomas D. *Free Men All: The Personal Liberty Laws of the North, 1780–1861*. Baltimore: Johns Hopkins University Press, 1974.

Parrish, William E. *Frank Blair: Lincoln's Conservative*. Columbia: University of Missouri Press, 1998.

———. *Turbulent Partnership: Missouri and the Union, 1861–1865*. Columbia: University of Missouri Press, 1963.

Phillips, Christopher. *Damned Yankee: The Life of General Nathaniel Lyon*. Columbia: University of Missouri Press, 1990.

———. *Missouri's Confederate: Claiborne Fox Jackson and the Creation of Southern Identity in the Border West.* Columbia: University of Missouri Press, 2000.

———. *The Rivers Ran Backwards: The Civil War and the Remaking of the American Middle Border.* New York: Oxford University Press, 2016.

Phillips, Ulrich B. "The Central Theme of Southern History," *American Historical Review* 34, no. 1 (October 1928): 30–43.

Pitcaithley, Dwight T. *The U.S. Constitution and Secession: A Documentary Anthology of Slavery and White Supremacy.* Lawrence: University Press of Kansas, 2018.

Radan, Peter, *Creating a More Perfect Slaveholders' Union: Slavery, the Constitution, and Secession in Antebellum America.* Lawrence: University Press of Kansas, 2023.

Robinson, Michael D. *A Union Indivisible: Secession and the Politics of Slavery in the Border South.* Chapel Hill: University of North Carolina Press, 2017.

Sacco, Nicholas W. "The Contested Memories of General Nathaniel Lyon in St. Louis." *Muster-Journal of the Civil War Era.* https: journalofthecivilwarear.org/2019/05the-contested-memories-of-general-nathaniel-lyon-in st-louis/.

———. "Searching for Compromise: Missouri Congressman John Richard Barret's Fight to Save the Union." *The Confluence* 10, no. 1 (Fall/Winter, 2018/2019): 5–32.

Shalhope, Robert E. *Sterling Price: Portrait of a Southerner.* Columbia: University of Missouri Press, 1971.

Stack, Joan. "The Rise and Fall of General Nathaniel Lyon in the Missouri State Capitol." *Gateway* 33 (2013): 60–67.

INDEX

abolition/abolitionists/abolitionism, xv, xxi–xxiii, xxvi–xxvii, xl, 1, 8, 20, 24, 33, 35–36, 39, 68, 72–74, 77–78, 81, 89, 94, 97, 136, 141, 152, 163, 171, 180, 192; amendment, 152; societies, 44, 80, 179
Abolition Party, 74, 86, 98, 150
abolition societies, 44, 80, 179
Adams, Charles F., 69
Adams, John, 71
Adams, John Q., 82, 224
Africa, 33, 112, 137, 176
African question, 191
African race, 169
African slaves/slavery, xxii, 4, 169, 193
Alabama; secession of, xxv, 52, 144, 168–69, 200
Alamo, 196
Allen, J. S., 204
American Party, 51, 84, 98, 119, 149–50, 277n49
American Revolution, 28, 51, 70, 76, 97, 136
Anderson, Thomas L., xxv–xxvi, 51
Andrew, James O., 98
Anthony, Henry B., 45
Anti-Slavery Society of New England, 72
Arkansas, xxxiv, 66–67, 121–22, 138, 198, 235; army/troops, xxxviii, 234, 236, 239, 247; secession of, 43, 225; slavery in, 108
Arnold, Benedict, 177
Articles of Confederation, xxxii, 159

Atchison, David, R., 165, 243
Augusta College, 101

barbarism, 197, 269n3
Barret, John R., xxvi–xxvii, 68–69, 96
Bast, George, xvii, 93, 111, 202, 204
Bates, Edward, 83, 110, 229
Bates, Frederick, 110
Bell, John, xx–xxi, 176
Benjamin, Judah, 187–89, 281n86
Bible, 68, 72
Bigler, William, 49
Birch, James H., 137, 205, 218–19, 240
Black Republicans, 24, 194
Blair, Francis P., Jr., xviii, xxxiv–xxxvii, 77, 227
Bogy, Joseph, 229
Border State Convention, xxxi, 117, 122, 126–28, 133
Border states, xxvii, xxx, 6, 14–15, 42, 57–58, 66–67, 85–87, 125, 127, 134, 142, 156, 176, 179, 198; compromise in, 133, 203, 223; cooperation of, 24, 67; neutrality of, xxxi; slavery in, 81, 264n8; slavery losses in, 30, 179
Breckinridge, John C., xx–xxi
Breckinridge, Samuel M., 217
Bright, Jesse D., 45
Broadhead, James O., 175, 229
Brown, John, xxx, 24, 39, 72, 81, 153, 164; death of, 259n40
Buchanan, James, xix–xx, xxv, 34, 37, 173; administration, 96; election of, 98, 138, 179, 274n7, 276n34

Burke, Edmund, 37, 200
Burlingame, Anson, 82
Burr, Aaron, 177

Calhoun, John C., 41; theory of nullification xxxii, 195
California, 3, 90; admission of, xix, 29, 137
Cameron, Simon, xxxiv
Camp Butler, Illinois, xxxv
Camp Jackson, xviii, xxxv–xxxvi, 221, 236
Canada, 30, 114, 148, 177; Canadian provinces, 217
Centre College, 170
Charleston, 40, 89, 146, 149, 168, 174, 214; Harbor, xviii, xxxiv, 222
Chase, Salmon P., 181
Chenault, John R., 110
Chicago Platform. *See* Republican Party
civil war, xxxvii, xxxix, 8, 17, 24, 28, 37, 45, 57, 65, 77, 79–80, 86, 88, 115–16, 123, 129, 161, 170–73, 211, 226–28, 234; horrors/terrors of, xxvi, xxx, xxxviii, 59, 67, 116, 223, 227
Clark, John B., xxvi, 60
Clay, Henry, xviii, xxiii, 15, 80, 98, 137, 150, 177, 194, 198
Clifford, John H., 164
Coalter, John D., 102, 106
Cobb, Howell, 96
Cobb, Mildred Lewis, 96
Cobb, Thomas, R. R., 96
Collamer, Jacob, 29
Colorado Territory; organization of, xxix, 205
Comingo, Abram, 170
Compromise of 1850, 60, 72, 150, 273n52
Conant, Horace, xxxvii
Confederate Army, 27, 184, 247; flag, xxxvi

Confederate Constitution; and Fifth Amendment, xxvi; slavery, xxv–xxvi, 258n25
Confederate States of America/Confederacy, xvii, xxiii–xxiv, xxvi, xxix, xxxiii–xxxiv, xxxvii, xl–xli, 9, 16, 20, 25, 27, 58, 68, 85, 93–96, 101, 111, 114, 146, 149, 172, 176, 198, 206, 211–12, 232, 237, 245–47
constitutional guarantees, 11, 18, 37, 55, 61–62, 192
Constitutional Union Party/candidate, xxviii, 11, 94
Corwin, Thomas; proposed constitutional amendment, xxiv, xxxi, xxxix, 69, 174, 176, 205, 275n29, 283n109
cotton states, 7, 57, 84, 86–87, 167, 206
Crawford, Andrew J., 211
Crisp, John T., 248
Crittenden, John J.; proposed constitutional amendment, xxiii–xxvi, xxx–xxxi, 24, 36, 45–46, 51, 60, 65–66, 102, 105, 111, 116–17, 122, 129–30, 132–40, 142, 151, 170–72, 174–76, 196, 202–03, 275n29, 279n70
Cuba, xx, 108, 147, 277n47, 279n70
Curtis, George W., 74

Dakota Territory, 170; organization of, xxix, 205
Davis, H. Winter, 84
Davis, Jefferson, xvii, xxxiv, xl, 93, 142, 173, 243; proposed constitutional amendment, xxv
Declaration of Independence, xx, 31, 74–77, 175, 180
Democratic Party, xxxiii, 4, 28, 88, 98, 149–50; convention of, 149; election of 1860, xx

District of Columbia, 191; slavery in, xxiii, 13, 33, 35, 80, 82, 156, 182, 272n50
Doniphan, Alexander, W., 101–2, 106, 110
Doolittle, James R., 30
Dred Scott case/decision. *See* US Supreme Court
Douglas, Stephen A., xx–xxi, 31, 149–50, 181
Douglass, William, 110, 229

Election of 1856, 98
Election of 1860, xix–xxi, xxvii, 15
emancipation, xix, xl, 78, 272n50; compensated, 262n80
Emigrant Aid Societies, 13, 36, 43, 99
England/Great Britain, 15, 39, 95, 148–49, 203
Everett, Edward, 176

fanaticism/fanatics, xxv, 12, 144; northern, xxii–xxiii, xxvii, xxxv, 3–5, 7, 51–52, 54, 59, 64, 68, 73, 77, 118, 191, 193, 218, 221, 223; southern, 191
Farnsworth, John F., 64
Fifth Amendment. *See* US Constitution
Fillmore, Millard, 24, 138, 151
Fitch, Graham N., 45
Florence, Thomas, 63
Florida, 15, 87, 95, 188; acquisition of, xxv, 186, 216; secession of, xxv, 24, 42, 52, 144, 200; territory of, 80
Fort Columbus, 40
Fort McHenry, 40
Fort Moultrie, 24
Fort Pickens, 172
Fortress Monroe, 40
Fort Scott, 246

Fort Sumter, xvii, xxxiv–xxxv, 40, 172, 221–22
Founding Fathers, xv, xxxiii
France, 10, 142, 149
Free Soil Party, xxvi
Fremont, John C., 98, 182
Frost, Daniel M., xxxiv–xxxv
Fugitive Slave Act/Law of 1850, xxx, 30, 135, 138–39, 154, 192; execution/enforcement of, xxv, 23, 38, 43–44, 46, 55, 63, 113, 148, 151, 176, 208; violation/nullification of, xxvi, 146
fugitive slaves, 266n6, 267n9; rescue of, xxxi–xxxii, 13; return/rendition of xxiv, 51, 63, 130, 181

Gamble, Hamilton R., xxx–xxxi, xxxix, 110–11, 122, 129,132, 229, 233; as governor, xviii, xxxviii–xl, 240–41
Gantt, Thomas T., xxix, xxxii–xxxiii, 158, 168
Gardenhire, James, xxi
Garrison, William L., 163, 192, 201
George the Third, 200
Georgia; secession of, 24, 42, 97, 101, 168, 206, 274n9
Giddings, Joshua R., 33, 74, 88, 180
Gilmer, John A., 67
Glenn, Luther, xxviii, xxix, 93–94, 96, 205–6
Grant, Ulysses S., 170, 261n63
Greeley, Horace, 88
Green, James S., xxiv–xxv, 38, 165
Gulf of Mexico, 186
Gulf States, 57, 206
Guthrie, James, 105

Hale, John P., 201
Hall, Willard P., xxxix, 110, 205, 229
Hall, William A., 110, 229
Hamlin, Hannibal, 100

Hampden-Sydney College, 110
Harney, William S., xvii–xviii, xxxiv, xxxvi–xxxvii, 227
Harney-Price Agreement, xxxvi
Harpers Ferry, Virginia, xxx
Hartford Convention, 212
Helper, Hinton R., 72, 78–79, 81–82, 99, 271n37
Henderson, John B., xxix, 110, 143, 205–6, 217, 229
Hendrick, Littleberry, 229
Hill, Benjamin H., 168
Hoar, Samuel, 181–82
Hoard, Charles B., 66
Holmes, John, 71
Home Guards, xxxiv, xxxvii, 94, 227
Hough, Harrison, xxx, 102, 110, 117
house divided, 31, 64, 120, 155, 267n11
Houston, Sam, 142, 277n40
Howell, William J., 205
Hunter, Robert M. T., xxiii

irrepressible conflict, 31, 45, 53, 82, 89, 120, 133–34, 155, 267n11

Jackson, Andrew, 24, 211, 224
Jackson, Claiborne F., xxii, 11, 67, 175, 184, 221–22; as secessionist, xvii–xviii, xxii, xxiv, xxviii, xxxiii–xl, 226, 234; election of, xxi; in exile, xl, 11, 243–45, 247; removal of, 184
Jackson, Hancock L., xxi
Jackson-Napton Resolutions, xxi, 67, 270n18
James, Lucy A., 51
Japan, 108
Jay, John, 33, 82
Jefferson, Thomas, 10, 70, 175, 224, 264n10
Jenkins, Albert G., 49
Junkin, Benjamin F., 63

Kansas, xviii, 13, 23, 36, 43, 46, 77, 99, 208; organization of, xix, 208; statehood, xix, xxxiv, 84, 138
Kansas-Nebraska bill/Act, 138, 150, 276n35
Kilgore, David, 63, 66, 72
King Cotton, 148
Knott, James P., 205

Lake Itasca, 171
Lemmon Slave Case, 268n19
Letcher, John, 24
Lincoln, Abraham, 82, 88, 110, 131, 134, 163, 173–74, 229, 235; administration, xx, xxii, xxix, xxxi, xxxiii, xxxvii–xli, 185, 222–23; at Cooper Union, 24; call for troops, xvii, xxxiv–xxxv, 221; election/victory, xv, xviii–xix, xxiii, xxvi, 11, 23, 32, 44, 61, 64, 74, 100, 139–40, 143, 155, 172, 181, 194; inauguration/inaugural address, xxiv, 24, 53, 93, 95, 223; position on Negro equality, xxiv, 27, 31–32, 64–65, 74–76; position on slavery, xviii, xxiv, xi, 31, 69, 77–80, 82, 84, 96, 100
Lincoln-Douglas Debate, 271n31
Linton, Moses L., 173
Locke, John, 193
Lord North, 200
Louisiana, xxiii, 138, 187–88; purchase of, 216, 267n16; secession of, 142, 144; slavery in, 33; troops, xxxviii
Lovejoy, Owen, 201
Lowe, Samuel A., xxviii
Lyon, Nathaniel, xviii, xxxiv–xxxviii, 221, 226–29

Marvin, Asa C., 205
Mason, James M., 47
Massey, Benjamin F., 229, 237
McKenty, Jacob. K, 63

Mexico, xxi, 13; war with, 101, 216
Miles, William P., 163
Minnesota Territory; slavery in, xix, 159
Minute Men, xxxiv
Mississippi; secession of, xxiii, xxv, 20, 23, 52, 144
Mississippi River, xvii, 41, 58, 148, 171, 190, 200
Missouri Compromise, xix, 60, 65, 70–71, 138, 155, 166, 209
Missouri Compromise line, xviii, 13, 28–29, 56, 65–66, 83, 174, 209
Missouri State Convention, xviii, xxxiv, xxxvi, xxxviii, 19, 21, 94, 102, 205, 221; Committee on Federal Relations, xxx–xxxi, xxxiii, 110, 130, 172, 174, 183, 202, 204, 219, 240; election of delegates, xxviii
Monroe, James, 70
Montgomery, James, 24, 39, 43
Moss, James H.; amendment of, xxx–xxxi, 129–30, 170, 172, 174, 177
Mullanphy, Bryan, xxxiv
Mullanphy, John, xxxiv
Mullanphy, Mary, xxxiv

Napton, William B., xxi
Nebraska Territory; organization of, 138, 208; slavery in, xix
Negro/racial equality, xxvii, 60, 74–77, 81, 150–51, 180–82, 270
neutrality, xxxi, xxxiii, xxxvi–xxxvii, xl, 7, 170, 173–74, 177, 227
Nevada Territory; organization of, xxix, 205
New Mexico Territory, xviii–xix, 36, 80, 83, 101, 137–38; slavery in, 83, 200, 283n106
New York Tribune, 23, 152
Noell, John William; proposed constitutional amendment, xxiv–xxv, 49–50

Northwest Ordinance of 1787/1789, 159, 209
nullification, 174–75, 210–11, 213, 227, 284n115; doctrine of 131

Ohio River, 171
Oliver, Mordecai, xxxix
Ordinance of secession, xl–xli, 97, 101, 146, 157, 168–69, 206, 247
Oregon Territory, 201; organization of, 29, 196; slavery in, xix, 154, 159, 165–66
Orr, James Lawrence, 276n39
Orr, Sample, xxi, xxviii, 11, 94, 175

Palmer, George W., xxiv, 268n24
Parker, Theodore, 81
personal liberty laws/bills, xxiii, xxv, xxxii, 23, 27, 29, 55, 63, 77, 81, 154, 158, 164–65, 174, 176, 278n52, 279n62
Pettus, John J., 20
Phillips, Wendell, 163, 192, 201
Planter's House Hotel, xxxvii
Polk, James K., 29, 166
Polk, Trusten, xxi, xxiii–xxv, 1, 27, 69; expulsion from Senate, 143, 205; proposed constitutional amendment, 35, 49
Pomeroy, William G., 110
popular sovereignty, xxi, 149, 209, 276n35
Price, Sterling, xxviii, xxxvi–xxxviii, 68, 110, 205, 227, 284n6
Pugh, George E., 31

Redd, John T., xxx–xxxiii, 110, 117, 152, 158–60, 164–66, 178, 184, 186–87, 189, 204
Republican Party, xix, xxi–xxii, xxx, 1, 24, 36, 59–69, 72–74, 76, 78, 84, 90, 99, 119, 135, 140, 161, 163, 195, 198–99, 208; Chicago Platform/convention,

Republican Party (*cont.*)
    xix, xxvi, xxix, 31–32, 60–61, 69, 74, 76, 84, 87–88, 96, 100, 104, 120, 141, 163–64, 172, 174–75, 179–83, 194, 200–201, 205, 207; position on equality, 73–74; position on slavery, xxii, xxiv, xxvi–xxvii, xxix, xxxiii, 11, 69, 72, 77–78, 80–83, 85, 89, 96, 100, 150, 152, 156, 166, 174, 178, 185, 192, 202, 205, 207, 217
Reynolds, Thomas C., xxi, 21–22, 236
Rhett, Robert B., 163
Rocky Mountains, 3, 103, 197
Rodman, Francis, 247
Rollins, James S., 1
Russell, Daniel R., xxiii, xxviii–xxix, 20
Russia, 108, 149

Sawyer, Samuel L. 110
Sayre, Kitchell S., 177–78
Scott, Dred, 72
secession; as heresy, xxii, xxix, xxxi, 143, 145, 170, 173, 201, 207; as revolution, 9, 62, 86, 114, 140; movement, 22, 176; right of, xxvii, 38–39, 41, 62, 152, 157, 160–61, 163, 169, 173, 200–201, 212, 214; voluntary, 1–2, 9
secession commissioners, xxiii, xxviii–xxix, 20, 93–94, 96
Secession Winter, xviii, xxvi, 49, 51, 260n46
servile insurrection, 34, 64, 77, 119, 182
Seward, William H., 23, 32, 44, 68–69, 73, 77–78, 82, 84, 88, 100, 181, 198, 201
Shaw, Lemuel, 164, 297n62
Sheeley, James K., 217
Sherman, John, 62, 83, 86–87
Sioux Tribe, 170
slave/s; as property, xix–xx, xxv–xxvi, 16, 32–35, 38, 51, 53–56, 60, 67, 74, 78, 80–81, 85–86, 105, 120, 135–36, 139, 146, 148, 178, 182, 203, 217, 219; insurrection, 182
slavery, 203; abolition/end of, 78, 80–81, 113, 152, 156, 183; as sin, 77, 81, 89, 112, 179, 192–93; numbers of, 34; value of, xl, 16, 30, 35, 55, 85, 124, 136, 264n11, 265n14
slave trade, 82, 156, 182; international, 7, 102, 200
Snead, Thomas L., xxxvii, 226
South Carolina, xxiii, xxix, 39–40, 86–87, 95, 174, 176, 181–82, 188, 210, 213; secession of, xvii, xxv, 7, 15, 24, 41–42, 52, 89, 144, 146, 167, 173, 200
sovereignty, 118, 160, 185; nature of xxxiii, 160–61, 189–90, 215; popular, xxi, 149, 209; state, xviii, xxviii, xxxii, xxxv, 93, 186–87, 212, 214, 223, 239, 248
Spain, xx
Stanton, Benjamin, 65
St. Domingo, horrors of, 180, 280n76
Stephens, Alexander, 168
Stevenson, John D., 22
Stewart, Robert M., xxi–xxii, xxvii, 1, 11, 205
St. Louis; Germans in, xvii; Republicans in, 25; secessionist sentiment in, xxxiv
St. Louis Arsenal, xvii, xxviii, xxxiv–xxxv, 221
St. Louis Mercantile Library, xxviii, 259n34
St. Louis University, xxvi, xxxv, 68; medical school, 173
Stockton, Robert F., 131
Sumner, Charles, 77, 80, 100, 201
superior race, 194, 197, 201

Taney, Roger B., xviii, 195
Tappan, Lewis, 163

tariff/revenue/duties, 38, 55, 105, 146, 172, 174, 189–90, 206–7, 211, 216; Act of 1828, 213
telegraph/telegrams, 134, 168
territories, western/common, xix, xxvi, 6, 61, 124, 137, 139, 195; organization of, xxix, xxxiii, 143, 159, 165–66, 174, 185, 196, 201, 205, 208, 217; slavery in, xv, xviii, xix–xxi, xxv, xxvii, xxix, xxxii–xxxiii, 4, 13, 17–18, 31–36, 44, 51, 54–56, 60, 62–63, 82–84, 86, 89, 96, 99–100, 105, 112–13, 120, 130, 134, 136, 138, 143, 149–50, 154–56, 158, 165–66, 171–72, 175–77, 182, 185, 192, 194–97, 203, 205, 207, 209, 217
Texas, xix, 43, 188, 196; annexation of, xxv, 9, 50, 60, 84, 142; debt of, 216; division of, 137; secession of, xxvi, 144
Thomason, Hugh F., 50
Tindall, Jacob T., 110
Toombs, Robert, xxv
transcontinental railroad, 39
Transylvania University, 173
treason, 21, 41, 64, 71, 119, 157, 173, 208, 214
Tucker, Henry, 184
Tucker, J. W., 235
Turkey, 108

underground railroad, 27, 30, 57, 77
University of Georgia, 96
US Congress; Committee of Thirty-Three, 50, 60, 69, 90, 174–76
US Constitution, xviii, xx, xxix, xxxii–xxxiii, xxxviii, 1–2, 4, 12, 17, 31, 33, 36–37, 42, 46, 51–54, 56, 59, 61–62, 65, 70, 72–74, 77, 82–83, 85, 88, 89–90, 94, 97, 101–2, 143–44, 151–52, 156, 160, 163–64, 168, 180, 182, 186, 188–90, 190, 193–95, 199, 210, 214–15, 222–24; amending of, xvi, xxii, xxiv, 12, 18, 27, 35, 45, 50–51, 57–58, 81, 104, 120, 126, 135, 140, 150, 178, 183, 213; and secession, xv, 114, 116, 173, 185, 216; as compact, 152, 158, 212–13, 260n46; Fifth Amendment, xxii, xxv–xxvi, xxx; fugitive slave clause, xxiii, xxxii, 29–31, 54, 63, 76, 153, 162; perpetuity of, 50; recognizing property in/protection of slaves, xv, xix, xxv–xxvi, 4, 33, 55, 67, 74, 80; reserved powers/rights, 157, 186–88, 203, 215; subversion/violation of, xxxiii, xli, 29, 32, 78, 88, 112, 153–54, 156–57, 159, 165–66, 178, 181, 183, 187, 244, 248; three-fifths compromise, xxvi, 258n25
US Military Academy, 184
US Supreme Court, xix, xxix–xxx, xxxiii, 36, 56, 62, 72, 82–83, 96, 112, 154, 185, 199, 209, 214, 217; *Dred Scott* case/decision, xviii–xx, xxv, xxix, xxxiii, 65, 96, 110, 195–96; reorganization/reform of, 32, 64, 82–83, 86, 183
US Union/American flag, 7, 13, 23, 33, 52, 57, 86, 88–89, 103, 124, 129, 144, 147, 151, 177, 200
Utah Territory, xviii–xix, 191

Vallandigham, Clement, 49
Vest, George G., 95
Virginia; secession of, 224–25

Wade, Benjamin F., 28, 34, 201
Walker, David, 234
Washington, George, 24, 69–70, 99, 113, 211, 224
Washington Peace Conference, xli, 102, 106, 141
Watkins, Nathaniel W., 110

Webster, Daniel, 15, 24, 28–29, 137, 194–95
Webster's dictionary, 177
Welch, Aikman, 217
white supremacy, xv, xviii, xxviii, 69, 258n28
Wigfall, Louis T., 142
Wigwam, 180
Wilmot Proviso, xxxiii, 60, 175, 185, 196–97, 199, 201, 260n52

Wilson, Henry, 82, 100
Wilson, Robert, xxviii
Wilson's Creek, xxxviii
Wise, Henry, A., xxv
Wright, Uriel, xxxii–xxxiii, 184–85, 202, 205

Yale College, xxiii, 27
Yancey, William L., 144, 163, 167, 277n45

www.ingramcontent.com/pod-product-compliance
Lightning Source LLC
Chambersburg PA
CBHW020246010526
44107CB00002B/126